AF784942

Dear Janet,

Your's and Ron's friendship has been a gift I will always treasure.

With deep affection and thanks.

Tom

NEOLIBERALISM AND THE ROAD TO INEQUALITY AND STAGNATION

In memory of Ron Blackwell (1946–2018):
friend, mentor, and teacher.

Neoliberalism and the Road to Inequality and Stagnation

A Chronicle Foretold

Thomas I. Palley

Founding Co-editor of the Review of Keynesian Economics *and an Independent Economist*

Edward Elgar
PUBLISHING

Cheltenham, UK • Northampton, MA, USA

Published by
Edward Elgar Publishing Limited
The Lypiatts
15 Lansdown Road
Cheltenham
Glos GL50 2JA
UK

Edward Elgar Publishing, Inc.
William Pratt House
9 Dewey Court
Northampton
Massachusetts 01060
USA

A catalogue record for this book
is available from the British Library

Library of Congress Control Number: 2021947645

This book is available electronically in the **Elgar**online
Economics subject collection
http://dx.doi.org/10.4337/9781802200089

Printed on elemental chlorine free (ECF)
recycled paper containing 30% Post-Consumer Waste

ISBN 978 1 80220 007 2 (cased)
ISBN 978 1 80220 008 9 (eBook)

Printed and bound in the USA

Contents

About the Author

Thomas I. Palley is an independent economist and author living in Washington, DC. He is a founder and co-editor of the *Review of Keynesian Economics*. Most recently, he was Senior Economic Policy Adviser to the AFL–CIO. In the past, he has held positions as Chief Economist with the US–China Economic and Security Review Commission, Director of the Open Society Institute's Globalization Reform Project, and Assistant Director of Public Policy at the AFL–CIO.

Dr. Palley holds a BA degree from Oxford University and an MA degree in International Relations and PhD in Economics, both from Yale University. His recent books are *From Financial Crisis to Stagnation: The Destruction of Shared Prosperity and the Role of Economics* (Cambridge University Press, 2012); *Financialization: The Economics of Finance Capital Domination* (Palgrave Macmillan, 2013); and *The Economic Crisis: Notes from the Underground* (CreateSpace, 2012). He is also the author of *Plenty of Nothing: The Downsizing of the American Dream and the Case for Structural Keynesianism* (Princeton University Press, 1998) and *Post Keynesian Economics* (Macmillan Press, 1996). He also co-edited with Gustav Horn *Restoring Shared Prosperity: A Policy Agenda from Leading Keynesian Economists* (CreateSpace, 2013).

Dr. Palley has published over 150 articles in a wide range of academic journals, as well as publishing numerous book chapters, newspaper op-eds, and articles in popular magazines. His op-eds and recent articles are available at www.thomaspalley.com.

Preface

This book consists of essays written over the past 27 years. The essays anticipated how neoliberalism would lead to increased economic inequality and stagnation, and they provided an explanation of imminent major developments in real time.

I cannot say I have had much (or even any) impact on economics and economic policy, but I can say I have persistently anticipated with considerable accuracy the major economic developments of the neoliberal era. As far as I am aware, that is something no mainstream economist has done.

In economics, not only is there need to get the outcome right, there is also need to get the story right. Mainstream economists occasionally call the correct outcome, but on closer inspection their story does not add up in terms of the evidence. That makes their calls just a matter of good fortune.

In Oscar Wilde's play *The Importance of Being Earnest*, Lady Bracknell remarks: "To lose one parent, Mr. Worthing, may be regarded as a misfortune; to lose both looks like carelessness." In economics one might paraphrase that as: "To get it wrong once may be regarded as a misfortune; to get it wrong over and over again looks like ideologically blinded theory." The fact that the analysis in this book has gotten it so right in advance of events, and the fact that mainstream economics has gotten it so wrong, speaks to the correctness of the book's theoretical perspective and the failure of mainstream economic theory.

In a less politicized discipline that record might lead to a change of theoretical paradigm. However, economics is highly politicized because how we explain the economy is of critical significance to the powers that be as it provides justification for existing economic arrangements and outcomes. Additionally, mainstream economists have nothing to gain and much to lose from a change of paradigm, which incentivizes their opposition to change.

But enough said. Readers of the book can judge for themselves. I put the case in their hands.

Tom Palley
Washington, DC
March 2021

Acknowledgements

The editors and publishers wish to thank the authors and the following publishers who have kindly given permission for the use of copyright material:

Dollars & Sense: 'Labor in the Global Economy: The Globalization Clock, May/June 2006, 12–13. Revised in 2018 and republished as 'The Globalization Clock', Article 7.1 in *Real World Globalization*, 19th edition, edited by Armağan Gezici, Elizabeth T. Henderson, Jeannette Mitchell, Jawied Nawabi, and the Dollars and Sense Collective, Economic Affairs Bureau Inc., December 2020, 177–9.

Internationale Politik und Gessellschaft (*International Politics and Society*): 'A Labor Perspective on Globalization', April, 2009, 22–39.

New School Economic Review for: 'America's Exhausted Paradigm: Macroeconomic Causes of the Financial Crisis and Great Recession', **4** (1), 2010, 15–43.

Oxford Academic: 'Europe's Crisis Without End: The Consequences of Neoliberalism', *Contributions to Political Economy*, **32**, (2013), 29–50.

Pontifical Academy of Social Sciences: 'The Economics of Globalization: Problems and Policy Responses', in *Toward Reducing Unemployment*, 5th Plenary Session, Vatican City, 1999, 202–216 [originally 185–205].

Real-World Economics Review: 'After the Bust: The Outlook for Macroeconomics and Macroeconomic Policy', **49**, March, 2009, 22–35; 'Fixing the Euro's Original Sins: the Monetary–Fiscal Architecture and Monetary Policy Conduct', **81**, September, 2017, 1–12.

Routledge: 'The US Economy: Explaining Stagnation and Why it Will Persist', in A. Gallas, H. Herr, F. Hoffer and C. Scherrer (eds), *Combatting Inequality: The Global North and South*, London, 2016, 113–31.

Science Direct: 'The Rise and Fall of Export-led Growth', *Investigación Económica*, **LXXI** (280), April–June, 2012, 141–61.

Taylor and Francis Group: 'Capital Mobility and the Threat to American Prosperity', *Challenge*, **37** (6), November/December, 1994, 31, 34–9, 'Economic Contradictions Coming Home to Roost? Does the U.S. Economy Face a Long-Term Aggregate Demand Generation Problem?', *Journal of Post Keynesian Economics*, **25** (1), Fall, 2002, 9–32; 'The Questionable Legacy of Alan Greenspan', *Challenge*, **48** (6), November/December, 2005, 17–31; 'Developing the Domestic Market', *Challenge*, **49** (6), November/December, 2006, 20–34; 'The U.S. Economy after Bush, *Challenge*, **51** (6), November/December, 2008, 26–37; 'The

Fallacy of the Revised Bretton Woods Hypothesis: Why Today's System is Unsustainable and Suggestions for a Replacement', *International Journal of Political Economy*, **36** (4), Winter, 2007–2008, 36–52; 'The European Monetary Union Needs a Government Banker', *Challenge*, **54** (4), July/August, 2011, 5–21; 'Inequality and Stagnation by Policy Design: Mainstream Denialism and its Dangerous Political Consequences', *Challenge*, **62** (2), 2019, 128–43.

The New School for Social Research: 'The Free Trade Debate: A Left Keynesian Gaze', *Social Research*, **61** (2), Summer, 1994, 379–94. Copyright © The New School. Published with permission by Johns Hopkins University Press.

Thomas Palley and Gustav A. Horn: 'The War of Ideas: A Comparison of the US and Europe', in *Restoring Shared Prosperity: A Policy Agenda From Leading Keynesian Economists*, CreateSpace.com, 2013, 289–93 [originally 7–14].

Every effort has been made to trace all the copyright holders but if any have been inadvertently overlooked the publishers will be pleased to make the necessary arrangement at the first opportunity.

[1]

Introduction: neoliberalism as a variety of capitalism

1. What is neoliberalism?

This book is about the neoliberal economy and how it has delivered economic inequality and stagnation. Neoliberalism is a political economic philosophy that consists of two claims, one political and the other economic.[1] The political claim is that a free market *laissez-faire* economy is necessary for the promotion and protection of individual liberty. The economic claim is that a free market *laissez-faire* economy is the best way of delivering economic prosperity since it ensures economically efficient outcomes.[2]

There are multiple features to note about those two claims. First, free markets are central to neoliberalism, being essential for its claims about both liberty and economic efficiency. Second, given the importance of free markets in the neoliberal argument, it is easy to understand why business, wealthy interests, and high income earners all tend to strongly support neoliberalism. Third, mainstream economics is central to neoliberalism as it provides the intellectual support for the claim about markets and economic efficiency. Fourth, an important innovation of neoliberalism is its extension of economics into the political sphere via its claim about the importance of markets for liberty. That extension has been critical in widening the popular political appeal of neoliberalism.

Given the current ideological dominance of neoliberalism it is easy to take its claims for granted. However, stop to scratch the surface and serious problems quickly emerge. First, the claim about economic efficiency rests on mainstream neoclassical economics which is highly contested (even if that contest is significantly suppressed by university economics departments). Critics claim the neoclassical theoretical model is an ontologically impossible fiction which describes an economy that can never be (Albert, 2012 [1963]; Hein and Lavoie, 2016, p.262). If correct, that undermines the model's real world relevance.

Second, neoliberalism's political claims are contentious. Though it makes sense that free markets promote liberty, a market economy also needs government and behavioral restraints to function well. That points to a significant tension between liberty and free markets.

Additionally, liberty needs more than free markets, and what it needs may be at odds with free markets. In particular, liberty needs political support, which may not be forthcoming if free market outcomes are deemed unjust and unacceptable. The *de jure* right to liberty is unlikely to endure if it is associated with an economic system that generates outcomes that render many unable *de facto* to enjoy that right.

2. The politics of the neoliberal era

The neoliberal era is widely identified as formally beginning with the November 1980 election of Ronald Reagan in the United States (US).[3] In fact, the actual transition to neoliberalism had already begun under President Carter (1977–1980) whose administration inaugurated both the deregulation and monetarist anti-inflation macroeconomic policies which have been hallmarks of the neoliberal era.

That is a small historical detail, but it is not innocuous. Instead, it shows neoliberalism has been a bipartisan political project in the US, supported by both Republicans and the elite segment of the Democratic Party. Such bipartisanship is also true of Europe. However, there the bipartisanship came later when European Social Democratic political parties shifted right and adopted a softened version of neoliberalism, both as an electoral strategy to beat back European conservatives and because they were intellectually captured by the softened vision of neoliberalism. Politically, that softened vision is referred to as the "Third Way". In the UK it was implemented by Prime Minister Tony Blair in the 1990s. And in Germany it was implemented by Chancellor Gerhard Schröder in the 2000s.

The global bipartisan nature of the neoliberal project is extremely important. It explains why neoliberalism has been so enduring despite its awful economic consequences. Bipartisanship transformed the politics of the era, creating a politics in which the choice was between right and center-right economic policy. There was no political space for alternative policies, and everything to the left of center-right was labeled as left or extreme left, which is still the prevailing situation. That transformation has hobbled the possibility for alternative social democratic inclined policies.

Furthermore, the bipartisan pattern is paralleled in the economics profession, with parallel consequences. Thus, mainstream economics thinking was captured by the Chicago School of economics and the MIT School of economics. The former represented the right and is associated with the hard neoliberalism of the Republican Party and European conservative parties. The latter represented the center-right and is associated with the softer neoliberalism of the Democratic Party's elite and the European Third Way movement. That capture of economics has served to delegitimize and exclude alternative economic points of view which advocated different theoretical perspectives and different economic policies.

The combination of the neoliberal bipartisanship of politics and the neoliberal intellectual capture of economics explains why it has been so hard to overturn neoliberalism, despite its manifest increased inequality and tendency to economic stagnation. This capture of the top of society has trickled down to influence thinking throughout society, including even those who have been adversely impacted by neoliberalism. That has hugely compounded the difficulty of overturning neoliberalism as not only is it supported from the top by those who have benefitted from it, it is also supported from the bottom by some of those who have been adversely impacted.

Once an ideology is adopted by society and becomes dominant, it becomes akin to an article of faith. At that stage, it has to be lived through and disproved by experience before it can be rejected. Until then, both logical arguments and accumulating evidence are ignored. The former fails against faith, while the latter lacks persuasive power as the evidence is still tentative.

Even when the analytic verdict is in, the outcome remains uncertain. That is because elite interests who benefit from the ideology will fight to sustain it, while opponents of the ideology and those who have been injured by it may not converge on a shared new direction.

That situation might be said to characterize the current moment. The result can be an unhappy and politically contested period. The old regime may hang on despite the misery and discontent it has produced. Alternatively, a new regime may struggle to form, but it will suffer from lack of political strength. That can show up in the form of fractures within or counter-attacks from the old regime. In a worst case scenario, it can result in irrational alliances between the injured and cynical elements of the elite who are intent on retaining power. In that event, politics can be diverted down the path of intolerance and scapegoating, rather than addressing the underlying causes of distress.

3. Neoliberalism as a variety of capitalism

The above observations on the politics of the neoliberal era have critical implications for understanding the neoliberal economy. First, they make clear that the neoliberal economy is a political creation rather than a natural order. That may sound obvious *ex-post*, yet it is easily lost sight of owing to economists' claims re laws of economics that parallel physical laws and economists' language of "natural" rates of unemployment, interest, and growth.

The deregulation of markets, the creation of an integrated global economy via the process of globalization, and the creation of hugely valuable property rights in the form of copyrights and patents are all the result of political interventions. That fact of political creation is not unique to neoliberalism. Rather, it applies to all economic orders, which argues for conceiving modern economies as varieties of capitalism (VoC). Neoliberalism is a particular VoC.

Second, though the rhetoric of neoliberalism proclaims it promotes competitive "free" markets, the reality is often substantially different. Copyright and patents explicitly confer monopoly power, the antithesis of free markets. In an economic world dominated by large corporations, deregulating labor markets and weakening worker rights or facilitating corporate global mobility tends to deliver markets in which the power of the already powerful is further increased.

Third, being a political creation, neoliberalism is pushed and supported by those whose interests it advances. That tends to be corporations, the wealthy, and the highly paid.

Fourth and most importantly, if neoliberalism is a politically created VoC, it can be politically reshaped into another VoC. Society can choose what type of economy it wants, drawing on both past experience and the exercise of current imagination. That said, the possibilities are not unlimited. Instead, they are constrained by society's current economic endowment and by basic economic principles as identified by economic theory.

Furthermore, shifting from one VoC to another can involve significant transition costs as prior business practices and production networks have to be re-engineered and reconfigured. Those transition costs can be large and can serve as a deterrent to change, which makes them a mechanism for "locking-in" a particular VoC (Palley, 2017/18).

The great deception of the politics of the neoliberal era is the closing down of the economic possibility space. That deception has been fed by mainstream economics via its imposition of the neoliberal model as the ideal economy. Thus, mainstream economics imagines a fictitious perfect economy (the so-called Arrow–Debreu competitive general equilibrium economy) which corresponds to the ideal neoliberal economy. That ideal is then asserted to be the unique ideal economy. Moreover, that ideal is claimed to be viable on grounds that the imagined Arrow–Debreu model is derived from the theory that mainstream economics uses to analyze the real world.

The irony is the imagined model is ontologically impossible. That impossibility, in turn, casts grave doubt on mainstream economic theory. The bitter double irony is that instead of disqualifying mainstream economic theory, the mainstream ideal has been accepted as a real world guide. Worse yet, the neoliberal era has seen governments actively trying to implement this flawed ideal. In effect, acting on the advice of mainstream economists, governments have paved the neoliberal road to inequality and stagnation.

4. Deconstructing the neoliberal model

Neoliberalism is a political economic philosophy that implicates the entirety of the political economic system. The scale and scope of its impact makes it hard to encompass and treat comprehensively. One helpful step is to deconstruct the system to identify the component parts.

Figure 1.1 provides such a deconstruction. It shows a nexus of bidirectional impacts between the four components which are identified as the neoliberal economy, economics, domestic politics, and international political economics. At the center of the system is the neoliberal economy from which ramify impacts that affect economics, domestic politics, and the international arena. The outer components also impact each other and all impacts are bi-directional, reflecting how each component affects others.

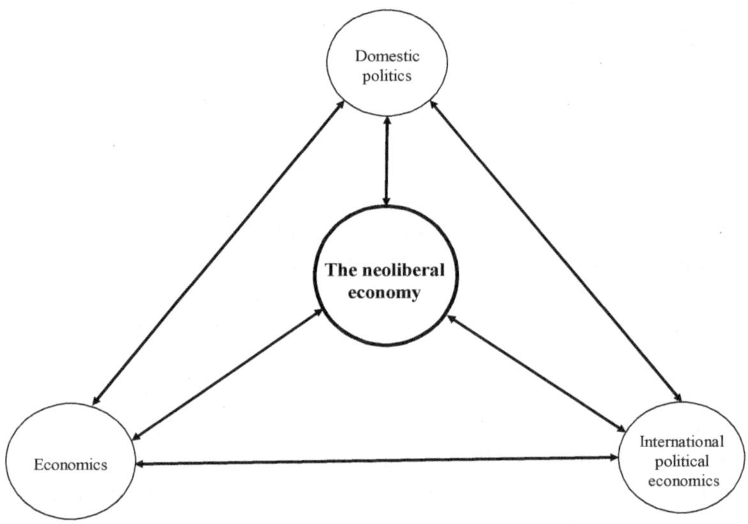

Figure 1.1 Neoliberalism and the political economic system

The neoliberal economy impacts domestic politics via its impact on the distribution of economic power, and via the economic outcomes it generates which generate political responses. The economy is itself impacted by domestic politics via economic policy which affects the structure, the rules, and the performance of the economy.

The neoliberal economy impacts economics by affecting the economic research agenda. Even more profoundly, economics impacts the neoliberal economy since the latter is built on blueprints provided and justified by economists. The ideas of economists also ramify through society, thereby impacting the perceptions, thinking, and behaviors of economic agents within the economy.

The neoliberal economy also affects and is affected by international developments. The process of globalization has been a key feature of the neoliberal era. It has transformed both the US domestic economy and the international economy, giving rise to a global reconfiguration of production arrangements and increased international trade (Palley, 2018).

Turning to the outer edge of Figure 1.1, economics affects domestic politics via its impact on understandings of the economy and economic policy. Conversely, politics impacts economics via its promotion of particular research agendas and points of view within economics. Just as the rise of Keynesian economics was fueled by the politics of the inter-war (1930s) and post-World War II years, so too the rise of neoliberal economics has been fueled by society's political turn to neoliberalism.

Economics also impacts the international economy via its impact on policy thinking regarding how to organize the international economy. The expansion of free trade and the liberalization of international financial capital mobility have been key developments of the neoliberal era, and those developments have been significantly influenced by the policy advice of mainstream economists. Conversely, developments in the international economy (e.g. the rise of multi-national corporations or the rise of China and the economic success of East Asian nations) feedback to influence economics.

Lastly, domestic politics are impacted by international events, and vice-versa. Globalization and the economic rise of China have had significant impacts on domestic politics, and domestic politics have had significant impacts on the international economic and political order. Thus, China was brought into the global economy by the US granting it permanent normal trading relations (PNTR) status in 2000. Now, China's astonishing rise is provoking an economic and national security backlash in US politics.

5. The analytical complexity of neoliberalism

The mapping in Figure 1.1 points to the complexity of neoliberalism as a political economic phenomenon. The political economics of neoliberalism consists of multiple interacting moving parts, each of which is integral to the story. That complexity makes it difficult to analyze.

The economy cannot be understood without reference to politics, and politics cannot be understood without reference to the economy. The international economy (i.e. globalization) is also an important part of the story. In the background, is the critical role of economics which has justified and designed the neoliberal model, and economics is itself subject to socio-political influences.

The critical role of economic ideas in the neoliberal economy is especially complicated and difficult to grasp. Economics has constructed an image (substantially based on its extensive use of mathematics) whereby it claims parallels with physics. Physics explains the natural world, while economics claims to scientifically describe the economic world.

That frame has led to the belief that mainstream economics provides "truth" about the economy. By implication, that means other economic perspectives are in error. All of that is sealed by the institution of the economics textbook. What is included therein is deemed truth: what is excluded is deemed error or, worse yet, denied of existence.[4] That social reality is a central part of the difficulty in analyzing neoliberalism. As noted above, mainstream economics provides the justification and design of the neoliberal economy. However, to understand the neoliberal economy it is necessary to step outside mainstream economics, look at the economy with a different theoretical lens, and insert mainstream economics into the economy as an ingredient explaining the neoliberal economy.

Such deconstructive thinking is totally alien to economists, given their belief that they hold the truth. It is also resisted by most of society. Elites resist it for reasons of economic self-interest, while society as a whole resists it owing to the simplicity and comfort offered by the notion that the conventional wisdom is the truth. That societal disposition makes it hard to get a hearing for an alternative perspective, yet the record documented in this book is strongly supportive of the latter.

The left Keynesian perspective has repeatedly identified imminent major developments, and has not had to reinvent itself with each successive crisis. That contrasts with mainstream economics which has persistently failed to anticipate imminent major developments, and has had to significantly reinvent itself after each crisis in order to provide explanations of those crises.

6. Additional perceptual complications

In addition to the above analytic complexities, the neoliberal economy adds some further perceptual complications. First, the neoliberal economy is prone to extended asymmetric boom–bust cycles, which complicates discussion. The business cycle has lengthened, with the four business cycles of the neoliberal era (1982–1990, 1991–2001, 2001–2007, 2009–2020) averaging approximately nine years. The asymmetric aspect reflects the fact that the expansions (i.e. recovery and boom) tend to be gradual and long-lived, whereas the busts tend to be sharp and deep. That structure of asymmetrically long expansions obstructs pointing out the fundamental failings of the neoliberal model since most of the time the economy is in recovery and hope springs eternal.

Second, the cycle is significantly associated with financial markets, especially the stock market, which colors understanding. During the boom the real economy does alright, but the stock market does spectacularly. During the bust, the real economy and stock market crash together, but the stock market recovers much faster with the assistance of the Federal Reserve bank and other country central banks. That pattern tilts reporting on the neoliberal economy, as economists and the chattering class (i.e. reporters and commentators) tend to be beneficiaries of the stock market's performance.

Third, mainstream economics has difficulty with the notion of a neoliberal "regime", and that difficulty is compounded by the fact that the regime has been long-lived (it began in 1980). The idea of long-lived economic regimes is conceptually at odds with mainstream economics, which does not conceive of regimes and varieties of capitalism. For mainstream economists, there is just the market economy. Moreover, the market economy is viewed as rapidly adjusting to equilibrium, so that it quickly gravitates back to equilibrium in response to any disturbance.

However, in sharp contrast with that theoretical belief, the neoliberal economy exhibits the characteristics of a slowly deteriorating and unstable system. The busts have been getting deeper, and the recoveries have been getting weaker and slower to take hold. The busts have also needed increasingly large government intervention to put in place a floor and reset the economy. Those patterns are obscured by the long expansions and the long-lived nature of the regime. The longevity is not due to underlying good health. Instead, it is because the neoliberal economy has lived off credit and previously accumulated capital and productive structures. The reliance on credit is evidenced by the massive increase in indebtedness and debt ratios across every sector of the economy – households, non-financial corporations, the financial sector, government, and the foreign sector.

Metaphorically, it is as if the neoliberal economy has masked its shortfalls by running up its credit card. If one starts with a good credit record and a large borrowing limit, that process can go on for a very long time, while simultaneously spawning the appearance of prosperity – especially when accompanied by asset price inflation. However, the below the surface reality is very different as financial contradictions and proclivities to instability build.

Fourth, and lastly, the bipartisanship of politics and the economics profession has played into the perceptual problem by making it difficult to surface any of the above. The political–intellectual consensus in favor of neoliberalism has been overwhelming, which has discredited critique. It has also occupied most of the public discourse space, thereby restricting visibility of critique which has been pushed to the margins of discourse.

7. Structure and content of the book

Figure 1.1 provides an overarching mapping of the political economics of neoliberalism. The balance of the book focuses squarely on "the neoliberal economy" which is at the center of Figure 1.1, and it also addresses the impact of "international" developments via economic globalization. To a lesser degree, the book also focuses on the linkage between "economics" and "the neoliberal economy". That additional focus is inevitable because, as noted earlier, mainstream economics is deeply implicated in the making of the neoliberal economy.

The main body of the book consists of nineteen chapters, divided into four parts titled The United States, Europe, The Global Economy, and The War of Ideas. The chapters consist of essays, written over many years, in which the analysis and (most of) the predictions have been borne out with striking accuracy. That fact speaks to the correctness of the underlying analysis, and the essays constitute a form of supportive evidence in themselves as they were written in advance of developments. That is something mainstream economists cannot claim.

Chapters 2–7 explore the evolution of the neoliberal economy in the US. That evolution has been marked by increased financial instability, increased income inequality, and the emergence of proclivity to economic stagnation.

Chapters 8–10 explore the evolution of the neoliberal economy in Europe, with an additional explicit focus on the problems generated by the introduction of the euro. The euro is the European common currency that was introduced in 1999. It was designed from scratch along neoliberal lines, in accordance with the recommendations of mainstream macroeconomic theory, and it has been the source of significant economic and political difficulties.

Chapters 11–17 explore developments associated with economic globalization. As with the euro, the design of that process has been guided by mainstream economic thinking. And as with the euro, globalization has also been the source of significant economic and political difficulties.

Chapters 18–20 discuss "the war of ideas", and it is here that the intersection between economics and the neoliberal economy is especially important. As argued earlier, the neoliberal economy is a variety of capitalism which has been politically created. Just as the economy was made in the image of neoliberalism, so too it can be remade in the image of another design. The implication is that society is engaged in a war of ideas regarding what theoretical model and vision of the economy will prevail. Economics is deeply implicated in that, and today's mainstream economics can be expected to instinctively align with the neoliberal vision owing to its ideological foundation.

How the war of ideas evolves is unpredictable. It involves the entirety of society, with the economics profession being a critical participant that occupies a strategically important place.

The economic consequences of neoliberalism (increased inequality, financial instability, and proclivity to stagnation) are now clear – so much so that mainstream economists are looking to reverse engineer their theoretical models to allow for the possibility of such outcomes. However, the political consequences are only just beginning to work themselves out. The timescale for political developments is longer as the economic consequences must first manifest themselves, be felt, and then politically processed.

The indications are that neoliberalism has triggered a powerful and dangerous political drift to intolerant democracy, or even authoritarianism bordering on fascism. That drift is evidenced by recent political developments in Europe, which include Brexit in the UK and the ascension of far right politics in Germany, France, Italy, and Spain. In the US the drift is evident in the political rise of Donald Trump and the transformation of the Republican Party.

The drift to authoritarianism fits into the framework described in Figure 1.1, and reflects the impact of the neoliberal economy's adverse outcomes on domestic politics. However, the explication of that drift must await another book. There is too much in Figure 1.1 for a single book, showing again how difficult it is to succinctly capture the entirety of neoliberalism's impacts.

Notes

1. Palley (2012, Chapter 2) provides a fuller discussion of the history of neoliberalism and critiques thereof.
2. Economists call such outcomes "Pareto optimal". Given the initial endowment of resources, the current state of technology, and the current distribution of ownership of resources, a free market economy supposedly ensures output is produced at the lowest private economic cost and all opportunities for mutually beneficial exchange are taken up.
3. Some might argue that the formal inauguration of the neoliberal era should be identified with the May 1979 election of Margaret Thatcher as Prime Minister in the United Kingdom (UK). However, it is doubtful the global economy would have embraced neoliberalism without the US doing so, given the latter's enormous weight in all things economic. That reasoning makes the US the true political fulcrum of neoliberalism, which goes with its role as the intellectual fulcrum.
4. The view that economics parallels physics and provides truth is not restricted to mainstream economics. Many critics of mainstream economics also subscribe to that view, only they see their version of economics as being the truth. That points to an indelible need for a pluralistic economics, but this is a minority belief – especially in practice.

References

Albert, H. (1963 [2012]), "Modell-Platonismus. Der neoklassiche Stil des ökonomischen Denkens in Kristischer Beluchtung," in F. Karrenberg and H. Albert (eds.), *Sozialwissenschaft und Gesellachaftsgestaltung – Festschrift für Gerhard Wesser*, Berlin: Duncker und Humblot, 45–76. Translated by Arnold, D. and Maier-Rigaud, F. as "Model Platonism: Neoclassical thought in critical light," *Journal of Institutional Economics*, 8(3), 295–323.

Hein, E. and Lavoie, M. (2016), "Interview with Thomas I. Palley: 'We need to confront more forcefully the neoclassical position and show the absolute impossibility of the world it describes!'," *European Journal of Economics and Economic Policy*, 13(3), 255–264.

Palley, T. I. (2012), *From Financial Crisis to Stagnation: The Destruction of Shared Prosperity and the Role of Economics*, Cambridge University Press, February.

Palley, T. I. (2017/18), "A theory of economic policy lock-in and lock-out via hysteresis: Rethinking economists' approach to economic policy," *Economics: The Open-Access, Open-Assessment E-Journal*, 11, 1–18.

Palley, T. I. (2018), "Three globalizations, not two: Rethinking the history and economics of trade and globalization," *European Journal of Economics and Economic Policy*, 15(2), 174–192.

PART I

THE UNITED STATES

[2]

THOMAS I. PALLEY

Economic contradictions coming home to roost? Does the U.S. economy face a long-term aggregate demand generation problem?

Abstract: *Many argue that the current recession is the product of a temporary stock market wobble. This paper argues that the U.S. economy confronts deeper-seated problems concerning the aggregate demand generation process. For two decades, these problems have been obscured by a range of demand compensation mechanisms—rising consumer debt, a stock market boom, and rising profit rates. Now, these mechanisms are exhausted. Fiscal policy adjustments and dollar depreciation are the only stable exits from this impasse, but they must be accompanied by measures rectifying the income distribution imbalances at the root of the problem. Absent this, deficient demand will reassert itself.*

Keywords: *aggregate demand, debt, income distribution, saving rates, stock market.*

The U.S. economy slowed dramatically in the second half of 2000, and formally entered recession in March 2001. Now there are indications that the recession may be ending, though dangers of a double-dip or W-recession still abound. Even if this pessimistic double-dip scenario does not transpire, there is a danger that the economy may find itself trapped in a jobless recovery or growth recession such as obtained in the early 1990s. Recalling that period, the recession was declared to be formally over in March 1991, but the unemployment rate did not actually start falling until October 1993.

Chairman of the Federal Reserve Alan Greenspan has himself acknowledged in Humphrey-Hawkins testimony to the Congress (February 2002) that the recovery may be tepid. His reasoning is that since the recession

The author is Director of the Globalization Reform Project with the Open Society Institute, Washington, DC. A version of the paper was originally presented at the Eleventh Annual Hyman P. Minsky Conference, held at the Levy Economics Institute, April 26, 2002.

0160–3477 / 2002 $9.50 + 0.00.

has been so mild, with spending on housing and consumption remaining strong, there is little pent-up demand to propel a vigorous recovery. This paper challenges this "lack of pent-up demand" hypothesis and instead argues that the danger of a lasting growth recession reflects the emergence of systemic contradictions in the U.S. economy that pose a long-term aggregate demand generation problem.

The aggregate demand generation thesis maintains that for the last 20 years demand growth has been generated by an increasingly unsustainable process that rests on rising stock prices, rising household debt, mortgage refinancing driven by disinflation, and falling household saving rates. These processes have helped cover up the aggregate demand implications of deteriorating income distribution, but they are now exhausted. The stock market remains at extremely high valuation levels on a historical basis, which means that covering the shortfall of aggregate demand with further equity price increases enjoins the contradiction of an asset price bubble. Consumer borrowing has also offset the problem of aggregate demand, but consumers are now approaching debt ceilings, and further rapid growth of borrowing risks a consumer debt crisis. Saving rates are close to zero and, therefore, have little room left for further decline. Finally, the pool of high interest rate mortgages suitable for refinancing has been eroded by successive waves of refinancing, leaving a much smaller base on which to pin demand growth fueled by reduced mortgage interest burdens.

The bottom line is that the boom of the 1990s may have been built on a combination of forces that are unsustainable. These forces helped cover up the contradictions between deteriorated income distribution and aggregate demand generation, but further staving off these contradictions is only possible at the cost of deepening existing unstable financial positions.

Income distribution: the dog that hasn't barked—yet

The deterioration of U.S. income distribution is a phenomenon that has been proceeding steadily for the last 20 years, and it is well documented (see Mishel et al., 2000). Between 1979 and 1999 the top one-fifth of families increased their income share from 41.4 percent to 47.2 percent, whereas the share of income going to the bottom 60 percent of families fell from 34.5 percent to 29.8 percent. The ratio of family income of the top 5 percent relative to the lowest 20 percent increased from 11.4 in 1979 to 19.1 in 1999. Over the same period, family income of the top one-fifth grew by 42 percent, whereas that of the bottom 60 percent grew by just 3.3 percent. This worsening of family income distribution was accompanied by generalized income and wage stagnation. Whereas median family income had grown at an annual rate of 2.75 percent between 1947 and 1973, it grew at only 0.52 percent per year between 1973 and 1999—and this at a time when female labor force participation was increasing and average hours worked grew by over 10 percent.[1] Real average hourly earnings of production and nonsupervisory workers (who constitute roughly 80 percent of employment) grew at an annual rate of 2.25 percent between 1947 and 1973, but then fell at an annual rate of 0.12 percent between 1973 and 1999.

These trends in the distribution of family income and average hourly real wage growth have been amplified by shifts in the functional distribution of income, which have raised the profit share at the expense of the labor share. Table 1 shows business cycle peak-to-peak profit rates. The pretax profit rate rose from 9.2 percent in 1979 to 12.1 percent in 1999—a 31.5 percent increase, and the posttax profit rate rose from 4.9 percent in 1979 to 8.1 percent in 1999—a 65 percent increase. Side by side, the profit share also increased, rising from 17.7 percent in 1979 to 20.5 percent in 1999—a 15.8 percent increase.

Figure 1 places these income distribution trends in a unified framework and illustrates how working families have been squeezed at two margins. First, the shift toward profit income has reduced the wage share. Second, within the wage share component there has been a shift away from production and nonsupervisory workers to managerial workers. These two trends have added up to increased family income inequality. However, whereas the increased profit share has been relatively unproblematic and may even have yielded benefit in the form of increased investment spending, the changed composition of the wage share has been unambiguously damaging.

An old adage is that a mass-production economy needs mass-consumption markets to support it. Behind this claim lies the implicit belief that robust mass-consumption markets rest on a healthy distribution of income. Yet, despite the clear worsening of income distribution, the last two business cycles have seen the U.S. economy still generate substantial increases in aggregate demand. This has cast doubt on the core Keynesian proposition that market economies are prone to failure regarding aggregate demand generation, as well as casting doubt on the claim that income distribution matters for aggregate demand.

[1] All of the above numbers either are taken directly from Mishel et al. (2000) or are based on calculations using their numbers.

Table 1
Profit rates and shares at business cycle peaks, 1959–1999

Corporate sector profit rates	1959	1969	1973	1979	1989	1999
Pretax (percent)	12.0	12.5	10.9	9.2	10.0	12.1
After tax (percent)	6.4	6.8	6.0	4.9	5.7	8.1
Income shares						
Profit share (percent)	21.9	19.7	18.2	17.7	18.2	20.5
Labor share	78.1	80.3	81.8	82.3	81.8	79.5

Source: Mishel et al. (2000, p. 91).

Figure 1 The division of gross domestic product

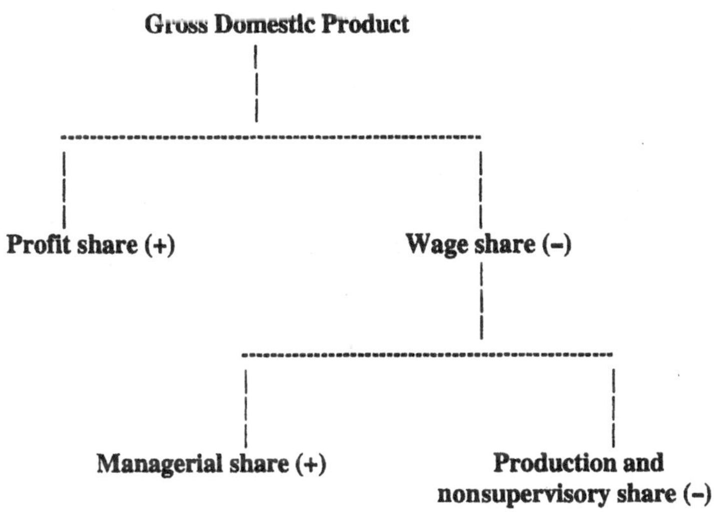

Note: Signs in parentheses represent direction of change in shares 1979–1999.

The argument that is developed below maintains that both Keynesian claims remain solidly intact—market economics can have a problem generating sufficient aggregate demand, and income distribution matters for aggregate demand. Making this argument involves showing how the process of demand generation over the last two business cycles has served to mask the impact of deteriorating income distribution. Moreover, this existing process is unsustainable. Consequently, the U.S. economy now confronts the risk of systemic demand shortage.

The recession of 2001 has already contributed to a revival of public awareness of Keynesian-styled concerns with deficient aggregate demand—though it is also the case that this awareness is still often coded as a problem of excess capacity (*BusinessWeek,* April 9, 2001).[2] However, the linkage between "sustainable" aggregate demand generation and income distribution remains less understood.

The generation of aggregate demand: what has covered for worsening income distribution?

Whereas much has been written about the causes of worsening income distribution and stagnating wages, little has been written as to why the deterioration of income distribution has failed to impact aggregate demand.[3] For Chicago school economists, the fact that the income distribution/aggregate demand dog has not barked is of little surprise since they discount the problematic of aggregate demand, believing that all households have a common propensity to consume regardless of income level.[4] However, for Keynesian economists, accounting for this silence is important, and explaining the absence of demand effects of deteriorated income distribution is a necessary step in making the claim of a contradicted economy.

At the most abstract level, the reason the demand effects of deteriorating income distribution have not yet shown up is because modern financialized economies possess many margins of compensation, and these margins can operate for lengthy periods of time before they are

[2] The one place where the problem of aggregate demand shortage is openly expressed is in connection with the global economy. For the last several years, the United States has acted as global buyer of last resort, providing demand in an otherwise demand-short global marketplace. Now there are fears that a U.S. slowdown could cut global demand, thereby triggering recession in East Asia and Latin America (for example, see *The Economist,* March 31, 2001).

[3] The reasons for the deterioration of income distribution and the stagnation of average hourly wages are deeply contested. The mainstream of the economics profession maintains that it is the result of a shift in the composition of labor demand away from unskilled to skilled workers (Bound and Johnson, 1992; Katz and Murphy, 1992). An alternative view is that it is due to changed labor market bargaining conditions resulting from reduced union density, weakened labor market institutions that underpin the wage floor, globalization, and less robust macroeconomic conditions (Palley, 1998a).

[4] This belief is based on Friedman's (1956) permanent income theory of consumption.

exhausted.[5] These margins of compensation have served to mask and keep at bay the problem of demand shortage.

Federal budget deficits

One of the most important margins of adjustment has been the growth of debt—both public and private. The worsening of U.S. income distribution gathered steam in the 1980s, but this coincided with the enormous Reagan administration budget deficits. Between 1980 and 1990, gross federal debt jumped from $909.1 billion to $3,206.6 billion, and during this period, the federal government ran budget deficits every year. In absolute terms, the deficit (on a fiscal year basis) peaked at $221.2 billion in 1986, and over the course of the decade it averaged (on a National Income and Product Accounts [NIPA] basis) 3.4 percent of the gross domestic product (GDP). The federal deficit, funded by a growing federal debt, therefore served to inject demand into the economy. This contributed to offsetting the negative demand impact of the shift in income distribution from low income/higher propensity to consume households to high income/lower propensity to consume households.

Whereas public sector deficits were an important engine of aggregate demand in the 1980s, this engine began to slow down in the 1990s as the government deficit started falling and the federal budget began its steady climb toward surplus. This change in direction of federal financial policy began with the Omnibus Budget Reconciliation Act of 1993, but it is important to recognize that deficits persisted through 1997. Thus, although the size of the federal stimulus to aggregate demand was falling during this period, it remained positive. The impact on aggregate demand only turned negative in 1998 with the emergence of the first federal budget surplus in over a generation.[6]

[5] For historians, with their longer time horizons, such a process of gradual deepening of contradictions is readily plausible. However, economists, with their emphasis on fast-adjusting competitive markets and "Chicago school"-styled rational expectations, find such descriptions profoundly problematic. Instead, they maintain that rational agents will extrapolate forward and see how the current economic configuration implies future trouble—albeit 20 years away. These same agents will then unravel the implications of future trouble through a process of backward recursion, thereby bringing it into the present and forcing markets to confront the problem today. Such reasoning explains why the economists are resistant to casting policy arguments in a historical, structural frame of reference.

[6] Prior to 1998, the last time the federal government ran a surplus was in 1969.

Declining private sector saving

Large federal deficits for most of the last 20 years have been one important factor maintaining aggregate demand in the presence of deteriorating income distribution. A second, even more important factor has been changed private sector saving behavior that has made for a steady decline in the private sector's saving rate. Moreover, the decline in the private sector saving rate accelerated in the 1990s just as the federal government began to reverse its financial course, so that the private sector stepped in and more than compensated for the declining size of the federal deficit in generating aggregate demand. The change in private sector saving behavior is illustrated in Figure 2, which shows the private sector deficit, the government deficit, and the current account deficits as shares of GDP from 1959 to 1999. In 1992 the private sector had a net financial surplus, defined as the difference between total private sector saving and investment, of 4.2 percent of GDP. However, by 2000, this surplus had been transformed into a deficit of 6.2 percent of GDP. Thus, in the space of just eight years, the annual private sector saving rate had fallen by an amount equal to 10.4 percent of GDP.[7]

Godley (2000) has emphasized the current size of the private sector deficit. At 6.2 percent of GDP, the private sector is now issuing liabilities at a rate that exceeds growth of income, giving rise to a rapidly rising liability-to-income ratio, which Godley concludes is likely to prove unsustainable. Godley's analysis is conducted at a highly aggregative level and focuses on the private sector as a whole. However, it is useful to decompose the private sector into component parts, as this serves to link with other analyses, which have emphasized the significance of household debt in the business cycle (Palley, 1994, 1998a). It also sheds further light on the mechanisms that have helped defer the aggregate demand impact of worsened income distribution, as well as shedding light on why the current configuration is unsustainable.

The private sector balance is defined as

$$\text{private sector balance} = \text{private sector saving}(S) - \text{private sector investment } (I), \tag{1}$$

[7] From the national income account identities, the private sector deficit is defined as

$$\text{private sector deficit } (S - I) = \text{government balance } (G - T) + \text{current account balance } (X - M).$$

Figure 2 The private sector, government, and current account deficits as shares of GDP, 1959–2000

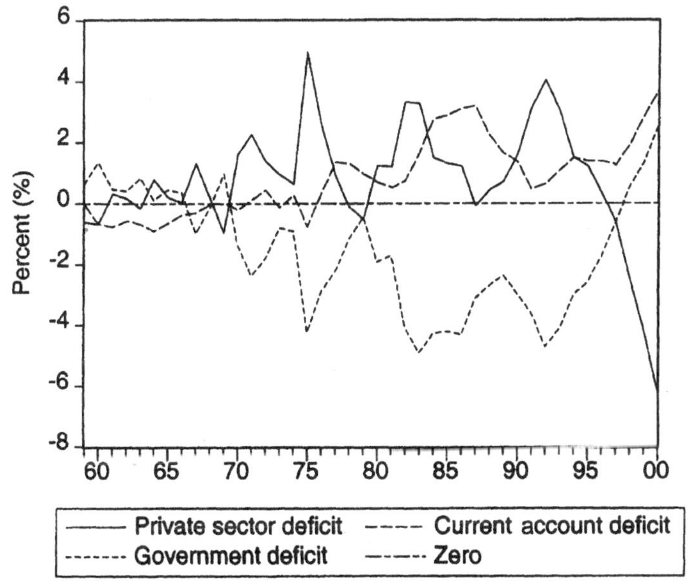

where saving and investment are defined as shares of nominal GDP. Figure 3 shows the evolution of private sector saving and investment as shares of GDP. The figure shows a dramatic decline in the private sector saving rate since 1984 and a recovery in the private sector investment share after 1990. The implication is that both saving and investment behavior have contributed to maintaining robust demand. Rising investment spending has directly fueled aggregate demand, whereas a declining private sector saving rate has fueled consumption spending. However, the private sector saving rate has fallen to historical record lows, whereas the investment share remains well within the bounds of normal highs. This indicates that changed saving patterns have played the greater role.

The private sector saving share can in turn be decomposed into personal and business components so that the private sector saving share becomes defined as

$$\text{private sector saving} = \text{personal saving} + \text{business saving}. \quad (2)$$

Figure 4 shows personal and corporate saving as shares of GDP. This figure sheds important light on the process of private sector demand generation. The business sector saving share has been largely unchanged,

Figure 3 Private sector saving and investment as shares of GDP, 1959–2000

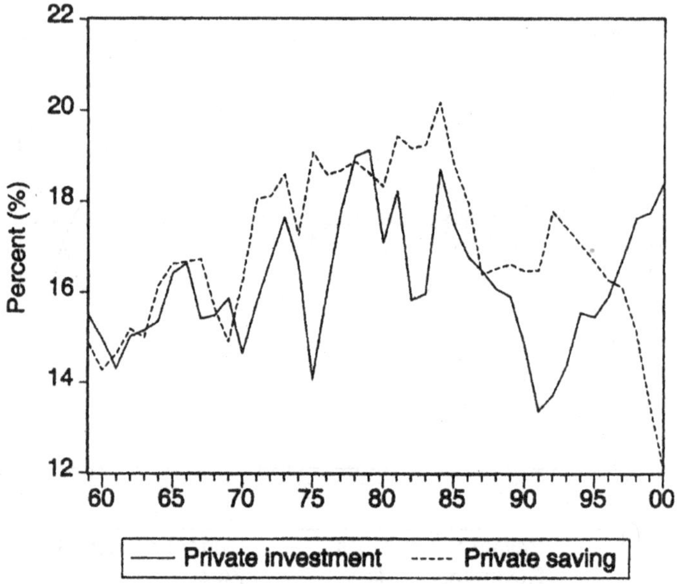

Figure 4 Personal and business sector saving as shares of GDP, 1959–2000

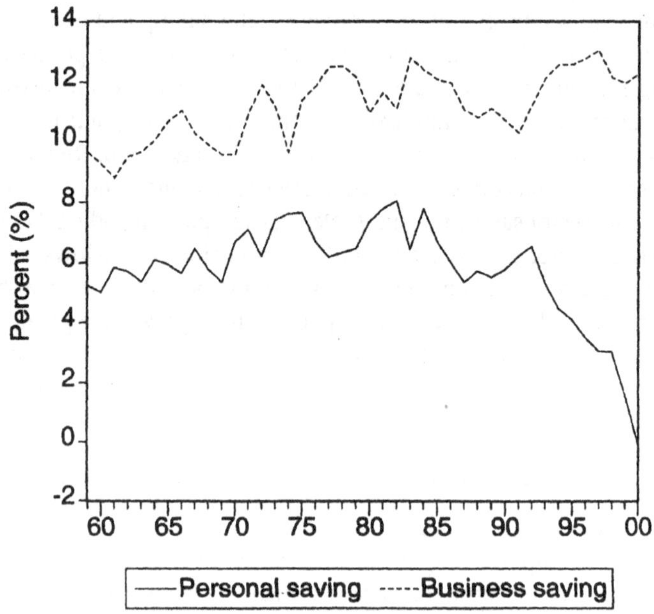

and all the change in the private sector saving share has therefore been driven by a collapse in the personal saving share. Prior to 1980, personal saving was slightly above 5 percent of GDP, but since then it has steadily drifted down, and in the last quarter of 2000 and the first quarter of 2001, it actually turned negative. Few countries have experienced negative personal saving rates. Two that have are Norway and Sweden in the second half of the 1980s, and both experienced severe, hard landings.[8]

Finally, the share of personal saving can in turn be written as

$$\begin{aligned}&\text{personal saving share}\\&= \text{personal saving/personal disposable income}\\&\times \text{personal disposable income/GDP.}\end{aligned} \tag{3}$$

Figure 5 shows the evolution of these two components of the personal saving share. This figure shows how the decline in the personal saving share has been driven by falls in both the rate of saving out of personal disposable income (a behavioral propensity) and the personal disposable income share of GDP. The decline in the personal saving rate began in the early 1980s and has proceeded steadily. The decline in the personal disposable income share began in 1990, and it reflects the twin influences of a shift to a government budget surplus and a rising business sector saving rate. From a historical perspective, it is again noteworthy that the personal disposable income share is well within the normal range, whereas the personal saving rate is abnormally low. This raises questions as to whether such a low saving rate is sustainable.

Household sector debt

The decline in the personal saving rate has helped finance household sector consumption spending. Another development is the increase in consumer debt, and household borrowing has financed additional consumption spending. Figure 6 shows the evolution of the household debt-to-personal disposable income ratio. This figure shows a cyclical pattern around an upward trend, and the ratio now stands at a record high level.

Figure 6 reveals two important features. The first is the rising trend of the household debt–income ratio. This rising trend reflects the extensive

[8] A number of other countries (Canada, Australia, New Zealand, Sweden) also have unusually low personal saving rates today. If the low saving rate augurs trouble—for reasons discussed below—these economies may also find themselves hit by hard landings.

Figure 5 Personal disposable income as a share of GDP and personal saving as a share of personal income, 1959–2000

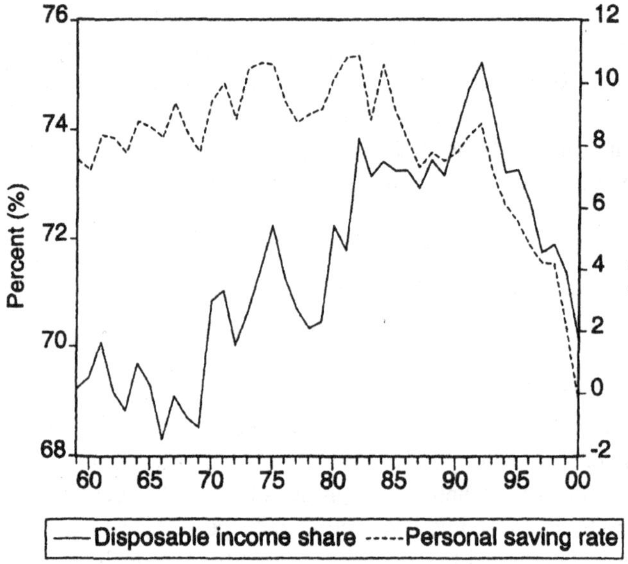

Figure 6 Ratio of total household sector debt to personal disposable income, 1966–2000

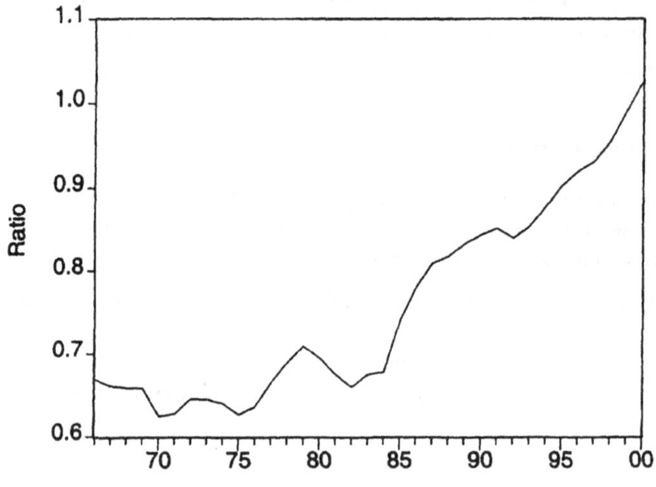

process of financial innovation in the U.S. economy over the last 25 years. Such innovation has given households increased access to credit, thereby increasing their ability to borrow to finance consumption. The increased use of credit cards, with their extensive credit facilities, is one example of this innovation. A second example is home equity loans, which have allowed households to tap wealth that was previously illiquid. These innovations have come on stream steadily and have been gradually and continuously diffused into the economy. This long and steady process has been a critical factor explaining how demand problems have been kept at bay. Indeed, the continuing importance of home equity loans has been shown in the current recession, and may help explain why it has been so mild. With housing prices remaining robust throughout the recession, households have been able to access home equity loans to sustain consumption spending despite job losses.

The second important feature of Figure 6 is that it shows that the debt-to-income ratio rose rapidly in the 1990s. Borrowing has therefore risen faster than income, and this at a time when national income has been rising rapidly. In 2000, the debt–income ratio was 1.02, which is 22 percent higher than its previous cyclical peak of 0.834 in 1989. The scale of the increase suggests that households may now be approaching their debt ceiling ratios, and this promises to put a stop to using debt-financed consumer spending to compensate for the deteriorated underlying aggregate demand generation process.[9]

Figure 6 provides data on the economy average debt–income ratio. This average ratio may conceal deeper problems. Household sector saving can be decomposed into two parts:

$$\begin{aligned}\text{household saving} &= \text{saving of creditor households}\\ &\quad + \text{saving of debtor households}.\end{aligned} \tag{4}$$

In effect, there are two types of households—financially affluent households and financially strapped households. The former have positive savings, whereas the latter have negative saving and borrow from the financially affluent. Financial distress in the strapped group of households may be much more advanced than is suggested by aggregate numbers.

Evidence for this proposition comes from the Federal Reserve's 1998 Survey of Consumer Finances (2000). Table 2 decomposes the results

[9] The exact level of this ceiling is impossible to predict, as the ceiling has risen with every cycle, owing to the gradual diffusion of financial innovations within retail financial markets, which has more and more households taking advantage of them. It is this type of change that makes forecasting business cycles so difficult.

Table 2
Household debt distribution by income

Household type	Average income ($)	Average debt ($)	Average mortgage ($)	Average other debt ($)	Debt share (%)	Mortgage share (%)	Other share (%)	Debt/ income	Mortgage/ income	Other/ income
Less than $50,000 (66.2% of households)	23,090	68,918	36,305	32,614	46	45	48	2.98	1.57	1.41
More than $50,000 (33.8% of households)	112,232	157,681	87,417	70,264	54	55	52	1.40	0.78	0.63
					100	100	100			

Source: Author's calculations based on Federal Reserve 1998 Survey of Consumer Finances.

of the survey into households earning less that $50,000 and households earning more than $50,000. For households earning less than $50,000, the debt-to-income ratio was 2.98; for households earning more than $50,000 it was 1.40. In 1999, the median family income was $48,950. Putting the pieces together indicates the divided state of household sector finances. The top half of households have debt burdens that are unproblematic, but the bottom half have heavy burdens.

Two important implications follow. First, interest rate cuts may be relatively ineffective in stimulating consumer borrowing because the top half of households are not liquidity-constrained and have little demand for new borrowing. Side by side, the bottom half of households are constrained, but credit risk is more important than the cost of wholesale financial funds in setting their interest rates. This means that the marginal impact of Federal Reserve interest rate cuts is likely to be small. The second implication is that reducing debt burdens to create the conditions for another expansion of consumer lending could take considerable time, and during this period of transition the economy is vulnerable to a vicious circle of lending contraction—which is the twin of the recent virtuous circle of lending expansion. Thus, a contraction of income causes an increase in the debt–income ratio, which lowers lending and income, thereby further raising the debt–income ratio. This is the model of the debt-driven business cycle presented in Palley (1994).

Finally, an interest rate mechanism that has been critical in spurring household-consumption spending is mortgage refinancing. This has reduced household interest burdens, freeing income for consumption spending. The last 20 years have witnessed a steady secular decline in mortgage interest rates. The average annual rate on a new 10-year mortgage peaked at 15.14 percent in 1982, and then fell to 9.19 percent in 1988. There was a small increase back to 10.13 percent in 1989 as the Fed tightened, but the rate then fell in fairly steady fashion to 7.04 percent in 1999, and in 2001 it was 7 percent.[10] This secular decline in long-term rates, driven by disinflation and the unwinding of the Fed's earlier tight monetarist positions, has made for a steady stream of mortgage refinancing waves. Each wave has served to reliquefy the household sector, helping sustain consumer spending. When faced by aggregate demand weakness, the Fed has simply had to lower interest rates, thereby triggering a new refinancing wave.

[10] *Economic Report of the President*, February 2002, p. 406.

Now this process of disinflation-based mortgage refinancing may be exhausted. Mortgage interest rates have been around 7 percent for the last four years, and getting further significant stimulus will require them to fall to around 6 percent. This is certainly feasible and could happen if there is a significant lasting economic downturn. However, initially, credit markets stand to be resistant as inflation expectations will have to adjust down. Thus, the mortgage interest rate response may be slow in coming, as was the case in 2001, when long-term rates remained essentially unchanged even as short-term rates plummeted. Second, with many households now heavily extended through home equity loans, many will find it difficult to refinance. Third, with housing prices at record levels, a downturn could impose equity losses on many homeowners, and this too will make refinancing problematic. In sum, though there may exist room at the margin for some further mortgage-refinancing stimulus, this mechanism is likely to be less powerful than in the past.

Investment exhilarationism

An examination of the household sector shows how reduced saving rates and increased consumer borrowing have been important factors offsetting the negative demand effects of worsened income distribution. A second important factor has been increased investment spending, which has risen steadily over the course of the 1990s. Investment spending as a share of GDP bottomed at 13.4 percent in 1991, but then rose to 18.4 percent in 2000. Two principal factors can be identified with this rise—one systemic, the other temporary—and both are riven by contradiction. This suggests that any further increase in the investment share is unlikely.

On the temporary side, the rise in investment spending in the second half of the 1990s was helped by the exuberance promoted by "New Economy" chatter. An examination of the record of investment spending shows a dramatic acceleration in 1997 of spending on equipment and software. This acceleration transformed what had previously been a subpar business cycle expansion into a record expansion. However, the exuberance that drove this spending had the hallmarks of a bubble, and it has now become evident that translating new economy developments into private profit is a difficult task. With the bursting of the bubble's expectations and the stark realization about the difficulties of turning new economy developments into profits, growth of investment spending on equipment and software has fallen dramatically and has actually turned negative. The new conditions suggest that it will be hard to maintain existing levels of investment spending, let alone grow them, and this points to an urgent need for new sources of aggregate demand generation.

On the systemic side, the rising investment share of GDP has also been driven by the rising profit share and rising profit rates that were documented in Table 1. These favorable capital income trends have increased incentives to invest, and they correspond to a regime that Bhaduri and Marglin (1990) term "exhilarationist." In such a regime, rising profitability spurs an increase in investment that more than compensates any reduction in consumption spending attributable to worsened income distribution. However, the critical unknown is whether exhilarationist regimes (high profit rate/high profit share) are permanently sustainable, or whether the initial rise in investment and profit rates eventually peters out. This can occur if the worsening of income distribution—be it the result of a shift to profits or a shift within the wage distribution to upper income groups—results in a situation in which there is insufficient aggregate demand to absorb the additional capacity created through new investment. At this stage, excess capacity would begin to emerge, competitive pressures would start to erode profit rates, and investment spending would be scaled back. The extensive presence of excess manufacturing capacity both domestically and internationally suggests that this could be happening.[11]

The role of the stock market

The stock market boom of the last 20 years has been another prominent feature of the U.S. economy, and it has played an important role in explaining both the declining saving rate and the strength of investment. In January 1980, the Dow Jones index stood at 904, and by January 2000, it had reached 11,281. This tremendous increase in stock market values has provided another mechanism for compensating the negative aggregate demand effects of deteriorated income distribution. Moreover, the fact that the stock market has risen almost uninterruptedly for 20 years again serves to illustrate the long time period over which these demand compensation mechanisms can operate. However, as with consumer indebtedness, there are now indications that this mechanism may also be exhausted, with the market hitting a valuation contradiction. Even if corporate earnings are sustained, current price–earnings ratios look

[11] As of March 2000, total U.S. industry capacity utilization was 82.25 percent, and U.S. manufacturing capacity utilization was 81.6 percent.

rich, and the picture only gets worse if earnings start to fall because of deficient demand.

A second reason the stock market is unlikely to provide price appreciation on the scale enjoyed over the last 20 years is that part of the earlier rise in prices was due to a change in portfolio preferences. This had households shifting their wealth into stocks, and this shift was reinforced by changes in pension arrangements, which had firms shifting from defined benefit to defined contribution arrangements—such as 401(k) plans. Both of these shifts increased demand for stocks and drove up prices. However, both are also of a nonrepeatable nature and cannot therefore drive future stock price appreciation.

The increase in stock market prices has positively affected consumption spending through three channels—a wealth effect channel, a confidence channel, and an expectations channel. The wealth effect is the most widely recognized channel, yet it may in fact be the least important.[12] The wealth effect has rising equity prices contributing to greater household wealth, thereby encouraging households to consume more and save less.[13] This effect has likely grown in size given the extensive shift in the composition of household portfolios, which has resulted in more households owning stock. Moreover, this shift has been amplified by the spread of 401(k) saving plans and by the shift in pension arrangements toward defined contribution plans away from defined benefit plans. Both of these arrangements contribute to households directly owning more stock, and they also encourage households to view pension wealth as if it were standard private wealth. However, despite these changes, equity ownership still remains enormously concentrated at the top end of the income distribution, and for this reason it is unlikely that the wealth effect has been the main channel of transmission of a stock market effect.[14]

The second channel is the consumer confidence effect, which has consumers interpreting a rising stock market as an indicator of robust real

[12] It is important to distinguish between the "stock market wealth effect" and the "property market wealth effect." Whereas the aggregate impact of the stock market wealth effect has likely been small, the impact of the property market wealth effect has been huge. The evidence of the impact of property wealth on consumption is evident in home equity borrowing. Rising home prices have allowed consumers to take out home equity loans that have then financed consumption spending.

[13] Saving less also includes borrowing more since borrowing constitutes a form of negative saving.

[14] In 1998, the top 10 percent of households owned 86.1 percent of all common stock, including pensions (Mishel et al., 2000, p. 265).

economic conditions. Whereas the household wealth effect is restricted to operate only on households that own equities, the consumer confidence effect touches all households. Consequently, its impact can be far more widespread.

The third channel is the stock market expectations effect. This has households extrapolating current price gains into the future, leading them to believe that their future wealth will be significantly larger. Even households with small current holdings of equity can be significantly influenced by the expectations effect, and this means it can also be widespread. Thus, low-wealth households, believing that their small holdings will multiply in value over time, may increase consumption and reduce saving now.

Whereas the wealth effect is a stock market "price-level" effect, the confidence and expectations effects are driven by the "rate of change of stock prices"—that is, they depend on a rising stock market. This is a critical distinction. The latter two effects are probably the most significant because of their application to all households, and not just the wealthiest, but they require a steadily rising stock market. It is this feature that ultimately generates contradiction, since stock prices must eventually get pushed to implausibly high valuations. Once equity prices stop rising (note they do not even need to fall), the stock market confidence and expectations effects can even kick into reverse.

Finally, in addition to affecting consumption spending, the rising stock market may also have influenced aggregate demand through its effect on the cost of capital. The logic here is that rising stock prices lower the cost of equity capital, thereby encouraging firms to finance increased investment spending with new equity issues. This investment channel may have been particularly important in the information technology sector, which was marked by a tidal wave of initial public offerings (IPOs). However, even here it may not have been the cost of equity capital per se, but rather the irrationally exuberant expectations about the payoffs to new technology investment.[15] With these expectations now revealed as unjustified, investment in the new technology sector and stock prices of new technology sector companies have collapsed together.

All of these channels have enabled a rising stock market to help compensate for deterioration in the underlying demand generation process. However, for reasons discussed earlier, the stock market is unlikely to

[15] To the extent that investors had wildly optimistic expectations about future profitability in the new technology sector, the cost of equity capital (measured in terms of expected future profits given away) may even have been quite high.

repeat its past price appreciation, and it even risks price declines. This means that the stock market is also exhausted as an engine of demand compensation.

The trade deficit and the budget surplus

Whereas reduced household saving rates, increased household indebtedness, and a rising stock market have contributed to maintaining aggregate demand, the worsening of the U.S. trade deficit has contributed to draining aggregate demand out of the economy. However, just as there are doubts about whether the above processes of demand compensation can be maintained, so too are there doubts whether the trade deficit leak can be plugged in a non-destabilizing fashion.

For all of 2000, the United States ran a current account deficit of $435 billion, or 4.4 percent of GDP. On the surface it would appear easy to plug this demand leak by simply reducing imports. Here, the goal is to bring about a reduction of imports through expenditure switching (that is, shifting spending toward domestically produced goods). Lowering the exchange rate to accomplish this would seem the easiest way to accomplish such switching, but it is not problem free. First, a lower exchange rate stands to raise imported inflation, and this risks an errant Federal Reserve interest rate response. Second, a lower exchange rate and reduced U.S. imports stand to reduce global demand and trigger recession in the rest of the global economy, which in turn risks feeding back and amplifying the demand shortage in the U.S. economy. Over the last two decades, the United States has taken on the role of "buyer of last resort" for the global economy. Ending this role risks major global disruptions, particularly since the International Monetary Fund (IMF) and the World Bank have pushed developing countries to pursue development strategies predicated upon export-led growth. Putting the pieces together, it is unlikely that the United States can look to its external account to be the engine of demand growth. Instead, considerations of the external account actually show how contradictions in the aggregate demand generation process extend into the global economy.

The federal budget surplus has been another major source of demand leakage. In 2000, the total federal surplus was $236 billion, or 2.4 percent of GDP. Tax cuts and increased defense spending in 2001, combined with the automatic stabilizer design of the fiscal system, have eliminated this surplus and pushed the budget into approximate surplus. From a macroeconomic policy stance, these developments have been welcome and have helped mitigate the depth of the recession, and point to the continued efficacy and relevance of fiscal policy. But here too there are policy risks owing to continued flawed understandings of the economic impact of budget surpluses. In particular, most economists continue to argue that deficits are bad because they decrease national saving and capital accumulation, whereas surpluses do the reverse. Such thinking has elevated surpluses as a goal of policy, and this thinking is most deeply reflected in the commitment to prefund Social Security through large surpluses that will continue for almost two decades.

Although current political and economic conditions have reduced the budget surplus, the underlying misunderstanding remains intact. This gives rise to the following danger. In the event of a prolonged economic slowdown, the surplus is likely to start automatically and rapidly disappearing owing to falling incomes and tax receipts. At this stage policymakers may try to protect the surplus by cutting spending and raising taxes; evidence of the likelihood of such a response is provided by repeated discussions about spending triggers linked to deficit outcomes. Such a reaction would effectively reduce aggregate demand at a time of demand shortage, thereby amplifying the downturn.

Moreover, even if this worst-case scenario does not materialize, fiscal policy still looks to be calibrated to exert significant fiscal drag. Thus, the 2003 Bush administration budget (released February 2002) treats 4.9 percent unemployment as full employment and has budget policy calibrated to produce small rising surpluses at this benchmark. This means the economy stands to face a systematic head wind if it attempts to push below 4.9 percent unemployment.

Conclusion: economic policy in the contradicted economy

The 2001 U.S. recession has been demand-driven. The dominant view among economists is that the recession is a passing problem and that there is nothing wrong with the economy's underlying demand generating process. However, this paper has argued that the recession reflects considerably more intractable structural problems associated with the process of aggregate demand generation, and these problems are directly related to the severe worsening of income distribution that has taken place over the last 20 years.

The aggregate demand effects of the worsening of distribution have been kept at bay over two long business cycles through a number of mechanisms—reduced household saving rates, increased household borrowing, a rising profit share that has stimulated investment spending, and a prolonged stock market boom. The demographics of the "echo" baby boom have also helped. These combined mechanisms have been so powerful that they have even at times been capable of creating conditions verging on excess demand. However, the ending of the "Great Expansion" of the 1990s suggests that these mechanisms are approaching exhaustion, and the dangers posed by this exhaustion are compounded by the deflationary stance of fiscal policy and the intractable nature of the U.S. trade deficit. Together, these considerations suggest that the U.S. economy is entering a period when systemic demand shortage is likely to be the major difficulty.

The underlying policy problematic concerns how to restore a solid basis to the aggregate demand generation process. Tackling this problem involves the huge task of confronting the misguided intellectual understandings that now guide policy.

1. The easiest part of the problem is monetary policy where the Fed must implement a regime of low real interest rates. But low interest rates are unlikely to be sufficient, as shown by Japan's experience over the last half decade.
2. The problem of the federal on-budget surplus can be readily solved by a combination of tax cuts and spending increases. But here political conflicts intervene. The best policy would be a combination of immediate tax cuts aimed squarely at middle- and low-income households, and sustained spending to meet health, education, and infrastructure needs.
3. The problem of the off-budget Social Security surplus is deeply intractable, with policy-makers of all stripes committed to prefunding Social Security. Prefunding, whether it be through private saving accounts or the publicly owned Social Security Trust Fund, exerts a deflationary drag.[16]
4. Just as it is important to remedy the drag imposed by the budget surplus, so, too, there is a need to remedy the drag imposed by the trade deficit. The contradictions inherent in a trade strategy exclusively focused on import reduction suggest that the solution is to increase world demand growth and thereby raise demand for U.S. exports. However, expanding global demand and trade does not mean more trade agreements like the North American Free Trade Agreement (NAFTA). Instead, it means new development policies

[16] Both private and public prefunded systems exert a deflationary drag, but public systems have a range of other advantages associated with collective insurance and intergenerational income insurance (Palley, 1998b).

that pay attention to income distribution, and a new international financial architecture that provides stable flows of development capital. Such measures can allow developing countries to consume an increasing share of the goods they produce, while still retaining access to financial resources to fund their growth and development.

5. In addition to a pro-growth global economic agenda, there is also a need to remedy the overvalued dollar problem (Palley, 2001). The appreciation of the dollar over the last five years has directly affected U.S. manufacturing, which has been at the epicenter of the current recession. The U.S. economy has been the locomotive of the global economy, but the strong dollar has been cannibalizing that locomotive by undermining manufacturing jobs and investment. A gradual depreciation of the dollar, coordinated by the world's major central banks, can reverse this development without imposing financial disruptions. At the same time, it will bring terms-of-trade benefits to the rest of the world, which increase standards of living and alleviate burdens associated with servicing dollar-denominated foreign borrowing.
6. Each of the above measures can contribute to alleviating the underlying demand problem. Yet, at the end of the day, there is a need to repair U.S. income distribution. In particular, the traditional focus on the functional distribution of income (profits versus wages), but exclusive focus on profits, is too narrow. A healthy profit rate is good for investment and growth. U.S. profit rates are up and may have gotten a little out of line, warranting some downward reduction. But they are not steeply out of line, either historically or internationally. The real problem is the distribution of the wage share, which has shifted to upper income corporate managers and professionals at the expense of nonsupervisory and production workers. Remedying this calls for rebuilding the institutions that gird the labor market, including the minimum wage and union density. However, in today's globalized economy, these domestic institutions must be accompanied by core labor standards that can gird the new global economy.

The above set of policy prescriptions is summarized in Figure 7. Policymakers face choices regarding macroeconomic and microeconomic policy variables. The U.S. economy is currently positioned in box B—unsustainable growth. The European economy is positioned in box C—stagnation. Policy stands at a critical juncture. Failure to repair the damage done to income distribution risks setting in train forces of aggregate

Figure 7 The macroeconomic–microeconomic policy matrix

	Level playing field labor markets	Business-dominated labor markets
Expansionary macropolicy	A. Sustainable Growth	B. Unsustainable Growth (U.S.)
Contractionary macropolicy	C. Stagnation (Europe)	D. Deep Recession

Source: Palley (1998c).

demand stagnation that could trap the economy in prolonged and even deep recession. The needed policy mix is that described in box A (expansionary macroeconomic policy, level playing field labor markets), which produces sustainable growth. The challenge is getting there in the face of an economics profession and public understandings that lean to box D.

REFERENCES

Bhaduri, A., and Marglin, S. "Unemployment and the Real Wage: The Economic Basis for Contesting Political Ideologies." *Cambridge Journal of Economics,* 1990, *14* (4), 375–393.

Bound, J., and Johnson, G. "Changes in the Structure of Wages in the 1980s: An Evaluation of Alternative Explanations." *American Economic Review,* June 1992, *82* (3), 371–392.

Friedman, M. *A Theory of the Consumption Function.* Princeton: Princeton University Press, 1956.

Godley, W. "Drowning in Debt." Levy Institute Policy Note 2000/6, Annandale-on-Hudson, NY, 2000.

Katz, L.F., and Murphy, K.M. "Changes in Relative Wages, 1963–1987: Supply and Demand Factors." *Quarterly Journal of Economics,* February 1992, *107* (1), 35–78.

Mishel, L.; Bernstein, J.; and Schmitt, J. *The State of Working America, 2000/2001.* Ithaca, NY: ILR/Cornell University Press, 2000.

Palley, T.I. "Debt, Aggregate Demand, and the Business Cycle: An Analysis in the Spirit of Minsky and Kaldor." *Journal of Post Keynesian Economics,* Spring 1994, *16* (3), 371–390.

———. *Plenty of Nothing: The Downsizing of the American Dream and the Case for Structural Keynesianism.* Princeton: Princeton University Press, 1998a.

———. "The Economics of Social Security: An Old Keynesian Perspective." *Journal of Post Keynesian Economics,* Fall 1998b, *21* (1), 95–112.

———. "Restoring Prosperity: Why the U.S. Model Is Not the Right Answer for the U.S. or Europe." *Journal of Post Keynesian Economics*, Spring 1998c, *20* (3), 337–354.

———. "The Over-Valued Dollar: Policy Complacency and the Deepening of America's Slump." *New Economy*, December 2001, *8*, 242–247.

[3]

MANAGING AMERICA

The Questionable Legacy of Alan Greenspan

Thomas Palley

Alan Greenspan will retire soon, and many analyses, most of them swooning, will soon be upon us. This economist offers an original and perhaps lasting post-mortem on Greenspan's reign. He believes that Greenspan has been responsible for a new business cycle whose foundation is financial boom and cheap imports. The resulting borrowing is not a basis for stable future growth.

ALAN GREENSPAN was appointed chairman of the Board of Governors of the Federal Reserve on August 11, 1987, and for most of the eighteen years since then, he has been widely regarded as an oracle of economic policy. Now, with Greenspan preparing to step down and relinquish the reins of the Federal Reserve in 2006, it is timely to offer an assessment of his legacy.

The focus of the current assessment is Chairman Greenspan's impact on the goals and systemic conduct of Federal Reserve policy rather

THOMAS PALLEY is an economist in Washington, DC. He was the chief economist at the U.S.-China Economic and Security Review Commission and, earlier, the assistant director of economic policy at the AFL-CIO.

Challenge, vol. 48, no. 6, November/December 2005, pp. 17–31.

ISSN 0577–5132 / 2005 $9.50 + 0.00.

than his policy judgment. Much has been written on the question of whether Greenspan raised interest rates too abruptly in 1987, causing the stock market crash; whether he raised rates too much in 1988–89, causing the recession of 1990; whether he raised rates too much in 1994, causing the economic slowdown of that year; and whether he contributed to the stock market bubble of the late 1990s by keeping monetary policy too easy for too long. However, these episodes are not the focus of the current assessment. Instead, this assessment is structural in character, focusing on changes in the Federal Reserve's construction of monetary policy under Greenspan. To the extent that the above policy episodes matter, they do so because they illustrate the real consequences that follow from changes in policy construction initiated during his tenure.

That said, a first conclusion is that the Greenspan era has cemented a transformation of monetary policy whereby policy now privileges financial markets over employment and labor markets. Prior to 1980, monetary policy was significantly driven by labor market concerns and, in many regards, worked hand in hand with other elements of the policy apparatus to put a floor under labor markets. Now, monetary policy is significantly driven by financial market concerns and looks to put a floor under financial markets.

A second conclusion is that the policy transformation cemented by Alan Greenspan was begun by his predecessor, Paul Volcker, and in many respects it was Volcker who did the difficult political spadework that has enabled Greenspan's policy regime. Many progressives love to hate Greenspan as the representative of conservative financial market interests. Yet, the reality is that construction of today's monetary policy regime began under a Democratic administration, and it has been very much a bipartisan affair.

A third and final conclusion is that the U.S. economy is fragile, and a full assessment of the Greenspan era must therefore wait for what happens over the next few years. This policy transformation of the past twenty-five years has elevated the significance of finance in the U.S. economy. The process of transformation has provided an economic shot in the arm as American households have used their enhanced access to credit to finance increased consumption spending. The open question is what will be the long-term consequences of this increased financial access. The new economic regime clearly has a powerful financial accelerator powered by borrowing. The next few years will show whether or not it is sustainable once consumers and business have loaded up on debt.

Financial Markets and the New Business Cycle

Alan Greenspan took office in August 1987 when the Reagan economic expansion of the 1980s was still in process. That expansion was marked by several features that have come to delineate a new business cycle. Whereas earlier cycles were characterized by growth of manufacturing, the new business cycle has been marked by deindustrialization, growing trade deficits, and robust consumer spending financed by booming financial markets and growing household debt.

This new cycle emerged out of the deep recession of 1981, which saw large-scale deindustrialization, unemployment above 10 percent, and a brief flirtation with wage deflation. Thereafter, there followed a long economic expansion, but it was marked by robust appreciation of the dollar that contributed to record trade deficits and also caused a double-dip recession in the manufacturing sector. As a result, for the first time since before World War II, manufacturing employment failed to recover its previous peak employment level recorded in 1979.

On the financial side, the 1980s expansion saw a huge stock market boom, albeit briefly interrupted by the crash of October 1987. In addition, the decade witnessed the emergence of the corporate junk bond market, which gave rise to the phenomenon of leveraged buyouts. Household borrowing also rose to record levels relative to income, and there was a house price boom that eventually imploded in 1990. Finally, the expansion saw a sustained widening of income inequality, epitomized by the CEO pay explosion.

These features have been present in the business cycles that have since followed. In the 1990s, the Clinton business cycle began with a period of extended economic weakness that became known as "jobless recovery." When the boom eventually gathered steam in 1996, it was marked by an even more robust stock market expansion, and there was a repeat of the dollar appreciation that had been so damaging to U.S. manufacturing in the 1980s. As a result, the trade deficit rose to new highs, and manufacturing again failed to recover the peak employment level of the prior boom.

Similarly, under President George W. Bush there has been a second episode of jobless recovery. Like the recession of 1990–91, the recession of 2001 was supposedly short and shallow, yet it took four years for private-sector employment to recover its pre-recession peak. In foreign currency markets, the dollar continued to appreciate until early 2003, helping the trade deficit break records year after year. Manufacturing and manufacturing employment have therefore continued to find themselves in the economic crosshairs. On the financial side, the stock market's bounce back from its large fall in 2001 has provided some economic support, but this time around the principal driving financial force has been house price appreciation. This outcome has contributed to a construction boom, and it has also provided the wherewithal for further household borrowing that has financed another consumption binge and pushed household debt to record highs.

Though history never repeats itself precisely, the business cycles of Ronald Reagan, Bill Clinton, and George W. Bush bear robust structural similarities that unify them and distinguish them from the business cycles of the 1945–80 period. To summarize, these similarities include deindustrialization, overvaluation of the dollar, record trade deficits, widening income inequality, and stock market and housing price appreciation that have supported record consumer debt burdens. Thus, the foundation of the new business cycle is financial boom and cheap imports. Financial boom provides consumers with borrowed finance that funds spending, while cheap imports ameliorate the impact of widening income inequality, deindustrialization, and periodic bouts of increased economic insecurity.

Behind this new business cycle lies a new economic structure. Deregulated financial markets have ensured a proliferation of lenders providing easy access to credit, while financial product innovation (such as home equity loans) ensures a steady flow of credit leveraged against rising home prices. In goods markets, globalization of production and an overvalued dollar have ensured a steady flow of cheap imported consumer goods, and in future this flow stands to increasingly include services that are becoming more and more tradable.

The Role of Policy in the New Business Cycle

Much of the economic structure that supports the new business cycle would likely have come into being on its own as a result of market innovations. However, policy has also played a critical role by actively promoting the emergence of these structures. More importantly, there has been a refusal to contemplate new policies that would have moderated or altered these trends. This is where Chairman Greenspan's impact has been so critical.

As chairman of the Federal Reserve, Greenspan has consistently used his bully pulpit to promote the current path of globalization, and he has also thrown his support behind wide-ranging financial deregulation and bank mergers. However, the most important change under Greenspan has concerned the conduct of monetary policy. In the post–World War II era, the Fed's macroeconomic policy goals have always been a combination of full employment and price stability, and all Federal Reserve chairmen have wrestled with the problem of inflation. However, under Greenspan there has been a significant shift of policy weight toward concern with inflation. Between 1945 and 1979 the shadow of the Great Depression ensured that the weight placed on full employment was far greater than the weight placed on price stability, and attention to full employment concerns helped ensure that productivity gains were shared and supported rising real wages and a rising popular standard of living. Across the board, White House, Congress, and Federal Reserve policymakers felt the need to react to labor market weakness, an approach that was formally enshrined in the 1946 Employment Act that mandated that all branches of government work together toward full employment. In effect, the era was characterized by a labor market–centered policy regime that put a floor under employment and real wages.

The Greenspan era has seen a significant shift in policy focus. Whereas the earlier regime aimed at putting a floor under labor markets, the new regime aims at putting a floor under financial markets. The new regime manifests itself in several ways, the most noticeable feature of which is the prominence given to combating inflation. This objective has replaced the earlier regime's policy goals of full employment, easy job availability, and rising real wages. Indeed, rising wages are actively fought on the grounds that they are inflationary, but the same logic is never applied to rising profit rates.

This policy transformation has been justified by appeal to the theory of the natural rate of unemployment, a theory developed by Milton Friedman and his Chicago school colleagues. The theory maintains that there is a minimum unemployment rate below which the economy cannot go without producing ever-accelerating inflation. Initially, the theory was used to justify a floor on the unemployment rate and to retreat from earlier notions of full employment such as a level of job vacancies equal to the number of job seekers. Subsequently, it has been used to shift policy attention to inflation, which becomes the indicator of when full employment is breached. In this fashion, concern with inflation displaces a direct concern with unemployment, and it is the theory of the natural rate that is ultimately behind today's policy vogue of inflation targeting.

The theory of the natural rate has been extensively criticized on both theoretical and empirical grounds. At the theoretical level, it makes grand unrealistic assumptions about wage flexibility and the way labor markets work, and at the empirical level, it has been impossible to establish a tight, stable estimate. Indeed, the concept is more akin to religion than science since it is incapable of disproof.

Despite these scientific weaknesses, the theory has been adopted by the Greenspan Fed, with enormous consequences for policy. First, it has elevated the policy significance of inflation. This elevation has been compounded by shifting to a concern with expected inflation that is used to justify preemptive monetary policy strikes against inflation even before it has emerged. Such preemptive-strike thinking played a role in the interest-rate policy miscalculations of 1987 and 1994. A second problem is that it has made inflation the sole indicator for policy. This focus on inflation, then, explains the Federal Reserve's neglect of asset prices in the late 1990s (which are not included in inflation statistics), which allowed the stock market bubble—and may also be allowing a house price bubble now.

In addition to shifting away from direct concern with unemployment, the Federal Reserve's new policy regime turns a blind eye to the foreign-exchange value of the dollar despite its critical impact on manufacturing employment and the trade deficit. Indeed, to the extent that the Fed has even engaged the question of the dollar, it has tended to view the "strong dollar" as a bonus that helps contain inflation by putting the squeeze on prices of manufactured goods.

Finally, the new policy regime is evident in the Fed's deferential treatment of financial markets and its response to financial market crises. Having created deregulated, highly leveraged financial markets that are free to wheel and deal, the Fed is now implicitly obliged to obtain market approval or face the fallout of the markets' displeasure. And when financial markets get themselves into trouble, the Fed must now come to their assistance to save the system from itself. This happened in the crash of 1987, in the recession of 1991 when Citibank was granted temporary exceptional regulatory relief, in the peso crisis of 1994, and again in the Long Term Capital Management crisis of 1998.

It is important to recognize that this regime shift started under Paul Volcker, who promoted a policy of disinflation centered on high interest rates. Inflation is especially bad for financial market interests, as it erodes the value of financial assets. The 1970s saw a spike in inflation as business and workers tried to resolve who would bear the burden of rising oil prices and determine how slower productivity growth would be shared between wages and profits. The Volcker Fed initiated a period of high interest rates that was good for financial investors in two ways. First, high interest rates raised the unemployment rate, thereby effectively settling the income distribution conflict in favor of business. Second, high interest rates directly raised the returns to financial investors. In addition, the Volcker Fed began the process of financial market deregulation that has created the space for expanded provision of credit to households.

The shift initiated by Volcker was tectonic, and, in combination with Ronald Reagan's political rhetoric, it fractured the New Deal policy consensus that had ruled since 1945. In this regard, Volcker is a critical historical figure who oversaw the preliminary initiation of a new policy paradigm. Viewed in this light, Alan Greenspan's policy configuration can be thought of as a logical extension of the paradigm initiated by Volcker.

That said, there are also critical differences between Chairman Volcker and Chairman Greenspan. In particular, whereas the policies of the Volcker Fed were justified as a form of "crisis" response to the high inflation of the late 1970s, under Greenspan the appeal to a crisis justification has completely fallen away, and the policies have become a form of "business as usual" that is claimed to be good for Americans. What began under Chairman Volcker as an anti-inflation crisis regime has evolved under Chairman Greenspan into a de facto financial market–centered policy regime in which financial markets have replaced the labor market as the principal focus of policy.

Similarly, when it comes to deregulation, there are also large differences in approach between the two. Whereas Volcker's approach to deregulation was partial and very much circumstance-driven, Alan Greenspan's approach appears much more doctrinally driven. He has been aggressively promotional in his approach to eliminating regulatory limits and controls, as evidenced by his strong support for the repeal of the Glass-Steagall Act (1933), which divided financial power between commercial and investment banks.

Compounding these developments is the fact that the new policy priorities have been ensconced in an institutional framework that has become increasingly free of political accountability. Since its inception in 1913, the Federal Reserve has always been a relatively autonomous institution, evidenced in its part-public, part-private ownership structure. However, under Chairman Greenspan the political autonomy of the Fed has increased. Though still subject to congressional oversight through hearings first mandated by the Humphrey-Hawkins Act (1978), the Fed has established an expanded position of independence. Multiple factors have been at work. First, the fact that the Volcker-Greenspan regime has been a bipartisan creation has meant that neither major political party has significantly challenged the Fed, creating space for new practices to take root. Second, Greenspan's oracular status has made it politically difficult to criticize the Fed for even those few politicians who would like to do so. Third, academic economists have promoted the notion that monetary policy is highly technical and should be left to the experts. Fourth, economists and conservative public policy institutes have also promoted the notion that politicians are not capable of objectively overseeing monetary policy. Instead, it is asserted that monetary policy should be left to independent central bankers, who will conduct it in a nonpartisan fashion that advances the national interest. The implication, never explicitly spelled out, is that central bankers are capable of objective nonpartisanship, but the rest of society is not.

This institutional and political setting has provided the Fed with a shield to ward off policy criticism, and the shield has been reinforced by Greenspan's brilliant use of the rhetoric of free competitive markets. This rhetoric implicitly presents the Fed as bowing out of markets and leaving the market to itself. Yet the reality is that the Fed is intervening, just as it always has in the post–World War II era. The difference is that it now intervenes on behalf of financial interests and financial wealth holders.

The new regime has momentous consequences. In the real economy, it has meant that full employment, robust real-wage growth, and a healthy manufacturing sector are no longer explicit policy priorities. In the financial economy, it has created a moral hazard among investors that generates asset price inflation. Since investors increasingly realize that the stability of the system is configured around asset prices, they realize the Fed cannot afford to let asset prices go to hell in a hand basket, and they have an incentive to put everything in stocks and other such assets. Moreover, this incentive also encourages debt bubbles, since economic agents have an incentive to finance their asset purchases with debt, thereby maximizing their gain from asset price inflation. Finally, the new regime may have had collateral effects on social attitudes toward risk sharing, perhaps most clearly reflected in the debate surrounding social security privatization. In that discussion, the construction of a new policy regime conducive to asset price inflation may have encouraged people to think that the stock market is a perpetual motion machine that generates appreciation without regard to the performance of the real economy.

Is the New Regime Sustainable?

The unusually weak recovery from the recession of 2001 suggests that the regime constructed over the course of the Greenspan era may be unsustainable. Despite the Fed's pushing interest rates to forty-five-year lows of 1 percent and the federal government's running a budget deficit of close to 4 percent of gross domestic product, the recovery has been the weakest in the post–World War II era, and the economy has kept hitting fresh "soft spots."

Ideologically grounded belief in the benefits of globalizing production has encouraged neglect of the trade deficit and the overvalued dollar, with catastrophic consequences for manufacturing. The prolonged weakness in manufacturing has in turn made for weakness in business investment spending, thereby compounding the obstacles to robust recovery. While low interest rates may have helped support consumer spending, they may also have created a new problem in the form of a housing price bubble. The good side of the bubble is that rising home equity has created wealth that has financed consumer spending and helped recovery. The bad side is that it has led to the buildup of debt secured on an asset whose price can fluctuate significantly. This is a feature that the Federal Reserve has consistently overlooked. Households own "flexible price" assets, but they are taking on "fixed value" debts, which exposes them to a major financial mismatch. Should the price of those assets fall, they will still owe the debts, but they will be less able to cover them with asset sale proceeds.

In a sense, the need for recourse to artificially low interest rates points to the contradiction in the current policy regime. Low rates have been used in the hope of jump-starting sustained recovery, but they have also triggered a debt-financed housing price bubble. That result means trouble down the road when debt has to be repaid and assets come to be cashed in. Driving up prices today beyond what is economically warranted tomorrow has severe consequences.

There are two core problems with today's system. First, owing to flawed international economic policies governing trade and the value of the dollar, too much spending is leaking overseas through purchases of imports. This outcome reduces domestic job creation—though it is good for foreign economies. Second, the long-term decline in real-wage growth and the widening of income inequality have called for household borrowing to fill the demand gap these trends created. Over time, such borrowing needs ever-lower interest rates to be sustained, but eventually it will hit the wall as households reach their borrowing limits, and interest rates hit the market floor determined by default risk.

These considerations point to a potential contradiction. Borrowing is a powerful economic stimulant that finances spending. At the same time, borrowing results in the accumulation of debt, and debt is a drag on the economy because it requires interest-service payments. The Greenspan era has been marked by the creation of a new financial regime characterized by a massive increase in borrowing by all sectors, and rising borrowing has made for robust economic growth. The open question is what will happen as accumulated debt burdens begin to exert a drag. Analytically speaking, the economy may exhibit robustness and vitality along the transition path from the old regime to the new, but once that transition is completed, the new regime may turn out to be economically fragile.

A Suggested Agenda for the Next Fed Chairman

The restoration of soundly based and widely shared prosperity will need an economic program that includes rules for labor markets, corporate governance, international trade, and financial markets. As one of the nation's preeminent policy-making institutions, the Federal Reserve has an important role to play, especially as regards the financial markets piece of that program.

A first important contribution that the next chairman can make is to use the Fed's bully pulpit to shape opinion supportive of a new policy configuration. Formally, the Fed controls monetary policy and has an important role in financial regulation. However, the Fed does far more than that through its influence over the shaping and coordination of elite policy opinion. This influence works through the research activities conducted by hundreds of Federal Reserve economists, Fed conferences and publications, and Fed links into the business community. Via these activities, the Fed contributes to shaping and legitimizing understandings of the economy that in turn drive policy.

As the senior and most visible executive of this powerful institution, the chairman of the Federal Reserve can powerfully influence the direction of this opinion-shaping power. Not only has Greenspan used this power to promote financial policy that is friendly to financial interests, he also has used it to address all manner of policy questions unconnected to the Fed's main mandate. These issues have included promoting trade liberalization, regressive social security reform, tax cuts favoring the wealthy, and even an attack on the economic merits of the minimum wage. Looking to the future, Alan Greenspan's replacement should be a person who will use the Fed's pulpit in a way that is more in tune with the Fed's institutional traditions and that is less economically ideological.

With regard to management of financial markets, the problem of asset price bubbles points to a need to regain control over the financial system to prevent its creating excessive liquidity that generates asset price inflation. At the policy level, the problem is that the Fed has relinquished all of its tools except interest rates, so that it must now manage activity in both the real economy and financial markets with just one instrument—interest rates. If it uses interest rates to target asset prices, it risks tanking manufacturing and the broader economy—what can be termed the "blunderbuss effect." Conversely, if it ignores asset prices, it risks an unstable asset price bubble and debt buildup.

The Fed's shortage of policy tools is a direct result of policies pursued during the Greenspan era. During this period the Fed has given up on quantitative regulatory controls, and even where controls remain, it has ideologically refused to use them. A case in point is margin requirements on debt-financed equity purchases that the Fed could have used to chill the stock market bubble of 1999–2000, but Chairman Greenspan resisted doing so.

In the wake of two decades of financial deregulation and innovation, the Fed needs some policy instrument innovation of its own. One such tool is adjustable, asset-based reserve requirements. Such requirements oblige financial institutions to hold cash reserves against different asset classes. The level of reserves would be adjustable and set by the Fed. Thus, if the Fed wanted to reduce speculation in a particular asset class, it would raise the cash reserve requirement for holding that type of asset and thereby cool speculation in that asset. For instance, if the Fed wanted to cool housing speculation, it would raise reserve requirements on mortgages. This action would de facto raise the cost of mortgages, since banks would have to hold more cash for each mortgage they issued, but the level of interest rates for other types of loans would be unchanged, thereby avoiding the blunderbuss effect.

A popular fallacy is that financial markets can no longer be regulated. However, the reality is that it is possible to invent new market-consistent controls over the financial sector. Some analysts have criticized Chairman Greenspan for lowering the federal funds interest rate to 1 percent in the last recession and leaving it at this low rate for too long. The argument is that this decision created a housing price and debt bubble. My personal view is that the chairman did the right thing to stop the recession from developing into an extended slump—though that may still happen. Instead, the real criticism of Alan Greenspan is his long-term promotion of a financial system that is unstable and his refusal to maintain existing instruments of financial control and to develop new ones. Asset price inflation and debt accumulation are the natural outcomes of the new policy regime, but the new policy structure gives the Fed only the blunderbuss of interest rates to control these processes.

Politics, Ideas, and the Greenspan Era

Over the past eighteen years Chairman Greenspan has been an enormously influential policymaker. It is important to recognize that his importance and position are not just the products of his own accomplishment. Instead, they should be understood in a broader context of politics and ideas. The new business cycle that the Fed has helped create is not a partisan affair. Rather, its creation has been supported by both Republican and Democratic administrations, and there has also been significant (but not universal) bipartisan support in Congress. Indeed, the creation of this new business cycle was, as noted, already well in hand under Volcker, Greenspan's predecessor, who was appointed by Democratic President Jimmy Carter. As for Greenspan, he was first appointed chairman of the Fed by Republican Ronald Reagan, and then successively reappointed by Republican George H. Bush, Democrat Bill Clinton (twice), and Republican George W. Bush. The net result is that there has been little competition in the political market for policy. Should America's new business cycle unravel, it will open a historic opportunity to challenge the existing policy configuration. The question is, will progressives be equipped with an inspiring and coherent economic vision backed by a consistent set of economic policies that can take advantage of that moment?

This consideration leads to the fundamental observation that ideas matter, something that conservatives have long appreciated and which was emphasized in Richard M. Weaver's canonical conservative text *Ideas Have Consequences* (1948). Volcker's anti-inflation program, which set the stage for Greenspan's tenure, grew out of intellectual work on inflation, the natural rate of unemployment, and competitive free markets. Policy independence for the Federal Reserve has been supported by academic work that emphasizes government policy incompetence. These features point to a symbiotic relationship between ideas, politics, and economic outcomes. Ideas shape politics and outcomes and are in turn shaped by them. This contribution of ideas is often obscure and difficult to track at any given moment, and for this reason politicians are inclined to dismiss their importance. Keynes acerbically captured this reality:

> [T]he ideas of economists and political philosophers, both when they are right and when they are wrong, are more powerful than is commonly understood. Indeed, the world is ruled by little else. Practical men, who believe themselves to be quite exempt from any intellectual influences, are usually the slave of some defunct economist. (Keynes 1936, 383)

Ideas are the spectacles through which we see the world, and different spectacles reveal a different world. Progressive political leaders and policy advisers, critical of the legacy of Chairman Greenspan, would do well to recognize this reality as they attempt to chart a new course in the post-Greenspan era.

For Further Reading

Galbraith, J.K. 1997. "Time to Ditch the NAIRU." *Journal of Economic Perspectives* 11 (winter): 93–108.

Keynes, J.M. 1936. *The General Theory of Employment, Interest and Money.* London: Macmillan.

Palley, T.I. 2004. "From Keynesianism to Neo-liberalism: Shifting Paradigms in Economics." In *Neo-liberalism: A Critical Reader,* ed. Alfredo Saad-Filho and Deborah Johnston. London: Pluto Press.

——. 2003. "Asset Price Bubbles and the Case for Asset Based Reserve Requirements." *Challenge* 46, no. 3 (May–June): 53–72.

——. 1999. "The Structural Unemployment Policy Trap: How the NAIRU Can Mislead Policymakers." *New Economy* 6 (June): 79–83.

——. 1998. "Zero Is Not the Optimal Rate of Inflation." *Challenge* 41, no. 1 (January–February): 7–18.

——. 2000. "Chairman Greenspan Wants Your Job: New Rules for a New Federal Reserve." *American Prospect,* October 23, 26–28.

[4]

International Journal of Political Economy, vol. 36, no. 4, Winter 2007–8, pp. 36–52.

ISSN 0891–1916/2008 $9.50 + 0.00.
DOI 10.2753/IJP0891-1916360403

THOMAS I. PALLEY

The Fallacy of the Revised Bretton Woods Hypothesis

Why Today's Global Financial System Is Unsustainable and Suggestions for a Replacement

In a series of papers, Dooley, Folkerts-Landau, and Garber (2003, 2004a, 2004b) have suggested that today's international financial system has structural similarities with the Bretton Woods arrangement that held sway between 1946 and 1971. Export-led growth by developing countries figures heavily in their analysis, and the authors have done a major service by reminding the economics profession of export-led growth and the possibility that it can have significant international macroeconomic effects.[1]

This article agrees with Dooley, Folkerts-Landau, and Garber's emphasis on export-led growth but challenges their comparison of today's system with the Bretton Woods system. It also differs regarding their conclusion that today's system is sustainable for the medium term and instead argues that the system is prone to a crash. Other authors (Eichengreen 2004; Goldstein and Lardy 2005) have also argued that

Thomas Palley is affiliated with Economics for Democratic and Open Societies, Washington, DC 20010. This article was originally prepared for a workshop called "Currency Conflicts and Currency Cooperation in the Global Economy," Institute for European Studies, University of British Columbia, Vancouver, Canada, on February 9–10, 2006. It was also released as Public Policy Brief No. 85 (2006) by the Levy Economics Institute of Bard College.

the system will crash, but their arguments are different. In particular, they focus on the sustainability of financing for the U.S. trade deficit, whereas this article focuses on the demand-side inadequacies of the system. The article also explores the politics supporting the current system, as well as speculating about the future of the dollar's dominant reserve currency status. The paper concludes with suggestions for a global system of managed exchange rates that should replace the current system.

The Revised Bretton Woods Hypothesis

The hypothesis put forward by Dooley, Folkerts-Landau, and Garber (2003, 2004a, 2004b) is that today's international financial system has structural resemblances with the earlier Bretton Woods system. That earlier system was one of fixed exchange rates and, according to their analysis, was a center–periphery system in which the post–World War II United States was the center, while war-ravaged Europe was the developing periphery. Within this framework, the United States proceeded to run progressively growing trade deficits with Europe that eventually caused the system's demise, but that demise was slow in coming.

Dooley, Folkerts-Landau, and Garber argue that today's global financial system has strong resemblances with this earlier system, with the United States still the center but East Asia (especially China) now playing the role of the periphery. China has an explicitly fixed exchange rate vis-à-vis the dollar, whereas other East Asian economies actively manage their exchange rates to prevent them from appreciating against the dollar. In addition, the East Asia region is running huge trade surpluses with the United States.

The economic logic behind the new system is that East Asian economies are pursuing export-led growth in which exports are the engine of growth. Lacking sufficiently robust domestic demand, they need exports to keep their factories operating. Export success then serves to attract large-scale foreign direct investment that creates jobs, builds manufacturing capacity, and transfers technology. Moreover, foreign investors finance this capital accumulation by providing the foreign exchange to purchase the capital goods. They also organize its transfer, installation, and operation. In this fashion, countries acquire jobs and a modern internationally competitive manufacturing sector.[2]

The price the periphery must pay is exports to the center. This explains why savings flow north from poor to rich, rather than from rich to poor as predicted by conventional intertemporal consumption smoothing models of the international economy. Moreover, because international competitiveness is key to export-led growth, countries actively pursue policies aimed at maintaining undervalued exchange rates. This explains China's refusal to revalue its exchange rate despite its massive and growing trade surplus, and it also explains the pattern of accumulation of dollar-denominated official reserves throughout East Asia.

The Misplaced Analogy with Bretton Woods

Dooley, Folkerts-Landau, and Garber's (2003, 2004a, 2004b) analogy of the present system with Bretton Woods rests on a number of similar macroeconomic patterns, including quasi-fixed exchange rates and the fact of persistent and growing U.S. trade deficits financed by the periphery. However, the analogy is wrong and ignores the fundamentally different microeconomic regimes governing the two periods.

Three significant differences between today's system and the earlier system exist. First, today's trade deficits are the result of an export-led growth predicated on undervalued exchange rates, yet the purpose of Bretton Woods was to prevent "beggar-thy-neighbor" trade based on competitive devaluation such as had afflicted the international economy in the Great Depression era. Though Germany's exchange rate alignment in the old Bretton Woods system came to be significantly undervalued, that was not the case for the United Kingdom. Moreover, the Bretton Woods system had formal provisions whereby countries with structural trade deficits could devalue.

Second, the current period shows multinational corporations shifting to China to establish state-of-the-art export platforms whose production is intended for export back to the center (the United States). This contrasts with the 1950s and 1960s when American multinationals established production facilities in Europe for purposes of supplying the European market. Companies such as Ford, General Motors, and IBM produced in Europe for Europe, not for export back to the United States. Likewise, European capital accumulation was primarily intended for European markets.

Third, the growing U.S. trade deficits of the 1960s were driven by full employment in the United States, with growing wages, a growing manufacturing sector, and increasing manufacturing employment. This contrasts with current trade deficits that are driven by debt-financed consumption spending supported by a house price bubble, and these deficits are also displacing U.S. manufacturing. Whereas the U.S. trade deficits of the 1960s were consistent with a robust and stable aggregate demand generation process, the current system is hollowing out the income and aggregate demand generation process and eroding manufacturing capacity.

Why the New Regime Will Fail

Dooley, Folkerts-Landau, and Garber (2003, 2004a, 2004b) maintain that the new system is sustainable and can last for another decade. In terms of their Bretton Woods analogy, the situation is closer to 1958 than 1968 (the Bretton Woods system collapsed in 1971). The reason for this stability is that the new arrangement suits both U.S. and East Asian interests—particularly those of China. The steady flow of imports that constitute the U.S. trade deficit supply a stream of cheap consumption goods that lowers consumer prices, keeping inflation down. This enables the Fed to hold the line on interest rates despite reduced unemployment rates. Furthermore, East Asian countries contribute to the favorable interest rate environment by recycling their trade surpluses into U.S. Treasury bonds as part of their strategy of keeping their currencies undervalued vis-à-vis the dollar.

East Asia benefits from exporting to the United States, which keeps its factories fully employed. Export success in turn spurs domestic and foreign direct investment in manufacturing, fuelling growth and development. For China, this is especially important because it needs to create jobs rapidly to absorb rural migration to the cities. If jobs are not forthcoming, this could trigger social and political unrest that would pose a threat to Communist Party rule. These benefits mean that East Asian governments are willing to continue accumulating U.S. financial assets, ensuring a sustainable stream of financing for the U.S. trade deficit at current interest rates and exchange rates. For East Asian countries, portfolio risk and return are not the driving force of their financial investment decisions and therefore do not enter their calculations. Economic growth is.

This configuration of national economic interests is underwritten politically by U.S. multinationals. Given their East Asian investments and the profitability of subcontracted production, these corporations are willing to do the political lobbying in Washington that heads off "protectionist" pressures generated by the trade deficit and U.S. deindustrialization. Finally, the fact that the dollar is no longer officially convertible into gold adds extra stability to the system and closes the weakness that brought down the original Bretton Woods system.[3]

Existing Arguments Regarding Why the System Is Unstable

Dooley, Folkerts-Landau, and Garber's (2003, 2004a, 2004b) claim regarding the stability of the new system has been challenged by several authors. Eichengreen (2004) argues that the system will collapse because of inconsistencies between the system and individual country financial interests. Although it is true the system delivers export-led growth for East Asian economies, countries are obliged to accumulate massive dollar reserves. These accumulations are unwise from a portfolio standpoint, lacking diversification and exposing countries to massive capital losses (equal to several percentage points of gross domestic product [GDP]) should the dollar ever fall in value. As a result, individual countries have an incentive to diversify their reserve holdings even though they benefit from the system as a whole. In effect, a classic cartel problem exists with individual members having an incentive to cheat on the system.

Eichengreen's analysis raises two serious objections. The first concerns his argument that placement of reserves elsewhere by East Asian countries will bring down the system. The principal option is the euro. Purchasing of other East Asian currencies—especially the yen—is also an option, as is buying gold, commodities, and real assets such as equities. However, these diversification activities do not necessarily fatally wound the system.

Selling dollars and buying euros will appreciate the euro vis-à-vis the dollar, undermining European international competitiveness and exporting deflation and unemployment to Europe. However, the dollar will retain roughly the same parity against East Asian currencies. Because the United States is their principal export market, all East Asian economies have an incentive not to let their currency appreciate too much against the dollar or against the currencies of rival East Asian economies. These incentives provide a centripetal force that stabilizes the system.

Similarly, purchases of commodities and equities may cause commodity and asset price inflation, but they also leave the dollar exchange rate essentially unchanged. In addition, to the extent that East Asian countries do sell Treasury bonds, this will drive up U.S. interest rates, thereby providing an incentive to remain invested in dollars.

A second objection concerns Eichengreen's assumption that East Asian economies ultimately face capital losses on their dollar reserve holdings. This assumption tacitly assumes the conclusion that the system is unstable. In fact, it is quite possible that China could end up reaping large capital gains on its holdings. The logic is as follows. China is resisting exchange rate appreciation to preserve its export-led growth model. Yet, at the same time it is gradually working toward international opening of its capital markets. Such opening could eventually trigger a depreciation of renminbi if Chinese wealth-holders exit the domestic system for purposes of economic and political portfolio diversification.[4] In this event, China will make large capital gains on its reserve holdings, and it will gain a second wind for its export led-growth program.

This scenario should be extremely troubling to U.S. policymakers concerned about America's industrial base, yet the U.S. Treasury Department is actively promoting such an outcome by demanding capital market openness. Once China liberalizes its capital markets and floats its exchange rate, the United States will no longer be able to claim that China is manipulating its exchange rate, and international legal grounds for action against China will disappear. Yet, capital market opening and renminbi depreciation are the diametric opposite of what the United States needs. The U.S. problem is with the trade balance and the exchange rate, and that calls for Chinese revaluation without capital market opening. The Treasury's policy promises to aggravate both the exchange rate and trade balance problems.

The U.S. Treasury's policy stance repeats the mistakes made with Japan in the early 1980s. At that time Japan was running a large trade surplus and was relatively financially closed. The U.S. Treasury pushed Japan to open its financial markets, which it did. As a result, undiversified Japanese wealth-holders exited Japan looking to invest overseas, causing the yen to fall and increasing Japan's trade surplus.

Goldstein and Lardy (2005) provide a second line of criticism of Dooley, Folkerts-Landau, and Garber's stability claim. Their analysis is a combination of positive and normative arguments that say not only will the system break down because of costs to China of maintaining it, but it is also in China's best interests that it do so. The principal focus of their analysis is the high cost to Chinese authorities of sterilizing monetary inflows into China. To prevent exchange rate appreciation, China's central bank sells renminbi, which increases the money supply and poses inflationary dangers. To sterilize this money supply increase, the bank then sells domestic bonds and soaks up excess liquidity. However, this in turn drives up interest rates and distorts financial signals. To counter this, the central bank has turned to administrative controls such as higher reserve requirements on commercial bank deposits and higher administered deposit rates to attract and retain bank deposits. But Goldstein and Lardy believe that at the end of the day these measures will prove inadequate and China will suffer from a combination of costly inflation and financial system distortions that misallocate and waste resources. They believe these prospective costs will compel China to abandon its undervalued exchange rate.

Goldstein and Lardy's other arguments against the existing system's stability and sustainability include challenging the underlying premise of Dooley, Folkerts-Landau, and Garber's hypothesis (that FDI-driven export-led growth is critical for China's industrialization), the capital-loss-on-reserves argument put forward by Eichengreen (2004), and an argument that revaluation will yield large terms of trade gains for China. This is because revaluation will lower the domestic cost of commodity and capital goods imports but will not have a large effect on Chinese manufactured exports because they consist mostly of processed products based on imported inputs.

Goldstein and Lardy's arguments are subject to important counter-arguments.[5] First, the sterilization-cost argument is essentially a monetarist one, yet the empirical link between the money supply and inflation is known to operate over a long and variable time horizon. China's administrative controls have worked well so far, and they may continue to work with the assistance of minor adjustments. Second, China's stiff resistance to revaluation provides a "revealed preference" statement by China's economic policy authorities showing that the contribution from export-led manufacturing growth is very important. Third, as noted above, it cannot simply be assumed that China will end up suffering capital losses on its reserve holdings. Fourth, China has an alternative plan for dealing with financial sector resource misallocation: partial privatization of its banks. The goal is for Western banks to modernize and improve the banking systems credit allocation function. The financial system can thereby be modernized, while simultaneously retaining the existing export-led growth strategy, which China's authorities view as helping the industrial sector and promoting capital accumulation and job creation.

A New Explanation of Instability

Dooley, Folkerts-Landau, and Garber (2003, 2004a, 2004b), Eichengreen (2004), and Goldstein and Lardy (2005) all focus on the sustainability of the supply of financing for the U.S. trade deficit. Dooley, Folkerts-Landau, and Garber believe this supply is sustainable because it meets the needs of supplier (surplus) countries. Eichengreen and Goldstein and Lardy believe it is not. This article argues that the system is indeed unsustainable and will crash but not for reasons of supply of finance. Rather, it is for reasons associated with the sustainability of the demand side of the system. This demand-side weakness has been overlooked because of failure to understand the microeconomic workings of the current regime.

These workings are shown in Figure 1. The key insight is that the financing of export-led growth and the U.S. trade deficit is a two-stage intermediated transaction. One half of the process involves a transaction between governments and financial intermediaries (i.e., banks) in U.S. financial markets. The other half of the process involves a transaction between U.S. banks and ultimate U.S. borrowers (i.e., consumers). The international transaction can be loosely identified with the supply of credit from East Asian economies to the U.S. economy, whereas the domestic transaction can be loosely identified with the demand for and provision of credit within the U.S. economy. The system can break down in either the international or domestic credit market. Thus far, attention has exclusively focused on the international credit market and possible withdrawal of financing by foreign lenders. However, the real nonsustainability may lie on the domestic credit market side.[6]

Export-led growth relies on selling goods in the U.S. market, but to sell, there must be a buyer. For the past several years the U.S. consumer has been that buyer and is even sometimes characterized as the global economy's "buyer of last resort." This consumer spending has been significantly financed by borrowing, which in recent years has been supported by a housing price bubble.

At this stage, there are several factors that could end the consumption boom. One possibility is that the Federal Reserve may overshoot with its interest rate tightening campaign, triggering a recession. A second possibility is that local American banks may tighten lending standards and reduce lending because they see households as financially overextended and housing collateral as overvalued. A third possibility is that

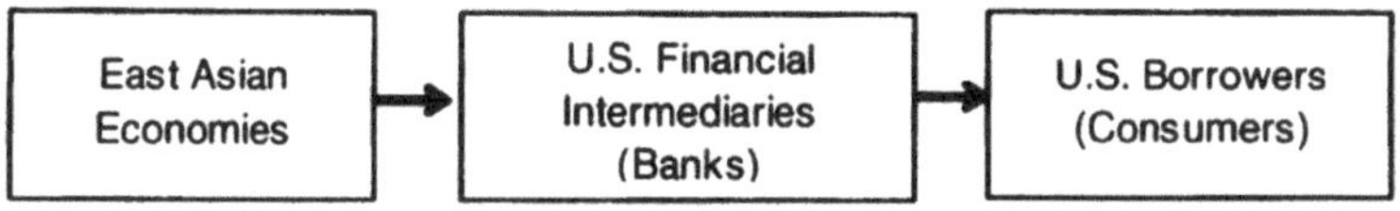

Figure 1. **Microeconomic Workings of the Current Regime**

consumers may voluntarily reduce spending. One reason is that the housing price bubble may be topping out, thereby eliminating future gains to borrow against and even possibly imposing losses. A second reason is that U.S. households face adverse wage and income pressures generated by international outsourcing. These pressures have been spreading from the manufacturing sector to the larger service sector.

If U.S. consumption spending falls, East Asian exports will fall. When that happens, the willingness of East Asian economies to finance the U.S. trade deficit becomes redundant. At that stage, international financing is no longer a binding constraint. Instead, the constraint will lie in the U.S. goods and domestic credit markets, and East Asian economies can do nothing to force those transactions by providing credit to banks. It is the borrower and local bank that must seal that deal. The bottom line is that the system is vulnerable to a crash that originates within the United States and about which East Asian economies can do little. Indeed, the competitive pressures unleashed by export-led growth and outsourcing are part of the constellation of forces making for such a crash.

What Happens If the U.S. Economy Sinks into Recession?

In the event that the United States falls into a consumer-led recession, East Asia is likely to be significantly impacted. This contrasts with the U.S. recession of 2001, which was an investment-led recession that left East Asia relatively unscathed because it largely exports consumer goods. A first impact would be felt via reduced exports, which would lower employment. A second impact would be felt via reduced foreign direct investment. With excess capacity and diminishing exports, multinationals would have reduced incentives to make new investments in East Asia.

The United States is also likely to find it difficult to escape a consumer-led recession. It broke out of the previous recession through the combination of a budget U-turn from large surplus to large deficit, a significant reduction in interest rates that spurred mortgage refinancing, which in turn reliquified household balance sheets, and consumer borrowing collateralized by a house price bubble. Today, these options are no longer available, and the only significant space for policy stimulus is for the Federal Reserve to reverse itself and cut rates. However, such rate cuts will likely be much less effective than previously. One reason is the stock of high interest mortgages has already been depleted and refinanced. The second reason is that lenders will be less inclined to lend given households' more financially stretched positions. Third, house prices have already risen and are more likely to go down than up. The net result is that interest rate reductions are likely be akin to "pushing a string."

That raises the question of what will happen to the dollar. Diminished U.S. economic prospects are likely to promote some portfolio shifting toward Europe and Japan. However, the reliance of Europe and Japan on exports to the United States means they too will be adversely impacted by a U.S. recession, which will reduce the incentive to shift into euro and yen investments. Side by side, the East Asian countries will be even keener to retain competitiveness given they will already be suffering diminished exports. That suggests they will continue to restrict appreciation against the dollar. The net result is that the dollar may not fall very much, making it harder for the United States to beat the recession. The prognosis is therefore one of prolonged slump.

Whither the Dollar? Some Longer-Term Reflections

Adopting a longer time horizon, there is the question of the future of the dollar and whether it will continue to retain its unique status atop the global economy. Today, the U.S. dollar is the world's premiere currency, with approximately two-thirds of world official foreign exchange holdings in dollars. Moreover, countries appear willing to run sustained trade surpluses with the United States in return for additional dollar holdings.

The conventional explanation of the dollar's reserve currency status is a "medium of exchange" story. The United States has historically been the largest and richest currency area, with the largest share of world output and trade. This has provided incentives for other countries to use dollars. A second related explanation is the "portfolio" theory whereby foreign investors have an incentive to hold dollar-denominated investments because the United States is the world's largest economy. This gives them ownership of a piece of the U.S. economy so that they share in U.S. economic growth and also diversify their investments. This portfolio effect is further strengthened by the perceived relative political stability of the United States compared to many other countries. It is also strengthened by the fact that many governments overissue their own money and create high inflation, encouraging foreign citizens to protect themselves by holding dollars instead of domestic currency.

A third theory of reserve currencies, associated with the political left, is based on U.S. military power and the Pax Americana. The argument is that U.S. military power provides the security that protects the global market system, and New York is the new Rome. Countries such as Saudi Arabia hold reserves in dollars because New York is a political safe haven and because that is how they help cover the costs of enforcing the Pax Americana.

These three theories are mutually reinforcing. Thus, to the extent that the dollar is widely used and is also a safe haven, investors will tend to rush into dollars in times of uncertainty. Consequently, central banks in other countries need to accumulate large dollar reserve holdings to protect against financial disruptions that result from sudden exits by investors, as happened in East Asia in 1997. According to these theories the dollar is likely to continue to maintain its unique status as the United States looks to remaining the largest economy, a stable society, and the sole superpower for the foreseeable future. Moreover, the dollar has established a lead position in the network of international exchange that will be hard to reverse.

However, there is a third unrecognized theory that can be labeled the buyer-of-last-resort theory of reserve currencies. Put bluntly, the reason other countries run trade surpluses with the United States and accumulate dollars is their failure to generate adequate consumption spending in their own markets—be it due to poor income distribution or bad domestic economic policies. This forces them to rely on the American consumer, and it is the foundation of the need for export-led growth in East Asia.

The economic logic is simple. Countries need exports to provide demand. That prompts them to keep their currencies undervalued in order to maintain export competitiveness, and that in turn forces them to channel their trade surpluses into dollars to keep the dollar overvalued. The buyer-of-last-resort theory therefore explains both the continuing strong demand for dollars despite the U.S. trade deficit and the dollar's dominance in official foreign exchange holdings. Ironically, America's dispensation from trade deficit discipline stems from other countries' failure to develop an equivalent of the American consumer. Countries want to industrialize with full employment, but they lack adequate internal demand. Consequently, they must rely on the U.S. market.

Conventional theory says the dollar will only lose its dominance when countries' portfolios become saturated with dollar holdings. At that stage they will cease buying and may even sell dollars, causing a fall of the dollar. The problem with this story is that countries have no incentive to sell dollars, as this would kill the golden goose of export-led growth. The buyer-of-last-resort theory suggests a different take. According to this perspective, the dollar could topple if countries manage to develop their own consumption markets. Euroland is most capable of doing this, but it has been hindered by policymaking that has been obsessed with inflation and afraid of growth. China is also working on growing its domestic market, but it will need to improve its income distribution in a way that links income distribution to productivity.[7]

More generally, the buyer-of-last-resort theory suggests focusing on the relative size of markets. As other economies grow faster than the United States, that will automatically tend to diminish the significance of the U.S. market. A deep U.S. recession will also shrink the relative size of the U.S. market and amplify this force, and it would diminish portfolio interest in accumulating U.S. financial holdings.

Finally, such a transition whereby the world loses its unlimited appetite for dollar-denominated investments is likely to be painful for both the global and the U.S. economy. First, transitions are generally difficult and subject to unexpected disruption. Second, a transition away from the dollar is likely to take place in an environment of global demand shortage so that all countries will likely suffer negative employment consequences. This cautionary longer term prognosis reinforces the case for policy change.

Wanted: A New Global Financial Architecture

Dooley, Folkerts-Landau, and Garber (2003, 2004a, 2004b) have sought to justify the current global financial architecture by arguing that it provides significant welfare benefits for all parties involved and that the reserve accumulation of East Asian countries has a sensible microeconomic logic. Thus, they argue that the surpluses earned by East Asian economies represent a means of acquiring foreign exchange collateral needed to underwrite foreign direct investment in those economies. From their point of view, the system should be left as is.

One problem with this collateral argument is that it is distinctly odd that Japan is still accumulating collateral. A second problem is that it does not accord with the historical record of how the new system took off after the East Asian financial crisis of 1997. The accumulation of official reserves by East Asian countries was never driven by a desire to accumulate collateral to underwrite FDI. Instead, it was initially driven by a desire to protect against the possibility of future capital flight. From this perspective the current system is an accidental product, the result of state policy responses to unwelcome market developments. Viewing the system as the product of optimizing markets is the disease of modern economists who interpret everything in this light.

Today's global financial system is problematic because it is likely unstable and unsustainable and because it promotes export-led growth that in turn fosters deflation (Blecker 2000; Palley 2003). In particular, excessive emphasis on exports hollows out the income and aggregate demand generation process in the United States via deindustrialization and outsourcing. This points to the need to shift from export-led growth to domestic demand-led growth (Palley 2002, 2006c) and for a new global financial architecture that accompanies that change. The global economy papered over the problems revealed by the 1997 East Asian financial crisis, but this papering has in turn caused new problems. A new financial architecture, addressing both the root cause of the 1997 East Asian financial crisis and the problems that have emerged since, is therefore needed.

The core problems of the international financial system concern capital mobility and exchange rates. Destabilizing capital mobility was the core problem behind the East Asian financial crisis, and exchange rates are the core problem behind today's global financial imbalances. The Bretton Woods system was one of fixed exchange rates and tight capital controls. In today's world, neither is feasible nor desirable. Instead, a contemporary financial architecture should involve managed capital mobility and managed exchange rates. Particularly important is the need to recognize that the existing system is a problem for both periphery and center. After the East Asian crisis there was a tendency to talk as if only the periphery needed change. The reality is both need change.

Many ideas for redesigning the global financial architecture have been proposed. Blecker (1999), Griffiths-Jones and Kimmis (1999), and Palley (1999) provide treatments that deal with governing and improving the quality of capital flows. Their collective proposals include improved prudential regulation, Chilean-style speed bumps that implicitly tax short-term inflows, currency transaction taxes, domestically imposed reserve requirements on lenders, and obligations for lenders to hedge foreign currency lending on behalf of borrowers.

The 1997 financial crisis was centered on capital mobility. Today's problem is gross trade imbalances. These imbalances have elevated the significance of exchange rate misalignments, pointing to the need for a system of managed exchange rates that promotes exchange rate stability. The obvious candidate is some form of crawling band target zone system as proposed by Williamson (1985, 1999), Bergsten, Davanne, and Jacquet (1999), Grieve Smith (1999), and Weller and Singleton (2002).

Such a system involves choice of a number of parameters that would need to be negotiated by participants. These include the target exchange rate, size of the band in which the exchange rate could fluctuate, and whether the band would be hard or soft. A hard band is automatically and decisively defended; a soft band is one that allows for marginal temporary deviations outside the band while retaining a commitment to bring the exchange rate back within the band when market conditions are most conducive. A fourth parameter is the rate of crawl. This involves determining the rules governing the adjustment of the target and band. Issues here concern the periodicity of adjustment and the rule governing adjustment of the nominal exchange rate.

Regarding the target exchange rate, a sensible candidate is the notion of fundamental equilibrium exchange rates proposed by Williamson (1994). The basic notion is that participating countries select a set of exchange rates consistent with their targeted current account and GDP outcomes.[8]

Finally, rules of intervention to protect the target exchange rate need to be agreed on. Historically, the onus of defending the exchange rate has fallen on the country whose exchange rate is weakening. This requires the country to sell foreign exchange reserves to protect the exchange rate. Such a system is fundamentally flawed because countries have limited reserves, and the market knows it. This gives speculators an incentive to try and "break the bank" by shorting the weak currency, and they have a good shot at success given the scale of low-cost leverage that financial markets can muster. Recognizing this, the onus of exchange rate intervention needs to be reversed so that the strong currency country (the central bank whose exchange rate is appreciating) is responsible for preventing appreciation, rather than the weak currency country being responsible for preventing depreciation. Because the strong currency bank has unlimited amounts of its own currency for sale, it can never be beaten by the market. Consequently, once this rule of intervention is credibly adopted, speculators will back off, making the target exchange rate viable. Such a procedure recognizes and addresses the fundamental asymmetry between defending weak and strong currencies.

Conclusion: Beyond the Mentality of Policy Passivity

Today's global financial system is a haphazard, suboptimal creation. Whereas East Asian economies are strategically manipulating their exchange rates, U.S. policymakers have rejected intervention on the grounds that markets know best and should be left alone. This asymmetry has allowed East Asia to pursue neomercantilist policies that have contributed to today's massive global financial imbalances.

The U.S. policy mentality is at odds with reason and the evidence. There are many theoretical reasons for believing that foreign exchange markets are prone to herd behavior and strong empirical evidence that exchange rates depart from their theoretically warranted equilibrium levels—be they defined as purchasing power parity or as the exchange rate consistent with sustainable current account deficits. Also, from a realpolitik standpoint, it is unwise for a country to let itself be out-gamed by others.

East Asian policymakers are right to believe that they can improve economic outcomes through exchange rate intervention. As Williamson (1999) observes, policymakers that use theory to think sensibly about the exchange rate and how to manage it can do a better job than a pure unregulated float. The problem is that East Asia has gone about this intervention in an uncooperative manner, and that threatens disastrous outcomes.

Notes

1. Blecker (2000) and Palley (2003) have explored the global macroeconomic inconsistencies of export-led growth.

2. Dooley, Folkerts-Landau, and Garber (2003, 2004a, 2004b) emphasize the connection among exports, FDI, and growth. Goldstein and Lardy (2005) have rightly criticized them for overemphasizing the contribution of FDI to China's growth. That said, FDI is a critical component of China's capital and technology accumulation strategy. More important, the link that should be emphasized is between exports and industrial investment in general, with exports spurring both foreign direct investment and domestic manufacturing investment. Exports provide the classic "vent for surplus" in China's economy. China's entrepreneurial tradition makes it highly efficient at organizing capital accumulation. However, China has not yet put in place a domestic consumption market that can absorb the production China is capable of organizing. This point is emphasized in Palley (2006a).

3. President Nixon suspended the right of countries to convert official dollar reserves into gold on August 15, 1971, in the face of large gold conversions, especially by France.

4. Chinese wealth-holders will want to diversify for standard economic reasons as well as political reasons, given the questions about rule of law in China and the potential for future political instability.

5. These arguments are developed in greater detail in Palley (2006a).

6. These arguments are developed in two policy briefs in Palley (2005, 2006b).

7. Unions are the natural way to do this because they bargain for wages that firms can pay only if they have the underlying productive ability. However, this route to developing a domestic market may be blocked by China's totalitarian political system that fears unions.

8. Operationally, for the single-country case, this is done as follows. The first step is to empirically estimate a current account equation of the form $CA = \alpha_0 + \alpha_1 Y + \alpha_2 e + \alpha_X X$, where CA = current account, Y = GDP, e = exchange rate, and X = vector of exogenous variables. This estimated equation is then solved to yield the fundamental equilibrium exchange rate (e^*) consistent with the target current account (CA^*), target GDP (Y^*), and given levels of exogenous variables, yielding $e^* = -\alpha_0/\alpha_2 - \alpha_1 Y^*/\alpha_2 + CA^*/\alpha_2 - \alpha_X X/\alpha^2$.

In a multicountry exchange rate system, these equations must be estimated and solved simultaneously across countries to ensure a consistent set of exchange rates. Moreover, it is necessary for countries to agree on a consistent set of national current account targets as not all countries can run surpluses.

References

Bergsten, C.F.; O. Davanne; and P. Jacquet. 1999. "The Case for Joint Management of Exchange Rate Flexibility." Institute for International Economics Policy Brief 99–9, Washington, DC: Available at www.iie.com/publications/papers/wp/1999/99-9.htm.

Blecker, R.A. 1999. *Taming Global Finance: A Better Architecture for Growth and Equity*. Washington, DC: Economic Policy Institute.

———. 2000. "The Diminishing Returns to Export-Led Growth." Paper prepared for the Council of Foreign Relations Working Group on Development, New York.

Dooley, M.P.; D. Folkes-Landau; and P. Garber. 2003. "An Essay on the Revised

Bretton Woods System." Working Paper 9971, National Bureau of Economic Research, Cambridge, MA (September).

———. 2004a. "Direct Investment, Rising Real Wages, and the Absorption of Excess Labor in the Periphery." Working Paper 10626, National Bureau of Economic Research, Cambridge, MA (July).

———. 2004b. "The U.S. Current Account Deficit and Economic Development: Collateral for a Total Return Swap." Working Paper 10727, National Bureau of Economic Research, Cambridge, MA (August).

Eichengreen, B. 2004. "The Dollar and the New Bretton Woods System." Available at www.econ.berkeley.edu/~eicheng/policy/cityuniversitylecture2jan3-05.pdf.

Goldstein, M., and N. Lardy. 2005. "China's Role in the Revived Bretton Woods System: A Case of Mistaken Identity." Working Paper no. 05-02, Institute for International Economics, Washington, DC (March).

Grieve Smith, J. 1999. "A New Bretton Woods: Reforming the Global Financial System." In *Global Instability: The Political Economy of World Economic Governance*, ed. J. Michie and J. Grieve Smith. London: Routledge.

Griffith-Jones, S., and J. Kimmis. 1999. "Stabilizing Capital Flows to Developing Countries." In *Global Instability*, ed. J. Michie and J. Grieve Smith.

Palley, T.I. 1999. "International Finance and Global Deflation: There is an Alternative." In *Global Instability*, ed. J. Michie and J. Grieve Smith.

———. 2002. "A New Development Paradigm: Domestic Demand-Led Growth" *Foreign Policy in Focus* (September). Available from www.fpif.org.

———. 2003. "Export-Led Growth: Is There Any Evidence of Crowding-Out?" In *Globalization, Regionalism, and Economic Activity*, ed. P. Arestis et al. Cheltenham, UK: Edward Elgar.

———. 2005. "Two Views About a Possible Hard Landing: Foreign Flight Versus Consumer Burnout." December 23. Available at www.thomaspalley.com.

———. 2006a. "External Contradictions of the Chinese Development Model: Export-Led Growth and the Dangers of Global Economic Contraction." *Journal of Contemporary China* 46 (February): 69–88.

———. 2006b."Export-Led Growth: The Elephant in the Room." January 13. Available at www.thomaspalley.com.

———. 2006c. "Developing the Domestic Market." *Challenge* 49, no. 6 (November–December): 20–34.

Weller, C., and L. Singleton. 2002. "Reining in Exchange Rates: A Better Way to Stabilize the Global Economy." Briefing Paper no. 131, Economic Policy Institute, Washington, DC (September).

Williamson, J. 1985. *The Exchange Rate System*, rev. ed. Washington, DC: Institute for International Economics.

———. 1994. *Estimating Equilibrium Exchange Rates*. Washington, DC: Institute for International Economics.

———. 1999. "Crawling Bands or Monitoring Bands: How to Manage Exchange Rates in a World of Capital Mobility." Policy Brief 99-3, Institute for International Economics, Washington, DC. Available at www.iie.com/publications/pb/pb99-3.htm.

[5]

The Presidential Agenda Issue

The U.S. Economy After Bush

Thomas Palley

The Bush-Cheney years have been marked by a disappointing economic performance, reflected in a business cycle expansion that is by many measures the weakest since World War II. Moreover, not only has the expansion been weak, it also appears to be ending with a severe financial crisis and the possibility of a prolonged economic slump. Putting a bottom to the slump will be the next president's most immediate task. However, there is a deeper question, argues the author. How can we restore sustainable growth that generates shared prosperity? It will require more than a return to the economic policies of the 1990s.

On January 20, 2009, George W. Bush will vacate the presidency of the United States. But he leaves a deeply troubled economy with both short-term and long-term challenges. The short-term challenge is putting a bottom under the economy. The long-term challenge is arguably greater—generating sustainable growth that also provides shared prosperity.

The Bush-Cheney years have been marked by an extremely poor

***THOMAS PALLEY** is an economist and author of* Plenty of Nothing: The Downsizing of the American Dream *(Princeton University Press, 2000). He was chief economist on the U.S.-China Economic and Security Review Commission and currently runs Economics for Democratic and Open Societies. He posts a weekly blog at www.thomaspalley.com.*

Challenge, vol. 51, no. 6, November/December 2008, pp. 26–37.

ISSN 0577–5132 / 2008 $9.50 + 0.00.
DOI: 10.2753/0577–5132510602

economic performance, reflected in a business cycle expansion that is by many measures the weakest since World War II. Moreover, not only has the expansion been weak, it also appears to be ending with a severe financial crisis and the possibility of a prolonged economic slump.

The question we now face is whether the Bush administration's economic failure was caused by specific policy failures or by exhaustion of the economic-growth paradigm that has framed policy over the last thirty years.

Democrats may have been united regarding the Bush administration's failure. But many of them also subscribed to the paradigm. New Democrats argue that after the current slump, it will be back to business as usual. Progressive Democrats argue that the current growth paradigm is exhausted. It never generated shared prosperity, and now it is also being shown to be unsustainable.

For many progressives, the bursting of the house price bubble signals the end of the age of Milton Friedman. That era of market fundamentalism was launched on the back of Ronald Reagan's political rhetoric and sustained by Alan Greenspan's asset bubble monetary policies. Because of market fundamentalism's ideological hold on the public's mind, change was not possible until the experiment had been shown to fail.

That has now happened, creating a political opportunity to revive and modernize the New Deal economic paradigm developed by Franklin Roosevelt's administration, which proved so successful in the thirty years after World War II. Such a revived policy paradigm must:

- Rebuild the wage structure and reestablish labor market mechanisms that ensure that wages of ordinary workers grow with productivity
- Commit monetary policy to full employment, and break with the aversion to full employment instilled by the flawed notion of a natural rate of unemployment
- Address the corrosive effects of globalization that have undermined employment security among workers and fostered a race to the bottom among corporations

- Inaugurate effective mechanisms of international economic cooperation regarding monetary policy, exchange rates, and capital flows to prevent future exchange-rate misalignments and global financial imbalances
- Invest in America's infrastructure—including education and health facilities and transportation
- Shift the American economy to a sustainable "green" trajectory that addresses the problem of climate change
- Establish efficient mechanisms for financing social security and health care that do not cut benefits, ensure coverage of all, and do not raise employment costs and thus discourage job creation in the U.S. economy
- Restore effective regulatory control over the financial system
- Refashion corporate governance so that corporations again contribute to maximum sustainable, shared prosperity rather than maximizing short-term profits and paying excessive salaries to top management.

Reality and Perception

One difficulty in writing about the Bush record is that despite the truly poor performance, for much of his administration the United States has been portrayed as enjoying boom-time prosperity. This distortion reflects two factors.

First, since November 2001 the economy has formally been in expansion mode, albeit one of the weakest expansions in history. That expansion was driven by a house-price bubble and consumer borrowing that fueled an unsustainable "feel good" consumption boom. This boom created an illusion of sustainable prosperity that was difficult to pierce.

Second, during this period there was a recovery in stock prices that accompanied the house-price bubble. Moreover, what income growth there was went largely to the top of the income distribution. Both of these developments benefited the "chattering class" (i.e., economic pundits and the media), which likely colored reporting on the economy.

The Bush administration pursued policies aimed at benefiting corporations and the rich, but those policies also produced an initial flourish of prosperity. That made these policies difficult to counter politically, despite their negative long-term economic consequences—the benefits were front-loaded, while the huge costs would only come later.

The Economic Record

By many measures President Bush's economic record is the weakest since World War II. Growth of national output has been far below the postwar business cycle average, and the same holds for growth of business fixed investment. The business investment share of output has also fallen, which augurs poorly for the future. That is because business investment is the main driver of productivity growth and rising living standards.

In labor markets, an extended period of jobless recovery followed the end of the last recession, in November 2001. In past business cycles, it has taken an average of twenty-one months to regain the employment lost during recession. This time it took forty-seven months. Moreover, job losses in the last recession were not that large, which indicates just how weak this expansion was.

Another indicator of the extent of labor market weakness is the large decline in the employment/population ratio relative to its previous 2001 peak. This decline suggests considerable hidden unemployment that is not recorded in the official U.S. unemployment rate.

Wage and salary growth have also lagged far behind the nine other business cycles since 1948. Most tellingly, the current cycle looks like it will be the first in which median family income (i.e., the income of the family in the middle of the income distribution) fails to recover the peak level of the previous business cycle. That will be a major rupture in American history, which has always been marked by rising median family income.

Manufacturing has been an area of particular devastation. In January 2001 manufacturing employment was 17.1 million; in June 2008 it was 13.5 million. That difference amounts to a loss of 3.6 million manufacturing jobs, equal to 18 percent of all manufacturing jobs at the start of the administration.

Manufacturing's experience marks another first in U.S. economic history—the first time ever that manufacturing employment has not increased during an economic expansion. Before 1980, manufacturing jobs increased in economic expansions, and they also hit new record peaks in each expansion. After 1980, manufacturing jobs still increased in expansions, but manufacturing failed to recover all the jobs lost in the prior recession and therefore failed to recover previous peak employment levels. Since 2001, manufacturing has not only lost jobs in recession, it has continued losing jobs in the expansion. That is unprecedented.

With regard to the international economy, the trade deficit broke all records, rising from $365 billion in 2001 to $753 billion in 2006, when it equaled 6 percent of gross domestic product.

The government budget has also been in persistent large deficit. As a result, between 2001 and 2007 the federal debt rose from 57 percent of gross domestic product to 65 percent. This trend promises to complicate future fiscal policy.

Finally, a continuing rise in income inequality has come on top of the rise in income inequality experienced over the prior twenty-five years. Thus, according to Internal Revenue Service (IRS) data, the top 1 percent of income earners received 22 percent of gross income in 2006, matching the previous record for inequality set in 1929. Given this rise in income inequality, it is perhaps not surprising that business profit growth has been spectacular and far above normal.

Explaining the Economy's Terrible Performance

Statistics provide a photo of the economy's performance, but that begs the question of why economic performance has been so weak.

The key here is the unbalanced character of the expansion. The roots of this unbalanced expansion lie in manufacturing's failure to participate in the recovery, owing to the trade deficit, the overvalued dollar, and offshoring of production by U.S. corporations.

The overvalued dollar meant that much consumer spending was drained offshore in the form of spending on imports. That outcome created jobs in other countries but not in U.S. manufacturing. Meanwhile, excess manufacturing capacity discouraged investment, while the steady stream of manufacturing job losses held down wages. Manufacturing investment was further undermined by corporations' shifting production to East Asia to take advantage of low-cost labor and the region's undervalued exchange rates.

The Federal Reserve responded to this weakness by lowering interest rates to 1 percent, thereby triggering a housing boom. Rising house prices and low interest rates in turn spurred a debt-financed consumption boom.

This configuration generated a distorted expansion. On one hand, the trade deficit and offshoring of production meant persistent job losses in manufacturing and weak business investment spending. On the other hand, low interest rates fueled a house price bubble that spurred a housing construction boom. Rising house prices then provided backing for a debt-financed consumption binge that sucked in even more imports.

During this period the Fed kept interest rates low for fear that if it raised them, consumption spending would slow and the economy would fall back into recession. Rather than confronting the unbalanced and unsustainable nature of the expansion, Federal Reserve Chairman Alan Greenspan chose to underwrite it.

The net result was huge trade deficits that undermined manufacturing, a housing bubble that pushed prices far above sustainable valuations, and an unsustainable rate of borrowing that has ultimately left consumers heavily burdened with debt.

The implosion of the house price bubble brought this process to an abrupt end. That is because it removed the asset price inflation that supported the construction boom and the borrowing behind consumer spending.

The Economic Outlook

The U.S. economy is now heavily debt burdened. It has relied on consumer spending to fuel growth, but consumers are now constrained. They have large debts and low accumulated financial saving, and the value of their principal asset (houses) is falling.

The financial sector is also extremely vulnerable. It lent heavily to finance the housing boom and now faces huge mortgage-default losses. Those losses could wipe out the banking sector's net worth.

This situation is driving a credit crunch whereby credit supplies dry up, putting further downward pressure on house prices and also limiting normal business activity. This pattern generates a vicious circle. Tight credit undermines asset prices and business activity, which strengthens the rationale for tight credit.

Under these conditions, a return to the consumer-led growth model of the past two decades is highly implausible. Instead, households face growing financial stress, as does the financial sector. All indicators point to trouble. The index of leading economic indicators is down, consumer confidence is at near-record lows, house prices are falling, and the economy has lost jobs in each of the last seven months.

Inflation is also working against recovery. Energy and commodity price inflation mean that prices are rising faster than wages, which is equivalent to a tax on consumers that weakens spending. It is also spooking financial markets, pushing up mortgage interest rates and thereby intensifying downward pressure on house prices. That stands to deepen the slump in construction, consumer distress, and financial-sector distress.

Balanced against this array of negatives, two positives could help build an economic bottom. One positive is the fall in the dollar, which has made the United States more internationally competitive. This should contribute to strong export growth, and it could also strengthen manufacturing investment if corporations relocate back to the United States to take advantage of America's renewed international competitiveness. The downside is that a weaker dollar could undermine other economies that rely on exports to the U.S. market.

A second positive is the reversal of the recent speculative spike in oil and commodity prices. That should reverse some of the adverse inflationary pressures described above.

Recommendations for the Next President

The next president will face two immediate challenges. The first is to stop the economic rot. The second is to jump-start the economy.

With regard to stopping the rot, that process is already under way. The Federal Reserve has backstopped Wall Street by giving investment banks and primary government bond dealers access to credit from the Fed. Likewise, the Fed has moved to ensure a continuing flow of credit to the housing market by giving mortgage finance giants Fannie Mae and Freddie Mac access to the same credit facilities. The Treasury also now has the ability to provide capital to Fannie and Freddie should they need it. In addition, a bailout has been designed that will stabilize and reliquify the banking system by recapitalizing banks and by purchasing some bad assets of banks.

Funding is also in place to help reduce the foreclosure problem, which is putting downward pressure on house prices. That is because Congress has provided funds to buy foreclosed homes and also to help households negotiate mortgage reductions.

Jump-starting the economy is going to require policy action on multiple fronts. One recommendation is another round of fiscal stimulus, this time more focused on infrastructure and less focused on tax cuts. Such infrastructure construction not only adds to economic activity now, it increases future productive capacity.

Fiscal stimulus should also include federal funding assistance to state governments. Most states are constitutionally obliged to run balanced budgets, and falling state tax revenues are driving expenditure cuts that amplify the downturn. The federal government can counter this with block grant transfers.

Because of the immediate cost of the financial system bailout, the new president will face enormous pressure from fiscal conservatives and the bond market to scale back any fiscal stimulus. That pressure must be rejected. The real economy is suffering from significant demand weakness and the only effective tool is fiscal policy. Failure to use fiscal policy to support the real economy will boomerang back and undermine the financial sector, thereby also undermining the bailout.

A second measure is to continue extending the duration of unemployment insurance (UI) benefits. UI benefits go to those who need them and who spend them, making them a twofer. That is, they are targeted to the needy, and they yield strong demand stimulus at small cost. In addition, policy should further raise the minimum wage and permanently index it to the median wage so that it contributes to a robust wage floor. Increasing wages is important for reviving demand and offsetting the effects of inflation. A higher minimum wage does this, directly helping the wages of those at the bottom and also generating ripple effects up the wage structure. Moreover, this is a good time to raise the minimum wage, as the decline in the dollar has relaxed pressures of international competitiveness.

Third, the next president will need to pressure the Federal Reserve to resist prematurely raising interest rates. A growing group within the Fed now wants to raise rates to placate Wall Street and fight inflation. That group is wrong, as higher interest rates will do little to lower inflation caused by a commodity speculation and adjustment of the dollar.

Fourth, there is a continuing urgent need for China, Japan, and several other East Asian economies to revalue their exchange rates. Their undervalued exchange rates were a critical factor in distorting the economic expansion and creating an unbalanced global economy, and global balance cannot be restored until they revalue.

Failed Policy or Failed Paradigm?

Whereas there is agreement on many of the policies needed to stop the rot and jump-start the economy, there is enormous division regarding the ultimate causes of the Bush administration's failure and how to restore sustainable growth that generates shared prosperity.

On one side, of course, are the Republicans, who want largely to extend the Bush policies. This is the worst of possibilities. But the Democrats are also divided. At one end are Robert Rubin, Larry Summers, and the "New Democrats." According to this group, the Bush administration's economic paradigm has been basically sound. Thus, the administration has continued with trade liberalization and globalization; emphasized financial innovation and deregulation; supported the Federal Reserve's emphasis on the dangers of inflation; and promoted labor and product market flexibility.

For New Democrats, the administration's failure stems from lost budget discipline, combined with inegalitarian tax and social policy. According to New Democrats, rising income inequality is largely due to technological change that has increased the demand for skills. This calls for "helping hand" programs that offer income support and retraining assistance to those who are displaced. Such social policy should be financed with progressive taxation. In sum, the New Democrat position is that if America restores long-term budget discipline and implements helping-hand programs, it can be back to business as usual.

On the other side are Progressive Democrats, who maintain the current economic paradigm is fundamentally flawed. The Bush administration has been a mean-spirited extension of this paradigm, but not a radical departure. Rising income inequality, wage stagnation, excessive debt growth, asset price inflation, widening trade deficits, and manufacturing decline have been features of the American economic landscape for thirty years. The Bush administration deepened these features, but they were already present in the Clinton and Reagan years.

From a progressive standpoint, the problem is a flawed economic paradigm that triumphed some thirty years ago with the elections of Ronald Reagan and Margaret Thatcher. The post-1980 U.S. business cycle has relied on financial booms and cheap imports. Financial booms have provided collateral to support increased borrowing that has financed spending on consumption. Increased borrowing has also been supported by easing of credit standards and by financial innovations that have widened access to credit. Meanwhile, cheap imports have ameliorated the effects of wage stagnation.

This pattern contrasts with the pre-1980 business cycles that rested on wage growth tied to productivity growth and full employment. Strong domestic demand conditions, combined with full employment, encouraged investment, which increased productivity and fueled higher wages.

The shift from the old to the new business cycle was the result of political change associated with Reagan's election in 1980. That inaugurated a period in which business has been ascendant and labor battered. Economists such as Milton Friedman intellectually rationalized the shift.

The old business cycle rested on the combination of New Deal institutional innovations that strengthened labor, plus demand-management measures pioneered in Keynesian economics. The new business cycle rests on policies that have sought to erode and repeal New Deal institutions, and demand management has been redirected to lowering inflation rather than securing full employment. Indeed, the language of full employment has been discarded.

The economic policies behind the new business cycle undercut workers and strengthen the power of corporations. Workers are boxed in on every side by the push for small government, labor market flexibility, abandonment of full employment as a policy goal, globalization, and the elevation of short-term profit over long-term gain. Neither public-sector nor private-sector workers can escape the pressure. The only way out is a new policy paradigm that rebalances the relationship between corporations, workers, and government.

Conclusion

The "failed paradigm versus failed policy" debate is critical, but it remains unresolved. That explains the deep economic policy divisions within the Democratic Party.

A major obstacle for Progressive Democrats is the intellectual dominance of neoliberal economics, which suffocates articulation of an alternative paradigm. Thus, neoliberalism reinterprets bad economic outcomes as instances of "market failure," when the real issue is how to institutionally order and manage modern capitalist economies so that they produce shared prosperity.

Interestingly, a similar debate lurks in Europe, but political conditions are slightly different. George Bush is a polarizing failed president who has created political opportunity for a debate over economic paradigm. However, intellectually the United States is unprepared for such a debate. In Europe, the conditions are reversed. Europe's stronger tradition of social democracy means greater intellectual readiness to engage in a debate about economic paradigm. However, Europe is still muddling along politically, which prevents a clear political framing of the problem.

To conclude, both the United States and Europe face a danger that the dominant economic paradigm is flawed and exhausted. It has never been able to produce growth with shared prosperity, and now its capacity to produce growth with inequality is also exhausted. Yet political resistance to changing the paradigm may still be too strong, and intellectual awareness of alternative possibilities not sufficiently developed. The implication is that both the United States and Europe could face an extended period of economic stagnation and political discontent.

[6]

New School Economic Review, Volume 4(1), 2010, 15-43

AMERICA'S EXHAUSTED PARADIGM: MACROECONOMIC CAUSES OF THE FINANCIAL CRISIS AND GREAT RECESSION[1]

Thomas Palley

ABSTRACT

This paper traces the roots of the current financial crisis to a faulty U.S. macroeconomic paradigm. One flaw in this paradigm was the neoliberal growth model adopted after 1980 that relied on debt and asset price inflation to drive demand in place of wage growth. A second flaw was the model of U.S. engagement with the global economy that created a triple economic hemorrhage of spending on imports, manufacturing job losses, and off-shoring of investment. Financial deregulation and financial excess are important parts of the story, but they are not the ultimate cause of the crisis. These developments contributed significantly to the housing bubble but they were a necessary part of the neoliberal model, their function being to fuel demand growth by making ever larger amounts of credit easily available. As the neoliberal model slowly cannibalized itself by undermining income distribution and accumulating debt, the economy needed larger speculative bubbles to grow. The flawed model of global engagement accelerated the cannibalization process, thereby creating need for a huge bubble that only housing could provide. However, when that bubble burst it pulled down the entire economy because of the bubble's massive dependence on debt. The old post-World War II growth model based on rising middle-class incomes has been dismantled, while the new neoliberal growth model has imploded. The United States needs a new economic paradigm and a new growth model, but as yet this challenge has received little attention from policymakers or economists.

I. INTRODUCTION

The current financial crisis is widely recognized as being tied to the bursting of the house price bubble and the debts accumulated in financing that bubble. Most commentary has therefore focused on market failure in the housing and credit markets. But what if the house price bubble developed because the economy needed a bubble to ensure continued growth? In that case the real cause of the crisis would be the economy's underlying macroeconomic structure. A focus on the housing and credit markets would miss that.

Despite the relevance of macroeconomic factors for explaining the financial crisis, there is resistance to such an explanation. In part, this is because such factors operate indirectly and gradually, while microeconomic explanations that emphasize regulatory failure and flawed incentives within financial markets operate directly. Regulatory and incentive failures are specific, easy to understand, and offer a concrete "fixit" agenda that appeals to politicians who want to show they are doing something. They also tend to be associated with tales of villainy that attract media interest (such as Bernie Madoff's massive Ponzi scheme or the bonus scandals at AIG and Merrill Lynch). Finally, and perhaps most important, a microeconomic focus does not challenge the larger structure of economic arrangements, while a macroeconomic focus invites controversy by placing these matters squarely on the table.

But, an economic crisis of the current magnitude does not occur without macroeconomic forces. That means the macroeconomic arrangements that have governed the U.S. economy for the past 25 years are critical for explaining the crisis. Two factors in particular have come into play. The first concerns the U.S. economic growth model and its impact on the pattern of income distribution and demand generation. The second concerns the U.S. model of global economic engagement and its impact on the structure of U.S. economic relations within the global economy.

The macroeconomic forces unleashed by these twin factors have accumulated gradually and made for an increasingly fragile and unstable macroeconomic environment. The brewing instability over the past two decades has been visible in successive asset bubbles, rising indebtedness, rising trade deficits, and business cycles marked by initial weakness (so-called jobless recovery) followed by febrile booms. However, investors, policymakers, and economists chose to ignore these danger signs, resolutely refusing to examine the flawed macroeconomic arrangements that have led to the cliff's edge. It is time to take a step back and look at how we got ourselves in this precarious position. Then perhaps we can figure out where to go next.

II. THE FLAWED U.S. GROWTH MODEL

Economic crises should be understood as a combination of proximate and ultimate factors. The proximate factors represent the triggering events, while the ultimate factors represent the deep causes. The meltdown of the subprime mortgage market in August 2007 triggered the current crisis, which was amplified by policy failures such as the decision to allow the collapse of Lehman Brothers. However, a crisis of the magnitude now being experienced requires a facilitating macroeconomic environment. That macroeconomic environment has been a long time in the making and can be traced back to the election of Ronald Reagan in 1980 and the formal inauguration of the era of neoliberal economics.

a. The Post-1980 Neoliberal Growth Model

The impact of the neoliberal economic growth model is apparent in the changed character of the U.S. business cycle (Palley, 2005). Before 1980, economic policy was designed to achieve full employment, and the economy was characterized by a system in which wages grew with productivity. This configuration created a virtuous circle of growth. Rising wages meant robust aggregate demand, which contributed to full employment. Full employment in turn provided an incentive to invest, which raised productivity, thereby supporting higher wages.

After 1980, with the advent of the new growth model, the commitment to full employment was abandoned as inflationary, with the result that the link between productivity growth and wages was severed. In place of wage growth as the engine of demand growth, the new model substituted borrowing and asset price inflation. Adherents of the neoliberal orthodoxy made controlling inflation their primary policy concern, and set about attacking unions, the minimum wage, and other worker protections. Meanwhile, globalization brought increased foreign competition from lower-wage economies and the prospect of off-shoring of employment.

The new neoliberal model was built on financial booms and cheap imports. Financial booms provide consumers and firms with collateral to support debt-financed spending. Borrowing is also sustained by financial innovation and deregulation that ensures a flow of new financial products, allowing increased leverage and widening the range of assets that can be collateralized. Meanwhile, cheap imports ameliorate the impact of wage stagnation, thereby maintaining political support for the model. Additionally, rising wealth and income inequality makes high-end consumption a larger and more important component of economic activity, leading to the development of what Ajay Kapur, a former global strategist for Citigroup, termed a "plutonomy."

These features have been visible in every U.S. business cycle since 1980, and the business cycles under presidents Reagan, Bush *père*, Clinton, and Bush *fils* have robust commonalities that reveal their shared economic paradigm. Those features include asset price inflation (equities and housing); widening income inequality; detachment of worker wages from productivity growth; rising household and corporate leverage ratios measured respectively as debt/income and debt/equity ratios; a strong dollar; trade deficits; disinflation or low inflation; and manufacturing job loss.

The changes brought about by the post-1980 economic paradigm are especially evident in manufacturing employment (see tables 1 and 2). Before 1980, manufacturing employment rose in expansions and fell in recessions, and each expansion tended to push manufacturing employment above its previous peak.[2] After 1980, the pattern changes abruptly. In the first two business cycles (between July 1980 and July 1990) manufacturing employment rises in the expansions but does not recover its previous peak. In the two most recent business cycles (between March 1991 and December 2007), manufacturing employment not only fails to recover its previous peak but actually falls over the entirety of the expansions.

Table 1. Manufacturing Employment by Business Cycle, October 1945 -January 1980

Trough	**Employment** *(Millions)*	**Peak**	**Employment** *(Millions)*	**Change** *(Millions)*
Oct. 1945	12.5	Nov.1948	14.3	1.8
Oct. 1949	12.9	Jul.1953	16.4	3.5
May 1954	15.0	Aug.1957	15.9	0.9
Apr. 1958	14.5	Apr.1960	15.7	1.2
Feb. 1961	14.8	Dec.1969	18.6	3.8
Nov.1970	17.0	Nov.1973	18.8	1.8
Mar.1975	16.9	Jan.1980	19.3	2.4

Source: National Bureau of Economic Research, Bureau of Labor Statistics and author's calculations.

Table 2. Manufacturing Employment by Business Cycle, July 1980 -December 2007

Trough	**Employment** *(Millions)*	**Peak**	**Employment** *(Millions)*	**Change** *(Millions)*
July 1980	18.3	July 1981	18.8	0.5
Nov.1982	16.7	July 1990	17.7	1.0
Mar.1991	17.1	Mar.2001	16.9	-0.2
Nov.2001	15.8	Dec.2007	13.8	-2.0

Source: National Bureau of Economic Research, Bureau of Labor Statistics and author's calculations.

The great myth about manufacturing, which has been hard to puncture, is that the observed pattern of decline is a natural and benevolent outcome of manufacturing's relatively higher rate of productivity growth. The confusion stems from the fact that higher productivity growth does mean manufacturing's employment share tends to decline naturally. However, a smooth long run declining employment share brought about by investment and innovation that creates a more efficient manufacturing sector is a fundamentally different proposition from decline caused by adoption of a policy paradigm that dismantles the manufacturing sector by encouraging off-shoring and undermining competitiveness.[3]

The reality is the break in the historical pattern of manufacturing employment growth shown in Tables 1 and 2 reflects a changed policy paradigm that first undermined manufacturing and eventually undermined the entire economy. This changed policy paradigm is perhaps most clearly illustrated by the change in policy attitudes toward the trade deficit.

Under the earlier economic model, policymakers viewed trade deficits as cause for concern because they represented a leakage of aggregate demand that undermined the virtuous circle of growth. However, under the post-1980 model, trade deficits came to be viewed as semi-virtuous because they helped to control inflation and because they reflected the choices of consumers and business in the marketplace. According to neoliberal economic theory, those choices represent the self-interest of economic agents, the pursuit of which is good for the economy. As a result, the trade deficit was allowed to grow steadily, hitting new peaks as a share of GDP in each business cycle after 1980. This changed pattern is illustrated in table 3, which shows the trade deficit as a share of GDP at each business cycle peak.

Table 3. The U.S. Goods Trade Deficit by Business Cycle Peaks, 1960 Ȇ2007

Peak year	Trade deficit ($ millions)	GDP ($ billions)	Trade deficit/ GDP (%)
1960	3,508	526.4	0.7
1969	91	984.6	0.0
1973	1,900	1,382.7	0.1
1980	-25,500	2,789.5	-0.9
1981	-28,023	3,128.4	-0.9
1990	-111,037	5,803.1	-1.9
2001	-429,519	10,128.0	-4.2
2007	-819,373	13,807.5	-5.9

Source: Economic Report of the President, 2009 and author's calculations.

The effect of the changed growth model is also evident in the detachment of wages from productivity growth, as shown in table 4. It is also evident in rising income inequality, as shown in table 5. Between 1979 and 2006, the income share of the bottom 40 percent of U.S. households decreased significantly, while the income share of the top 20 percent increased dramatically. Moreover, a disproportionate part of that increase went to the 5 percent of families at the very top of income distribution rankings.[4]

Table 4. Hourly wage and productivity growth, 1967–2006 (2007 dollars)

Period	Productivity growth	Hourly wage growth	Productivity - wage gap
1967–73	2.5%	2.9%	-0.4
1973–79	1.2	-0.1	1.3
1979-89	1.4	0.4	1.0
1989-2000	1.9	0.9	1.0
2000-06	2.6	-0.1	2.7

Source: Lawrence Michel, Jared Bernstein, and Heidi Shierholz, *The State of Working America 2008/2009* (Ithaca, NY: ILR Press, forthcoming).

Table 5. Distribution of Family Income by Household Income Rank, 1947–2006

Year	Bottom 40%	Next 40%	Next 15%	Top 5%
1947	16.9%	40.1%	25.5%	17.5%
1973	17.4	41.5	25.6	15.5
1979	17.0	41.6	26.1	15.3
1989	15.2	40.2	26.7	17.9
2000	14.1	38.1	26.6	21.1
2006	13.5	38.0	27.0	21.5

Source: Lawrence Michel, Jared Bernstein, and Heidi Shierholz, *The State of Working America 2008/2009* (Ithaca, NY: ILR Press, forthcoming).

b. The Role of Economic Policy

Economic policy played a critical role in generating and shaping the new growth model, and the effects of that policy boxed in workers.[5] The four sides of the neoliberal policy box (see figure 1) are globalization, small government, labor market flexibility, and retreat from full employment. Workers are pressured on all four sides, and it is this pressure that led to the severing of the wage/productivity growth link.[6]

Figure 1. The NeoLiberal Policy Box

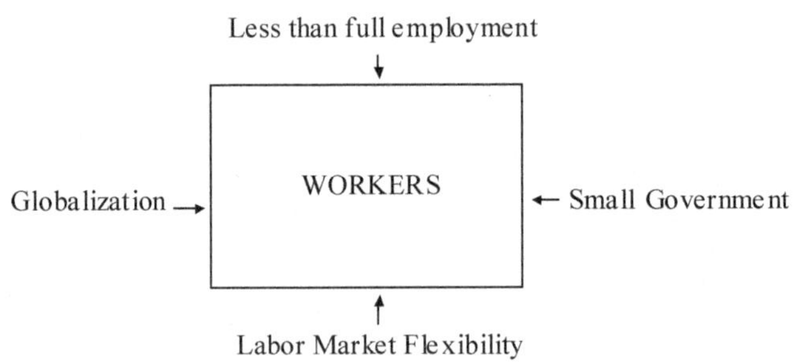

Globalization, in part spurred by policies encouraging free trade and capital mobility, means that American workers are increasingly competing with lower-paid foreign workers. That pressure is further increased by the fact that foreign workers are themselves under pressure owing to the so-called Washington Consensus development policy, sponsored by the International Monetary Fund (IMF) and the World Bank, which forces them into the same neoliberal box as American workers. Thus, neoliberal policies not only undermine demand in advanced countries, they fail to compensate for this by creating adequate demand in developing countries. This is clearly evident in China which has been marked by rising income inequality and a sharp decline in the consumption to GDP ratio.[7] The net result of global implementation of neoliberal orthodoxy is the promotion of deflationary global economic conditions.

Small government policies undermine the legitimacy of government and push privatization, deregulation, and light-touch regulation. Though couched in terms of liberating the economy from detrimental governmental interference, "small government" policies have resulted in the erosion of popular economic rights and protections. This is exemplified by the 1996 reform of U.S. welfare rights. Moreover, the government's administrative capacity and ability to provide services have been seriously eroded, with many government functions being outsourced to corporations. This has led to the creation of what the economist James Galbraith (2008) terms the "predator state," in which corporations enrich themselves on government contracts, while the out-sourced workers employed by these corporations confront a tougher work environment.

Labor market flexibility involves attacking unions, the minimum wage, unemployment benefits, employment protections, and employee rights. This is justified in the name of creating labor market flexibility, including downward wage flexibility, which according to neoliberal economic theory is supposed to generate full employment. Instead, it has led to wage stagnation and widening income inequality.

Abandonment of full employment means having the Federal Reserve emphasize the importance of keeping inflation low over maintaining full employment. This switch was promoted by the economics profession's adoption of Milton Friedman's (1968) theory of the natural rate of unemployment, which claims monetary policy cannot affect long-run equilibrium employment and unemployment.

The new theory dramatically changed macroeconomic policy. First, talk of full employment was abandoned in favor of talk about the natural rate of unemployment. Second, natural rate theory justified labor market flexibility policies as the only way to lower unemployment. Third, since monetary policy could do nothing to permanently lower unemployment, natural rate theory pushed a focus on low and stable inflation, a logic which in recent years has been used to push the adoption of formal inflation targets. Of course, no Federal Reserve Chairman was so politically inept as to publicly announce the abandonment of full employment as a policy goal. Instead, the new theory provided Federal Reserve policymakers with political cover for increased tolerance of unemployment, which contributed to undermining workers' bargaining power regarding wages (Palley, 2007).[8]

c. *The Neoliberal Bubble Economy*

The implementation of neoliberal economic policies destroyed the stable virtuous circle growth model based on full employment and wages tied to productivity growth, replacing it with the current growth model based on rising indebtedness and asset price inflation. Since 1980, each U.S. business cycle has seen successively higher debt/income ratios at end of expansions, and the economy has become increasingly dependent on asset price inflation to spur the growth of aggregate demand.

Table 6 shows the rising household debt to GDP ratio and rising nonfinancial business debt to GDP ratio under the neoliberal growth model. Compared to the period 1960-1981, the period 1981-2007 saw enormous increases in the debt/GDP ratios of both the household and nonfinancial corporate sectors.

Table 6. Household Debt/GDP and Non - Financial Corporation Debt/GDP Ratios by Business Cycle Peaks, 1948 Ğ2007

Year	GDP ($ billions)	Household debt (H) ($ billions)	H/GDP	Non-financial Corp debt (C) ($ billions)	C/GDP
1960	526.4	215.6	0.41	201.0	0.38
1969	984.6	442.7	0.45	462.0	0.47
1973	1,382.7	624.9	0.45	729.5	0.53
1981	3,128.4	1,507.2	0.48	1662.0	0.53
1990	5,803.1	3,597.8	0.62	3,753.4	0.65
2001	10,128.0	7682.9	0.76	6,954.0	0.69
2007	13,807.5	13,765.1	1.00	10,593.7	0.77

Source: FRB Flow of Funds Accounts and author Õs calculations.

Table 7 shows the rising household debt service ratio, measured as the ratio of debt service and financial obligations to disposable personal income. That this ratio trended upward despite a huge decline in nominal interest rates is evidence of the massively increased reliance on debt by households. In 1980 the average prime rate charged by banks was 15.27 percent: in 2007 it was 8.05 percent.

Table 7. Household Debt Service and Financial Obligations Ratio (DSR)

Year	**1980. q3**	**1991. q3**	**2001. q4**	**2007. q4**
DSR	10.9%	12.0%	13.4%	14.3%

Source: Federal Reserve Board.

Table 8 shows the pattern of house price inflation over the past 20 years.[9] This table is revealing in two ways. First, it shows the extraordinary scale of the 2001–06 house price bubble. Second, it reveals the systemic role of house price inflation in driving economic expansions. Over the last 20 years, the economy has tended to expand when house price inflation has exceeded CPI (consumer price index) inflation. This was true for the last three years of the Reagan expansion. It was true for the Clinton expansion. And it was true for the Bush-Cheney expansion. The one period of sustained house price stagnation was 1990-95, which was a period of recession and extended jobless recovery. This is indicative of the significance of asset price inflation in driving demand under the neoliberal model.

Table 8. CPI Inflation and Home Price Inflation Based on the S&P/Case-Shiller National Home Pricc Values Index

Period	**1987.q1 Ğ 1990.q1**	**1990.q1 Ğ 1995.q1**	**1995.q1 Ğ 2001.q1**	**2001.q1 Ğ 2006.q1**
Average home price inflation (%)	6.7	0.6	5.7	10.9
Average CPI Inflation (%)	4.5	3.5	2.5%	2.5
Excess house inflation (%)	2.2	-2.9	3.2	8.4

Source: S&P/Case-Shiller index and author's calculations.

Along with rising debt ratios, households progressively cut back on their savings rates, as shown in table 9. This reduction provided another source of demand.

Table 9. Personal Savings Rate (PSR)

Period	**1960**	**1969**	**1973**	**1980**	**1981**	**1991**	**2001**	**2007**
PSR (%)	7.3	7.8	10.5	10.0	10.9	7.3	1.8	0.6

Source: Economic Report of the President, table B.30 (2009).

The logic of the neoliberal growth model rests on redirecting income from lower- and middle-income households to corporate profits and upper-income households. Asset prices are bid up by a host of measures, including higher profits, savings by the super-rich that are directed to asset purchases, borrowing to buy assets, and such institutional changes as the shift from traditional defined benefit pension plans to defined contribution – such as 401(k) – pension plans. Consumption is maintained by lower household savings rates and by borrowing that is collateralized by higher asset prices. The reduction in savings rates is partly a response to squeezed incomes and partly rationalized on the grounds that households are wealthier because of higher asset prices (including house prices).

The problem with the model is that it is unsustainable. Maintaining growth of spending on consumption requires continued excessive borrowing and continued reduction in savings rates. Continued excessive borrowing requires ever increasing asset prices and debt/income ratios: hence, the systemic need for bubbles (which eventually burst). Meanwhile, when the savings rate hits zero, little further reduction is possible. Consequently, both drivers of demand eventually exhaust themselves.

The current financial crisis is different and deeper from earlier crises in two ways. First, the impact of earlier burst bubbles – such as the 2001 stock market and dot-com bubbles – was contained because their debt footprint was not that deep. Though financial wealth was destroyed and economic activity was temporarily restrained, the financial system remained intact. However, the housing bubble of 2001-2007 was debt financed and massive in size, and its bursting pulled down the entire financial system. Second, the drivers of aggregate demand are now exhausted because of the scale of debt accumulation and the rundown of the savings rate. In earlier crises, households still had unused borrowing capacity they could call upon and room to further reduce their saving. Both of those channels are now exhausted, making recovery a much more difficult task. Indeed, if households try to rebuild their financial worth that will increase savings rates, which will further deepen and prolong the downturn.

The economic growth model adopted after 1980 lasted far longer than it might have been expected to because of our capacity to expand access to debt and increase leverage. That is the real significance of deregulation and financial innovation, which had a functional role in sustaining the neoliberal model. However, delaying the day of reckoning also made it more severe when it arrived. When the subprime detonator set off the financial crisis, the economy's financial structure – 25 years in the making and integrally linked to the economic logic of the neoliberal growth model – proved to be extremely fragile and akin to a house of cards.[10]

III. The Flawed Global Economic Engagement Model

Though prone to instability (i.e., to boom and bust), the neoliberal growth model might have operated successfully for quite a while longer were it not for a U.S. economic policy that created a flawed engagement with the global economy. This flawed engagement undermined the economy in two ways. First, it accelerated the erosion of household incomes. Second, it accelerated the accumulation of unproductive debt – that is, debt that generates economic activity elsewhere rather than in the United States.

The most visible manifestation of this flawed engagement is the goods trade deficit, which hit a record 6.4 percent of GDP in 2006. This deficit was the inevitable product of the structure of global economic engagement put in place over the past two decades, with the most critical elements being implemented by the Clinton administration under the guidance of Treasury Secretaries Robert Rubin and Lawrence Summers. That eight-year period saw the implementation of the North American Free Trade Agreement (NAFTA), the adoption after the East Asian financial crisis of 1997 of the "strong dollar" policy, and the establishment of permanent normal trade relations (PNTR) with China in 2000.

These measures cemented the model of globalization that had been lobbied for by corporations and their Washington think-tank allies. The irony is that giving corporations what they wanted undermined the neoliberal model by surfacing its contradictions. The model would likely have eventually slumped because of its own internal dynamic, but the policy triumph of corporate globalization accelerated this process and transformed it into a financial crash.

a. The Triple Hemorrhage

Flawed global economic engagement created a "triple hemorrhage" within the U.S. economy. The first economic hemorrhage, long emphasized by Keynesian economists, was leakage out of the economy of spending on imports. Household income and borrowing was significantly spent on imports, creating incomes offshore rather than in the United States. Consequently, borrowing left behind a debt footprint but did not create sustainable jobs and incomes at home.

The second hemorrhage was the leakage of jobs from the U.S. economy as a result of offshore outsourcing, made possible by corporate globalization. Such off-shoring directly reduced the number of higher-paying manufacturing jobs, cutting into household income. Moreover, even when jobs did not move offshore, the threat of off-shoring could be used to secure lower wages, thereby dampening wage growth and helping sever wages from productivity growth (Bronfenbrenner, 2000; Bronfenbrenner and Luce, 2004).

The third hemorrhage concerned new investment. Not only were corporations incentivized by low foreign wages, foreign subsidies, and under-valued exchange rates to close existing plants and shift their production offshore, they were also incentivized to shift new investment offshore. That did double damage. First, it reduced domestic investment spending, hurting the capital goods sector and employment therein. Second, it stripped the U.S. economy of modern industrial capacity, disadvantaging U.S. competitiveness and reducing employment that would have been generated to operate that capacity.

A further unanticipated economic leakage from the flawed model of global engagement concerns energy prices. Off-shoring of U.S. manufacturing capacity has often involved the closing of relatively energy-efficient and environmentally cleaner production and its replacement with less efficient and dirtier foreign production. In addition, the shipping of goods from around the world to the U.S. market has compounded these effects. These developments added to energy demand and contributed to the 2005-2008 increase in oil prices, which added to the U.S. trade deficit and effectively imposed a huge tax (paid to OPEC) on U.S. consumers.

The flawed model of global economic engagement broke with the old model of international trade in two ways. First, instead of having roughly balanced trade, the United States has run persistent large trade deficits. Second, instead of aiming to create a global marketplace in which U.S. companies could sell their products, its purpose was to create a global production zone in which U.S. companies could either produce or obtain inputs from. In other words, the main purpose of international economic engagement was not to increase U.S. exports, but rather to substitute cheaper imported inputs for U.S. domestic production and to facilitate American-owned production platforms in developing countries that could export to the United States.

As a result, at the bidding of corporate interests, the United States joined itself at the hip to the global economy, opening its borders to an inflow of goods and exposing its manufacturing base. This was done without safeguards to address the problems of exchange rate misalignment and systemic trade deficits, or the mercantilist policies of trading partners.

The problem is that this new system created a widening hole in U.S. the economy by undermining domestic production, employment, and investment. That hole accelerated the contradictions in the neoliberal model but those contradictions were held at bay by ever more borrowing backed by asset price inflation. When these latter processes exhausted themselves the system collapsed, with the collapse taking the form of a financial crisis. Moreover, since the new arrangement had the global economy joined at the hip to the U.S. economy, this meant the global economy also cratered when the U.S. economy cratered.

b. NAFTA

The creation of the new system took off in 1989 with the implementation of the Canada-U.S. Free Trade Agreement that established an integrated production zone between the two countries. The 1994 implementation of NAFTA was the decisive next step, and in many regards NAFTA can be viewed as the first step along the path that ultimately led to the massive global trade imbalances that have so disrupted the U.S. and global economies.

With regard to specifics, NAFTA fused Canada, the United States, and Mexico into a unified North American production zone. More importantly, by including Mexico it joined developed and developing economies, thereby establishing the template U.S. corporations wanted.

NAFTA also dramatically changed the significance of exchange rates. Before, exchange rates mattered for trade and the exchange of goods. Now, they mattered for the location of production. That in turn changed the attitude of large U.S. multinational corporations (MNCs) toward the dollar. When U.S. companies produced domestically and looked to export, a weaker dollar was in their commercial interest and they lobbied against dollar overvaluation. However, under the new model, U.S. corporations looked to produce offshore and import into the United States. This reversed their commercial interest, making them proponents of a strong dollar. That is because a strong dollar reduces the dollar costs of foreign production, raising the profit margins on their foreign production sold in the United States at U.S. prices.

NAFTA soon highlighted this new dynamic because Mexico was hit by a financial crisis in January 1994, immediately after the implementation of the free trade agreement. To U.S. corporations, which had invested in Mexico and planned to invest more, the peso's collapse versus the dollar was a boon as it made it even more profitable to produce in Mexico and re-export to the United States. With corporate interests driving U.S. economic policy, the peso devaluation problem went unattended – and in doing so it also created a critical precedent.

The effects of NAFTA and the peso devaluation were immediately felt in the U.S. manufacturing sector in the form of job loss; diversion of investment; firms using the threat of relocation to repress wages; and an explosion in the goods trade deficit with Mexico, as shown in table 10. Whereas prior to the implementation of the NAFTA agreement the United States was running a goods trade surplus with Mexico, immediately afterward the balance turned massively negative and kept growing more negative up to 2007.

Table 10. US goods trade balance with Mexico before and after NAFTA ($ billions)
Source: Census Bureau.

1991	1992	1993	1994	1995	1996	2000	2005	2007
2.1	5.4	1.7	1.3	-15.8	-17.5	-24.5	-49.7	-74.6

These features helped contribute to the jobless recovery of 1993–96, though the economy was eventually able to overcome this with the stock market bubble that launched in 1996; the emergence of the Internet investment boom that morphed into the dot-com bubble; and the tentative beginnings of the house price bubble, which can be traced back to 1997. Together, these developments spurred a consumption and investment boom that masked the adverse structural effects of NAFTA.

c. *The Response to the East Asian Financial Crisis*

The next fateful step in the flawed engagement with the global economy came with the East Asian financial crisis of 1997, which was followed by a series of rolling financial crises in Russia (1998), Brazil (1999), Turkey (2000), Argentina (2000), and Brazil (2000). In response to these crises, Treasury Secretaries Rubin and Summers adopted the same policy that was used to deal with the 1994 peso crisis, thereby creating a new global system that replicated the pattern of economic integration established with Mexico.[11]

Large dollar loans were made to the countries in crisis to stabilize their economies. At the same time, the collapse of their exchange rates and the appreciation of the dollar was accepted and institutionalized in the form a "strong dollar" policy.[12] This increased the buying power of U.S. consumers, which was critical because the U.S. consumer was now the lynchpin of the global economy, becoming the buyer of first and last resort.[13]

The new global economic architecture involved developing countries exporting their production to the United States. Developing countries embraced this export-led growth solution to their development problem and were encouraged to do so by the IMF and the World Bank. For developing countries, the new system had a number of advantages, including the ability to run trade surpluses that allowed them to build up foreign exchange holdings to defend against capital flight; providing demand for their output, which led to job creation; and providing access to U.S. markets that encouraged MNCs to redirect investment spending toward them. The latter was especially important as it transferred technology, created jobs, and built up developing country manufacturing capacity.

U.S. multinationals were also highly supportive of the new arrangement as they now gained global access to low-cost export production platforms. Not only did this mean access to cheap foreign labor, but the overvalued dollar lowered their foreign production costs, thereby further increasing profit margins. Large importers, like the retailer Wal-Mart, also supported this arrangement. Furthermore, many foreign governments offered subsidies as an incentive to attract foreign direct investment (FDI).

In effect, the pattern of incentives established by the response to the East Asian financial crisis encouraged U.S. corporations to persistently downsize their U.S. capacity and shift production offshore for import back to the United States. This created a dynamic for progressively eroding U.S. national industrial capacity, while foreign economies were encouraged to steadily expand their capacity and export their way out of economic difficulties.

As with NAFTA, the adverse effects of this policy were visible almost immediately. As shown in table 11, the goods trade deficit took a further leap forward, surging from $198.4 billion in 1997 to $248.2 billion in 1998, and rising to $454.7 billion in 2000. In addition, as shown in table 12, there was a surge in imports from Pacific Rim countries. Part of the surge in the trade deficit was due to the boom conditions sparked by stock market euphoria, the dot-com bubble, and house price inflation, but the scale of the trade deficit surge also reflects the flawed character of U.S. engagement with the global economy.

Table 11. US Goods Trade Balance ($ billions)

1995	1996	1997	1998	1999	2000
-174.2	-191.0	-198.4	-248.2	-347.8	-454.7

Source: U.S. Census Bureau.

Table 12. US Goods Trade Balance with Pacific Rim Countries ($ billions)

1995	1996	1997	1998	1999	2000
-108.1	-101.8	-121.6	-160.4	-186.0	-215.4

Source: U.S. Census Bureau.

The proof of this claim is that manufacturing employment started falling despite boom conditions in the U.S. economy. Having finally started to grow in 1996, manufacturing employment peaked in March 1998 and started declining three full years before the economy went into recession in March 2001. That explains why manufacturing job growth was negative over the entirety of the Clinton expansion, a first in U.S. business cycle history.

As with NAFTA, these adverse effects were once again obscured by positive business cycle conditions. Consequently, the Clinton administration dismissed concerns about the long-term dangers of manufacturing job loss. Instead, the official interpretation was that the U.S. economy was experiencing – in the words of senior Clinton economic policy advisers Alan Blinder and Janet Yellen – a "fabulous decade" significantly driven by policy.[14] According to the ideology of the decade, manufacturing was in secular decline and destined for the dustbin of history. The old manufacturing economy was to be replaced by a "new economy" driven by computers, the Internet, and information technology.

d. China and PNTR

Though disastrous for the long-run health of the U.S. economy, NAFTA-style corporate globalization, plus the strong dollar policy, was extremely profitable for corporations. Additionally, the ultimate costs to households were still obscured by the ability of the U.S. economy to generate cyclical booms based on asset price inflation and debt. That provided political space for a continued deepening of the model, the final step of which was to incorporate China as a full-fledged participant.

Thus, corporations now pushed for the establishment of permanent normal trading relations (PNTR) with China, which Congress enacted in 2000. That legislation in turn enabled China to join the World Trade Organization, which had been established in 1996.

The significance of PNTR was not about trade, but rather about making China a full-fledged part of global production arrangements. China had enjoyed access to the U.S. market for years and its entry into the WTO did generate some further tariff reductions. However, the real significance was that China became a fully legitimate destination for foreign direct investment. That is because production from China was now guaranteed permanent access to the U.S. market, and corporations were also given internationally recognized protections of property and investor rights.

Once again the results were predictable and similar to the pattern established by NAFTA – though the scale was far larger. Aided by a strong dollar, the trade deficit with China increased dramatically after 2001, growing at a rate of 25 percent per annum and jumping from $83.1 billion in 2001 to $201.5 billion in 2005 (see table 13). Moreover, there was also massive inflow of foreign direct investment into China so that it became the world's largest recipient of FDI in 2002 – a stunning achievement for a developing country.[15] So strong was China's attractiveness as an FDI destination that it not only displaced production and investment in the United States but also displaced production and investment in Mexico (Greider, 2001).

Table 13. US Goods Trade Balance with China before and After PNTR ($ billions)

1998	1999	2000	2001	2002	2003	2004	2005	2007
-56.9	-68.7	-83.9	-83.1	-103.1	-124.1	-161.9	-201.5	-256.2

Source: U.S. Census Bureau.

According to academic and Washington policy orthodoxy, the new global system was supposed to launch a new era of popular shared prosperity. Demand was to be provided by U.S. consumers. Their spending was to be financed by the "new economy" based on information technology and the globalization of manufacturing, which would drive higher productivity and income. Additionally, consumer spending could be financed by borrowing and asset price inflation, which was sustainable because higher asset prices were justified by increased productivity.

This new orthodoxy was enshrined in what was termed the "New Bretton Woods Hypothesis," according to which the global economy had entered a new golden age of global development, reminiscent of the postwar era.[16] The United States would import from East Asian and other developing economies, provide FDI to those economies, and run large trade deficits that would provide the demand for the new supply. In return, developing countries would accumulate financial obligations against the United States, principally in the form of Treasury securities. This would provide them with foreign exchange reserves and collateral that was supposed to make investors feel secure. China was to epitomize the new arrangement.[17]

The reality is that the structure of U.S. international engagement, with its lack of attention to the trade deficit and manufacturing, contributed to a disastrous acceleration of the contradictions inherent in the neoliberal growth model. That model always had a problem regarding sustainable generation of demand because of its imposition of wage stagnation and high income inequality. Flawed international economic engagement aggravated this problem by creating a triple hemorrhage that drained consumer spending, manufacturing jobs, and investment and industrial capacity. This in turn compelled even deeper reliance on the unsustainable stopgaps of borrowing and asset price inflation to compensate.

As for developing economies, they embraced the post-1997 international economic order. However, in doing so they tied their fate to the U.S. economy, creating a situation in which the global economy was flying on one engine that was bound to fail. Consequently, far from creating a de-coupled global economy, it created a linked economy characterized by a concertina effect: when the U.S. economy crashed, other economies came crashing in behind (Palley, 2008b).

IV. America's Exhausted Macroeconomic Pcaradigm

The twin macroeconomics factors of an unstable growth model and of flawed global economic engagement were put in place during the 1980's and 1990's. However, their full adverse effects took time to build and the chickens only came home to roost in the 2001-2007 expansion. From that standpoint, the Bush-Cheney administration is not responsible for the financial crisis. Its economic policies can be criticized for mean-spiritedness and a greater proclivity for corporate favoritism, but they represented a continuation of the policy paradigm already in place. The financial crisis therefore represents the exhaustion of that paradigm rather than being the result of specific policy failures on the part of the Bush-Cheney administration (Palley, 2008c).

In a nutshell, the U.S. implemented a neoliberal growth model that relied on debt and asset price inflation. As the neoliberal model slowly cannibalized itself and became weaker, the economy needed larger speculative bubbles to grow. The flawed model of global engagement accelerated the cannibalization process, thereby creating need for a huge bubble that only housing could provide. However, when that bubble burst it pulled down the entire economy because of the bubble's massive dependence on debt.

In many regards the neoliberal paradigm was already showing its limits in the 1990's. An extended jobless recovery marked the business cycle of the 1990's when the term was coined and the boom was accompanied by a stock market bubble and the beginnings of significant house price inflation.

The recession of 2001 saw the bursting of the stock market and dot-com bubbles. However, although investment spending was hit hard, consumer spending was largely untouched, owing to continued household borrowing and continued moderate increases in home prices. Additionally, the financial system was largely unscathed because the stock market bubble involved limited reliance on debt financing.

Yet, despite the relative shallowness of the 2001 recession and aggressive monetary and fiscal stimulus, the economy languished in a second extended bout of jobless recovery. The critical factor was the trade deficit and off-shoring of jobs resulting from the model of globalization that had been decisively implemented in the 1990's. This drained spending, jobs, and investment from the economy, and also damped down wages by creating job insecurity.

The effects are clearly visible in the data for manufacturing employment. Manufacturing employment peaked in March 1998, shortly after the East Asian financial crisis and three years before the economy went into recession. Thereafter, manufacturing never really recovered from this shock and continued losing jobs throughout the most recent expansion (see table 14).

Table 14. US Manufacturing Employment (millions)

1997	1998	1999	2000	2001	2002	2003	2005	2007
17.42	17.56	17.32	17.26	16.44	15.26	14.51	14.32	13.88

Source: Economic Report of the President, 2009, table B -46.

The sustained weakness of manufacturing effectively undermined the economic recovery, despite expansionary macroeconomic policy. According to the National Bureau of Economic Research, the recession ended in November 2001, when employment was 130.9 million. Two years later (November 2003) total employment was 130.1 million, a decrease of 800,000 jobs. Over this period, manufacturing lost 1.5 million jobs, and total manufacturing employment fell from 15.83 million to 14.32 million.

The failure to develop a robust recovery, combined with persistent fears that the economy was about to slip back into recession, prompted the Federal Reserve to lower interest rates. Beginning in November 2000, the Fed cut its federal funds rates significantly, lowering it from 6.50 percent to 2.10 percent in November 2001. However, the weakness of the recovery drove the Fed to cut the rate still further, pushing it to 1.00 percent in July 2003, where it was held until June 2004.

Ultimately, the Federal Reserve's low-interest-rate policy succeeded in jump-starting the economy by spurring a housing price boom, which in turn sparked a construction boom. That boom became a bubble, which burst in the summer of 2007. What is important about this history is that the economy needed an asset price bubble to restore full employment, just as it had needed the stock market and dot-com bubbles to restore full employment in the 1990's.

Given the underlying structural weakness of the demand-generation process, which had been further aggravated by flawed globalization, a bubble was the only way back to full employment. Higher asset prices were needed to provide collateral to support borrowing that could then finance spending.

A housing bubble was particularly economically effective for two reasons. First, housing ownership is widespread so the consumption wealth effects of the bubble were also widespread. Second, higher house prices stimulated domestic construction employment by raising prices above the cost of construction. Moreover, the housing bubble was a form of "house price populism" that benefitted incumbent politicians who could claim credit for the fictitious wealth created by the bubble.

Some (Taylor, 2009) are now blaming the Federal Reserve for the bubble, but the reality is that it felt compelled to lower interest rates for fear of the economy falling back into recession. Additionally, inflation – which is the signaling mechanism the Federal Reserve relies on to assess whether monetary policy is too loose – showed no indication of excess demand in the economy. Indeed, all the indications were of profound economic weakness. Finally, when the Federal Reserve started raising the federal funds interest rates in mid-2004, the long-term rate that influences mortgages changed little. In part this may have been due to the Japan interest rate carry-trade and recycling of foreign country trade surpluses back to the United States, but the greater part was likely reflection of underlying weak economic conditions.

This reality is confirmed by a look back at the expansion of 2001-2007 compared to other expansions. By almost all measures it ranks as the weakest business cycle since World War II. Table 15 shows "trough to peak" and "peak to peak" measures of GDP growth, consumption growth, investment spending growth, employment growth, manufacturing employment growth, profit growth, compensation growth, wage and salary growth, change in the unemployment rate, and change in the employment/population ratio of this business cycle relative to other postwar cycles. The 2001-2007 cycle ranks worst in seven of the ten measures, and second worst in two measures. If the comparison is restricted to the four cycles lasting 27 quarters or more, the 2001-2007 cycle is worst in nine of ten measures, and best in one measure – profit growth. This weak performance occurred despite a house price and credit bubble of historic proportions. It is clear evidence of the structural weakness of the U.S. macroeconomic model and why a bubble was needed to sustain growth.

Table 15. Rank of Last Business Cycle Relative to Cycles since World War II (1 = best; 10 = worst)

	Expansion only (1 = best, 10= worst)	**Full Cycles (1 = best, 10= worst)**	**Full Cycles (1 = best, 4= worst)**
	All	**All**	**Cycles lasting more than 27 quarters**
Number of Cycles	10	10	4
Rank of 2001-07 cycle			
GDP growth	10	8	4
Consumption growth	9	9	4
Investment growth	10	9	4
Employment growth	10	9	4
Manufacturing employment growth	10	10	4
Profit growth	4	2	1
Compensation growth	10	9	4
Wage and salary growth	10	9	4
Change in unemployment rate	9	5	4
Change in Emp/population ratio	10	10	4

Source: Josh Bivens and John Irons, "A Feeble Recovery: The Fundamental Economic Weaknesses of the 2001-07 Expansion," EPI Briefing Paper No. 214 (Washington, DC: Economic Policy Institute, December 2008); and author's calculations.

V. Conclusion: Where Next?

Recognizing the role of macroeconomic factors in the current crisis raises critical questions. Deregulation and massive unsound lending by financial markets are important parts of the crisis story, but they were not the ultimate cause of the crisis. Instead, they facilitated the bubble and are better understood as being part of the neoliberal model, their function being to support demand growth based on debt and asset price inflation.

At this stage, repairing regulatory and microeconomic incentive failures can limit future financial excess. However, it will do nothing to address the problems inherent in the neoliberal U.S. growth model and pattern of global economic engagement. Worse, focusing on regulation diverts attention from the bigger macroeconomic challenges by misleadingly suggesting that regulatory failure is the principal cause of the crisis.

The case for paradigm change has yet to be taken up politically. Those who built the neoliberal system remain in charge of economic policy. Among mainstream economists who have justified the neoliberal system, there has been some change in thinking when it comes to regulation, but there has been no change in thinking regarding the prevailing economic paradigm. This is starkly illustrated in the debate in the United States over globalization, where the evidence of failure is compelling. Yet, any suggestion that the United States should reshape its model of global economic engagement is brushed aside as "protectionism.", which avoids the real issue and shuts down debate.

That leaves open the question of what will drive growth once the economy stabilizes. The postwar growth model based on rising middle-class incomes has been dismantled, while the neoliberal growth model has imploded. Moreover, stripping the neoliberal model of financial excess by means of regulation and leverage limits will leave it even more impaired. The U.S. economy needs a new growth model.

The outlines of that new model are easy to see. The most critical need is to restore the link between wages and productivity growth that drove the 1945-1980 virtuous circle model of growth. This will require creating a new policy box that takes workers out and puts corporations in.

The outlines of such a box are easy to envisage and involve restoration of worker bargaining power in labor markets through strengthened unions, a higher minimum wage, and stronger employee protections; restoration of full employment as a macroeconomic policy objective; restoration of the legitimacy of regulation and increased government provision of public goods; a new international economic accord that addresses the triple hemorrhage problem created by the flawed model of global economic engagement; and reform of financial markets and corporate governance that ensures markets and corporations work to promote national economic well-being.

While the economics are clear, the politics are difficult, which partially explains the resistance to change on the part of policymakers and economists aligned with the neoliberal model. The neoliberal growth model has benefitted the wealthy, while the model of global economic engagement has benefitted large multinational corporations. That gives these powerful political interests, with their money and well-funded captive think tanks, an incentive to block change. [18]

Judging by its top economics personnel, the Obama administration has decided to maintain the system rather than change it. The administration may yet manage to create another bubble, this time probably an interest-rate bubble in Treasury bonds that will weakly jump-start the borrowing cycle one more time. However, that will not fix the underlying structural problem, and delay may make its resolution more difficult by creating new financial facts in the form of more debt. Most importantly, even if the neoliberal model is revved up one more time, it will not deliver shared prosperity because it was never constructed to do so.

The bottom line of macroeconomic failure rooted in America's flawed economic paradigm is the ultimate cause of the financial crisis and Great Recession. Financial market failure played a role in the making of the crisis, but its role was part of a larger drama concerning the flawed paradigm. Now, there is a grave danger that policymakers will only focus on financial market reform and ignore reform of America's flawed economic paradigm. In that event, though the economy may stabilize, it will likely be unable to escape the pull of economic stagnation. That is because stagnation is the logical next stage of the existing paradigm.

END NOTES

[1] This paper was originally released in July 2009 by the New America Foundations' Economic Growth Program whose permission to use it is gratefully acknowledged. An abbreviated version of that paper was published in Empirica, Vol. 38(1), 2011.

[2] The 1950's are an exception because of the Korean War (June 1950-July 1953), which ratcheted up manufacturing employment and distorted manufacturing employment patterns.

[3] Defenders of the neoliberal paradigm argue that manufacturing has prospered and the decline in manufacturing employment reflects healthy productivity trends. As evidence, they argue that real manufacturing output has increased and remained fairly steady as a share of real GDP. This reflects the fact that manufacturing prices have fallen faster than other prices. However, this is due in part to hedonic "quality adjustment" statistical procedures that count improved information technology embodied in manufactured goods as increased manufacturing output. It is also due to increased use of cheap imported components that are not subject to the same hedonic statistical adjustments. As a result, the real cost of imported inputs is understated, and that has the effect of making it look as if real manufacturing output is higher. The stark reality is that the nominal value of manufacturing output has fallen dramatically as a share of nominal GDP. The United States has also become more dependent on imported manufactured goods, with imported manufactured goods making up a significantly increased share of total manufactured goods purchased. Moreover, U.S. purchases of manufactured goods have risen as a share of total U.S. demand, indicating that the failure lies in U.S. production of manufactured goods which has lost out to imports (Bivens 2004).

[4] Much attention is devoted to the issue of excessive CEO pay, and CEO pay is the poster child for the problem of income inequality. However, fixing CEO pay will not fix the problem. Instead, there is a deeper problem regarding the overall pay structure. That problem implicates far more than just the top one percent of households, and for that reason it will be politically difficult to remedy.

[5] Palley (1998) analyzes in detail how economic policy has impacted income distribution, unemployment, and growth. The metaphor of a box is attributable to Ron Blackwell of the AFL-CIO.

[6] There is a deeper political economy behind the neoliberal box that has been termed "financialization" (Epstein, 2001; Palley, 2008a). The policy agenda embedded in the box is driven by financial markets and corporations who are now joined at the hip, with corporations pursuing a narrow financial agenda aimed at benefiting top management and financial elites.

[7] See International Monetary Fund, "People's Republic of China: Staff Report for the 2006 Article IV Consultation" (Washington, DC, 2006).

[8] Full employment is difficult to define. One definition is wages are rising with productivity because workers are scarce and jobs plentiful. Using that definition, over the last the thirty years the U.S. has only enjoyed full employment for a brief period at the end of the 1990's.

[9] S&P/Case-Shiller index data is only available from 1987.

[10] This means the crisis is not a "pure" Minsky (1993) crisis. Minsky saw crises as the result of endogenous financial instability that developed over years. However, the current crisis is a crisis of the neoliberal model. That model fostered financial instability as a way of sustaining itself. Consequently, when the crisis hit it took on the appearance of a classic Minsky crisis but its real roots lie in the neoliberal model.

[11] It cannot be overemphasized that the policies adopted by Treasury Secretaries Robert Rubin and Lawrence Summers reflected the dominant economic paradigm. As such, Rubin and Summers had the support of the majority of the U.S. political establishment, the IMF and the World Bank, Washington's premier think tanks, and the economics profession.

[12] China had already gone this route with a large exchange rate devaluation in 1994. Indeed, there is reason to believe that that devaluation contributed to hatching the East Asian financial crisis by putting other East Asian economies under undue competitive pressures and diverting foreign investment from them to China.

[13] The strong dollar policy was also politically popular, constituting a form of exchange rate populism. Boosting the value of the dollar increased the purchasing power of U.S. consumers at a time when their wages were under downward pressure due to the neoliberal model. Households were under pressure from globalization, yet at the same time they were being given incentives to embrace it. This is why neoliberalism has been so hard to tackle politically.

[14] Blinder and Yellen (2001). To the extent there was concern in the Clinton administration about manufacturing, it was about the hardships for workers regarding job dislocations. Additionally, there was political concern that produced some sweet talk (i.e., invitations to policy consultations) aimed at placating trade unions. However, there was no concern that these outcomes were due to flawed international economic policy. Not only did this policy failure contribute to eventual disastrous economic outcomes, it may well have cost Vice President Al Gore the 2000 presidential election. The

Clinton administration's economic advisers may have downplayed the significance of manufacturing job loss but blue-collar voters in Ohio did not.

[15] *OECD Observer* 2003.

[16] See Dooley, Folkerts-Landau and Garber (2003); Dooley, Folkerts-Landau, and Garber (2004a); and Dooley, Folkerts-Landau, and Garber (2004b).

[17] For a critique of the New Bretton Woods hypothesis that explains why it was unsustainable see Palley (2006a).

[18] Even domestic manufacturers who are harmed by the international economic agenda may abstain from opposing that agenda because they are net beneficiaries from the overall neoliberal model.

BIBLIOGRAPHY

Blinder, A.S. and J. Yellen. 2001. The Fabulous Decade: Macroeconomic Lessons from the 1990's, New York Century Foundation.

Bivens, J. 2004. "Shifting Blame for Manufacturing Job Loss: Effect of Rising Trade Deficit Shouldn't Be Ignored," EPI Briefing Paper No. 149, Economic Policy Institute, Washington, DC.

Bivens, J. and J. Irons 2008. "A Feeble Recovery: The Fundamental Economic Weaknesses of the 2001–07 Expansion," EPI Briefing Paper No. 214, Washington, DC: Economic Policy Institute, December.

Bronfenbrenner, K. 2000. "Uneasy Terrain: The Impact of Capital Mobility on Workers, Wages, and Union Organizing", Report prepared for the United States Trade Deficit Review Commission, Washington, DC, September.

Bronfenbrenner, K., and S. Luce. 2004. "The Changing Nature of Corporate Global Restructuring: The Impact of Production Shifts on Jobs in the U.S., China, and Around the Globe", Report prepared for the U.S.-China Economic and Security Review Commission, Washington, DC, October.

Dooley, M.P., D. Folkerts-Landau, and P. Garber. 2003. "An Essay on the Revised Bretton Woods System," Working Paper 9971, Cambridge, MA: National Bureau of Economic Research, September.

Dooley, M.P., D. Folkerts-Landau, and P. Garber. 2004a. "Direct Investment, Rising Real Wages, and the Absorption of Excess labor in the Periphery," Working Paper 10626, Cambridge, MA: National Bureau of Economic Research, July.

Dooley, M.P., D. Folkerts-Landau, and P. Garber. 2004b. "The U.S. Current Account Deficit and Economic Development: Collateral for a Total Return Swap," Working Paper 10727, Cambridge, MA: National Bureau of Economic Research, August.

Epstein, G. 2001. "Financialization, Rentier Interests, and Central Bank Policy," manuscript, Department of Economics, University of Massachusetts, Amherst, MA, December.

Friedman, M. 1968. "The Role of Monetary Policy". *American Economic Review*, Vol. 58, 1-17.

Galbraith, J.K. 2008. *The Predator State: How Conservatives Abandoned the Free Market and Why Liberals Should Too*, New York: Free Press.

Greider, W. 2001. "A New Giant Sucking Sound," *The Nation*, December 13.

International Monetary Fund. 2006. "People's Republic of China: Staff Report for the 2006 Article IV Consultation," Washington, DC.

Minsky, H.P. 1992. "The Financial Instability Hypothesis," Working paper No. 74, The Jerome Levy Economics Institute of Bard College, New York, 1992 and published in Arestis P. and Sawyer M. (eds) 1993. *Handbook of Radical Political Economy*, Aldershot: Edward Elgar.

Michel, L., Bernstein, J. and H. Shierholz. 2009. *The State of Working America 2008/2009* Ithaca, NY: ILR Press.

OECD Observer. 2003. "China Ahead in Foreign Direct Investment," No. 237, May.

Palley, T. 1998. *Plenty of Nothing: The Downsizing of the American Dream and the Case for Structural Keynesianism*, Princeton, Princeton University Press.

Palley, T. 2005. "The Questionable Legacy of Alan Greenspan," Challenge, Vol. 48(6), 17-31.

Palley, T. 2006. "The Fallacy of the Revised Bretton Woods Hypothesis: Why Today's System Is Unsustainable and Suggestions for a Replacement," Public Policy Brief No. 85, The Levy Economics Institute of Bard College.

Palley, T. 2007. "Seeking Full Employment Again: Challenging the Wall Street Paradigm," Challenge, Vol. 50, 14-50.

Palley, T. 2008a. "Financialization: What It Is and Why It Matters," in: Eckhard Hein, Torsten Niechoj, Peter Spahn, and Achim Truger (eds.) *Finance-led Capitalism: Macroeconomic Effects of Changes in the Financial Sector*, Marburg, Germany: Metroplis-Verlag.

Palley, T. 2008b. "The Economic Concertina," *Comment Is Free*, September 7, http:/www.guardian.co.uk/commentisfree/2008/sep/07/economicgrowth.useeconomicgrowth ?gusrc=rss&feed=worldnews.

Palley, T. 2008c. "America's Exhausted Growth Paradigm," The Chronicle of Higher Education, April 11.

Taylor. J.B. 2009. "How Government Created the Financial Crisis," *Wall Street Journal*, Monday, February 3, A.19.

8 The US economy

Explaining stagnation and why it will persist

Thomas I. Palley

The crisis and the resilience of neoliberal economic orthodoxy

The financial crisis that erupted in 2008 challenged the foundations of orthodox economic theory and policy. At its outset, orthodox economists were stunned into silence as evidenced by their inability to answer the Queen of England's simple question to the faculty of the London School of Economics as to why no one foresaw the crisis (Greenhill, 2008). Six years later, orthodoxy has fought back and largely succeeded in blocking change of thought and policy. The result has been economic stagnation.

This chapter examines the major competing interpretations of the economic crisis in the USA and explains the rebound of neoliberal orthodoxy. It shows how US policy-makers acted to stabilise and save the economy, but failed to change the underlying neoliberal economic policy model. That failure explains the emergence of stagnation in the US economy – and stagnation is likely to endure. Current economic conditions in the USA smack of the mid-1990s. The 1990s expansion proved unsustainable and so will the current modest expansion. However, this time it is unlikely to be followed by a financial crisis because of the balance sheet cleaning that took place during the last crisis.

Competing explanations of the crisis

The Great Recession, which began in December 2007 and included the financial crisis of 2008, was the deepest economic downturn in the USA since the Second World War. The depth of the downturn is captured in Table 8.1, which shows the decline in GDP and the peak unemployment rate. The recession has the longest duration and the decline in GDP is the largest. The peak unemployment rate was slightly below the peak rate of the recession of 1981–1982. However, this ignores the fact that the labour-force participation rate fell in the Great Recession (i.e. people left the labour force and were not counted as unemployed) whereas it increased in the recession of 1981–1982 (i.e. people entered the labour force and were counted as unemployed).[1]

Table 8.2 provides data on the per cent decline in private-sector employment from business cycle peak to trough. The 7.6 per cent loss of private sector jobs

Table 8.1 Alternative measures of the depth of US recessions

Recession dates	*Duration*	*GDP decline (peak to trough)*	*Peak unemployment rate*
Nov 1948–Oct 1949	11 months	−1.7%	7.9% (Oct 1949)
July 1953–May 1954	10 months	−2.6%	6.1% (Sep 1954)
Aug 1957–April 1958	8 months	−3.7%	7.5% (July 1958)
April 1960–Feb 1961	10 months	−1.6%	7.1% (May 1961)
Dec 1969–Nov 1970	11 months	−0.6%	6.1% (Dec 1970)
Nov 1973–March 1975	16 months	−3.2%	9.0% (May 1975)
Jan 1980–July 1980	6 months	−2.2%	7.8% (July 1980)
July 1981–Nov 1982	16 months	−2.7%	10.8% (Nov 1982)
July 1990–March 1991	8 months	−1.4%	7.8% (June 1992)
March 2001–Nov 2001	8 months	−0.3%	6.3% (June 2003)
Dec 2007–June 2009	18 months	−4.3%	10.0% (Oct 2009)

Source: http://en.wikipedia.org/wiki/List_of_recessions_in_the_United_States

Table 8.2 US private employment cycles, peak to trough

Peak date (year – month)	*Employment peak (thousands)*	*Trough date (year – month)*	*Employment trough (thousands)*	*Percent change*	*Peak to trough duration (months)*
1948 – 9	39,489	1949 – 7	37,568	−4.8%	10
1953 – 7	43,813	1954 – 8	41,933	−4.3%	13
1957 – 4	45,537	1958 – 6	42,986	−5.5%	14
1960 – 4	46,278	1961 – 2	44,969	−2.8%	10
1969 – 12	58,763	1970 – 11	57,579	−2.0%	11
1974 – 6	64,363	1975 – 4	61,668	−4.2%	10
1980 – 3	74,695	1980 – 7	73,414	−1.7%	4
1981 – 8	75,448	1982 – 12	72,775	−3.4%	16
1990 – 4	91,274	1992 – 2	89,557	−1.9%	22
2000 – 12	111,681	2003 – 7	108,231	−3.1%	31
2008 – 1	115,610	2010 – 2	106,772	−7.6%	25

Source: Bureau of Labor statistics and author's calculations.

in the Great Recession dwarfs other recessions, providing another measure of its depth and confirming its extreme nature.

Broadly speaking, there exist three competing perspectives on the crisis (Palley, 2012a). Perspective one is the hardcore-neoliberal position which can be labelled the *government failure hypothesis*. In the USA, it is identified with the Republican Party and with the economics departments of Stanford University, the University of Chicago and the University of Minnesota. Perspective two is the softcore-neoliberal position, which can be labelled the *market failure hypothesis*. It is identified with the Obama administration, the Wall Street and Silicon Valley wing of the Democratic Party, and economics departments such as those at Massachusetts Institute of Technology, Yale and Princeton. In Europe it is identified with 'Third Way' politics. Perspective three is the progressive position, which is rooted in Keynesian economics and can be labelled the *destruction of shared prosperity hypothesis*. It is identified with the New Deal wing of the Democratic Party and the labour movement, but it has no standing within major economics departments owing to their suppression of alternatives to economic orthodoxy.

The hardcore-neoliberal *government failure* argument is that the crisis is rooted in the US housing bubble and its bust. The claim is that the bubble was due to excessively prolonged loose monetary policy and politically motivated government intervention in the housing market aimed at increasing ownership. With regard to monetary policy, the Federal Reserve pushed interest rates too low for too long following the recession of 2001. With regard to the housing market, government intervention via the Community Reinvestment Act and Fannie Mae and Freddie Mac drove up house prices and encouraged home-ownership beyond people's means.

The softcore-neoliberal *market failure* argument is that the crisis is due to inadequate financial sector regulation. First, regulators allowed excessive risk-taking by banks. Second, regulators allowed perverse incentive pay structures within banks that encouraged management to engage in 'loan pushing' rather than 'sound lending'. Third, regulators pushed both deregulation and self-regulation too far. Together, these failures contributed to financial misallocation, including misallocation of foreign savings provided through the trade deficit, which led to financial crisis. The crisis in turn deepened an ordinary recession, transforming it into the Great Recession, which could have become the second Great Depression if there had not been the extraordinary policy interventions of 2008–2009.

The Keynesian *destruction of shared prosperity* argument is that the crisis is rooted in the neoliberal economic paradigm that has guided economic policy for the past 30 years. An important feature of the argument is that, though the USA is the epicentre of the crisis, all countries are implicated as they all participated in the adoption of a systemically flawed policy paradigm. That paradigm infected finance via inadequate regulation, enabling financial excess that led to the financial crisis of 2008. However, financial excess is just one element of the crisis, and the full explanation is far deeper than just financial market regulatory failure.

According to the Keynesian *destruction of shared prosperity* hypothesis, the deep cause is generalised economic policy failure rooted in the flawed neoliberal economic paradigm that was adopted in the late 1970s and early 1980s. For the 1945–1975 period, the US economy was characterised by a 'virtuous circle' Keynesian growth model built on full employment and wage growth tied to productivity growth. This model is illustrated in Figure 8.1, and its logic was as follows: Productivity growth drove wage growth, which in turn fuelled demand growth and created full employment. That provided an incentive for investment, which drove further productivity growth and supported higher wages. This model held in the USA and, subject to local modifications, it also held throughout the global economy – in Western Europe, Canada, Japan, Mexico, Brazil and Argentina.

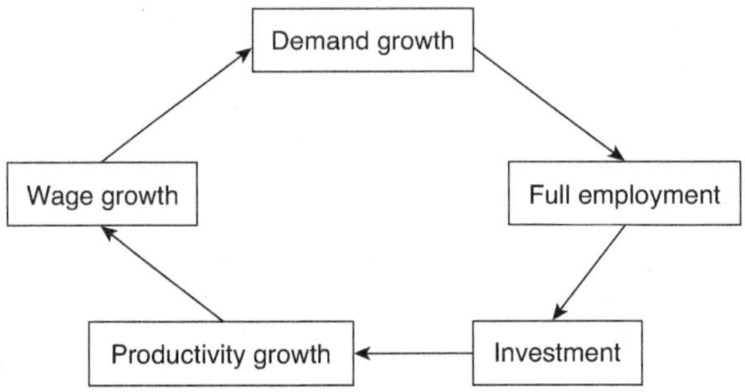

Figure 8.1 The 1945–75 virtuous circle Keynesian growth model

After 1980 the virtuous-circle Keynesian growth-model was replaced by a neoliberal growth-model. The reasons for the change are a complex mix of economic, political and sociological reasons that are beyond the scope of the current paper. The key changes wrought by the new model were: (1) abandonment of the commitment to full employment and the adoption of commitment to very low inflation, and (2) severing of the link between wages and productivity growth. Together, these changes created a new economic dynamic. Before 1980, wages were the engine of US demand growth. After 1980, debt and asset price inflation became the engine.

The new economic model was rooted in neoliberal economic thought. Its principal effects were to weaken the position of workers, strengthen the position of corporations, and unleash financial markets to serve the interests of financial and business elites. As illustrated in Figure 8.2, the new model can be described as a neoliberal policy box that fences workers in and pressures them from all sides. On the left-hand side, the corporate model of globalisation put workers in international competition via global production networks that were supported by free trade agreements and capital mobility. On the right-hand side, the 'small' government agenda attacked the legitimacy of government and pushed persistently for deregulation regardless of dangers. From below, the labour-market flexibility agenda attacked unions and labour-market supports such as the minimum wage, unemployment benefits, employment protections and employee rights. From

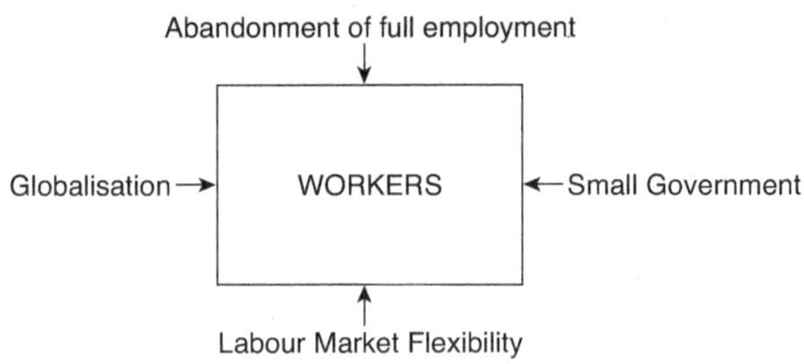

Figure 8.2 The neoliberal policy box

above, policy-makers abandoned the commitment to full employment – a development that was reflected in the rise of inflation targeting and the move towards independent central banks influenced by financial interests.

Corporate globalisation is a key feature. Not only did it exert downward inward pressures on economies via import competition and the threat of job offshoring, it also provided the architecture binding economies together. Thus, globalisation reconfigured global production by transferring manufacturing from the USA and Europe to emerging market economies. This new global division of labour was then supported by having US consumers serve as the global economy's buyer of first and last resort, which explains the US trade deficit and the global imbalances problem. This new global division of labour inevitably created large trade deficits that also contributed to weakening the aggregate demand (AD) generation process by causing a haemorrhage of spending on imports (Palley, 2015).

An important feature of the Keynesian hypothesis is that the neoliberal policy box was implemented on a global basis, in both the North and the South. As in the USA, there was also a structural break in policy regime in both Europe and Latin America. In Latin America , the International Monetary Fund (IMF) and the World Bank played an important role as they used the economic distress created by the 1980s debt crisis to push neoliberal policy. They did so by making financial assistance conditional on adopting such policies. This global diffusion multiplied the impact of the turn to neoliberal economic policy, and it explains why the Washington Consensus enforced by the IMF and the World Bank has been so significant. It also explains why stagnation has taken on a global dimension.

The role of finance in the neoliberal model

Owing to the extraordinarily deep and damaging nature of the financial crisis of 2008, financial market excess has been a dominant focus of explanations of the Great Recession. Within the *neoliberal government failure* hypothesis, the excess is attributed to ill-advised government intervention and Federal Reserve interest-rate policy. Within the *neoliberal market failure* hypothesis, it is attributed to ill-advised deregulation and failure to modernise regulation. According to the Keynesian *destruction of shared prosperity* hypothesis neither of those interpretations grasps the true significance of finance. The government failure hypothesis is empirically unsupportable (Palley, 2012a: Chapter 6), while the market failure hypothesis has some truth but also misses the true role of finance.

That role is illustrated in Figure 8.3 which shows that finance performed two roles in the neoliberal model. The first was to structurally support the neoliberal policy box. The second was to support the AD generation process. These dual roles are central to the process of increasing financial domination of the economy that has been termed 'financialisation' (Epstein, 2004: 3; Krippner, 2004, 2005; Palley, 2013).

The policy box shown in Figure 8.2 has four sides. A true box has six sides and a four-sided structure would be prone to structural weakness. Metaphorically

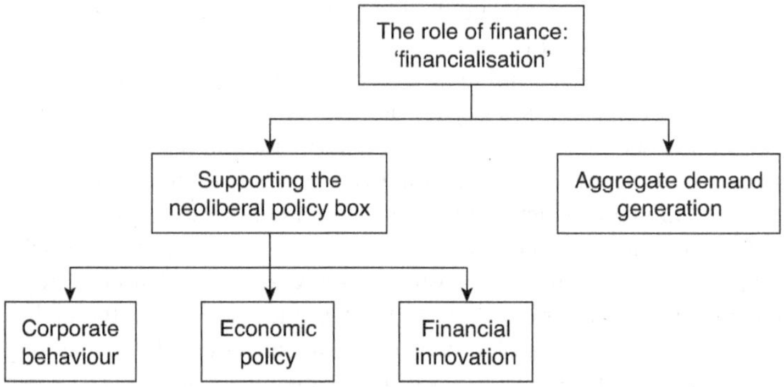

Figure 8.3 The role of finance in the neoliberal model

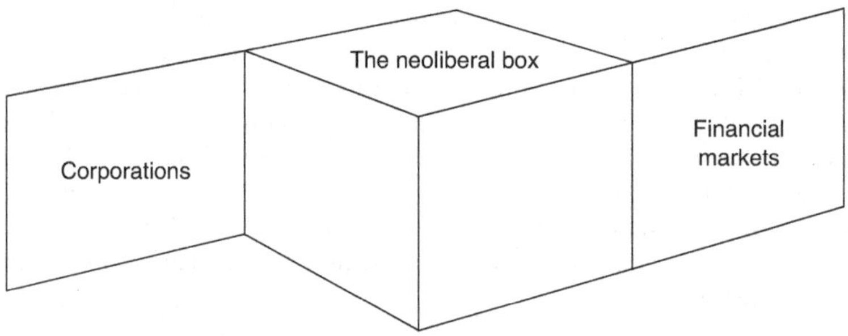

Figure 8.4 Lifting the lid on the neoliberal policy box

speaking, one role of finance is to provide support on two sides of the neoliberal policy box, as illustrated in Figure 8.4. Finance does this through three channels. First, financial markets have captured control of corporations via enforcement of the shareholder-value-paradigm of corporate governance. Consequently, corporations now serve financial market interests along with the interests of top management. Second, financial markets in combination with corporations lobby politically for the neoliberal policy mix. The combination of changed corporate behaviour and economic policy produces an economic matrix that puts wages under continuous pressure and raises income inequality. Third, financial innovation has facilitated and promoted financial market control of corporations via hostile takeovers, leveraged buy-outs and reverse capital distributions. Financial innovation has therefore been key for enforcing Wall Street's construction of the shareholder-value paradigm.

The second vital role of finance is the support of AD. The neoliberal model gradually undermined the income and demand generation process, creating a growing structural demand gap. The role of finance was to fill that gap. Thus, within the USA, deregulation, financial innovation, speculation and mortgage lending fraud enabled finance to fill the demand gap by lending to consumers and by spurring asset price inflation. Financialisation assisted with this process by changing credit market practices and introducing new credit instruments that made credit more easily and widely available to corporations and households. US consumers in turn filled the global demand gap, along with help from US and European corporations who were shifting manufacturing facilities and investment to the emerging market economies.

Three things should be emphasised. First, this AD-generation role of finance was an unintended consequence and not part of a grand plan. Neoliberal economists and policy-makers did not realise they were creating a demand gap, but their laissez-faire economic ideology triggered financial market developments that coincidentally filled the demand gap. Second, the financial process they unleashed was inevitably unstable and was always destined to hit the wall. There are limits to borrowing and to asset price inflation – and all Ponzi schemes eventually fall apart. The problem is the impossibility of predicting when they will fail. Third, the process went on far longer than anyone expected, which explains why critics of neoliberalism sounded like Cassandras (Palley, 1998: Chapter 12). However, the long duration of financial excess made the collapse far deeper when it eventually happened. It has also made escaping the after-effects of the financial crisis far more difficult as the economy is now burdened by debts and destroyed credit-worthiness. That has deepened the proclivity to economic stagnation.

Evidence

Evidence regarding the economic effects of the neoliberal model is plentiful and clear. Figure 8.5 shows productivity and average hourly compensation of non-supervisory workers (that is non-managerial employees who are about 80 per cent of the workforce). The link with productivity growth was severed almost 40 years ago and hourly compensation has been essentially stagnant since then.

Table 8.3 shows data on the distribution of income growth by business cycle expansion across the wealthiest top 10 per cent and bottom 90 per cent of households. Over the past 60 years there has been a persistent decline in the share of income gains going to the bottom 90 per cent of households ranked by wealth. However, in the period 1948–1979 the decline was gradual. After 1980 there is a massive structural break and the share of income gains going to the bottom 90 per cent collapses. Before 1980, on average the bottom 90 per cent received 66 per cent of business cycle expansion income gains. After 1980, on average they receive just 8 per cent.

Figure 8.6 shows the share of total pre-tax income of the top 1 per cent of households ranked by wealth. From the mid-1930s, with the implementation of the New Deal social contract, that share fell from a high of 23.94 per cent in 1928 to a low of 8.95 per cent in 1978. Thereafter it has steadily risen, reaching 23.5 per cent in 2007 which marked the beginning of the Great Recession. It then fell during the Great Recession owing to a recession-induced fall in profits,

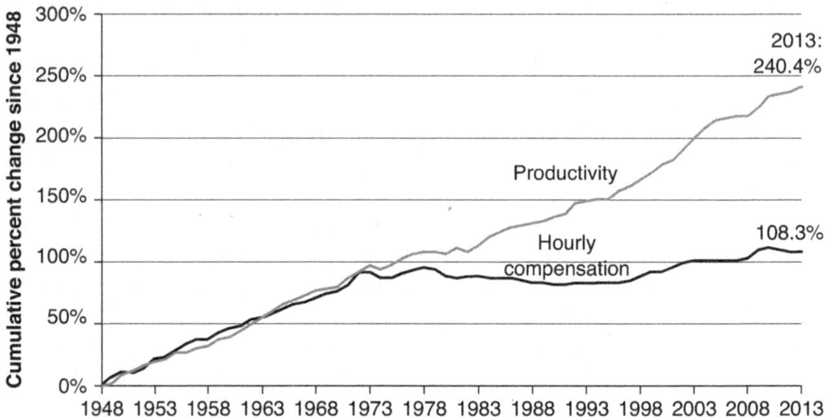

Figure 8.5 Productivity and real average hourly compensation of US non-supervisory workers, 1948–2013

Note: Data are for compensation of production/non-supervisory workers in the private sector and net productivity of the total economy. 'Net productivity' is the growth of output of goods and services less depreciation per hour worked.

Source: Economic Policy Institute analysis of unpublished Total Economy Productivity data from Bureau of Labor Statistics (BLS) Labor Productivity and Costs program, wage data from the BLS Current Employment Statistics, BLS Consumer Price Index and Bureau of Economic Analysis National Income and Product Accounts.

Table 8.3 Distribution of income growth by business cycle expansion across the wealthiest top 10 percent and bottom 90 percent of households

	'49–'53	*'54–'57*	*'59–'60*	*'61–'69*	*'70–'73*	*'75–'79*	*'82–'90*	*'91–'00*	*'01–'07*	*'09–'12*	*Average Pre-1908*	*Average Post-1980*
Top 10%	20%	28	32	33	43	45	80	73	98	116	34%	92%
Bottom 90%	80%	72	68	67	57	55	20	27	2	–16	66%	8%

Source: Tcherneva (2014), published in The New York Times, September 26, 2014.

but has since recovered most of that decline as income distribution has worsened again during the economic recovery. In effect, during the neoliberal era the US economy has retraced its steps, reversing the improvements achieved by the New Deal and post-Second World War prosperity, so that the top 1 per cent's share of pre-tax income has returned to pre-Great Depression levels.

As argued in Palley (2012a: 150–151), there is a close relationship between union membership density (i.e. the percentage of employed workers that are unionised) and income distribution. This is clearly shown in Figure 8.7, which shows union density and the share of pre-tax income going to the top 10 per cent of wealthiest households. The neoliberal labour-market flexibility agenda explicitly attacks unions and works to shift income to wealthier households.

Table 8.4 provides data on the evolution of the US goods and services trade balance as a share of gross domestic product (GDP) by business cycle peak.

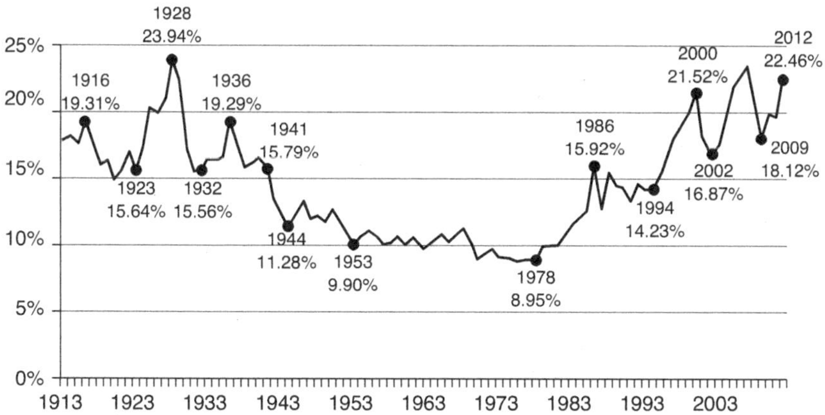

Figure 8.6 US pre-tax income share of top 1 percent (1913–2012)
Source: http://inequality.org/income-inequality/. Original source: Thomas Piketty and Emanuel Saez (2003), updated at http://em.lab.edu/users/saez

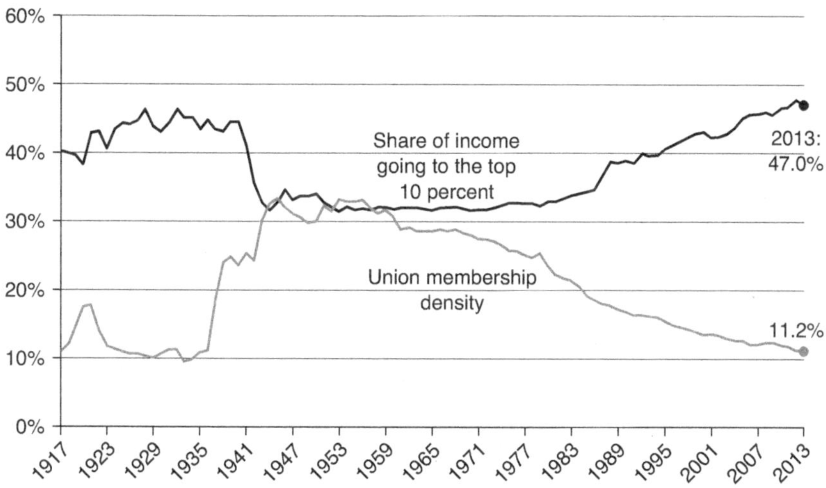

Figure 8.7 Union membership and the share of income going to the top ten percent of wealthiest households, 1917–2013
Source: Data on union density follows the composite series found in Historical Statistics of the United States; updated to 2013 from unionstats.com. Income inequality (share of income to top 10%) from Piketty and Saez, 'Income Inequality in the United States', 1913–1998, *Quarterly Journal of Economics*, 118(1), 2003, 1–39. Updated and downloadable data, for this series and other countries, is available at the Top Income Database. Updated January 2015.

Comparison across peaks controls for the effect of the business cycle. The data show that through to the late 1970s, US trade was roughly in balance, but after 1980 it swung to a massive deficit, which increased during each business cycle. These deficits were the inevitable product of the neoliberal model of globalisation

Table 8.4 The U.S. goods and services trade deficit/surplus by business cycle peaks, 1960–2007

Business cycle peak year	*Trade balance ($ millions)*	*GDP ($ billions)*	*Trade balance/ GDP (%)*
1960	3,508	526.4	0.7
1969	91	984.6	0.0
1973	1,900	1,382.7	0.1
1980	–25,500	2,789.5	–0.9
1981	–28,023	3,128.4	–0.9
1990	–111,037	5,803.1	–1.9
2001	–429,519	10,128.0	–.2
2007	–819,373	13,807.5	–5.9

Sources: Economic Report of the President, 2009 and author's calculations.

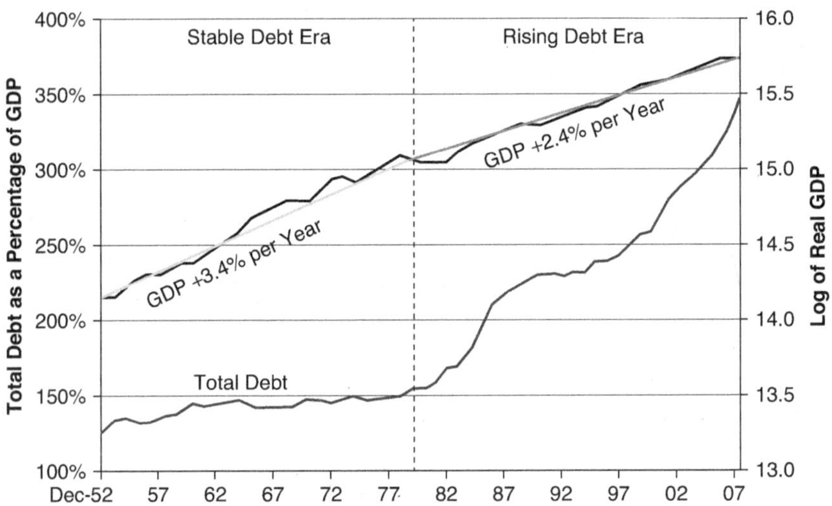

Figure 8.8 Total domestic debt and growth (1952–2007)
Source: Grantham, 2010.

(Palley, 2015), and they undermined the AD generation process in accordance with the Keynesian hypothesis.

Finally, Figure 8.8 shows total domestic debt relative to GDP and growth. This figure is highly supportive of the Keynesian interpretation of the role of finance. During the neoliberal era, real GDP growth has actually slowed but debt growth has exploded. The reason is that the neoliberal model did nothing to increase growth, but it needed faster debt growth to fill the demand gap created by the model's worsening of income distribution and creation of large trade deficits. Debt growth supported debt-financed consumer spending, and it supported asset price inflation that enabled borrowing, which filled the demand gap caused by the neoliberal model.

The debate about the causes of the crisis: why it matters

The importance of the debate about the causes of the crisis is that each perspective recommends its own different policy response. For *hardcore-neoliberal government failure* proponents, the recommended policy response is to double-down on the policies described by the neoliberal policy box and further deregulate markets; to deepen central bank independence and the commitment to low inflation via strict rules based monetary policy; and to further shrink government and impose fiscal austerity to deal with increased government debt produced by the crisis.

For *softcore-neoliberal market failure* proponents, the recommended policy response is to tighten financial regulation but continue with all other aspects of the existing neoliberal policy paradigm. That means continued support for corporate globalisation, so-called labour-market flexibility, low inflation targeting and fiscal austerity in the long term. Additionally, there is a need for temporary large-scale fiscal and monetary stimulus to combat the deep recession caused by the financial crisis. However, once the economy has recovered, policy should continue with the neoliberal model.

For proponents of the *destruction of shared prosperity* hypothesis, the policy response is fundamentally different. The fundamental need is to overthrow the neoliberal paradigm and replace it with a 'structural Keynesian' paradigm. That involves repacking the policy box as illustrated in Figure 8.9. The critical step is to take workers out of the box and put corporations and financial markets in so that they are made to serve a broader public interest. The key elements are to replace corporate globalisation with managed globalisation, thus blocking the 'race to the bottom' trade dynamics and stabilising global financial markets; restoring a commitment to full employment; replacing the neoliberal anti-government agenda with a social democratic government agenda; and replacing the neoliberal labour-market flexibility with a solidarity-based labour-market agenda. The goals are the restoration of full employment and the restoration of a solid link between wage and productivity growth.

Lastly, since the neoliberal model was adopted as part of a new global economic order, there is also need to recalibrate the global economy. This is where

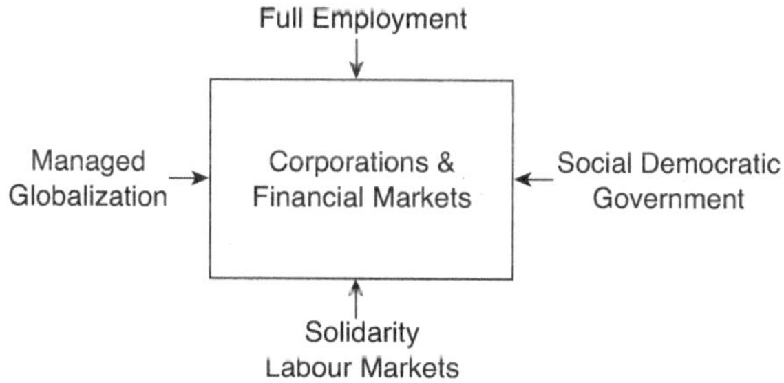

Figure 8.9 The structural Keynesian box

the issue of 'global rebalancing' enters: emerging market economies need to shift away from export-led growth strategies to domestic demand-led strategies, which poses huge challenges for many of them because they have configured their growth strategies around export-led growth based on selling to US consumers.

From crisis to stagnation: the failure to change

Massive policy interventions, unequalled in the post-war era, stopped the Great Recession from spiralling into a second Great Depression. The domestic economic interventions included the 2008 Troubled Asset Relief Program (TARP) that bailed out the financial sector via government purchases of assets and equity from financial institutions; the 2009 American Recovery and Reinvestment Act (ARRA) that provided approximately $800 billion of fiscal stimulus, consisting of approximately $550 billion of government spending and $250 billion of tax cuts; the Federal Reserve lowering its interest target to near-zero (0–0.25 per cent); and the Federal Reserve engaging in quantitative easing (QE) transactions that involve it purchasing government and private-sector securities. At the international level, in 2008 the Federal Reserve established a temporary $620 billion foreign exchange (FX) swap facility with foreign central banks. That facility provided the global economy with dollar balances, thereby preventing a dollar liquidity shortage from triggering a global wave of defaults on short-term dollar loans that the financial system was unwilling to roll over because of panic.[2] Additionally, there was unprecedented globally co-ordinated fiscal stimulus arranged via the G-20 mechanism.

Despite their scale, these interventions did not stop the recession from being the deepest since 1945, and nor did they stop the onset of stagnation. Table 8.5 shows how GDP growth has failed to recover since the end of the Great Recession, averaging just 2.1 per cent for the five-year period from 2010 to 2014. Furthermore, that period includes the rebound year of 2010 when the economy recovered from its massive slump owing to the extraordinary fiscal and monetary stimulus measures that were put in place.

Table 8.6 shows employment creation in the five years after the end of recessions, which provides another window on stagnation. The job-creation numbers show that the neoliberal model was already slowing in the 1990s with the first episode of 'jobless recovery'. It actually ground to stagnation in the 2001–2007 period, but this was masked by the house-price bubble and the false prosperity it created. Stagnation has persisted after the Great Recession, but the economic

Table 8.5 U.S. GDP growth

1961–1970	*1971–1980*	*1981–1990*	*1991–2000*	*2001–2007*	*2008–2009*	*2010–2014*
4.2%	3.2%	3.3%	3.5%	2.5%	−1.6%	2.1%

Source: Statistical Annex of the European Union, Autumn 2014 and author's calculations. The growth rate for 2014 is that estimated in October 2014.

Table 8.6 U.S. private sector employment creation in the five year period after the end of recessions for six business cycles with extended expansions

Recession end date	*Employment at recession end date (millions)*	*Employment five years later (millions)*	*Per cent growth in employment*
Feb 1961	45.0	52.2	16.0%
Mar 1975	61.9	74.6*	20.5%
Nov 1982	72.8	86.1	18.3%
March 1991	90.1	99.5	10.4%
Nov 2001	109.8	115.0	4.7%
June 2009	108.4	117.1	8.0%

Source: Bureau of labor statistics and author's calculations. * = January 1980 (the beginning of the next recession).

distress caused by the recession has finally triggered awareness of stagnation among elite economists. In a sense, the Great Recession called out the obvious, just as did the little boy in the Hans Andersen story about the emperor's new suit.

The persistence of stagnation after the Great Recession raises the question 'why?'. The answer is policy has done nothing to change the structure of the underlying neoliberal economic model. That model inevitably produces stagnation because it produces a structural demand shortage via (i) its impact on income distribution, and (ii) via its design of globalisation, which generates massive trade deficits, wage competition and offshoring of jobs and investment.

In terms of the three-way contest between the *government failure* hypothesis, the *market failure* hypothesis and the *destruction of shared prosperity* hypothesis, the economic policy debate during the Great Recession was cast as exclusively between government failure and market failure. With the Democrats controlling the Congress and Presidency after the 2008 election, the market failure hypothesis won out and has framed policy since then. According to the hypothesis, the financial crisis caused an exceptionally deep recession that required exceptionally large monetary and fiscal stimulus to counter it and restore normalcy. Additionally, the *market failure* hypothesis recommends restoring and renovating financial regulation, but other than that the neoliberal paradigm is appropriate and should be deepened.

In accordance with this thinking, the incoming Obama administration affirmed existing efforts to save the system and prevent a downward spiral by supporting the Bush administration's TARP, the Federal Reserve's first round of QE (November/December 2008) that provided market liquidity and the Federal Reserve's FX swap agreement with foreign central banks.

Thereafter, the Obama administration worked to reflate the economy via the passage of the ARRA (2009), which provided significant fiscal stimulus. With the failure to deliver a V-shaped recovery, candidate Obama became even more vocal about fiscal stimulus. However, reflecting its softcore-neoliberal inclinations, the Obama administration then became much less so when it took office.

Thus, the winners of the internal debate about fiscal policy in the first days of the Obama administration were those wanting more modest fiscal stimulus.[3] Furthermore, its analytical frame was one of temporary stimulus with the goal of long-term fiscal consolidation, which is softcore-neoliberal speak for fiscal austerity.

Seen in the above light, after the passage of ARRA (2009), the fiscal policy divide between the Obama administration and hardcore-neoliberal Republicans was about the speed and conditions under which fiscal austerity should be restored. This attitude to fiscal policy reflects the dominance within the Democratic Party of 'Rubinomics', the Wall Street view associated with former Treasury Secretary Robert Rubin, that government spending and budget deficits raise real interest rates and thereby lower growth. According to that view, the USA needs long-term fiscal austerity to offset social security and Medicare.

Side-by-side with the attempt to reflate the economy, the Obama administration also pushed for a major overhaul and tightening of financial sector regulation via the Dodd–Frank Act (2010). That accorded with the market failure hypothesis's claim about the economic crisis and Great Recession being caused by financial excess permitted by the combination of excessive deregulation, lax regulation and failure to modernise regulation.

Finally, and again in accordance with the logic of the market failure hypothesis, the Obama administration has pushed ahead with doubling-down and further entrenching the neoliberal policy box. This is most visible in its approach to globalisation. In 2010, free-trade agreements modelled after NAFTA were signed with South Korea, Colombia and Panama. The Transpacific Partnership (TPP) and the Transatlantic Trade and Investment Partnership (TTIP), two mega-agreements negotiated in secrecy and apparently bearing similar hallmarks to prior trade agreements, are also being pushed by the Obama administration.

The Obama administration's softcore-neoliberalism would have likely generated stagnation by itself, but the prospect has been further strengthened by Republicans. Thus, in accordance with their point of view, Republicans have persistently pushed the government failure hypothesis by directing the policy conversation to excessive regulation and easy monetary policy as the causes of the crisis. Consequently, they have consistently opposed strengthened financial regulation and demands for fiscal stimulus. At the same time, they have joined with softcore-neoliberal Democrats regarding doubling-down on neoliberal box policies, particularly as regards trade and globalisation.

Paradoxically, the failure to change the overall economic model becomes most visible by analysing the policies of the Federal Reserve, which have changed the most dramatically via the introduction of QE. The initial round of QE (QE1) was followed by QE2 in November 2010 and QE3 in September 2012, with the Fed shifting from providing short-term emergency liquidity to buying private sector financial assets. The goal was to bid up prices of longer-term bonds and other securities, thereby lowering interest rates on longer-term financing and encouraging investors to buy equities and other, riskier financial assets. The Fed's reasoning was lower long-term rates would stimulate the economy, and higher financial asset prices would trigger a positive wealth effect on consumption spending. This makes clear the architecture of policy. The Obama administration was to provide fiscal stimulus to jump start the economy; the Fed would use QE to blow air back into the asset price bubble; the Dodd–Frank Act (2010) would stabilise financial markets; and globalisation would be deepened by further NAFTA-styled international agreements. This is a near-identical model to that which failed so disastrously. Consequently, stagnation is the logical prognosis.

Déjà vu all over again: back to the 1990s but with a weaker economy

The exclusion of the *destruction of shared prosperity* hypothesis, combined with the joint triumph of the *market failure* and *government failure* hypotheses, means the underlying economic model that produced the Great Recession remains essentially unchanged. That failure to change explains stagnation. It also explains why current conditions smack of 'déjà vu all over again', with the US economy in 2014–2015 appearing to have returned to conditions reminiscent of the mid-1990s. Just as the 1990s failed to deliver durable prosperity, so too current optimistic conditions will prove unsustainable without deeper change.

The déjà vu similarities are evident in the large US trade deficit that has started to again deteriorate rapidly; a return of the over-valued dollar problem that promises to further increase the trade deficit and divert jobs and investment away from the US economy; a return to reliance on asset-price inflation and house-price increases to grow consumer demand and construction; a return of declining budget deficits owing to continued policy disposition toward fiscal austerity; a return of the contradiction that has the Federal Reserve tighten monetary policy when economic strength triggers rising prices and wages that bump against the ceiling of the Fed's self-imposed 2 per cent inflation target; and a renewal of the push for neoliberal trade agreements.

All of these features mean both policy context and policy design look a lot like the mid-1990s. The Obama administration saved the system but did not change it. Consequently, the economy is destined to repeat the patterns of the 1990s and 2000s. However, the US economy has also experienced almost 20 more years of neoliberalism, which has left its economic body in worse health than the 1990s. That means the likelihood of delivering another bubble-based boom is low, and stagnation tendencies will likely reassert themselves after a shorter and weaker period of expansion.

This structurally weakened state of the US economy is evident in the further worsening of income inequality that has occurred during the Great Recession and subsequent slow recovery. As shown in Figure 8.10, national income data show that the labour share has continued to fall during this period, hitting new post-war lows. Furthermore, earlier, Table 8.3 showed how the top 10 per cent of wealthiest households garnered 116 per cent of the income gains during the recovery period 2009–2012, implying that the bottom 90 per cent experienced falling income during this period.

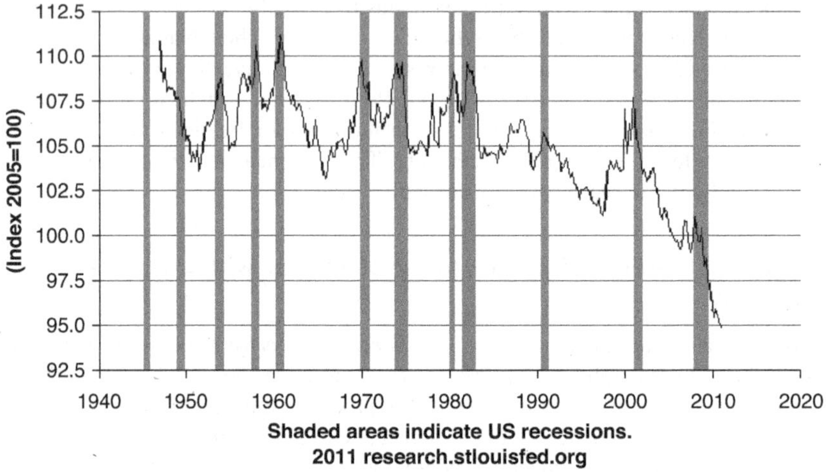

Figure 8.10 Labour share of US non-farm business GDP (%), 1945–2011
Source: Economist's View, June 16, 2011. Labour share consists of wages, salaries and pension benefits of non-supervisory workers.

This worsening of income distribution has multiple negative implications that promote stagnation via direct and indirect effects. With regard to direct effects, worsened income distribution shifts income from poorer low-saving households to richer high-saving households. That shift reduces consumption spending and aggregate demand. With regard to indirect effects, by lowering the incomes of poorer households (which tend to be borrowers), it reduces their borrowing capacity, which in turn reduces credit expansion via consumer- and mortgage-borrowing. This indirect effect helps explain why credit and mortgage growth have been sluggish despite much lower interest rates. QE aimed to stimulate household borrowing, but continued worsening of income distribution has undermined middle-class households' ability to do so. Furthermore, at the start of the recovery in 2009, households already had more debt that was accumulated over the 2000–2007 period than they did in the 1990s. That combination of further worsened income distribution and increased debt makes the possibility of another 1990s-style extended debt-driven expansion unlikely.

A second problem is the macroeconomic restraining effects of the Dodd–Frank Act (2010) financial sector reforms and increased regulation. These measures were necessary to limit the scope and space for financial excess that was a threat to the economy's stability. However, the neoliberal economic model needs asset-price inflation and borrowing to fill the demand gap created by worsened income distribution, the trade deficit and fiscal austerity. Ironically, the Dodd-Frank reforms of the financial sector limit the financial system's capacity to generate asset-price inflation and borrowing to fill that gap. That is another difference from the 1980s and 1990s, when the system was being deregulated to facilitate this demand-filling mechanism (see Palley, 2012a: Chapter 5). This is

Table 8.7 Contributions to per cent change in real GDP

	2008	*2009*	*2010*	*2011*	*2012*	*2013*	*2014*
1. Government consumption & investment spending	0.54	0.64	0.02	−0.65	−0.30	−0.39	−0.03
2. Net exports of goods & services	1.11	1.19	−0.46	−0.02	0.04	0.22	−0.22
3. Gross private investment spending	−1.71	−3.52	1.66	0.73	1.33	0.76	0.95
4. Consumption spending	−0.23	−1.08	1.32	1.55	1.25	1.64	1.72
GDP growth (= 1 + 2 + 3 + 4)	−0.3%	−2.8%	2.5%	1.6%	2.3%	2.2%	2.4%

Source: Bureau of Economic Analysis, GDP Report, Table 1.1.2.

an additional reason why the system is less capable of generating another credit bubble to drive economic expansion.

Lastly, weakness in the global economy resulting from the spread of the export-led growth model (Palley, 2012b) promises to weaken demand for exports by US firms, increase the intensity of import competition as foreign firms try to capture an increased share of the US market to compensate for weakness in their own domestic markets; and increase the grinding downward pressure on US wages via global wage competition as the threat of unemployment compels workers to accept lower wages.

These adverse developments combine with and amplify the existing structural drags inherent to the neoliberal model (that is, wage stagnation, deteriorated income distribution, proclivity to fiscal austerity, trade deficits, global wage competition, job and investment offshoring, etc.). The 1990s boom proved unsustainable despite more favourable conditions. Worsened current conditions suggest any new expansion will again prove unsustainable, will peter out in stagnation, and will be much weaker and of shorter duration.

These tendencies are already visible. Table 8.7 shows the contributions to GDP growth from different sources for the 2008–2014 period. Having been positive in the 2008–2010 period because of ARRA, government spending has begun to contract and become a drag on growth. The collapse of imports during the Great Recession helped strengthen growth by lowering the trade deficit, but as the economy and the dollar have strengthened, that impetus has fallen and reversed. Investment spending has made a positive contribution but the contribution has been weaker than in the 1990s. The one strengthening area is consumption spending, but the past two business cycles (1991–2001, 2001–2007) have shown that that alone is not sustainable.

Conclusion: stagnation rather than another financial crisis

The Great Recession has been followed by stagnation which is likely to endure. That is because of failure to change the structure of the underlying economic policy model. Policy saved the model but did not change it. The policy mix constituting the neoliberal model failed in the 1990s and 2000s under more favourable conditions (that is, less debt hangover, less destroyed consumer credit-worthiness, financial innovation that was beginning and had room to grow, and equity and house prices that were at a lower base with more room for increases, etc.). That suggests the model is destined to fail again.

However, this time it is less likely the expansion will end in a financial crisis because the resolution of the last crisis compelled the financial sector to massively strengthen its balance sheet. Instead, the expansion is likely to end with a stock-market correction and evaporation of growth, but that may take a couple of years to play out. That said, there are two scenarios that may end in financial crisis. The first is if the euro implodes as a result of the exit of an economically depressed and politically stressed member country. The second is if the Federal Reserve continues to pump up financial asset prices and the economy eventually hits an inflation threshold that triggers higher interest rates, which could then trigger an asset price melt-down.

Stagnation without financial crisis seems the most likely outcome for the US economy. The neoliberal economic model is unchanged and exhausted. That is symbolically paralleled by the political system in which the 2016 presidential election may well be between Hillary Clinton and Jeb Bush. One is the wife of former President Bill Clinton, while the other is the brother of former President George W. Bush. Together, Presidents Clinton and Bush presided over the entrenchment and implosion of the neoliberal model. Paralleling the economy, US politics also smacks of déjà vu all over again.

Notes

1 Over the course of the 1981–1982 recession, labour-force participation rose from 63.8 per cent to 64.2 per cent, thereby likely increasing the unemployment rate. In contrast, over the course of the Great Recession the labour-force participation rate fell from 66 per cent to 65.7 per cent, thereby likely decreasing the unemployment. The decrease in the labour-force participation rate was even sharper for prime-age (25–54 years old) workers, indicating that the decrease in the overall participation rate was not due to demographic factors such as an ageing population. Instead, it was due to a lack of job opportunities, which supports the claim that labour force exit lowered the unemployment rate.

2 The FX swaps with foreign central banks have been criticised as being a bail-out for foreign economies. In fact, they saved the US financial system which would have been pulled down by financial collapse outside the US. Many foreign banks operating in the USA had acquired US assets financed with short-term dollar borrowings. When the US money market froze in 2008, they could not roll over these loans in accordance with normal practice. That threatened massive default by these banks within the US financial system, which would have pulled down the entire global financial system. The Federal Reserve could not lend directly to these foreign banks and their governing central banks lacked adequate dollar liquidity to fill the financing gap. The solution was to lend dollars to foreign central banks, which then made dollar loans to foreign banks in need of dollar roll-over short-term financing.

3 Since 2009 there has been some evolution of policy positions characterised by a shift to stronger support for fiscal stimulus. This has been especially marked in Larry Summers, who was the Obama administration's chief economic adviser when it took office. This

shift has become a way of rewriting history by erasing the memory of initial positions. That is also true of the IMF, which in 2010–2011 was a robust supporter of fiscal consolidation in Europe.

References

Epstein, G. (2004) Introduction. In Epstein, G. (ed.) *Financialization and the World Economy*. Northampton, MA: Edward Elgar: 3–16.

Grantham, J. (2010) Night of the Living Fed. *GMO Quarterly Letter*.

Greenhill, S. (2008) It's Awful – Why Did Nobody See It Coming? *Daily Mail*, 5 November 2008.

Krippner, G. (2004) *What Is financialization?* Mimeo, Department of Sociology, UCLA.

Krippner, G. (2005) The Financialization of the American Economy. *Socio-Economic Review* 3: 173–208.

Mishel, L., Gould, E. and Bivens, J. (2015) *Wage Stagnation in Nine Charts*. Washington, DC: Economic Policy Institute.

Palley, T.I. (1998) *Plenty of Nothing: The Downsizing of the American Dream and the Case for Structural Keynesianism*. Princeton, NJ: Princeton University Press.

Palley, T.I. (2012a) *From Financial Crisis to Stagnation: The Destruction of Shared Prosperity and the Role of Economics*. Cambridge: Cambridge University Press.

Palley, T.I. (2012b) The Rise and Fall of Export-led Growth. *Investigación Económica*, LXX, 280: 15–35.

Palley, T.I. (2013) *Financialization: The Macroeconomics of Finance Capital Domination*. Basingstoke: Macmillan/Palgrave.

Palley, T.I. (2015) The Theory of Global Imbalances: Mainstream Economics vs. Structural Keynesianism. *Review of Keynesian Economics* 3(1): 45–62.

Tcherneva, P.R. (2014) Reorienting Fiscal Policy: A Bottom-Up Approach. *Journal of Post Keynesian Economics* 37(1): 43–66.

PART II

EUROPE

[8]

Contributions to Political Economy (2013) **32**, 29-50

EUROPE'S CRISIS WITHOUT END: THE CONSEQUENCES OF NEOLIBERALISM

THOMAS I. PALLEY

AFL-CIO

This paper argues that the eurozone crisis is the product of a toxic neoliberal economic policy cocktail. The mixing of that cocktail traces all the way back to the early 1980s when Europe embraced the neoliberal economic model that undermined the income- and demand-generation process via wage stagnation and widened income inequality. Stagnation was serially postponed by a number of developments, including the stimulus from German re-unification and the low interest rate convergence produced by creation of the euro. The latter prompted a 10-year credit and asset price bubble that created fictitious prosperity. Postponing stagnation in this fashion has had costs because it worsened the ultimate stagnation by creating large build-ups of debt. Additionally, the creation of the euro ensconced a flawed monetary system that fosters public debt crisis and the political economy of fiscal austerity. Lastly, during this period of postponement, Germany sought to avoid stagnation via export-led growth based on wage repression. That has created an internal balance of payments problem within the eurozone, which is a further impediment to resolving the crisis. There is a way out of the crisis. It requires replacing the neoliberal economic model with a structural Keynesian model; remaking the European Central Bank so that it acts as a government banker; having Germany replace its export-led growth wage suppression model with a domestic demand-led growth model; and creating a pan-European model of wage and fiscal policy coordination that blocks race to the bottom tendencies within Europe. Countries, particularly Germany, can implement some of this agenda on their own. However, much of the agenda must be implemented collectively, which makes change enormously difficult. Moreover, the war of ideas in favor of such reforms has yet to be won. Consequently, both politics and the ruling intellectual climate make success unlikely and augur a troubled future.

JEL Classification: E00; E31

I. EUROPE'S TOXIC POLICY COCKTAIL

This paper examines the causes of the eurozone crisis and the outlook for eurozone prosperity. Its conclusion is not optimistic and the eurozone likely faces a prolonged future of economic stagnation. The paper argues that the eurozone crisis is the

Received: 2 March 2013 Accepted: 11 March 2013

product of a toxic neoliberal economic policy cocktail. The mixing of that cocktail traces all the way back to the early 1980s, the defining moment being March 1983 when French President Francois Mitterrand initiated a turn away from Keynesian policies of reflation to neoliberal policies of austerity. That fateful turn symbolized the end of the Keynesian era in Europe and the beginning of the neoliberal era. The crisis is the culminating logic of 30 years of neoliberal policy.

The roots of the eurozone crisis therefore lie deep. That makes explaining the crisis a difficult task as it is easy to focus on more recent developments and mistake symptoms for causes. The crisis is best understood as the outcome of a process of 'policy sedimentation'. Measures put in place long ago set the course for economic stagnation. That stagnation was postponed by subsequent developments, but only at the cost of deepening the ultimate crisis and tendency to stagnation.

There are close analytic parallels with the U.S. crisis (Palley, 2009 [2011a], 2012). This reflects the fact that the global economic crisis is a crisis of neoliberalism which has been the guiding global economic ideology for the past 30 years. In the USA, as in Europe, there was also a change of economic policy paradigm, symbolized by the election of President Reagan in November 1980. That change saw the abandonment of the post-World War II Keynesian policy paradigm and its replacement with a neoliberal growth paradigm. A 30-year credit bubble papered over the demand shortage caused by worsening income distribution. That, in turn, created an unstable financial system which crashed when the credit bubble burst. Now, after the crisis, the U.S. economy is also stuck in stagnation because of deteriorated income distribution and a structural trade deficit that together undermine aggregate demand (AD).

Though the specific details are different, Europe exhibits an analytically similar narrative. However, the European story is complicated by the introduction of the euro. This added an additional dimension of institutional change that has proved catastrophic because it was shaped by neoliberal economic theory.

The sedimentation approach to understanding the eurozone crisis means there is no silver bullet to resolving it. Instead, there is need to reform or replace the series of policy and institutional changes put in place over the past 30 years. That is far easier said than done because of the problem of 'lock-in'. Once in place, it is extremely difficult and costly to make changes. For instance, with regard to the euro the intellectual issues are fairly simple (Palley, 2011b [2011c]). However, successful change will require political unanimity, which is an unlikely outcome. For that reason, as discussed in the conclusion, the most likely scenario is continued stagnation. Moreover, there is also a fair likelihood of a damaging 'black swan' political or economic shock that causes the euro to shrink or disintegrate at great economic cost.

II. OVERVIEW

The eurozone crisis is the product a neoliberal policy cocktail. Figure 1 illustrates the recipe behind this cocktail, the principal ingredients of which are flawed

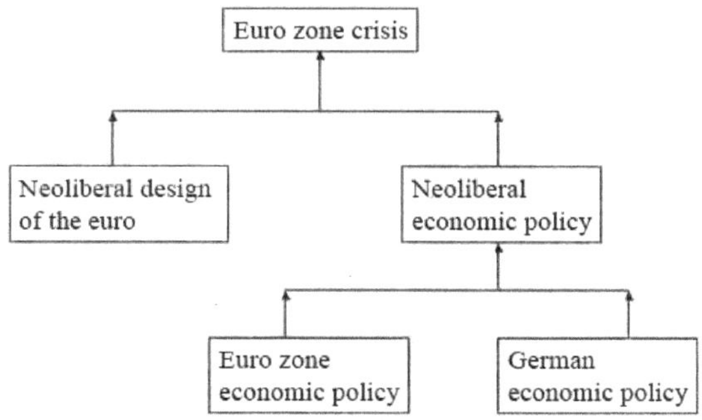

FIGURE 1. The toxic neoliberal cocktail: causes of the eurozone.

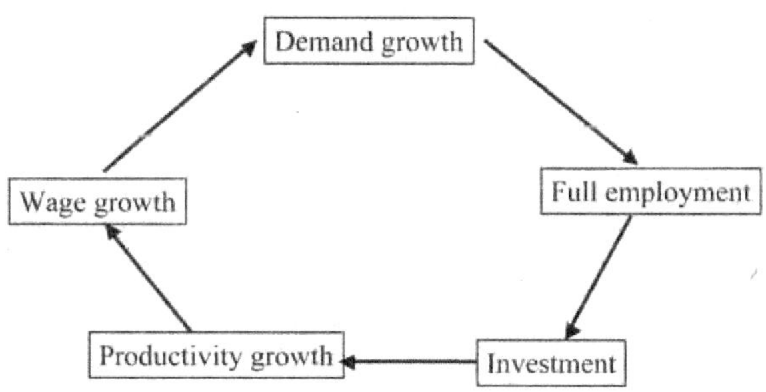

FIGURE 2. The Keynesian 'virtuous circle' growth model.

neoliberal institutional design combined with flawed neoliberal economic policies. The flawed institutional design concerns the architecture of the euro and the European Central Bank (ECB). The flawed economic policy can be decomposed into flawed European-wide policy and flawed German policy.

The flawed European-wide policy concerns the neoliberal labor market and macroeconomic policy strategy that has been persistently promoted since the early 1980s. The flawed German policy concerns Germany's reliance on export led growth based on domestic wage suppression. The combination of flawed policy plus flawed design explains how the crisis came about; why existing policy has been incapable of addressing the crisis; and why the future promises on-going economic crisis absent reform of the eurozone's economic policy configuration and monetary architecture.

2.a The shift from Keynesianism to neoliberalism

The workings of the post-World War II Keynesian growth model are illustrated in Figure 2. The model can be described as a 'virtuous circle' model built on full employment and wage growth tied to productivity growth. Its logic was as follows. Productivity growth drove wage growth, which in turn fuelled demand growth and created full employment. That provided an incentive for investment, which drove further productivity growth and supported higher wages.

After 1980 the Keynesian model was replaced by a neoliberal growth model. The key changes wrought by the new model were: (i) abandonment of the commitment to full employment and the adoption of commitment to very low inflation and (ii) severing of the link between wages and productivity growth. Together, these changes created a new economic dynamic. Before 1980, wages were the engine of demand growth. After 1980, finance and idiosyncratic factors became the engine.

The new economic model was rooted in neoliberal economic thought. Its principal effects were to weaken the position of workers; strengthen the position of business; and unleash financial markets to serve the interests of financial and business elites. The new model is illustrated in Figure 3 and it can be described as a policy box that fences workers in and pressures them from all sides. On the left-hand side, the corporate model of globalization put workers in international competition via global production networks that are supported by free trade agreements and capital mobility. On the right-hand side, the 'small' government agenda attacked the legitimacy of government and pushed persistently for deregulation regardless of dangers. From below, the labor market flexibility agenda attacked unions and labor market supports such as the minimum wage, unemployment benefits, employment protections, and employee rights. From above, policymakers abandoned the commitment to full employment, a development that was reflected in the rise of inflation targeting and the move toward independent central banks controlled by financial interests.

This shift to neoliberal policy created a new economic model that gradually cannibalized the income- and demand-generation process in the eurozone. However, the effects of this cannibalization process were obscured by positive temporary developments, including the launch of the euro in 1999 and the credit and property bubble it unleashed. Now that the credit bubble has burst, the combined effects of the turn to neoliberalism and the flawed design of the euro have created a deep structural crisis that will persist absent change of policy direction and profound reform.

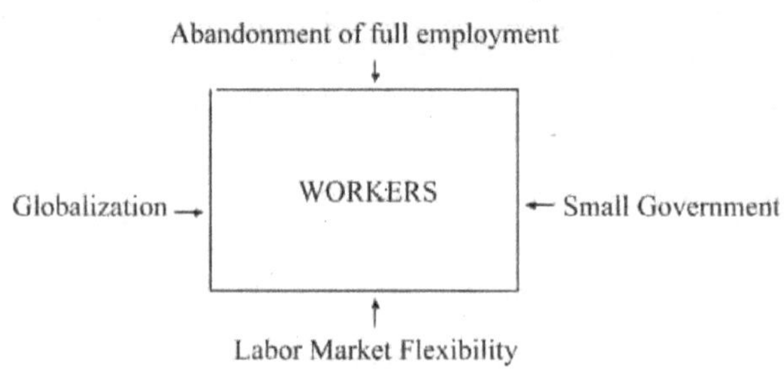

FIGURE 3. The neoliberal policy box.

2.b Germany's role

These underlying structural conditions regarding European macroeconomic policy and design of the euro are further aggravated by Germany's economic policy of export-led growth based on domestic wage suppression. However, as will be shown later, Germany's export-led growth strategy is not the principal cause of the crisis. Indeed, ironically, Germany stands to suffer significantly from the crisis which will undermine its export sales in Europe.

On the other hand, Germany is significantly to blame for blocking reform of the euro's architecture and for its demands for fiscal austerity from stricken eurozone economies as the price of financial support. This stance has kept in place the underlying structural problems. It has also amplified deflationary forces by compelling fiscal austerity in crisis countries, and by forcing them to pursue deflation (so-called internal price devaluation) in an attempt to sustain demand by reducing imports and increasing exports.

2.c The role of the Euro's neoliberal design

One of the great difficulties in discussing the eurozone crisis is that it has taken the form of a public debt crisis. For both politicians and the general public, appearance and correlation are taken as causation. As a result, government profligacy has become the 'fall guy' for the crisis, and that has driven a push for fiscal austerity that has made the crisis worse.

The reality is that the public debt crisis is just the latest phase of the crisis, rather than cause. Moreover, the reason there is a public debt crisis is the flawed institutional design of the euro. Figure 4 shows the sequence of the crisis beginning with the deep originating causes, moving to the 'Great Moderation' period that generated financial exuberance and real estate bubbles in the eurozone, followed by the financial crash and the private debt crisis, and leading to the current situation of a public debt crisis. This is a complicated sequence with a complicated transmission mechanism. That explains why it has been so hard to counter neoliberal populist rhetoric that government and welfare state profligacy is the cause of the crisis.

In fact, as is shown later, the statistics are very clear on the non role of fiscal excess. Except for Greece, the crisis countries (Greece, Ireland, Portugal, Spain, and Italy or GIPSI) exhibited a high degree of fiscal responsibility in the six years

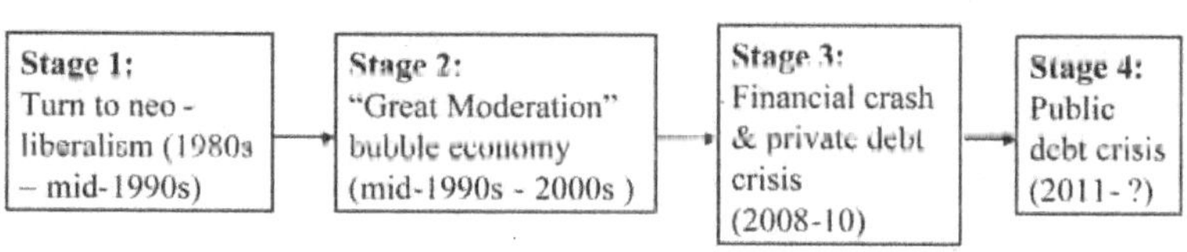

FIGURE 4. The causal sequence of the eurozone crisis.

prior to the crisis. Indeed, they can even claim to have been more responsible than Germany. However, with the onset of the crisis in 2008 they all plummeted into large-budget deficits. The message is not that they were fiscally irresponsible. Instead, it is that the economic model ruptured catastrophically and plunged them into budget deficit.

III. THE COMPLEX MECHANICS OF THE EUROZONE'S CRISIS

Rather than being the result of fiscal irresponsibility, the crisis is the product of the systems and policies put in place within the eurozone over the past 30 years. In the wake of an airplane crash the task is to find out what went wrong. That yields a parallel with the eurozone crisis where the task is to find out how and why the system failed.

3.a Stage 1: the turn to neoliberalism as originating cause

The eurozone's crisis and current predicament is rooted in the past, and understanding the crisis therefore requires going back in the past. A critical feature is that important factors explaining today's predicament were established long ago. However, those factors were obscured by later developments.

The starting point for the story is the turn away from social democratic Keynesianism to neoliberalism, symbolized by the election victories of Margaret Thatcher in 1979 and Ronald Reagan in 1980. In continental Europe this turn was symbolized by French President Mitterand's 1983 policy U-turn.

The turn to neoliberalism changed the economic policy configuration by adopting a labor market flexibility agenda aimed at weakening worker bargaining power; having monetary policy focus on inflation instead of full employment; and imposing fiscal austerity and central bank independence that aimed to shrink the social democratic state by financially constraining it.

In one form or another, this policy configuration was pushed throughout Europe. Though not explicitly expressed in such terms, the goal was to cow labor unions and redistribute income to capital. Analytically, the macroeconomic significance was it worsened income distribution by rupturing the link between productivity and real wage growth. That undermined the demand-generation process, which in turn undermined employment growth. The neoliberal model therefore created a growing 'structural demand gap' because the demand-generation process weakened relative to the growth of potential output.[1]

Table 1 provides data on the wage share. From 1960 to 1981 the wage share was roughly constant, but after 1981 it began a precipitous decline that continued

[1] The most vocal official proponent of the new economic policy strategy was the OECD. Its 'Jobs Strategy' (OECD, 1994) exemplifies the labor market flexibility agenda. That agenda was supported by almost the entirety of the economics profession and still is. It was contested by a handful of Keynesian economists.

TABLE 1.
Wage share as a percent of GDP

	1960–1970	1971–1980	1981–1990	1991–2000	2001–2010	1981	2010	Δ1981–2010
EU-15	71.5	72.9	70.1	67.6	66.1	73.6	66.1	−7.5
France	74.1	74.3	72.3	67.3	66.6	76.7	67.3	−9.4
Germany	67.8	70.4	67.4	66.6	64.1	70.6	63.6	−7.0
Italy	72.5	72.2	68.7	64.6	62.1	71.3	63.1	−10.2
Spain	70.5	72.4	68.3	66.9	62.6	73.0	61.1	−11.9
UK	72.9	74.3	72.8	71.9	71.4	75.2	73.0	−2.2
USA	70.0	69.9	68.3	67.1	63.7	69.1	63.7	−6.3

Based on compensation per employee.
Source: European Commission, ECFIN, Statistical Annex, Table 32, Autumn 2011.

through to end of the last business cycle expansion in 2007. The far-right column of Table 2 shows that between 1981 and 2010 the wage share declined 7.0 points of gross domestic product (GDP) in the EU-15; 9.4 points in France; 7.5 points in Germany; 10.2 points in Italy; and 11.9 points in Spain. Ironically, despite being viewed as the source of neoliberalism, the wage share in the UK and the USA has declined by less than in continental Europe and the UK has a far higher wage share.[2]

Table 2 provides data on the evolution of the unemployment rate. The shift to neoliberalism in the early 1980s is accompanied by a large jump in the unemployment rate. In continental Europe the jump is permanent. In the USA and the UK the unemployment rate backs down a little in the 1990s and 2000s, but as of 2010 it is back up and approximately the same as in continental Europe.

Tables 1 and 2 provide a clear picture of the effects of the shift to neoliberalism. That picture rejects the claims of mainstream economists and confirms the analysis of Keynesian economists (Palley, 1998, 1999, 2004 [2006]; Baker *et al.*, 2007), who have argued that the neoliberal model worsens income distribution, undermines the AD generation process, and increases the unemployment rate.

3.b Stage 2: Europe's 'Great Moderation' and bubble economy

Europe's turn to neoliberalism in the early 1980s undermined the European economy so that it never fully recovered from the dislocations of the 1970s. The

[2] There are two caveats to this. First, there have been significant changes in the distribution of the wage share between workers and managers that has contributed to income inequality, and this managerial pay effect may have been worse in the USA and UK. Secondly, the wage share is calculated using total compensation data, which includes fringe benefits such as health care. In the U.S. healthcare costs have risen astronomically so that workers have been forced to take compensation in the form of health insurance premiums. Moreover, on the basis of health and longevity data, those premiums appear to buy little in terms of additional health and longevity. These two factors tend to overstate the worker wage share in the USA and the UK.

TABLE 2.
Unemployment rate (%)

	1960–1970	1971–1980	1981–1990	1991–2000	2001–2010	2010
EU-15	2.2	4.0	8.5	9.2	8.0	9.6
France	1.8	4.1	8.7	10.6	8.9	9.8
Germany	0.6	2.2	6.0	7.8	8.8	7.1
Italy	4.9	6.1	8.6	10.4	7.8	8.4
Spain	2.4	5.4	15.6	15.7	11.9	20.1
UK	1.7	3.8	9.6	7.9	5.6	7.8
USA	4.8	6.4	7.1	5.6	6.1	9.6

Source: European Commission, ECFIN, Statistical Annex, Table 3, Autumn 2011.

TABLE 3.
The German federal government budget outcome as a percent of GDP, 1989–1996

	1989	1990	1991	1992	1993	1994	1995	1996
Budget	0.1	−1.9	−2.9	−2.5	−3.0	−2.3	−3.0	−3.4

Source: European Commission, ECFIN, Statistical Annex, Table 49, Autumn 2011.

critical significance of the turn was that it set in train developments that persistently eroded the wage share and raised unemployment. That created (i) a growing structural demand shortage and (ii) a growing pool of unemployed. However, these two features were obscured in the 1990s and 2000s by developments associated with the introduction of the euro (see below) which created a bubble economy, but they were not permanently solved. In effect, the bubble economy filled the demand gap but did not solve it. Consequently, with the implosion of the bubble economy the gap has come back to haunt Europe, which explains the baseline condition of stagnation.

In the 1990s and 2000s, the contradictions of the neoliberal model were kept at bay and the unemployment rate actually came down in the 2000s. The reason is Europe, like the USA, had a temporary 'Great Moderation' and bubble economy of its own that obscured the underlying trend to stagnation. The first temporary economic adrenaline shot came from German unification in 1990, which triggered a massive fiscal expansion to integrate the former East Germany. Table 3 shows the evolution of the German federal government's budget deficit. In 1989, the budget was in small surplus, but in 1990 it turned to deficit and the deficit then trended up for the next seven years, peaking at 3.4% of GDP in 1996. This generated large German fiscal stimulus that benefitted all of Europe since Germany is the largest economy in Europe.

The second temporary adrenaline shot came from the general lowering of interest rates that occurred during the 1990s, something that also happened in the USA. This is illustrated in Table 4 which shows how the German long-term nominal interest rate, which proxies for the European safe rate, trended down strongly. In 1990, the long-term rate was 8.7%. In 1999, it was 4.5%. Moreover, after rising slightly at the end of the 1990s business cycle expansion, German long-term interest rates resumed their downward slide and bottomed at 3.4% in 2005. This decline benefitted all eurozone countries as their interest rates are effectively priced off the German rate, with premiums reflecting differences in credit risk relative to Germany.

The third temporary adrenaline shot came from the introduction of the euro and the resulting convergence of European long-term interest rates across countries. This convergence between European periphery (Greece, Ireland, Portugal, Spain, and Italy) and center (Germany) interest rates is shown in Table 5. The critical implication is that the periphery enjoyed a double interest rate boon, which delivered a double dose of economic adrenaline that spurred a massive long running real estate and construction boom in the GIPSI countries. First, it benefitted from the decline in the general level of interest rates caused by the decline in German rates. Secondly, it benefitted from convergence between GIPSI country and German interest rates. This convergence is shown in the bottom row of Table 5 which reports the ratio of the average GIPSI long-term interest rate to Germany's long-term interest rate.

However, even as these interest rate developments were spurring growth, there continued to be background developments that were undermining the eurozone's economic integrity. In particular, Germany was focused on increasing its competitive advantage via policies of wage repression and domestic demand suppression. The objective was to spur the economy by increasing German exports. This relative wage repression is shown in Table 6 that shows nominal compensation growth per employee. In Germany, especially after 2000, nominal compensation growth slowed dramatically relative to its euro country partners. This is shown in the bottom row which reports the ratio of German nominal compensation growth to average eurozone 12 country compensation growth.

Table 7 shows country trade deficits and surpluses as a share of GDP, and it shows Germany was successful with its strategy of increasing its trade surplus. The German surplus jumps after 2000 and jumps again in 2004. Coinciding with this

TABLE 4.
The German long-term nominal interest rate (%), 1990–2007

	1990	1992	1994	1996	1999	2000	2001	2003	2005	2007
Rate	8.7	7.8	6.9	6.2	4.5	5.3	4.8	4.1	3.4	4.2

Source: European Commission, ECFIN, Statistical Annex, Table 49, Autumn 2011.

TABLE 5.
Long-term nominal interest rates (%), 1996–2005

	1996	1997	1998	1999	2000	2001	2002	2003	2004	2005
Germany	6.2	5.7	4.6	4.5	5.3	4.8	4.8	4.1	4.0	3.4
Greece	–	9.9	8.5	6.3	6.1	5.3	5.1	4.3	4.3	3.6
Ireland	7.2	6.3	4.7	4.8	5.5	5.0	5.0	4.1	4.1	3.3
Portugal	8.6	6.4	4.9	4.8	5.6	5.2	5.0	4.2	4.1	3.4
Spain	8.7	6.4	4.8	4.7	5.5	5.1	5.0	4.1	4.1	3.4
Italy	9.4	6.9	4.9	4.7	5.6	5.2	5.0	4.3	4.3	3.6
GIPSI average	8.5	7.2	5.6	5.1	5.7	5.2	5.0	4.2	4.2	3.5
Ratio GIPSI/Germany	1.37	1.26	1.21	1.12	1.07	1.08	1.05	1.02	1.05	1.02

Source: European Commission, ECFIN, Statistical Annex, Table 49, Autumn 2011.

TABLE 6.
Annualized growth of nominal compensation per employee (%)

	1991–2000	2001–2010
Germany	3.2%	1.1%
France	2.5	2.7
Greece	10.1	4.3
Italy	4.1	2.8
Ireland	4.9	4.1
Portugal	8.6	3.2
Spain	4.9	3.6
Euro area 12	3.5	2.4
Germany/EA-12	0.91	0.46

Source: European Commission, ECFIN, Statistical Annex, Table 29, Autumn 2011.

improvement in the German current account, the GIPSI countries experience a deterioration of their current account positions after 2004.The result of these developments was to drain demand from the periphery countries to the benefit of Germany. This did not matter as long as the financial and real estate boom continued so that credit was plentiful in the GIPSI economies. However, when the real estate bubble burst in 2008, it came home to haunt the eurozone as discussed in the following sections.

3.c Stage 3: The unraveling of Europe's Great Moderation

Europe's Great Moderation economy came to an abrupt end in 2008 with the implosion of the U.S. sub-prime market and the collapse of Fannie Mae, Lehman

TABLE 7.
Current account balances as percent of GDP, 2000–2007

	2000	2001	2002	2003	2004	2005	2006	2007
Germany	−1.8	−0.2	2.0	1.9	4.7	5.1	6.5	7.5
Greece	−12.0	−11.4	−12.7	−12.3	−10.5	−10.8	−13.0	−16.9
Ireland	−0.4	−0.5	−0.4	0.8	−0.1	−3.0	−3.7	−5.5
Portugal	−10.7	−10.6	−8.5	−6.7	−8.3	−10.4	−10.8	−10.2
Spain	−4.0	−4.3	−3.8	−4.0	−5.9	−7.5	−9.0	−10.0
Italy	−0.2	0.3	−0.3	−0.8	−0.4	−0.9	−1.5	−1.3

Source: European Commission, ECFIN, Statistical Annex, Table 44, Autumn 2011.

Brothers, and AIG. The unraveling of the bubble era economy has been far easier to understand in the USA. There, the financial crisis ended the asset price and consumer credit bubble that had filled the U.S. demand gap for two decades (Palley, 2009 [2011a], 2012). *Ex post,* the workings and flaws of the U.S. bubble economy are relatively easy to see.

In Europe, the unraveling has been far more complex and difficult to understand. That has fostered misunderstanding and helps explain why the crisis is so widely and mistakenly seen through the lens of a public debt crisis. The first misunderstanding of the crisis came from Germany's Social Democratic Finance Minister, Peer Steinbrück, who immediately declared 'The U.S. will lose its status as the superpower of the world financial system (September 25, 2008)'. From Steinbrück's point of view the crisis was a purely American phenomenon to do with the American model; the European economy was fine; and the eurozone stood to gain from the crisis. Such thinking could not have been more wrongheaded.

Moreover, a great irony is that though Germany has weathered the storm better than other European countries, its financial system was one of the first to feel the spreading shock waves of the global financial crisis. Thus, some of the earliest and largest European losses on U.S. sub-prime loans were felt by German banks. The first German banks to be hit with sub-prime investment losses were Sachsen LB and IKB Deutsche Industriebank which needed bailouts in 2007. By early 2009 massive losses had already been sustained by the major private label names in German banking (e.g. Deutsche Bank, Commerzbank, Dresdner Bank, and Hypo Real Estate) as well as the major landesbanks and co-operative banks (e.g. Bayern LB, West LB, and DZ Bank). The reason for this is simple. Germany was the country running the bulk of Europe's trade surplus so that U.S. payments for German exports were therefore channeled significantly through German banks. They became large investors in the U.S. sub-prime bubble, thinking it offered easy high returns. That tied the German financial system to the U.S. financial system, made Germany an early victim of the U.S. financial crisis, and provided an initial financial transmission mechanism between the USA and Europe.

These financial losses were just a precursor. The reality was Europe's problems were deeper than just exposure to collateral damage from the U.S. financial crash. Instead, Europe shared a common economic model with the USA and the foundations of that model were built on sand. In both regions wage stagnation, worsening income distribution, and growing employment insecurity had contributed to a growing structural demand gap. In both regions this reality was obscured by financial developments that plugged the gap via borrowing fueled by asset price inflation (especially real estate) and a 20 year-long persistent decline in nominal interest rates. In the USA, the demand gap was filled by an explosion in household borrowing fuelled by financial innovation and the house price bubble (Palley, 2009 [2011a], 2012). In Europe, the demand gap was filled by the cross-country nominal interest rate convergence promoted by the introduction of the euro. The important feature is both economic regions were destined to eventually hit stagnation owing to limits to artificially maintaining AD by borrowing, asset price inflation, and nominal interest rate reductions.

Though Minister Steinbrück claimed the crisis meant the end of dollar hegemony, the bitter irony is the eurozone was in far worse structural shape and more vulnerable than the U.S. because of its flawed monetary system that had been implemented in the late 1990s with the creation of the euro. Despite the fact Europe had not enjoyed as robust a boom as the U.S. because it had pursued tighter monetary and fiscal policy, Europe was more vulnerable to the slump caused by the financial crisis because of its weaker institutional structure. First, unlike the U.S. Federal Reserve, the ECB is prohibited from acting as a government banker that finances euro-member country government deficits. Secondly, unlike the USA, the eurozone lacks a federal fiscal policy aimed at macroeconomic stabilization of the entire region, in part via inter-country transfers that smooth differential impacts of business cycle shocks.

The fragility and vulnerability of the eurozone was quickly displayed in early 2009 when the U.S. Federal Reserve had to rescue the eurozone financial system via a series of non-market currency swaps arranged through the ECB. The bailout was needed because European banks had financed their massive involvement in the U.S. sub-prime and commercial property markets via short-term dollar denominated borrowing, rendering them insolvent when the U.S. commercial paper market froze and banks were unable to roll-over borrowings. Though the Federal Reserve acted out of self-interest with the goal of preventing European banks defaulting on their U.S. counterparts, it was still Europe that needed the rescue.

Finally, like the USA, Europe also has its own trade imbalances that undermine employment. However, here too Europe has found itself worse off. The USA has massive trade deficits with Europe and China. Europe has a trade surplus with the USA, a trade deficit with China, and large internal trade deficits between Northern and Southern Europe. Whereas the U.S. trade deficit is with countries with different currencies (e.g. China, Japan, Mexico, Canada, and Europe), the eurozone imbalances are between Germany and the GIPSI economies, which are locked together in a currency union. That makes remedying the eurozone's imbalance far more difficult.

For the USA, exchange rate depreciation can rapidly diminish the trade deficit, and thereby help stem the demand leakage from imports and investment diversion. For the eurozone, the Germany—GIPSI imbalance cannot be corrected in that way. Instead, either the periphery must undergo deflation relative to Germany, or Germany must undergo more rapid inflation relative to the periphery. Given high levels of domestic indebtedness, the former risks a cycle of destabilizing debt—deflation: the latter is opposed by German policymakers who have visceral resistance to inflation.

In sum, far from signaling the relative decline of the dollar, the crisis has been worse for the euro for three reasons: exposure of eurozone banks to the U.S. financial crisis; structural flaws within the euro's design; and the nature of the eurozone's internal trade imbalance. As a result, the crisis has imposed triple losses on the eurozone's financial system: losses from investments in the USA,; losses associated with the bursting of Europe's own real estate bubble; and losses caused by the transformation of Europe's private sector debt crisis into a public sector debt crisis.

3.d Stage 4: Public debt crisis as product of the Euro's flawed neoliberal design

The striking feature about the crisis is that it started as a private sector debt crisis in both the USA and the eurozone. However, unlike the USA, the crisis has jumped the line in the eurozone to become a public sector debt crisis. The fundamental reason for this difference is the eurozone's lack of a central bank that can act as government banker (Palley, 2011b [2011c]). This absence is due to the euro's flawed neoliberal design that prohibits the ECB from helping governments finance their deficits and manage their debts.

Tragically, this appearance as a public debt crisis has created a dangerous economic and political situation. That is because it has created space for neoliberal political elements to exploit the 'appearance' and push for a doubling-down on the long-standing agenda of fiscal austerity and attack on the social democratic state.

It is easy to show that government debt and fiscal excess are not the cause of the crisis. Table 8 shows central government financial balances as a percent of GDP for the period 2000–2011. It is striking for several reasons. First, Ireland and Spain both ran budget surpluses for much of the five-year period (2002–2007) before the crisis. Secondly, as shown in the last row of Table 8, the GIPSI countries ran smaller average budget deficits than Germany from 2002 to 2005, and thereafter the deficit positions were quite similar. Third, the large increase in government deficits in the GIPSI countries only comes in 2008, which is when their budget deficits increase enormously relative to Germany as shown in the bottom row.

The message from Table 8 is clear. Except for Greece, the GIPSI countries exhibited a high degree of fiscal responsibility in the six years prior to the crisis, and it is only with the onset of the crisis in 2008 that they plummeted into large budget deficits. The message is not that they were fiscally irresponsible. Rather, the message is that the model broke catastrophically and plunged them into budget deficit.

TABLE 8.
Central government financial balances as a percent of GDP, 2002–2011

	2002	2003	2004	2005	2006	2007	2008	2009	2010	2011
Germany	−3.6	−4.0	−3.8	−3.3	−1.6	0.3	0.1	−3.0	−3.3	−2.1
Greece	−4.8	−5.7	−7.4	−5.3	−6.0	−6.7	−9.8	−15.6	−10.4	−7.5
Ireland	−0.3	0.4	1.4	1.6	2.9	0.1	−7.3	−14.3	−32.4	−10.1
Portugal	−2.9	−3.1	−3.4	−5.9	−4.1	−3.2	−3.6	−10.1	−9.2	−5.9
Spain	−0.5	−0.2	−0.4	1.0	2.0	1.9	−4.2	−11.1	−9.2	−6.3
Italy	−3.0	−3.5	−3.6	−4.4	−3.3	−1.5	−2.7	−5.3	−4.5	−3.9
GIPSI average	−2.3	−2.4	−2.7	−2.6	−1.7	−1.9	−5.5	−11.3	−13.1	−6.7
GIPSI minus Germany	1.3	1.6	1.1	0.7	−0.1	−1.6	−5.4	−8.3	−9.8	−4.6

Source: OECD Economic Outlook 89 database, Annex Table 27.

Moreover, when the model broke it broke asymmetrically, plunging the GIPSI economies into massive deficit while Germany suffered much smaller increases in its budget deficit. In Ireland, the huge jump in the deficit in 2009 and 2010 was significantly due to the cost of public bailout of the banking system. Bank bailout costs have also impacted budget deficits in Spain.

Table 8 begins the task of demystifying the eurozone's crisis and why it has taken the shape of a public debt crisis. It definitively rules out fiscal irresponsibility. The true culprit is the design of the euro. How that design has created a public debt crisis is explained below.

The euro was introduced in 1999 which marked the high water mark of neoliberal economics. The neoliberal political project aimed to diminish the role of the state and enhance the power of the market. This goal is reflected in neoliberal monetary theory that guided the design of the euro. The theory argues the role of the central bank is to control inflation and the exchange rate, but there should be complete separation between the central bank and government finances.

By adopting this theory, the euro's architects intentionally changed the monetary—fiscal balance. Previous national monetary systems ensured 'fiscal dominance' whereby central banks served governments. The new euro system instituted 'central bank dominance' whereby governments were stripped of access to their own central bank that could help them finance budget deficits and manage interest rates on government debt.

How did the euro do this? It did so by creating a 'detached' central bank. The concept of a 'detached central bank' is fundamentally different from an 'independent central bank'. A detached central bank is prohibited from buying government debt. An independent central bank distances its decision making from government, but it is allowed to purchase government debt. Both the Federal Reserve and the Bank of England are significantly independent but they are not detached. The ECB is detached by design. The old national banking systems made European

TABLE 9.
Central government financial balances as a percent of GDP, 2002–2011

	2002	2003	2004	2005	2006	2007	2008	2009	2010	2011
Italy	−3.0	−3.5	−3.6	−4.4	−3.3	−1.5	−2.7	−5.3	−4.5	−3.9
Spain	−0.5	−0.2	−0.4	1.0	2.0	1.9	−4.2	−11.1	−9.2	−6.3
UK	−2.0	−3.7	−3.6	−3.3	−2.7	−2.8	−4.8	−10.8	−10.3	−8.7
USA	−4.0	−5.0	−4.4	−3.3	−2.2	−2.9	−6.3	−11.3	−10.6	−10.1

Source: OECD Economic Outlook 89 database, Annex Table 27.

governments masters of the bond market. The euro's architecture makes bond markets master of national governments. Under the old system of national money, central banks played a key government banker role by helping manage the government debt and finance spending, including financial sector rescues. The euro's neoliberal architecture cheats eurozone countries of such assistance.

This can be seen by comparing eurozone country experience with the USA and the UK. Tables 9 and 10 show country budget deficits and interest rates for the period 2002–2011. Spain was especially fiscally responsible before the crisis, and after the onset of the crisis Spain and Italy have run smaller deficits as a share of GDP than the USA and the UK. This is despite the fact that they have been forced to pursue policies of austerity that have caused deeper recession which has lowered GDP (i.e. the denominator). Yet despite this tighter fiscal policy, Spain and Italy have both had to pay higher long-term interest rates—and the differential worsened in 2012. The data clearly show that this has nothing to do with the so-called 'fiscal responsibility' and everything to do with the fact Spain and Italy do not have a national central bank that they can call on to lower rates.

Had the USA and the UK been subject to the same institutional constraints they too would have experienced public debt crises. However, because they have central banks that can act as government bankers they have avoided this. Instead, the Federal Reserve and Bank of England have lowered interest rates to near zero; have helped finance private sector financial bailouts; and have helped finance budget deficits at rock bottom interest rates.

GIPSI countries have had none of this assistance. Instead, Spain which had a fiscal position that was not so different from the USA and UK, has found its bonds are under attack. The euro's architecture means Spain has been without a central bank to defend the government, leaving its bond market open to speculative attack.

The problem of bond market attack is easy to understand if one thinks of a multiple equilibrium model of the bond market. A country can be subject to speculative attack that causes interest rates to jump which can trigger a self-fulfilling cycle. That is because higher interest rates raise the burden of debt, making it more likely the government will default, which then justifies high interest rates. The flaw in the euro

TABLE 10.
Long-term nominal interest rates (%), 2002–2011

	2002	2003	2004	2005	2006	2007	2008	2009	2010	2011
Italy	5.0	4.3	4.3	3.6	4.0	4.5	4.7	4.3	4.0	4.8
Spain	5.0	4.1	4.1	3.4	3.8	4.3	4.4	4.0	4.2	5.3
UK	4.9	4.5	4.9	4.4	4.5	5.0	4.6	3.6	3.6	3.8
USA	4.6	4.0	4.3	4.3	4.8	4.6	3.7	3.3	3.2	3.5

Source: OECD Economic Outlook 89 database, Annex Table 35.

system is that the ECB is not supposed to intervene in the bond market on behalf of specific governments under speculative attack.[3] Without a central bank, governments are reduced to the same bond market standing as provinces and large corporations—which is exactly what the euro's neoliberal architects intended.

IV. WHAT IS THE ROLE OF GERMANY'S EUROZONE TRADE SURPLUS?

In the wake of the crisis, one view that has gained increasing prominence is that the eurozone is suffering from a classic balance of payments crisis—albeit one that is taking place within the confines of a currency union. This view has been popularized by Wolf (2011), the prominent economics correspondent of *The Financial Times*:

> The fundamental difficulty throughout has been the failure to understand the nature of the crisis ... As Thomas Mayer of Deutsche Bank notes, 'below the surface of the euro area's public debt and banking crises lies a balance-of-payments crisis caused by a misalignment of internal real exchange rates.' The crisis will be over if and only if weaker countries regain competitiveness.

The balance of payments crisis interpretation has also been embraced by Krugman (2012):

> As a consequence of these inflows, costs and prices rose, manufacturing became uncompetitive, and nations that had roughly balanced trade in 1999 began running large trade deficits instead ... If the peripheral nations still had their own currencies, they could and would use devaluation to quickly restore competitiveness. But they don't, which means that they are in for a long period of mass unemployment and slow, grinding deflation.

In effect, this balance of payments crisis interpretation blames Germany and satellite northern eurozone economies (Austria, Belgium, and the Netherlands) for the crisis. The argument is that Germany's export-led growth model predicated on wage repression hollowed out GIPSI economies by creating trade deficits that made those

[3] This was the initial position of the ECB at the onset of the crisis, though that position has softened considerably over the course crisis. The ECB now seems willing to intervene when speculation threatens the integrity of the euro. That is an improvement, but it is a long way away from an optimal position that has the central bank act as a government banker.

countries vulnerable. It also worsened income distribution within Germany and undermined German domestic demand, thereby undercutting an important support of the European economy.[4]

Whereas the evidence (see Tables 6 and 7) shows clearly that Germany has engaged in wage repression and export-led growth which has suppressed German domestic demand and prejudiced the wider European economy, that does not mean this is the cause of the crisis. Instead, the structural balance of payments problem that now grips Europe is the dog that barked after the crisis.

Some micro evidence that the balance of payments did not cause the crisis is provided by Table 7. Italy and Ireland are both crisis countries. However, Table 7 shows that Italy's trade deficit on the eve of the crisis was a very manageable 1.3% of GDP. Ireland's deficit was larger at 5.5% of GDP, but in prior years it had been much smaller and only jumped to unsustainable levels in 2007.

Instead, the current account deficits that built up in the years preceding the crisis reflect how the GIPSI countries benefitted during the period of Europe's 'Great Moderation' from low interest rates and easy finance. In effect, the Great Moderation period had the crisis countries trade real estate assets in exchange for goods.[5] When the flow of money chasing real estate dried up, the model blew up and the real estate bubble burst, sending real estate asset prices into reverse. A consequence of that blow-up was also a domestic banking crisis, but its effects have been largely contained by government and ECB support for the banking sector.

At this stage, the GIPSI economies are held back by demand shortage. Though bank lending is down, it is not because of lack of supply of finance, but rather because of lack of credit demand combined with bankers' fears about the quality of credit demand. The private sector is burdened by accumulated debt and deteriorated income distribution, while the public sector is burdened by fiscal austerity resulting from the flawed design of the euro.

What then is the role of the eurozone's internal balance of payments disequilibrium? Its significance is not that it caused the crisis, but rather that it now constitutes an additional impediment to escaping the crisis. The impediment is threefold. First, Germany's wage repression continues to undermine demand in Europe's largest economy at a time when demand shortage is Europe's pressing problem. Secondly, the structural trade deficit drains demand from the eurozone's crisis countries, further undermining their economies. Thirdly, by undermining crisis country economies, the trade deficits worsen their budget deficits at a time when the market, the ECB, the IMF, and the European Commission are pushing for deflationary fiscal consolidation. That worsening of budget positions reinforces demands for fiscal austerity, which only worsens Europe's demand shortage. It is easy to mistake

[4] Bibow (2012) provides a detailed argument in favor of the hypothesis that the eurozone crisis is a balance of payments crisis manufactured by Germany.

[5] The UK can be viewed as having operated on a similar type of model for decades. In the UK's case, it involves gradually selling central London and leading British firms (e.g. Cadbury and ICI) to foreign nationals and foreign corporations.

these balance of payments related impediments as causes of the crisis when they are after the fact factors.

V. WHAT SHOULD BE DONE?

The above diagnosis of the causes the eurozone crisis paves the way for prescription. This section identifies a four part program for escaping the crisis and restoring European full employment with shared prosperity.

(1) The first critical component is the reversal of Europe's turn to neoliberalism that occurred 30 years ago. Earlier, the paper described the neoliberal growth model in terms of a policy box that pressures workers from all sides. The way forward is to replace the neoliberal box with a structural Keynesian box (Palley, 2009 [2011a], 2012) that repacks the policy box as illustrated in Figure 5. The critical feature is to take workers out of the box and put corporations and financial markets in so that they are again made to serve a broader public interest. The key elements are to replace corporate globalization with managed globalization; restore a commitment to full employment; replace the neoliberal anti-government agenda with a social democratic government agenda; and replace the neoliberal labor market flexibility with a solidarity-based labor market agenda. The critical goals are restoration of full employment and restoration of a solid link between wage and productivity growth.

(2) The second critical element is to reform the euro's design. The euro is a good idea because it provides transaction and pricing efficiencies, and it also solves the problem of exchange rate speculation which was historically a very serious for European economies because they are small and open. The problem is the ECB is prohibited from acting as government banker for individual member countries. That prohibition is appropriate as the ECB should not give special treatment and intervention subsidies to individual countries. Doing so could establish dangerous incentives as countries would have an incentive to engage in populist fiscal policy, knowing the ECB would come to the rescue. And that would result in monetary instability.

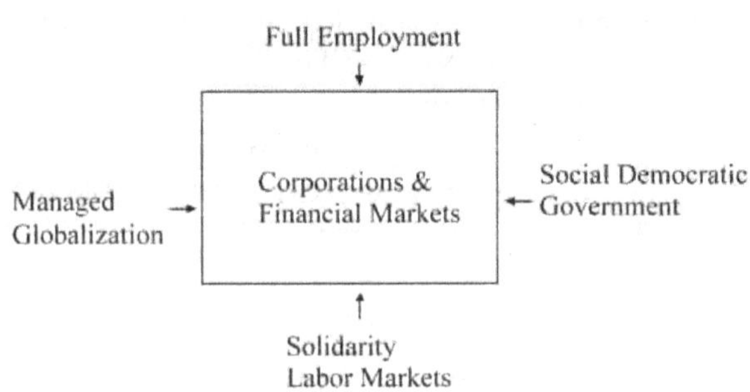

FIGURE 5. The structural Keynesian box.

The challenge is to design a system in which the ECB helps finance and defend governments, but without incentives for country fiscal irresponsibility. My proposed solution (Palley, 2011b [2011c]) is a new public finance architecture that includes the creation of a European Public Finance Authority (EPFA), which would issue European bonds jointly and severally backed by all member countries. The critical feature that distinguishes this proposal is the ECB would have the right to buy and sell EPFA bonds. The EPFA would work as follows: (i) It would have the right to sell new EPFA bonds at its discretion. (ii) All bond proceeds would be paid directly to national governments. (iii) The ECB would have the right to buy and sell EPFA bonds. (iv) EPFA would be governed by finance ministers of eurozone member countries, representing their national governments. (v) Voting rights within the EPFA would be allocated on a per capita basis. (vi) Distribution of bond proceeds would also be on a per capita basis, as would payment of debt interest. In effect EPFA would serve as a trust entity with regard to bond issues, receiving interest service from countries and distributing interest payments to bond holders.

The important feature of EPFA is that it would create a European bond without any trace of national identity so the ECB favors none. EPFA bonds can then be legitimately traded by the ECB. That creates the space for open market operations and allows the ECB to take on the role of government banker for Europe, which fills the missing feature in the current institutional set-up. EPFA would be able to help finance annual budget deficits for countries, and annual bond issues could vary with the state of the overall Eurozone economy. All member countries would receive payments on a per capita basis. Countries that received payments in excess of their own needs could retire their own sovereign debt or build up a sovereign wealth fund by acquiring the national debt of other countries.

In this fashion, an ECB—EPFA system would give back to the eurozone a policy architecture similar to that enjoyed by the USA and the UK. The ECB would be responsible for monetary matters including interest rates. It would also retain responsibility for exchange rates. The EPFA would have responsibility for issuing eurozone bonds. All spending decisions would remain entirely in the hands of national governments as proceeds from bond sales would be paid to governments.

(3) The third critical element is to reverse Germany's model of export-led growth based on wage repression. Germany is the largest most prosperous economy in Europe. Instead of seeking to be pulled along by the eurozone and the global economy, it must become a locomotive for growth. Doing so requires Germany shift to a domestic demand-led growth strategy. That requires both real and nominal wage growth. Real wages must grow with productivity, and there is also room to increase real wages to reverse some of the increase in profit share over past 30 years. Higher nominal wages are needed so that Germany reduces the competitive pressure and drain of demand on Europe's crisis countries. Rather than having the crisis countries gain competitiveness via price deflation, Germany should instead raise its prices. That achieves relative price adjustment without deflation which would trigger destructive debt-deflation dynamics.

(4) The final piece of the program is coordinated European fiscal expansion and real wage determination. In many regards, European economic integration is akin to globalization as it unifies economies with different characteristics and different levels of development. This process of unification can easily unleash 'race to the bottom' dynamics whereby countries seek to gain competitive advantage in unified product and service markets via adverse competition.

Such adverse competition can take a host of the forms including tax competition that favors capital income and prejudices labor income; suppression of labor, environmental, and regulatory standards; suppression of government social and educational spending; suppression of public investment; and wage repression. All of these features have been visible in the process of globalization, and they have also been present in the European integration project. This has contributed to Europe's demand problem by fostering wage stagnation and increased income inequality. It has also undermined the political willingness of countries to regulate capital for fear of deterring investment.

Restoring European shared prosperity requires putting in place institutional arrangements that block these adverse competitive dynamics. In particular, there is need for increased fiscal coordination to prevent an austerity race to the bottom, and increased wage bargaining coordination that harmonizes wage increases in an upward direction. A European minimum wage system (Palley, 2011d) can play an especially critical role with regard to this latter need.

VI. CONCLUSION: WHERE NEXT?

To conclude, Europe was long headed for economic stagnation because of its embrace of the neoliberal economic model that undermined the income- and demand-generation process. That stagnation was serially postponed by a number of developments, including the stimulus from German re-unification and the low interest rate convergence produced by creation of the euro. The latter prompted a 10-year credit and asset price bubble that created fictitious prosperity, particularly in the GIPSI countries.

However, postponing stagnation in this fashion has had costs since it worsened the ultimate stagnation by creating a large buildup of debt that now over-hangs the economy. Additionally, the creation of the euro, which also helped postpone stagnation, has left behind a flawed monetary system that fosters public debt crisis and the political economy of fiscal austerity. Lastly, during this period of postponement, Germany sought to avoid stagnation via export-led growth based on wage repression. That has created an internal balance of payments problem within the eurozone, which is a further impediment to resolving the crisis.

There is a way out of the crisis. It requires replacing the neoliberal economic model with a structural Keynesian model; remaking the ECB so that it can act as government banker; having Germany replace its export-led growth wage suppression model with a domestic demand-led growth model; and creating a pan-European model of policy and wage coordination that blocks off race to the bottom tendencies within Europe.

Countries, particularly Germany, can implement some of this agenda on their own. But much of this agenda must be implemented collectively, either because countries are now locked into institutional arrangements (such as the euro) or because markets threaten to punish individual countries that try to go it alone. This makes change enormously difficult because political consensus that borders on unanimity is needed. Moreover, the war of ideas in favor of such reforms has yet to be won. Consequently, both politics and the ruling intellectual climate make success unlikely.

Europe confronts three possible future scenarios. By far the most likely is prolonged stagnation, with on-going bursts of mini-crisis that compel policymakers to make small reforms which are just enough to preserve the euro. By far the least likely is that policymakers enact the type of reform program described above that can restore full employment with shared prosperity. The third scenario, with an in between likelihood, is that Europe is hit by a political or economic 'black swan' event that leads to country exit from the euro, causing it to shrink or disintegrate completely. This last scenario would likely be very economically disruptive and costly.

REFERENCES

Baker, D., Glyn, A., Howell, D. & Schmitt, J. (2007) Are protective labor market institutions at the root of unemployment? A critical review of the evidence. *Capitalism Soc.*, **2**, 1–71.

Bibow, J. (2012) The Euro Debt Crisis and Germany's Euro Trilemma. Working paper No. 721. New York: Levy Economics Institute of Bard College, Annandale-on-Hudson.

Krugman, P. (2012) What ails Europe? *New York Times*, February 26.

Organization for Economic Cooperation and Development. (1994) *The OECD jobs Study.* Paris: OECD.

Palley, T. I. (1998) Restoring prosperity: why the U.S. model is not the right answer for the U.S. or Europe. *J. Post Keynesian Econ.*, **20**, 337–354.

Palley, T. I. (1999) The myth of labor market flexibility and the costs of bad macroeconomic policy: U.S. and European unemployment explained. *Jobswunder USA* (Lang, S., Mayer, M.Scherr, C. eds). Munster: Westfalisches Dampfboot.

Palley, T. I. (2004, [2006]) The causes of high unemployment: Labor market sclerosis versus macroeconomic policy. *Challenging the Market: The Struggle to Regulate Work and Income* (Stanford, & Vosko, eds). Montreal& Kingston, Canada: McGill-Queens University Press. Also published as: The causes of high unemployment: labor market sclerosis versus macroeconomic policy. *Wages, Employment, Distribution and Growth* (Hein, Heise & Truger eds). London: Palgrave/Macmillan, 2006, pp. 20–48.

Palley, T. I. (2009, [2011a]) *America's Exhausted Paradigm: Macroeconomic Causes of the Financial Crisis and Great Recession.* Washington, DC: New American Contract Policy Paper, New America Foundation. July 22. Shortened version published as America's flawed paradigm: Macroeconomic causes of the financial crisis and Great Recession. *Empirica*, **38**, 3–17.

PALLEY, T. I. (2011b, [2011c]) The European Union needs a government banker. *Challenge*, **54**, 5–21. Also published as: Monetary union stability: the need for a government banker and the case for a European Public Finance Authority. *WSI Mitteilungen*, **6**, 297–303.

PALLEY, T. I. (2011d) A global minimum wage system. *Financial Times Economists' Forum*, July 18.

PALLEY, T. I. (2012) *From Financial Crisis to Stagnation: The Destruction of Shared Prosperity and the Role of Economics*. Cambridge: Cambridge University Press.

WOLF, M. (2011) Thinking through the unthinkable: fundamental difficulty has been failure to understand the crisis. *Financial Times*, November 8.

doi:10.1093/cpe/bzt004

[9]

Crises

The European Monetary Union Needs a Government Banker

Thomas Palley

Many economists contend that the European Monetary Union is in serious danger. This economist argues that it needs a fiscal authority to issue Europe-wide bonds that the European Central Bank can trade so that the bank can lower country funding costs and counter bond market speculation.

The financial crisis of 2008 began as a private-sector financial crisis. However, in many countries it has morphed into a public-sector financial crisis owing to large budget deficits caused by reduced tax revenues, temporary fiscal stimulus, and large bailouts of the financial sector, combined with long-standing adverse trends in the ratio of public debt to the gross domestic product (GDP).

The crisis has raised a host of issues regarding the merits of fiscal policy and the limits to debt-financed budget deficits. In Europe, it has raised another issue regarding fiscal policy and monetary unions. The standard argument (De Grauwe 1994; Kenen 1969) is that monetary

THOMAS PALLEY is an associate at the New America Foundation in Washington, DC.

Challenge, vol. 54, no. 4, July/August 2011, pp. 5–21.

ISSN 0577–5132 / 2011 $9.50 + 0.00.
DOI: 10.2753/0577-5132540401

unions (especially nonoptimal currency unions) need a system of fiscal transfers. That is because regions are likely to be hit by asymmetric shocks, and those shocks can be softened by interregional transfers, which substitute for capital and labor mobility. Europe lacks such a system, and euroskeptics therefore claim it needs to establish one, or else some member countries may be compelled to exit the euro.

The current paper offers another interpretation of the euro's monetary union problem, which is that it lacks a government banker. The euro solved Europe's problem of exchange-rate speculation by creating a unified currency with a single exchange rate managed by the European Central Bank (ECB). However, in doing so, it replaced the exchange-rate speculation problem with a bond-market speculation problem. That is because countries lost their national central banks, which were able to issue money and assist in managing interest rates and financing government.

The paper argues that this flaw in the euro's structural architecture can be remedied by the creation of a European Public Finance Authority (EPFA) that would have discretionary power to issue bonds that would be jointly and severally backed by eurozone member countries. In effect, the EPFA would function as the public finance sibling of the ECB, which manages monetary conditions.

Neoliberal Economics and the Euro's Design

The euro was created in an era of neoliberal political and intellectual dominance. Neoliberal political theory argues for diminishing the role of the state and enhancing the power of the market, and within monetary theory this is expressed by claims that:

1. Fiscal policy is ineffective.
2. Money is neutral, and the only effect of money growth is inflation.
3. The real economy quickly and automatically returns to full employment in response to negative demand shocks.

These theoretical claims shaped the euro's design and are reflected in the legal arrangements governing both the ECB and ECB policy. The essential feature was a change in the monetary-to-fiscal balance that followed from prohibiting central bank involvement with public finances.

Under the old system of national money, central banks played a key role in helping to manage the public debt, finance budget deficits, and finance rescues of the financial sector. The euro's architecture undermined this government banker function by stripping national central banks of the ability to issue means of payment. That has contributed to the public debt crisis centered in the PIIGS (Portugal, Ireland, Italy, Greece, and Spain) countries. In contrast, the United States and the UK have been able to use the Federal Reserve and Bank of England to push interest rates to near zero, to help finance private-sector financial bailouts, and to engage in quantitative easing of bond purchases that have helped finance budget deficits at rock-bottom interest rates. For the United States and the UK, that has lowered the budget cost of the crisis and helped to avoid a public debt crisis of confidence.

In effect, national monetary systems make national governments master of the bond market, whereas the euro's architecture makes the bond market master of national governments. Given the dominance of neoliberal economic thinking, this was an intended outcome of the euro's design.

Figure 1 shows alternative monetary–fiscal institutional structures. The government budget can be "unrestricted" or subject to "deficit rules." The central bank can play the role of "government banker," or it can be "detached." The concept of detached captures a situation where the central bank is unconnected to government. The critical feature is that the central bank is not allowed to buy government debt, which makes the concept of a detached central bank qualitatively different from the concept of central bank independence. The latter corresponds to a situation in which government distances itself from central bank decision making but central banks are allowed to purchase government debt.

The modern era of pure fiat money (i.e., the era since the end of the gold standard in the 1930s) has been characterized by the combination "unrestricted deficits–government banker," which corresponds to

		Government budget rules	
		Unrestrained deficits	Deficit rules
Central bank	Government banker	United States, United Kingdom	United States with a balanced budget rule
	Detached	Euro countries ex-Maastricht	U.S. states and euro countries with Maastricht

Figure 1. Alternative Monetary–Fiscal Institutional Structures

the current U.S. and UK arrangements. In recent years governments, including the UK, have allowed central banks to become more independent, but they are not detached.

Within the United States there has been a long-standing push to impose budget rules in the form of a balanced-budget requirement, which would push the United States into the northeast quadrant. The southeast quadrant of deficit rules and detached central bank effectively constitutes the situation of many U.S. states that have no central bank and are subject to balanced-budget requirements. The southeast quadrant also captures the formal situation of eurozone member countries. Within these countries the formal shells of central banks remain, but they are now regulatory agencies rather than central banks that issue means of payment. Along with this situation, the Maastricht treaty imposes a budget deficit rule allowing eurozone countries average budget deficits of up to 3 percent of GDP. However, the current crisis has proved so serious that the Maastricht treaty budget-deficit provisions have essentially been ignored, and eurozone countries have been allowed to ignore budget rules, placing them in the southwest quadrant.

Detached Central Banks and the Problem of Bond Market Instability

Although euro countries have been allowed (at least for the moment) to ignore budget rules, they are still subject to monetary governance via a detached central bank. The problem with such governance is that central banks are prohibited from buying government debt, leaving government bond markets open to speculative attack. In effect, the euro solved the problem of exchange rate speculation and replaced it with the problem of bond market speculation.

The Technical Appendix provides a simple model of the problem of bond market speculation. The basic logic of the problem is as follows. Government bond investors in euro countries aim to earn a risk-adjusted expected return equal to that which they could earn on safe bonds. This implies the condition

$$E(R) = 1 + i^* + z \qquad (1)$$

where $E(R)$ = expected return from holding risky country bonds, i^* = interest rate on safe bonds, z = required risk premium to hold risky country bonds.

If the return on safe bonds exceeds the risk-adjusted expected return on a country's bonds, the country bond interest rate rises as agents sell the country's bonds to buy safe bonds.

The core problem is that expected return on country bonds can be volatile due to shifts of confidence, and it can also be nonlinear with respect to the country bond interest rate. The economic logic of nonlinearity is the result of competing effects. On the one hand, a higher domestic interest rate directly raises the expected return on a country's bonds. On the other hand, higher interest rates can also reduce the expected return due to increased default risk from higher debt-service burdens and from adverse impacts of higher interest rates on the economy.

Figure 2 provides a graphic analogue of the model in which there are four equilibrium points. Equilibrium A is the stable "good" equilibrium with low country interest rates. Equilibrium B is the unstable low-interest-rate equilibrium. Equilibrium C is the stable "bad" equilibrium with high country interest rates, and equilibrium D is the unstable high-interest-rate equilibrium. PIIGS countries can be thought of as trapped in the bad high-interest-rate equilibrium given by C or D. The policy challenge is to move them to A.

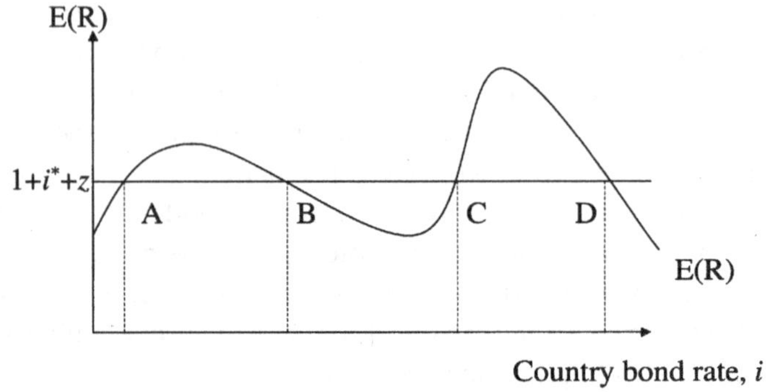

Figure 2. The Determination of Country Bond Rates

In the context of the eurozone, the safe bond interest rate, i^*, can be identified with the interest rate on German bunds. Given that Germany is the strongest and largest eurozone economy, bunds are regarded as the safest bond. To a degree, as with money (Menger 1892), there may even be an element of self-fulfilling prophecy. Having become the standard of safety, money flocks to that safe standard, thereby increasing the liquidity of bunds and further driving down the German interest rate. That improves Germany's fiscal situation, which further increases the perceived safety of bunds. By becoming the safe standard, Germany gets to enjoy a premium ranking and a form of bond-ranking seignorage.

The multiple-equilibrium character of the model means it may exhibit hysteresis. For instance, suppose financial panic causes a sudden jump in the risk premium, z. In this event, country bond rates may jump from the low-interest-rate good equilibrium at A to the high-interest-rate bad equilibrium at C or D. However, once the panic is over and the risk premium drops back, a country can remain trapped in the high-interest-rate equilibrium.

A similar outcome can occur if there is a sudden deterioration in confidence about future conditions in a country's economy. In this event, the *E(R)* function shifts down. If the downward shift is large enough, the country's domestic interest rate may jump to the bad high-interest-rate equilibrium, where it can remain stuck. That is because high interest rates create a self-fulfilling prophecy of increased likelihood of default, which means investors demand high interest rates to compensate for that increased risk.

The flaw in the system is that a government under speculative attack cannot use its central bank to intervene in the bond market and reduce the stock of outstanding debt. Without a central bank, governments are reduced to the same bond market standing as provinces and large corporations. That opens them to speculation and the vagaries of market discipline, and causes them to run on debt just like any other borrower.

The euro's constitution prohibits the ECB from intervening to protect national government bonds. That prohibition is justified, as the ECB should not give special treatment and intervention subsidies to individual countries, as it could establish dangerous incentives. Countries would have an incentive to engage in populist fiscal policy, with low taxes and large budget deficits, knowing the ECB would come to their rescue. With all countries subject to the political pull of such behavior, that would generate monetary instability. The trouble is that this prohibition also leaves euro countries financially exposed.

A New European Public Finance Architecture

The problem with the euro's architecture is that there is no institution to defend national bond markets. That restricts governments' ability to make optimal use of deficit financing, and it also exposes national bond markets to bond market vigilante discipline. This flaw can be remedied by creating a new public finance architecture that includes a European Public Finance Authority (EPFA), which would issue European bonds jointly and severally backed by all member countries. The critical feature of this proposal is that the ECB would have the right to buy and sell EPFA bonds.

The proposed public finance architecture consists of three pillars and is illustrated in Figure 3. First, countries would retain the right to issue their own sovereign bonds that they alone would back. These national bonds would be analogous to U.S. state and munici-

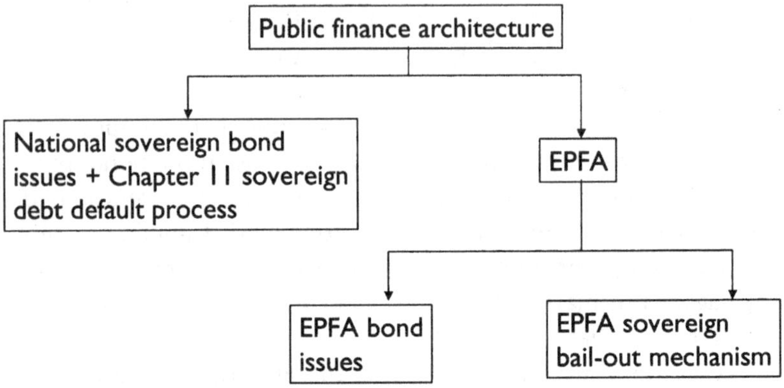

Figure 3. The Proposed New Eurozone Public Finance Architecture

pal bonds. They would be also subject to some form of sovereign debt default process that could be invoked in situations of extreme national financial distress, but EPFA bonds would be excluded. A sovereign default mechanism of this sort has been proposed by Gianviti et al. (2010). This default process would be similar to the chapter 9 provision in U.S. bankruptcy law governing default by states and municipalities. With markets aware *ex ante* of this possibility, standard bond market discipline would apply to this portion of the public finance architecture.

Second, eurozone member countries would create an EPFA that would issue jointly and severally backed bonds and operate as follows: (1) The authority would be able to sell new bonds of all maturities at its discretion. (2) Bond sale proceeds would be paid over to national governments. (3) The ECB would have the right to buy and sell already issued EPFA bonds. (4) The EPFA would be governed by finance ministers of eurozone member countries, representing their national governments. (5) Voting rights within the EPFA would be allocated across countries on a per-capita basis. (6) Distribution of bond sale proceeds would also be on a per-capita basis, as would countries' obligation to pay debt interest on EPFA bonds. In effect EPFA would serve as a trust entity with regard to EPFA bond issues, receiving interest service from countries and distributing those payments to bond holders.

The third pillar of the public finance architecture would have EPFA oversee a European sovereign bailout fund that could make emergency loans to member countries. This fund would be financed by sale of EPFA bonds. The important feature is that access to the fund would be subject to economic policy conditionality imposed by EPFA. In effect, the fund would be a form of European International Monetary Fund (IMF) (Gros and Mayer 2010; Palley 2010). In the current crisis Greece has turned to the IMF for emergency financing. That has been a mistake. At the political level it diminishes the global standing of the euro. At the economic level, it is unnecessary. The IMF cannot produce euros, which are produced only by the eurozone monetary system. Consequently, Europe can organize its own bailouts without recourse to the IMF. Indeed, interest payments on IMF loans are a form of tax leakage out of the European economy and are therefore bad at a time of demand shortage.

There are several important features of the proposed EPFA. First, and, most important, it creates a European bond without any trace of national identity. That bond can therefore be legitimately traded by the ECB without violating the "no bailout of countries" clause, which in turn creates space for open market operations. Consequently, the ECB can take on the role of government banker for Europe, a feature that is missing in the current institutional design.

Second, the EPFA would be able to help finance annual budget deficits for countries via annual bond issues that could vary with the state of the overall eurozone economy. All member countries would receive payments on a per capita basis. Countries that received payments in excess of their own needs could retire their own sovereign debt or build up a sovereign wealth fund by acquiring the national debt of other countries.

Third, there would be a small element of fiscal transfer via population growth because of the per capita formulation. Slow-growing-population countries would tend to see their debt obligation fall over time, while fast-growing-population countries would see their debt obligation rise. Germany is a slow-growing-population country and would therefore benefit from this. However, it would effectively be lending its creditworthiness to others to bring down their cost of credit so that these countries would still be individual beneficiaries. Moreover, the overall eurozone economy would also benefit by the strengthening of public finances.

Fourth, the EPFA would advance the political project of a democratic federal Europe, which is also widely viewed as being part of the core justification for the euro. It would be democratic because people of all countries would be treated equally via the EPFA voting structure, and it would be federal because of its unified frame that applies to all. As noted by Nutti (2011), a full system of fiscal federalism, with fiscal transfers between countries, might evolve later. However, that is a separate decision that would rest on the evolution of political sentiments within eurozone countries.

Policy Conduct in an ECB–EPFA System

An ECB–EPFA system would create a eurozone policy architecture similar to that enjoyed by the United States and the UK. The ECB, like the Federal Reserve and the Bank of England, would be responsible for monetary matters, including interest-rate policy. It would also retain responsibility for exchange rates. The EPFA would have responsibility for issuing eurozone bonds. Since all proceeds from bond sales would be paid to national governments, spending decisions would remain entirely in the hands of government.

The critical innovation is that the ECB would be allowed to buy and resell EPFA bonds at its discretion as part of its normal management of monetary conditions. It would therefore be able to conduct open market operations, something it rightly cannot do with individual country bonds. Moreover, it would be able to conduct open market operations across the entire EPFA maturity spectrum, thereby affecting the term structure of interest rates.

Figure 4 shows the major monetary responsibilities envisioned for the ECB under the new architecture. The first responsibility would be exchange-rate policy regarding the euro. The second responsibility would be eurozone interest-rate policy. In addition to being able to

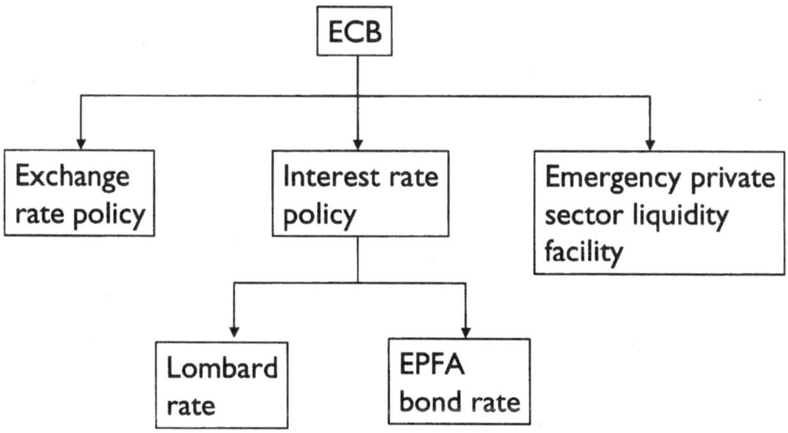

Figure 4. Monetary Policy Responsibilities of the ECB

set the ultrashort overnight interest rate via its Lombard lending facility, the ECB would be able to conduct interventions along the entire term structure of EPFA bonds. In emergency situations it could also undertake quantitative easing actions. EPFA bonds would essentially determine the risk-free interest rate for the eurozone, and all other bonds, including eurozone country sovereign bonds, would base their price on them. This is exactly how the U.S. monetary system operates. The third responsibility would be a facility providing emergency liquidity to the private financial sector. This would be analogous to the type of lending facilities the Federal Reserve established in the heat of the financial crisis of 2008–9.

A comparison of Figures 3 and 4 shows symmetry between the proposed EPFA and the ECB. The EPFA would essentially manage public finances, issuing European bonds and providing a sovereign emergency financing facility. The ECB would manage interest rates, and as part of that responsibility it would play the role of Europe's government banker. It would also provide an emergency financing facility for the private financial sector.

As part of this system, it would be desirable for policy coordination between the ECB and EPFA, as public finance policy and monetary policy should work together. Thus, EPFA willingness to help finance country budget deficits should be contingent on the ECB's assessment of monetary policy needs, and vice versa.

A major strength of the proposed architecture is that it has no arbitrary contraints such as the Maastricht treaty's 3 percent budget-deficit limit. Those restraints have been extremely unpopular politically, as they are seen as undermining sovereignty and the democratic process. Moreover, they have proved impossible to enforce, as countries have ignored them in times of economic stress. Consequently, they have yielded no benefits and only costs.

However, some form of constraint is needed, or else individual countries will be tempted to ignore the debt sustainability implications of their budget policies. The proposed architecture imposes restraints at three different levels. First, EPFA bond financing would be available only if agreed to by majority voting of finance ministers whose countries contain a majority of the eurozone population. Consequently, such a process enhances democracy rather than impeding it. Moreover, countries that did not support EPFA bond issues could use their proceeds to pay down their own sovereign debt. As that debt will carry a higher risk rating than EPFA bonds, they would gain by lowering their overall debt service.

A second level of restraint would operate via the sovereign bailout fund. That is because countries needing to use the fund would be subject to EPFA-imposed policy conditionality. That conditionality would again be democratically imposed, as it would be determined by majority opinion of finance ministers governing EPFA. The third level of restraint would be via market discipline operating in the market for individual country sovereign bonds.

These restraints mean that budget discipline would be maintained but without the public finance disadvantages of the current system. That system completely separates public finances from central banking by constitutionally barring the ECB from buying government debt. Consequently, it reduces national government to having the same bond market standing as provinces and corporations, and that is proving disastrous.

After it is fully in place, the EPFA would assist countries with normal budget-deficit financing. However, there would be an initial transition period in which countries would be able to swap national debt for EPFA debt. This transition process would work as follows. EPFA would sell bonds and use the proceeds to buy country bonds on a per capita basis. Those country bonds would then be canceled, and EPFA member countries would be responsible for their per capita share of EPFA debt service. Through the transition process countries like Luxembourg, which has little national debt to be canceled, would be credited with EPFA bonds that would offset their excess EPFA debt obligations.

Comparison to the "Blue" Bond Proposal

Almost twenty years ago, Stuart Holland (1993), an economic adviser to Jacques Delors, who served as president of the European Commission, proposed the idea of "Union" bonds issued by a European Investment Fund as a means of transferring member states' national debt to the European Union. That idea was not adopted, but it has recently resurfaced in connection with the eurozone's public debt crisis.[1] De Grauwe and Moesen (2009) propose a common eurobond. Building on that proposal, Delpla and von Weizsacker (2010) have recently proposed the idea of "blue" bonds that individual eurozone countries could issue and which would be jointly and severally guaranteed by other eurozone countries. The idea is to enable highly indebted member countries to access the better credit rating of financially stronger countries, thereby lowering their interest burden and improving their fiscal position.

Though having some similarities of appearance with the blue bond proposal, the current EPFA proposal is in fact fundamentally different. The most fundamental difference is that the ECB would able to buy and sell EPFA bonds and therefore manage the eurozone term structure of interest rates. Why is it able to do so under the EPFA proposal and not under the blue bond proposal? The answer is because EPFA bonds have no taint of national identification, owing to the bond issuance process that ensures all countries will receive equal per-capita funding. That means ECB purchases of EPFA bonds would benefit all countries similarly and would not violate the ECB's no-bailout clause. This contrasts with the blue bond proposal, in which individual countries would decide how many blue bonds to issue, and blue bonds would retain a national identification tag. Consequently, ECB blue bond purchases would benefit the country whose bonds were purchased. The blue bond proposal therefore remains stuck in the current system of national bonds, the only change being that part of those bonds would have a European guarantee.

The second advantage is that the EPFA would continuously issue bonds as part of assisting eurozone countries with normal budget-deficit financing. The goal is to make this a normal element of public finance. That contrasts with the blue bond proposal, which is inspired by the crisis and conceptualized as a crisis measure. For it, the goal is to help crisis countries swap existing high-yield debt for lower-yield debt by giving them partial access to Germany's credit rating.

The third advantage of the EPFA proposal is that it does away entirely with Maastricht-styled restrictions like the 3 percent deficit rule. Within the EPFA proposal, all budget disciplines operate via the EPFA democratic decision-making process or via market discipline. Contrastingly, the blue bond proposal would continue Maastricht deficit limits and would impose a ceiling (the suggested number is 60 percent of GDP) on a country's ability to issue blue bonds.

In sum, the EPFA proposal goes beyond the blue bond proposal because it aims to reshape the euro's financial architecture by restoring the role of government banker to the central bank. In effect, it fundamentally changes the euro's architecture by discarding its neoliberal design that separates the ECB from public finances. Like the blue bond proposal, the proposed EPFA provides debt interest relief to crisis countries by giving them access to lower-interest European bond credit. However, it also gets rid of undemocratic sovereignty violating Maastricht-style restrictions and enables the ECB to act as government banker and to conduct open market operations in EPFA bonds.

Conclusion

This article concerns both theory and policy. With regard to theory, it is about the stability of monetary unions and the need for a government banker that manages the bond market. With regard to policy, it offers a specific proposal for stabilizing the euro by creating a eurozone government banker.

There seems to be accumulating evidence that the current architecture of the euro is unstable, and it will likely fall apart unless changes are made. The source of that instability is high interest rates on highly indebted countries, which creates unsustainable debt burdens. Remedying that problem requires a central bank that acts as government banker and pushes down interest rates to sustainable levels. This can be accomplished by the EPFA.

Analytically, the article offers a third path for the euro. The current path, which includes modifications like the blue bond proposal, aims to continue with the Maastricht architecture, which imposes numerical caps on budget deficits and debts and separates the ECB from public finances. A second path is for a fiscal transfer union. A third path, proposed here, is for a full monetary and public finance union that abandons Maastricht-style quantitative restrictions but does not include fiscal transfers.

The debate over the euro's financial architecture is not limited to economics. It also has significant political implications. That is because the current neoliberal-inspired euro architecture, which imposes a complete separation between the central bank and public finances, puts governments under continuous additional financial pressures. Over time, that pressure is likely to make it difficult to maintain the European social democratic welfare state. This presents a political reason for reforming the euro and creating an EPFA that supplements the economic case for reform.

Note

1. Thanks are due to Mario Nutti (2011) for making me aware of the connection between Holland's (1993) proposal and current proposals.

For Further Reading

De Grauwe, P. 1994. *The Economics of Monetary Integration.* Oxford: Oxford University Press.

De Grauwe, P., and W. Moesen. 2009. "Gains for All: A Proposal for a Common Eurobond." *Intereconomics* (May/June): 132–35.

Delpla, J., and J. von Weizsacker. 2010. "The Blue Bond Proposal." Bruegel Policy Brief 2010/3, Bruegel Institute, Brussels, May.

Gianviti, F., A.O. Krueger, J. Pisani-Ferry, A. Sapir, and J. von Hagen. 2010. "A European Mechanism for Sovereign Debt Crisis Resolution: A Proposal." Bruegel Institute, Brussels, November 9.

Gros, D., and T. Mayer. 2010. "Disciplinary Measures." *Economist,* February 18, www.economist.com/node/15544302?story_id=15544302/.

Holland, S. 1993. *The European Imperative: Economic and Social Cohesion in the 1990s.* Foreword by Jacques Delors. Nottingham, UK: Spokesman Press.

Kenen, P. 1969. "The Theory of Optimum Currency Areas: An Eclectic View." In *Monetary Problems of the International Economy,* ed. R. Mundell and A. Swobodaa, 41–60. Chicago: University of Chicago Press.

Menger, K. 1892. "On the Origin of Money." *Economic Journal* 2: 239–55.

Nutti, D.M. 2011. "Euro Sovereign Debt: Would a Single European Bond Work?" Available at http://dmarionuti.blogspot.com/2011/02/single-european-sovereign-bond-pie-in.html.

Palley, T.I. 2010. "Euroland Is Being Crucified Upon Its Own Cross of Gold." *FT Economists' Forum,* February 10, http://blogs.ft.com/economistsforum/2010/02/euroland-is-being-crucified-upon-its-cross-of-gold/.

Technical Appendix

The problem of bond market speculation can be captured by the following simple model. Government bond investors in euro countries aim to earn a risk-adjusted expected return equal to that which they could earn on safe bonds, implying the following condition:

$$1 + i^* + z = E(R) \tag{A.1}$$

where i^* = safe bond interest rate, z = risk premium required for investing in a country's bonds, and $E(R)$ = expected return to investing in a country's bonds. The expected return to individual euro country bonds is given by

$$E(R) = p(Y(d(i,..),i,..),iD/Y(d(i),i,...), Z)X + [1 - p(Y(d(i), i,..), iD/Y(d(i),i,...),Z)][1 + i] \tag{A.2}$$

where $p(.)$ = probability of default, i = country interest rate, d = budget surplus/deficit, D = debt-to-GDP ratio, Z = confidence variable, and X = payment in default state. The probability of default is such that $0 < p < 1$, and the default payment is such that $0 < X < 1$.

Signs above functional arguments represent assumed signs of partial derivatives. An increase in the country interest rate directly increases the probability of default by increasing the government's debt service burden (iD). However, there are conflicting effects on Y. On the one hand, a higher interest rate directly lowers private-sector demand. On the other hand, balanced against this is a positive demand effect from higher interest payments that works via the budget deficit since interest payments are transfer payments.

The model is closed by adding a dynamic interest-rate-adjustment mechanism given by

$$di/dt = f(1 + i^* + z - E(R))\ f(0) = 0,\ f' > 0,\ f'' > 0 \qquad \text{(A.3)}$$

If the return on safe bonds exceeds the risk-adjusted expected return on a country's bonds, the country bond interest rate rises as agents sell the country's bonds to buy safe bonds.

Figure 2 in the main text provides a graphical analogue of the model. Equation (A.2), describing the expected return function, is the critical equation. This expected-return function can be volatile due to shifts of confidence (Z) and also nonlinear with respect to the country bond interest rate. The economic logic of nonlinearity is because of competing effects. On the one hand, a higher domestic interest rate raises the expected return on a country's bonds. On the other hand, higher interest rates can also reduce the expected return due to increased default risk from higher debt-service burdens and adverse impacts on income. Consequently, depending on the sensitivity of the p function and the sensitivity of Y to increases in i, the slope of the ER function can change signs.

real-world ***economics review***, issue no. 81

Fixing the euro's original sins: the monetary – fiscal architecture and monetary policy conduct[1]

Thomas Palley [Washington, DC]

You may post comments on this paper at
https://rwer.wordpress.com/comments-on-rwer-issue-no-81/

Abstract

The euro zone (EZ) was created in January 1999. Its weak economic performance is significantly due to the euro's neoliberal monetary architecture and the design of monetary policy. Those features undermine national political sovereignty and consign the EZ to severe economic under-performance, which in turn fosters political demands for exit from the euro. Escaping this dynamic requires restoring fiscal space to EZ countries, and also changing the design of EZ monetary policy. The paper shows how this can be done. It decomposes the challenge of reform into generic problems related to the neoliberal construction of monetary policy, and specific problems concerning the euro as a currency union. The currency union problems are further decomposed into "money – fiscal policy" architecture problems and specific monetary policy conduct problems.

1. The euro's twin original sins

The euro is afflicted by twin original sins: rupture of the money – fiscal policy link and adoption of neoliberally designed monetary policies. Those twin sins have contributed to generating dismal economic outcomes, which have fostered ugly political conditions that echo the 1930s and risk causing the euro to disintegrate.

This paper shows the euro's twin original sins can be fixed in a politically viable manner. As regards economics, the euro is a monetary phenomenon, which means that getting the monetary architecture right is the *sine qua non* for success. Other economic policy adjustments can then further strengthen the euro zone's (EZ's) economic performance, but without the right monetary architecture economic success will inevitably prove elusive.

As regards politics, the fundamental problem is the EZ consists of national political sovereigns that have been required to surrender monetary sovereignty. However, those national political sovereigns need a degree of monetary sovereignty in order to defend their public finances and pursue expansionary fiscal policy in times of economic distress. The EZ's architecture makes little provision for this, because of a combination of fears of moral hazard from country bail-outs and intellectual blindness. Fixing the EZ's monetary architecture and restoring a degree of monetary sovereignty is essential for creating the policy space needed by national governments to make the euro politically viable.

2. Diagnosing the EZ's problems

The euro was introduced in January 1999. As shown in Table 1, its macroeconomic performance was barely satisfactory prior to the financial crisis of 2008, but it has been dismal since. Since peaking in the 1960s, EZ average GDP growth each decade fell steadily through

[1] An earlier version of this paper was published in H. Herr, J. Priewe, and A. Watt (eds.), *Saving the Euro: Redesigning Euro Area Economic Governance*, Social Europe Publishing, 2017.

the 1990s. The introduction of the euro saw a brief uptick, but growth has collapsed since the 2008 financial crisis. That story is mirrored in the unemployment rate which steadily increased through to the 1990s, then fell slightly with the euro's advent, but surged to sustained record highs after the financial crisis.

Table 1 EZ output growth and unemployment rate

	Region	1961-70	1971-80	1981-90	1991-98	1999-2008	2009-2015
Average GDP growth rate at 2010 market prices (%)	EZ-12	5.3	3.4	2.4	1.9	2.1	0.1
	EZ-19					2.1	0.1
Average unemployment rate (%)	EZ-12	2.3	4.0	8.5	10.0	8.5	10.8
	EZ-19					8.7	10.8

Source: Statistical Annex of the European Economy, Spring 2016 (Tables 3 and 10) plus author's calculations

Behind this data is a dismal economic policy history. That history begins with the adoption of tough anti-inflation policy in the late 1970s, which turned into neoliberalism in the early 1980s. Consequently, Europe never fully recovered from the dislocations of the 1970s. The neoliberal turn was further locked in place in the 1990s with the first steps to monetary union via the Maastricht Treaty and its imposition of strict euro zone economic convergence criteria, requiring a deflationary policy posture to meet them. Come the euro, there was a brief boom in the 2000s fueled by the intersection of low interest rates and speculation. However, when the bust arrived with the 2008 crisis, the design flaws in the euro's monetary architecture and policy conduct surfaced with a vengeance. Those flaws are systemic and remain largely unresolved. Consequently, they now pose an existential threat to the euro.

The weakness of the EZ's economic performance is significantly rooted in its monetary architecture and monetary policy conduct. As regards architecture, the design of the euro's monetary policy institutions has massively shrunk the space for national fiscal policy and also exposed government finances to market instability. Under the old system of national currencies, each country government had a central bank that acted as the "government banker". Thus, national central banks helped governments finance their budget deficit, and also defended government bonds against speculative attack. This government banker function was completely and mistakenly ignored by the euro's creators, thereby weakening governments' ability to finance fiscal policy and giving financial markets massive power over them (Palley, 2011a, 2011b).

Simultaneously, EZ monetary policy conduct has been sub optimal. It was blind to asset price bubbles before the crisis; was slow to respond in the crisis; and the two percent inflation target risks being an unnecessary brake on performance if the EZ escapes the current stagnation.

Figure 1 outlines the nature of the problem. It decomposes the challenge of EZ monetary reform into generic problems related to the neoliberal construction of monetary policy, and specific problems concerning the euro as a currency union. The currency union problems are then further decomposed into architecture problems and conduct of policy problems.

Figure 1 A diagnosis of the failings afflicting the EZ's monetary architecture and policy

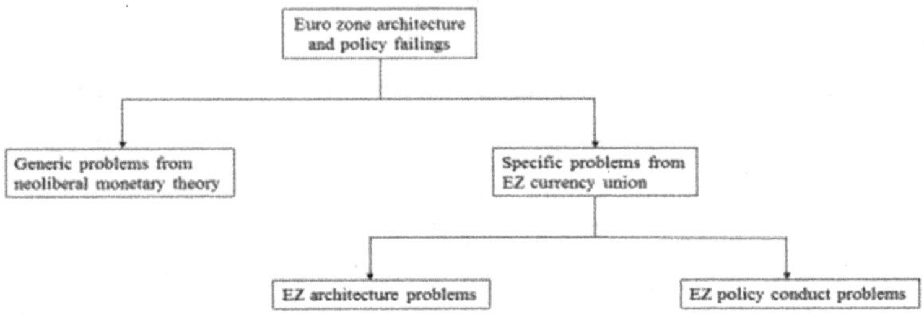

3. New Classical economics and the origins of the euro zone's monetary architecture and policy failings.

To understand the EZ's failings and the case for reform, it is necessary to begin with new classical economics which inspired and underlies the EZ's architecture and policy conduct. New classical macroeconomics (i.e. Chicago School macroeconomics) has under-pinned neoliberal economic policy, and it asserts:[2]

A) Money and inflation are neutral and have no effect on the real economy;

B) Inflation is caused exclusively by money supply growth;

C) The real economy automatically and quickly returns to full employment in response to negative shocks via price and nominal wage adjustment;

D) Financial markets are efficient and stable and determine a natural interest rate that delivers full employment;

E) Fiscal policy is ineffective.

Given the above theoretical framework, optimal policy involves having an independent central bank implement a credible transparent interest rate rule aimed at targeting stable low inflation. According to the policy rule, the equilibrium short-term interest rate should equal the inflation target plus the estimated natural real rate of interest. Furthermore, inflation targeting, implemented via the interest rate rule, is all that is needed to secure full employment because the economy goes there automatically and quickly.

This view of economic theory and optimal policy was hegemonic in the 1990s when the euro was designed and implemented, and it remains hegemonic today – albeit with less self-confidence. Its hegemonic standing meant that Social Democrats (like Jacques Delors and Wim Duisenberg) also accepted it. Consequently, it provided the theoretical template for designing the euro zone's architecture and policy conduct.

[2] Though somewhat more caveated today, new classical macroeconomics remains mainstream economists' dominant theoretical frame, which explains their incapacity to understand the problems of the EZ and resistance to reform. New classical macroeconomics' standing in relation to mainstream macroeconomics parallels the standing of neoclassical competitive general equilibrium theory to mainstream microeconomics.

real-world **economics review**, issue no. 81

3.a) Generic problems of new classical monetary policy

The new classical construction of monetary policy and central banking produces three grave generic problems that have afflicted monetary policy in both Europe and elsewhere. The first problem concerns mistakenly low inflation targeting. The problem stems from Milton Friedman's (1968) natural rate of unemployment hypothesis which claims money and inflation have no permanent real effects. Consequently, there is no trade-off between inflation and unemployment so that the long-run Phillips curve is vertical. This contrasts with the Keynesian view that a trade-off exists and the Phillips curve is negatively sloped because modest inflation helps grease the wheels of labor market adjustment (Tobin, 1972; Palley, 1994, 2012).

Figure 2 shows the new classical and Keynesian Phillips curves. Neoliberal macroeconomics recommends an ultra-low inflation target (π^*). The argument is that inflation is undesirable and confers no unemployment gain because the economy always gravitates to the natural rate of unemployment (u^*). From a Keynesian perspective, that will cause significant unnecessary unemployment as inflation of π^* implies a higher unemployment rate ($u^1 > u^*$) according to the Keynesian Phillips curve.

Figure 2 New classical (neoliberal) vs. Keynesian Phillips curves

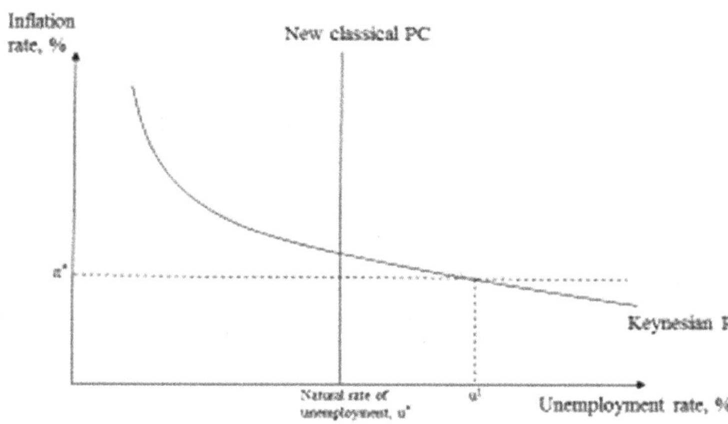

A second generic problem concerns central bank support for the so-called "labor market flexibility agenda" which aims to diminish workers' rights, protections and bargaining power. Natural rate theory argues the natural rate of unemployment is determined by frictions and rigidities within the labor market. Those frictions and rigidities are argued to include trade unions, minimum wages, unemployment insurance, and worker rights and protections. Since central banks believe in natural rate theory, that explains why they have persistently and vigorously lined up in support of the "labor market flexibility agenda" which has contributed to wage stagnation and increased income inequality.

The third generic problem of neoliberal economics is its belief that "flexible" labor markets and interest rate policy, targeted on low stable inflation, are all that is needed to ensure full employment. This belief stems from the assumptions of new classical economics about the economy's adjustment capacities and the character of financial markets. The important implication is it predisposes central banks against the need for financial market regulation or the need to intervene in asset markets to address asset price bubbles (Palley, 2003, 2006a). It also explains the retreat from and resistance to quantitative monetary policy (e.g. regulation of the asset side of banks' balance sheets), which was an important component of policy in the "golden age" three decades after World War II.

3.b) EZ monetary architecture problems: the rupture of the money – fiscal policy link

The major monetary architectural problem of the EZ concerns its divorce of the monetary authority from national fiscal authorities (Goodhart, 1998). From a new classical perspective, this divorce is inconsequential because fiscal policy is ineffective and increases in the money supply only cause inflation. Consequently, there is no need for money-financed fiscal policy and a hard divorce of the monetary and fiscal authorities is desirable.

According to new classical economics, if governments want to run budget deficits they should compete for finance with the private sector in financial markets. That is the efficient way to allocate capital. Additionally, in the context of a currency union, divorce of the monetary and fiscal authority is needed to prevent fiscal moral hazard. If member countries know the central bank will step in and finance their deficits, that would provide an incentive for countries to run larger and larger deficits.

The divorce of the monetary authority (i.e. the central bank) from the fiscal authority (i.e. the national state) is predicated on the assumptions that fiscal policy is ineffective, money financed deficits only cause inflation, and financial markets are stable and efficient. Once those assumptions are rejected, the new classical monetary architecture becomes dangerously dysfunctional.

The loss of national central banks and the divorce between monetary policy and fiscal policy leave national governments dependent on financial markets for their budget deficit financing needs. Consequently, governments may be unable to finance needed expansionary fiscal policy (Goodhart, 1998). Additionally, financial markets will have the power to veto fiscal policy via bond market sell-offs, and governments will also lack the means (i.e. a central bank under their control) to intervene and stabilize national financial markets in the event of financial panic (Palley, 1997). That is exactly what has happened in the EZ after the financial crisis of 2008.

3.c) EZ monetary policy conduct problems: too low an inflation target

As regards the conduct of EZ monetary policy, the generic policy problem of excessively low inflation targeting is amplified in a currency union (Palley, 1997, 2006b). This is illustrated in Figure 3. For new classical economists, a non-optimal currency union may increase the natural rate of unemployment for the currency union as a whole ($u^*_{PRE} < u^*_{POST}$). However, from their perspective, there is no cost in sticking with the pre-existing inflation target since monetary policy cannot affect the new natural rate of unemployment. In sharp contrast, a Keynesian perspective counsels differently. The Phillips curve shifts right from KPC_{PRE} to KPC_{POST}, so that preventing further increased unemployment requires the currency union to adopt a higher inflation target. If the target is unchanged and held at π^* after monetary union, the unemployment rate will rise to $u^2 > u^1$.

Figure 3 The effect of currency union on the Phillips curve

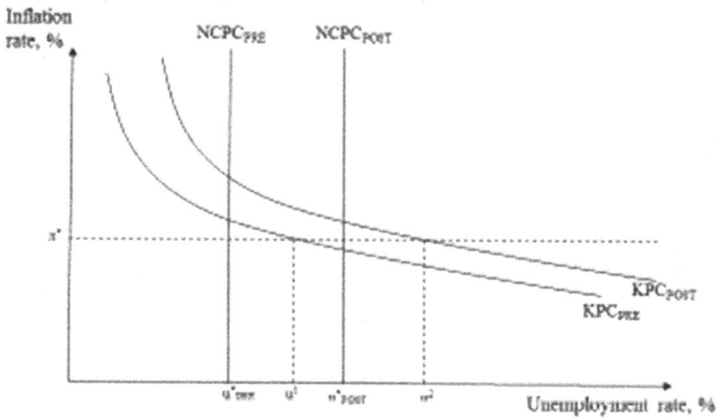

Additionally, the higher unemployment caused by the EZ's low inflation targeting problem has been further compounded by the fact that Germany's Bundesbank monetary policy was adopted as the template for the euro. The Bundesbank has long been dominated by monetarist thinking that is staunchly opposed to inflation. Its monetarist approach was imported into the ECB in the form of an inflation target mandating less than 2 percent inflation. In effect, the creation of the euro was used to lower the EZ's overall inflation target ($\pi_{POST} < \pi_{PRE}$) as shown in Figure 4. That caused an even larger increase in EZ unemployment to $u^3 > u^2$.

Figure 4 The effect of adopting the Bundesbank's ultra-low inflation target

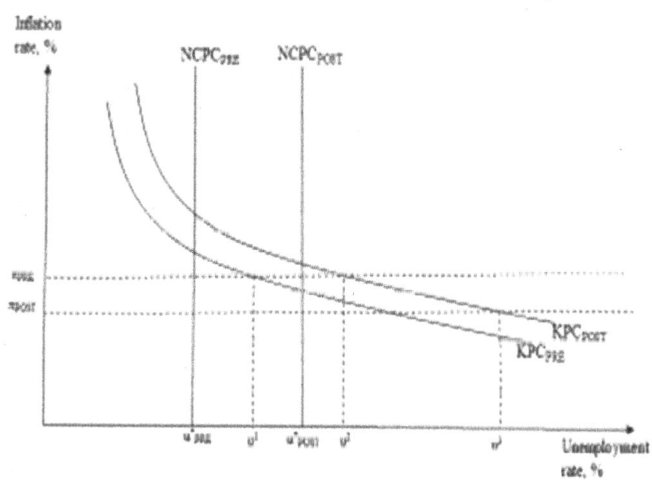

In sum, from a Keynesian perspective, not only did monetary policy fail to raise the inflation target to combat higher unemployment caused by monetary union creating a more diverse economy with more dispersed economic outcomes, it lowered the inflation target for many member countries which had higher targets prior to the euro. That made for a double failure in the conduct of monetary policy.

4. The crisis and the failure of neoliberal economics

The financial crisis of 2008, the Great Recession, and the ensuing stagnation should have entirely discredited neoliberal economics. These events have shown financial markets can be unstable and can greatly misprice assets; economies do not automatically and quickly rebound to full employment; fiscal policy can be highly effective; and inflation is not exclusively and automatically generated by money supply growth. That speaks to remaking the EZ's monetary architecture and redesigning the conduct of monetary policy as events have shown the current architecture and policy design are founded on flawed theory.

5. Remedying the EZ's monetary architecture and monetary policy

5.a) Repairing the money – fiscal policy link via a financing union

The euro's divorce of the monetary and fiscal authorities has created grave problems for governments' ability to finance fiscal policy and defend against financial market speculators. The conventional wisdom is the EZ needs "fiscal union" to overcome these architectural failings, but EZ countries do not politically want that. Instead, I (Palley, 2011a; 2011b; 2016) have argued for a "financing union" that involves collective issuance of debt, the proceeds of which are distributed among members on a per capita basis.

A financing union would require establishment of a European Finance Authority (EFA) governed by the finance ministers of euro zone countries. The Finance Authority would issue bonds jointly and severally backed by all member countries, which the ECB could buy.

The Authority would engage in no spending, and would simply pay issue proceeds to member countries on a per capita basis, with countries liable for debt service on the same per capita basis. Each year the EFA would determine the appropriate budget deficit for the euro zone, issue bonds, and distribute the proceeds to member countries to use as they deemed fit.

Those countries wanting fiscal stimulus could spend the proceeds: others could use them to buy EFA bonds, thereby covering their obligation and leaving their net debt position unchanged.

Countries could also issue their own national bonds to finance additional stimulus over and above that financed by EFA, and these national bonds would constitute a form of junior national debt.

Lastly, an accompanying bankruptcy mechanism would be established. Country national debt would be subject to a junior bankruptcy mechanism similar to the Chapter 9 provision in US law for states and municipalities. EFA debt would be subject to a senior sovereign bail-out mechanism that could permit conditionality arrangements.

The financing union proposal has many significant advantages, but three stand out. First, it permanently remedies the euro's original sin, creating both a permanent policy mechanism for deficit financing and a bond that can be bought without qualification by the ECB. Second, it avoids the great political pitfall of fiscal unions regarding usurping control of the purse from the state or imposing transfers between countries. Countries choose how they spend EFA proceeds. Third, it reconnects money and the state without creating fiscal moral hazard as countries are not bailed out by the EFA or ECB.

5.b) Conduct of monetary policy: a higher inflation target

With regard to conduct of monetary policy, the first change should be a higher inflation target in the region of 3 – 5 percent. Some mainstream economists (Blanchard et al., 2010) are also moving in this direction. Their argument is that a higher equilibrium inflation rate is needed to raise nominal interest rates, thereby providing space for the central bank to lower interest rates if the economy gets in trouble.

Such support is welcome, even if the reasoning is stuck in failed monetary theory. However, it would be far better if the Keynesian Phillips curve rationale were adopted as that would also bury the natural rate of unemployment hypothesis. As long as central banks hold to that hypothesis, there will be a perennial risk that central banks are drawn back into actively supporting the mistaken and damaging labor market "flexibility" agenda.

5.c) Conduct of monetary policy: target the bond rate on newly issued EFM bonds.

A financing union would create a steady growing supply of EFA bonds, and the ECB could then target the long bond rate as well as set the short-term interest rate. Neoliberal monetary theory recommends targeting just the short-term interest rate. The assumption is the combination of efficient financial markets plus a credible transparent interest rate rule ensures long term interest rates reflect expectations of future short-term interest rates markets. Consequently, there is no need to target the long rate.

Such indirect management is unreliable and imprecise as it rests on markets having correct expectations and understandings of future policy. The behavior of financial markets should have punctured that belief long ago. In future, rather than relying on market expectations to determine long rates, the ECB should directly target long rates using EFA bonds as the benchmark (Palley, 2013).

5.d) Asset based reserve requirements (ABRR)

Interest rate targeting should be supplemented by a system of ABRR which would extend margin requirements to a wide array of assets held by financial institutions (Palley, 2000; 2003; 2004; 2006b; 2010). ABRR require financial firms to hold reserves against different classes of assets, with the regulatory authority setting adjustable reserve requirements on the basis of its concerns with each asset class. One concern may be that an asset class is too risky; another may be that an asset class is expanding too fast and producing inflated asset prices.

A system of ABRR that covers all financial firms has multiple policy benefits. Most importantly, it enables central banks to target sector imbalances without recourse to the blunderbuss of interest rate increases. For example, if a monetary authority was concerned about a house price bubble generating excessive risk exposure, it could impose reserve requirements on new mortgages. This would force mortgage lenders to hold some cash to support their new loans, raising the cost of such loans and cooling the market.

For the EZ, ABRR are additionally attractive because they can help address the policy instrument gap at the national level created by the euro's introduction (Palley, 2006b). That can be done by implementing ABRR on a geographic basis. For instance, requirements on new mortgage loans can vary by country, or even by region within countries.

5.e) Banking union

Just as the design of the EZ neglected fiscal policy and the need for a government banker, so too it neglected the problem of cross-country bank runs (as has happened with money fleeing from the EZ periphery crisis countries to Germany).

The ECB's TARGET2 balance system has plugged the hole by making liquidity available to banks losing deposits. However, it is an inefficient system that recycles liquidity *ex-post* rather than preventing its flight *ex-ante*. It also creates banking regulatory moral hazard across countries, since countries know their banks have access to emergency liquidity from the ECB. That speaks to the need for full banking union with deposit insurance and common regulatory standards and capital requirements for bank asset and liability structures.

6. Radical reform of central bank thinking: bring back pluralism and Keynesianism.

Lastly, there is need for profound radical reform of ECB thinking and practice. Over the last three decades, central banks have been arrogant and closed minded, ignoring all economists outside central banks' narrow sociological circle, and dismissing all who disagreed with their belief that low inflation targeting was sufficient. Events have proved central bank economists wrong and shown the assumptions of neoliberal monetary theory to be disastrously flawed.

At the euro's outset, the focus of mainstream economics was the EZ's properties as an optimal currency area (OCA), and mainstream discussion was conducted exclusively through that lens. The principal concern was the euro was not an OCA (see for instance Bayoumi and Eichengreen, 1992; 1994) The fear was individual countries within the EZ would suffer macroeconomic losses from giving up their own currency and surrendering the exchange rate and interest rate as tools of country economic policy. Those losses from not having one's own currency would outweigh trade and capital flow gains. Feldstein (1997) argued those costs of not being an OCA would cause the euro to ultimately fail in a few decades, possibly even generating military conflict within the EZ.

These mainstream concerns were generic and not policy helpful. They contrast with the concerns of Keynesians (Godley, 1992; Palley, 1997; Goodhart, 1998) who, not only identified the OCA aspects, but also correctly identified and emphasized specific flaws in the euro's neoliberal monetary architecture and monetary policy design.

Godley (1992) argued the euro had a blind spot regarding need for a European federal institution to undertake counter-cyclical fiscal policy:

> "The incredible lacuna in the Maastricht programme is that, while it contains the blueprint for the establishment and modus operandi of an independent central bank, there is no blueprint whatever of the analogue, in community terms, of a central government" (Godley, 1992, p.3).

Goodhart (1998) emphasized the importance of the link between the fiscal authority (i.e. the state) and the monetary authority (i.e. the central bank), and identified the dangers for financing fiscal policy of divorcing the monetary and fiscal authorities:[3]

> "In particular, the participating nation states will continue to have the main fiscal responsibilities; but in the monetary field, their status will have changed to a *subsidiary* level, in the sense that they can no longer, at a pinch, call upon the monetary authority to create money to finance their domestic national debt. There is to be an unprecedented divorce between the main monetary and fiscal authorities" (Goodhart, 1998, p.410).

Palley (1997, 2006a) identified the importance of the central bank's policy preferences and the interaction of those preferences with economic understandings of the Phillips curve. Making the euro successful required a higher inflation target. It also required introduction of quantitative monetary policy and ABRR to supplement interest rate inflation targeting policy, thereby giving member countries additional policy instruments to replace those lost owing to currency union.

Additionally, Palley (1997) argued the divorce of the monetary and fiscal authorities would give bond markets the power to discipline governments who pursue economic policies that financial markets dislike. That is because governments would no longer have a central bank to buy their bonds and protect against capital flight:

> "Thus, if financial capital dislikes the stance of national fiscal policy, there could be a sell-off of government bonds and a shift into bonds of other countries. This would drive up the cost of government borrowing, putting a break on fiscal policy" (Palley, 1997, p.156).

This feature is cruelly ironic as part of the intention of the European monetary union was to protect against capital market flight, such as had undermined the policies of France's President Mitterrand in the early 1980s.

In sum, the record clearly shows Keynesians had a far superior understanding of the monetary macroeconomics of currency unions and anticipated many of the operational problems of the euro. That suggests it is time to heed the Keynesians by reforming the EZ along the lines they have advocated.

More broadly, the superior analytical insights of Keynesians regarding monetary union provides another case study of mainstream economics failure, and adds to the record of failure which has been accumulating for three decades. Given that record, it is also time to

[3] Goodhart is perhaps the only establishment economist to have anticipated specific structural problems of the euro, as against generic concerns regarding the euro being a non-optimal currency area. That said Goodhart is a distinguished "grey beard" who was admitted to the circle of central bankers before the ideological boom came down in the 1980s and put an end to pluralism in economic thought.

break the new classical monopoly on monetary theory and monetary policy, and to open central banking to a wider range of perspectives.

References

Bayoumi, T. and Eichengreen, B. (1992), "Shocking Aspects of Monetary Union," Working Paper 3949, NBER, Cambridge: MA, January.

Bayoumi, T. and Eichengreen, B. (1994) "One Money or Many? Analyzing the Prospects for Monetary Unification in Various Parts of the World," *Princeton Studies in International Finance*, no. 76, September.

Blanchard, O., Dell'Arica, G., and Mauro, P. (2010) Rethinking Macroeconomic Policy, in Research Department, IMF, Washington DC, February, available at http://www.imf.org/external/pubs/ft/spn/2010/spn1003.pdf.

Godley, W. (1992), "Maastricht and All That," *London Review of Books*, Vol. 14 No. 19, 8 October.

Goodhart, C.A.E. (1998) "The Two Concepts of Money: Implications for the Analysis of Optimal Currency Areas," *European Journal of Political Economy*, 14 (3), 407-432.

Feldstein, M. (1997) "EMU and International Conflict," *Foreign Affairs*, Vol. 76, no. 6, November / December .

Friedman, M. (1968) "The Role of Monetary Policy", *American Economic Review*, 58 (May), 1-17.

Palley, T. I. (1994) "Escalators and Elevators: A Phillips Curve for Keynesians", *Scandinavian Journal of Economics*, 96 (1), 117-123.

Palley, T. I. (1997) "European Monetary Union: An Old Keynesian Guide to the Issues", *Banco Nazionale del Lavoro Quarterly Review*, vol. L, no. 201 (June), 147 164.

Palley, T. I. (2000) "Stabilizing Finance: The Case for Asset Based Reserve Requirements", *Financial Markets and Society*, The Financial Markets Center, Philomont, VA, August. http://www.thomaspalley.com/docs/articles/macro_policy/stabilizing_finance.pdf

Palley, T. I. (2003) "Asset Price Bubbles and the Case for Asset Based Reserve Requirements," *Challenge*, 46 (May–June), 53-72.

Palley, T. I. (2004), "Asset Based Reserve Requirements: Reasserting Domestic Monetary Control in an Era of Financial Innovation and Instability," *Review of Political Economy*, 16 (January), 43-58.

Palley, T. I. (2006a) "Currency Unions, the Phillips Curve, and Stabilization Policy: Some Suggestions for Europe," *Intervention: European Journal of Economics and Economic Policies*, 3(2), 351-69.

Palley, T. I. (2006b) "Monetary Policy in an Endogenous Money Economy", in Arestis and Sawyer (eds.), *A Handbook of Alternative Monetary Economics*, Edward Elgar: Cheltenham, U.K., p.242-257.

Palley, T. I. (2010) "Asset Price Bubbles and Monetary Policy: Why Central Banks Have Been Wrong and What Should Be Done", *Intervention: European Journal of Economics and Economic Policies*, 7(1), 91-107.

Palley, T. I. (2011a) "Monetary Union Stability: The Need for a Government Banker and the Case for a European Public Finance Authority", in IMK Working Paper 2, Dusseldorf, Germany, and published as "The European Union Needs a Government Banker", *Challenge*, 54 (July-August 2011), 5-21.

Palley, T. I. (2011b) „Stabiltät in der Währungsunion: Plädoyer für eine Staatsbank und eine Europäische Finanzagentur", *WSI Mitteiliungen*, 6 (June).

Palley, T. I. (2012) "The Economics of the Phillips Curve: Formation of Inflation Expectations versus Incorporation of Inflation Expectations", *Structural Change and Economic Dynamics*, 23(3) (September), 221-230.

Palley, T. I. (2013) "Monetary Policy and Central Banking after the Crisis: The Implications of Rethinking Macroeconomic Theory", in *The Handbook on Political Economy of Financial Crises*, Editors: Gerald Epstein and Martin Wolfson, Oxford: Oxford University Press, Chapter 31, p.624-643.

Palley, T. I. (2016) "Financing Unions vs. Spending Unions: How to Remedy the Euro Zone's Original Sin", *Social Europe*, 14 July, https://www.socialeurope.eu/2016/07/financing-vs-spending-unions-remedy-euro-zones-original-sin/

Tobin, J. (1972) "Inflation and Unemployment", *American Economic Review*, 62 (1972), 1-26, reprinted in *Essays in Economics: Volume 2*, New York: North-Holland, 1975, p. 33-60.

Author contact: mail@thomaspalley.com

SUGGESTED CITATION:
Thomas Palley, "Fixing the euro's original sins: the monetary – fiscal architecture and monetary policy conduct", *real-world economics review*, issue no. 81, xx September 2017, pp. xx-xx,
http://www.paecon.net/PAEReview/issue81/Palley81.pdf

PART III

THE GLOBAL ECONOMY

THOMAS I. PALLEY

Capital Mobility and the Threat to American Prosperity

If we continue with the economics of orthodoxy, we will further entrench deep, dangerous structural changes in our economy that will be difficult, and perhaps impossible, to reverse.

The nations of Western Europe and North America are beset today by persistent economic malaise. This debility has manifested itself in the form of stagnant wages and higher average rates of unemployment. Conventional economists attribute the malaise to massive technological change that has caused job losses and induced the obsolescence of skills. They claim that everything will ultimately work out for the best. Given time, they pronounce, society will once again enjoy full employment with even greater prosperity supported by improved technology.

There is a challenge to this view—namely, that the malaise is not self-correcting. Instead, it is the result of adverse structural changes in the relative bargaining strength of capital and labor. These changes are the result of increased "mobility" of both financial and physical capital which has caused a deterioration in the distribution of income in favor of profits and executive pay, and has reduced the share of wages. This, in turn, has diminished mass purchasing power, and has contributed to the emergence of global excess capacities and unemployment. Moreover, this shift in the balance of economic power has not only been felt by workers, but by national governments as well. Their sovereignty has been increasingly eroded by the power of capital.

Implementing new policies to confront and reverse these trends requires that we recognize the causes of the crisis. In the absence of this awareness, policy will continue to be driven by the damaging prescriptions of conventional economic theory. The stakes are enormous: The legacy of failure is a structure of political and economic imbalance that will continue into the next century.

The verities of the system

An essential ingredient for good policy analysis is a sound analytical framework. In this sense, theory should always precede policy—a prescription that calls for a brief characterization of the economy as it really works:

THOMAS I. PALLEY is Assistant Professor of Economics at the New School for Social Research in New York City.

• The levels of employment and output depend on the level of demand for goods and services. Shortages of demand tend to lower output and employment. Brisk demand tends to produce inflationary pressures.

• The level of demand depends importantly on the distribution of income between wages and profits. A high wage share tends to stimulate demand owing to its effect on consumption. However, to the extent that wages reduce profits, they can adversely affect investment spending, which reduces demand.

• The distribution of income depends on bargaining between workers and firms. The relative bargaining strengths of workers and firms depend importantly on the state of the economy, with unemployment serving to weaken worker power. Worker power is also affected by the ease with which firms can replace existing workers, and by labor laws that provide protections against employer sanctions.

• Firms are driven by the search for profits, and will therefore shift production to sites that contribute to earning the highest profits.

The arithmetic of transactions costs

Within the above bargaining framework, the realized pattern of income distribution depends importantly on the ease with which firms can shift production and fire workers. This, in turn, depends on "transactions" costs which firms must incur in implementing different strategies. These costs are multidimensional. For purely financial dealings, they include costs such as brokerage fees, commissions, official taxes, and charges such as stamp duties. With regard to the location of production, they include such costs as transportation (including shipping, breakage, and insurance), and costs of coordinating production across geographically dispersed locations. In the context of international trade, they also include tariffs. Finally, with regard to the replacement of workers, these costs include the value of production lost during the replacement period, as well as costs related to training new workers.

These costs are important because they have an important effect on the relative power of capital; they affect firms' abilities to shift production and to threaten employed workers with replacement by unemployed workers. To see the impact of these costs on economic outcomes, consider their impact on the working of financial markets. Suppose there are two types of investment of identical risk that yield returns of R_1 and R_2. If there are no transactions costs, then market forces will equalize the two rates of return. Economic logic dictates that, any time the returns differ, there will be an incentive for wealth owners to rearrange their portfolios by selling the low-return investment and buying the high-return investment. Now, suppose there are transactions costs of C associated with buying and selling investments. In that case, market forces will only ensure that the difference between the two rates of return is less than the transactions cost. If the rate differential is less than the transactions cost, it is not worth incurring the cost to get the higher rate.

Exactly the same logic applies to manufacturing firms and their choice of production location. Suppose firms can locate production in two possible sites. In site 1, they earn a profit rate of P_1; in site 2, they earn P_2. In the absence of transactions costs, market forces will tend to drive the profit rates toward equality. The traditional market mechanism applies here: As firms relocate to the site with the higher profit rate, wages and other costs are driven up, thereby reducing the profit rate. Correspondingly, as they exit the other site, wages and costs fall, thereby raising the profit rate at that site. However, if there are transactions costs attributable to relocation, then market forces will only ensure that the profit rate differential is less than the transaction costs. The economic logic here is exactly the same as in the earlier case: If the profit rate differential at the two sites is less than the transactions costs, it is not worth incurring the relocation costs.

Finally, the same logic applies to firms' decisions to replace their existing "insider" labor force with cheaper unemployed "outsider" workers. If there are no transactions costs, firms will replace insiders, as long as outsiders are willing to work for less. However, if there are replacement costs, then firms may stick with the more expensive insiders, because the wage savings from replacement do not cover the costs of replacement.

Distribution of income

What has this to do with the current economic crisis? The answer is that transactions costs have a critical affect on bargainning power, and therefore affect the distribution of income. Though conventionally discussed in the politically neutral terms of supply and demand, the determination of wages involves a process that implicitly pits firms against workers. Sometimes, workers are collectively organized in unions, but more often they are not. In this real world, transactions costs protect workers.

In the first instance, firms face a decision about the locus of production. For example, should firms place production in the United States? Or should they relocate it to Indonesia, where they can take advantage of cheap labor, mimimal social insurance taxes, fewer pollution mandates, and scant worker safety laws? Alternatively, should firms that operate in high labor-cost regions within the United States (such as the Northeast) move to low labor-cost regions (such as the Southeast)? In both cases, moving production creates significant labor cost savings, but this may not be sufficient because of transactions costs associated with the suspension of production. If these transactions costs are sufficiently high, firms will not relocate. However, once these transactions costs fall below a certain threshold, firms will relocate to take advantage of the lower labor costs. At this stage, workers at existing plants will either become unemployed, or firms will use the credible threat of moving to extract wage concessions. In either case, the net result is that wages are reduced and profits increased.

The same issues arise in connection with firms' threats to replace existing workers with unemployed workers as a means of winning wage concessions. Now, transactions costs associated with replacement protect employed workers. These costs include production lost during the replacement period, retraining costs, and costs associated with having an alienated workforce. If these costs are sufficiently large, then replacement threats will not be credible, and firms will be unable to secure wage concessions. However, if these costs fall below a critical threshold, such threats become credible. At this stage, existing workers must confront either being replaced by cheaper labor, or accepting a wage cut. Once again, the net result is a redistribution of income from wages to profits.

These examples illustrate the critical influence of transactions costs on the distribution of income. Applied to the problem at hand, the underlying thesis is that, over the last twenty-five years, there has been a tremendous decrease in transactions costs. This has eroded workers' bargaining power. The result has been wage stagnation and a shift in the distribution of income toward capital. In the United States, this redistributive process began to be visible in the 1970s (when real wage growth ceased), and then accelerated in the 1980s.

This redistribution of income has, in turn, had a depressing influence on demand for output, because workers tend to spend a greater fraction of their income (and to save proportionately less) than do the wealthy. This has caused an ongoing deterioration in the robustness of business conditions. Though punctured by intermittent cyclical recoveries, the overall trend has been downward. Moreover, this process has fed on a vicious spiral wherein worsening income distribution has weakened demand for output and has, thereby, put further pressure on firms to reduce costs.

The impact of technology

Technological advance has been one source of the decrease in transactions costs. Among financial firms, improvements in electronic communication and data processing have vastly reduced the costs of trading financial assets. The result has been quicker and cheaper adjustment of portfolios, and an increased ability to shift financial wealth between countries. In manufacturing, transactions costs have fallen because of technological developments that have facilitated management of production across multiple distant locations. Thus, whereas the multinational corporation was previously an organizational form restricted to the largest of business enterprises, it is widespread today. Another source of lower transactions costs has been the decline in shipping costs. This has facilitated production in sites that are geographically distant from core markets. It has also promoted a system of national and international subcontracting in which production is delegated to the cheapest producer. The role of the lead firm is thereby reduced to one of production coordination and the assembly of the components supplied by subcontractors. The outcome is a low-cost mobile production system that pits worker against worker across different regions and countries. Last, improved monitoring technologies have given management greater ability to observe workers and has, thereby, reduced workers' abilities to threaten noncooperation in response to wage stagnation.

The impact on government

Technological developments have undoubtedly contributed to substantial reductions in firms' transactions costs. However, another cause of reduced transactions costs has been government policy. In financial markets, the abolition of capital controls has facilitated the international movement of financial capital. National governments have also promoted the development of global securities trading in the anticipation of expanded employment in their own financial centers. In goods markets, governments have promoted free trade and reduced both tariffs and official red tape that obstruct the international movement of goods. These policies have affected government's relations with capital in regard to (1) the ability to tax capital income, and (2) the ability to pursue independent national economic policies.

Just as the reduction of transactions costs has hurt labor vis-à-vis business, so too has it hurt government's ability to raise revenues by taxing capital, and has forced it to look for replacement sources of revenue. This has resulted in the burden of taxation being increasingly shifted to labor. It has affected every level of government in the United States—from the federal, to the state, to the municipal. The desire to create jobs in this era of unemployment has pitted government against government in an auction of business tax exemptions and subsidies that are designed to attract businesses. A recent example of this was the bidding war that took place over the siting of Mercedes-Benz's proposed U.S auto-assembly factory. Alabama finally won the auction. Another example was the 1993 negotiation between United Technologies Corporation (UTC) and the state of Connecticut over tax exemptions. In that case, UTC used the threat of relocating production to either Georgia or Maine to win significant tax concessions. A similar tactic, pitting Connecticut against New York, was used by Travelers Insurance Company. At the national level, an example of this process has been the competition between member countries of the European Union over the siting of Japanese car plants. To the extent that tax concessions extorted in this fashion have produced revenue shortfalls, tax burdens have been shifted to households. Thus falling transactions costs have hurt workers by reducing wages and by raising the taxation of wage income.

Another way in which reduced transactions costs have affected government concerns the ability to pursue sovereign economic stabilization policies. In market-oriented economies with open international movement of financial capital, wealth-holders will shift funds across countries in order to earn the highest rates of return (adjusted for risk differences). Such behavior produces pressures for equalization of cross-country interest rates.

Where there are transactions costs, this equalization will be incomplete. From the standpoint of national economic policy, this is an enormous benefit, because it potentially allows governments to pursue independent monetary and fiscal policies. In a world with no transactions costs, market forces imply that interest rates across countries must be equal, so that governments inevitably lose control over the level of interest rates. However, if there are transactions costs, this permits small cross-country differences in interest rates. Transactions costs therefore reduce the vulnerability of sovereign macroeconomic policy to international movements of financial capital.

Policy considerations

Reduced transactions costs, arising from both technological innovations and officially sanctioned economic policies have served to increase capital mobility, and have raised the power of capital relative to both labor and government. Adverse effects on both the distribution of income and the distribution of tax burdens have ensued. These effects directly cause the current economic stagnation and economic insecurity that afflicts the industrialized world. This raises important questions concerning the appropriate policy stance toward transactions costs, globalization of markets, and capital mobility. However, the focus on the significance of transaction costs is lacking in the current policy agenda—a construct created exclusively on the basis of orthodox economic theory. The reason for its absence is that conflict and power are absent in the orthodoxy, so that the significance of transactions costs for power relations is moot.

The orthodox approach to transactions costs (the Chicago School) portrays them as a "friction" that inhibits the realization of the benefits of competition and trade. Orthodox theoreticians therefore recommend that policy should be aimed at eliminating such costs. However, these costs have important implications for the distribution of income, and for governments' ability to tax capital and conduct sovereign economic policy. Moreover, the distribution of income also has important effects on the level of aggregate economic activity.

All of these effects and linkages are completely neglected by orthodox theory, which has dominated economic policymaking. This has meant that policy has been directed toward the reduction of transactions costs, as evidenced by the push for elimination of controls on international capital movements, the encouragement of multinational production, and the movement to free trade. Recognizing that transactions costs are an important strategic variable with significant macroeconomic implications compels a reassessment of policy.

What is the best policy toward transaction costs? A good point of departure for addressing this question is to distinguish between domestic and international transactions. Prima facie, reduction of transactions costs (such as transportation within an economy) would appear to be a good thing, because it reduces the resources needed for transportation, and frees them for use in other activities. Similarly, increasing the mobility of production means that employment can potentially be moved to depressed areas, thereby increasing their prosperity. However, though reduced transactions costs bring benefits, they can also have significant negative consequences. In particular, as it becomes easier to shift production, the bargaining power of capital increases, because firms can effectively pit local workers against workers from different regions in a competition for jobs. This adversely affects the distribution of income, with potentially damaging consequences for national prosperity. Indeed, since the great oil shock of 1974, this has been a significant feature of the U.S. economic scene. Workers from the rust belt have been confronted by workers from the sun belt, as a means of extracting wage concessions.

Government as a moderating force

What can government do about this? What *should* government do? The first step must be the establishment of a national policy toward transactions costs. This policy must start from the premise that transactions costs are important, and that their elimination affects income distribution. In effect, transactions costs represent a form of property. Officially changing these costs is tantamount to a redistribution of property. Sometimes such redistributions can be desirable—sometimes not.

One important area for transactions-costs policy concerns labor markets and mandated employer contributions on behalf of workers. A recent adverse development that is part of the general move to subcontracting is the replacement of full-time workers with part-time and contract workers. For firms, there is an economic incentive to avoid costs such as health insurance and pension contributions. Counteracting this incentive therefore requires that firms be mandated to pay contributions for all workers, including part-time and contract workers. Thus, health insurance reform that imposes this could actually provide a huge unintended structural boost to prosperity.

Another recent adverse development is the massive increase in overtime work. The result has been that employed American workers are working longer than ever, at a time when unemployment and underemployment are rising. Once again, this increase is driven by firms' desires to avoid hiring additional workers, thereby avoiding additional social security and pension contributions. Indeed, there are many informal indications that much of this overtime work is involuntary. Workers are facing a choice of working longer or being replaced. Confronting this trend requires that overtime hours be considered analogous to the hiring of a new worker, so that firms would have to start making fresh contributions on all time over forty hours. Whether one agrees with the specifics of these particular proposals, it is clear that transactions costs matter. *A national transactions-costs policy is urgently needed.*

A second policy area concerns coordination of state government tax policy. Here, there is an urgent need to put an end to the auction of corporate tax exemptions and subsidies designed to attract new jobs. Considered as a whole, this is a zero-sum game. The only winner is the corporate sector; it ends up paying lower taxes. States that participate in such tax auctions simply siphon jobs from other states, and lower overall state tax revenues. Rectifying this problem requires formal coordination of taxation policies across states. This is the only way of resolving a situation in which all states are beset by the prisoner's dilemma. Each state has an incentive to break ranks to make itself better off. However, the net result is that all states break ranks, and make all worse off. Only coordination can prevent this outcome.

A third area that concerns the maintenance of policy sovereignty is the use of taxes to counter the effect of declining transactions costs in financial markets. Thus, placing a small tax on financial transactions that involve U.S. assets could help reduce speculative activity. But it is important that the tax be a "title" tax that is levied exclusively on U.S. assets, and payable upon registration of new title. If it is just a trading tax, trading would be driven overseas. This would harm employment without reducing speculative activity. Such title taxes might promote a shift to bearer bonds, but this could be mitigated by imposing a new issue tax on bearer bonds. Moreover, this step would have the added benefit of diminishing bearer issues, thereby reducing their availability for use in the international money-laundering business.

Trade policy

Clearly, domestic factors have played an important role in the worsening of income distribution. But so too has the growth of international trade and multinational production. It has increased the threat posed to American workers by the abundance of cheap foreign labor, and it necessitates a re-examination of trade policy.

From the standpoint of orthodox theory, increased international trade is an unambiguous good. Lower international transactions costs and increased multinational production are both seen as major sources of gain. Orthodox economists have persistently pushed for free trade and the elimination of tariffs. These policies have reinforced the secular reduction in transactions costs.

But the conventional approach to trade draws no distinctions between types of trade. Instead, it projects all trade as good: The greater the diversity of the trading partners, the greater are the benefits to trade. Thus, Americans supposedly have the most to gain from trading with countries like China, Mexico, and the Philippines. Nothing could be further from the truth. Instead, the benefits to trade depend importantly on whom one is trading with. Without doubt, trade can be enormously beneficial. These benefits include greater product diversity, lower prices attributable to economies of scale associated with larger markets, lower prices attributable to the fact that some countries have climatic and natural resource advantages in the production of certain commodities, and lower prices due to increased market competition.

But trade ceases to be a good when it rests exclusively on wage differentials. In that case, it becomes an implicit instrument for battering down wages and raising profits. We must reconsider trade policy. Where countries have similar wage structures, employee-protection laws, and environmental-protection laws, then free trade is desirable. Where countries differ in these regards, we need to be much more cautious. Free trade that is predicated exclusively on wage competition is entirely unacceptable. It represents a major threat to popular prosperity in America and Western Europe.

In light of the above, trade policy must distinguish between trade liberalizations with high-employment/high-wage (northern) economies and surplus-labor/low-wage (southern) economies. Where there are conditions of domestic monopoly or where countries have a natural advantage in the production of goods, free trade is desirable. Thus, U.S. consumers have clearly benefited from the effect of Japanese automobile market competition. So too, it makes no sense for the United States to try to produce coffee when Colombia has a natural climatic advantage. However, where the only reasons for trade are poverty-level wages and lack of obligations regarding pollution abatement, worker-safety standards, and health and social insurance costs, then free trade is unacceptable. Under such conditions, free trade will end up promoting a decline in the wages of American workers, as companies either transfer production overseas or use the threat of doing so to extract wage concessions. Moreover, to the extent that the system of social and environmental protections is viewed as a source of cost disadvantage and job loss, it will unleash political pressures for its repeal. In the realm of free trade, market forces promote the lowest common denominator.

Given these probable events, free trade is appropriate where the requisite criteria are satisfied. But, if the criteria are not met, countries should be subject to a "social" tariff designed to compensate for their exploitative economic conditions. As conditions in countries improve, this tariff could be lowered in order to provide an incentive mechanism for governments in underdeveloped countries to advance the welfare interests of workers. Moreover, the tariff proceeds could be used to provide aid for purchases of U.S. exports, thus helping both the U.S. economy and the economies of underdeveloped countries.

Workers and government versus business and capital

Orthodox economists see the current economic malaise as the temporary result of massive technological change that will ultimately contribute to even greater well-being. Though these may be difficult times, mass prosperity is not deemed to be endangered. This is a dangerous representation—one that derives from a fundamental misunderstanding of the workings of the market system. In particular, it ignores the significance of power and conflict over the distribution of income, and blithely assumes full employment—except when the black box of technology suddenly unleashes a wave of technical change. In reality, the last twenty years have brought a progressive shift of bargaining power away from workers and governments toward business and financial capital. This shift has occurred because of technological change and government policies, and it has adversely affected the distribution of income. The result has been an erosion in the robustness of business conditions that has undermined the foundations of mass prosperity.

Changing the way we understand our economy is of paramount importance. The stakes are enormous. Without such a change, there is little likelihood of putting in place policies to reverse this decline. Indeed, the situation is worse than that. If we continue with the economics of orthodoxy, we will continue with policies that have already exacerbated a difficult situation. These policies will further entrench deep structural changes that will be difficult, and perhaps impossible, to reverse.

The Free Trade Debate: A Left Keynesian Gaze

BY THOMAS I. PALLEY

FOLLOWING the intense debate and ultimate passage of the North American Free Trade Agreement (NAFTA), it has now emerged that the question of globalized free trade has become one of the principal issues on the economic policy agenda. Rather than the closing shot in the trade debate, NAFTA represents an opening shot in the establishment of an international trading structure for the twenty-first century. For this reason, debate over the consequences of free trade is more important than ever.

Yet even as the need for such a debate becomes evident, the monolithic character of the trade establishment within orthodox economics has largely prevented it from developing. In part, this can be attributed to the professionalization of economics which operates to exclude the voices of lay-persons, and it is noteworthy that the political debate over NAFTA was much more contested than the debate amongst economists. If the economist's principle of rational self-interest is to be believed, the extent of public opposition to NAFTA should itself be sufficient to cast doubt on the benefit to the public weal of the agreement. In addition, the narrowness of the free trade debate can also be interpreted as a reflection of the ideological character of orthodox trade theory, the basis of which is derived from *laissez-faire* microeconomic theory.

The monopolization of the free trade debate by orthodox

SOCIAL RESEARCH, Vol. 61, No. 2 (Summer 1994)

trade theorists has major ramifications for both public understanding of the economic consequences of global free trade and for the construction of policy recommendations. This is because the models that underlie free trade prescriptions assume full employment and characterize workers as being paid what they deserve. Such a construction contrasts with a "left Keynesian" view of the economy, in which unemployment is the rule, and in which wages depend on the outcome of wage bargaining. If the left Keynesian position is correct, reliance on orthodox analysis for guidance in the trade debate is likely to produce misguided and damaging policy. It is this concern that motivates the current paper.[1]

Characterizing the Economy

A left Keynesian characterization of the economy involves three axiomatic principles. These are:

(i) The level of employment and output depends on the level of demand for goods and services. Slack demand will tend to lower output and employment; brisk demand will tend to produce inflationary pressures on prices and wages.

(ii) The level of demand depends importantly on the distribution of income between wages and profits. High wages tend to stimulate demand because of their positive effect on the level of consumption.[2]

(iii) The distribution of income between wages and profits depends on bargaining between workers and firms. Conflict is an essential part of this bargain. Moreover, the relative bargaining positions of workers and firms depends importantly on the state of the economy and on labor laws protecting against employer sanctions and layoffs.

A Taxonomic Framework for Analyzing Free Trade

An immediate difficulty in assessing the welfare effects of free trade reforms concerns the questions of, first, whose welfare and, second, trade reform with whom? Real world economies are constituted by heterogeneous agents, and economies also differ in their typologies. Together, these features compel a recognition of heterogeneity in any legitimate analysis of trade reform. The taxonomic structure suggested by a left Keynesian gaze distinguishes (a) wage income versus profit income, and (b) high wage/high employment economies versus low wage/surplus labor economies.

Recognizing the tension between wages and profits deconstructs the myth of an automatic single national interest. It makes us see that the economy consists of a multitude of agents, the vast majority of whom rely exclusively on wages for their income. Contrastingly, profit income largely accrues to a small minority who are the wealthiest segment of society. Introducing this distinction means that any welfare assessment of free trade must explicitly confront the issue of income distribution, and any welfare conclusions are contingent on the interpretation placed on free trade's distributional effects. For left Keynesians, given that wage income represents the only source of income for the vast majority of people, the welfare effects of free trade reforms can largely be analysed by reference to their impact on employment and wages.

This contrasts forcefully with orthodox trade analysis which places little weight on the distinction between wage and profit income and uses the device of a "representative consumer" to pretend that all persons are the same. Orthodox theory then argues that if total national income is increased, the representative consumer must be better off, and, consequently, trade reform is beneficial. This difference is central to understanding the distinction between the left Keynesian gaze and the conventional gaze.

Just as there is heterogeneity *within* economies, so too there is heterogeneity *across* economies. This latter form of heterogeneity is also critical for assessing the impact of free trade reforms. From a left Keynesian gaze, free trade is often best when conducted between countries that share common characteristics. This contrasts with orthodox analysis, where the greatest gains to trade arise when countries have the greatest dissimilarities. Thus, from a left Keynesian perspective, Americans stand to gain the most from trade with groups such as the EEC countries; for orthodox trade theorists, Americans stand to gain the most from trade with such countries as India, Mexico, and the Philipines. This difference follows from differences in the criteria for assessing the welfare effects of trade reform and from differences in interpretation of how the economy works and how it is impacted by free trade.

For left Keynesians, a minimalist taxonomy involves distinguishing between "high wage/high employment (rich)" economies and "low wage/labor surplus economies (poor)." The former are typified by the industrialized economies such as the United States economy; the latter can be identified with the less developed countries. This distinction not only encompasses the distinction bewteen capital-abundant and capital-scarce economies, but it also captures the notion that economies are social systems, and that multiple facets of these systems are relevant for understanding the impact of trade liberalization. Thus, whereas othodox analysis focuses exclusively on relative endowments of capital and labor as the factor determining the pattern and impact of trade, the above rich/poor taxonomy incorporates the effects of a range of socio-economic characteristics including firms' social security and health cost obligations, their rights to pollute and obligations to prevent pollution, and employee protection and worker safety laws. In general, richer countries tend to impose heavier obligations on firms, have stronger anti-pollution laws, and have stonger employee protection laws than do poorer countries, reflecting the stronger position that workers in these countries have secured for themselves. The critical import of these socio-economic characteristics is that they significantly alter costs of production, thereby changing the international structure of both absolute and comparative advantage. As we shall see, these costs can deeply influence the pattern of international production and trade.

The Impact of Free Trade

The previous section outlined the difficulties associated with making welfare assessments of free trade and the necessity of analyzing free trade reforms within a context recognizing structural difference across countries. This section uses the suggested framework to analyze the potential impact of free trade reforms on rich economies such as the Unites States. The assessment of free trade, therefore, is predicated on the vantage of a rich country: the welfare effects of free trade on poor countries is another chapter. However, it is worth noting that poor countries may win or lose, and the change in their economic welfare depends on the specifics of their situation and the manner in which their welfare interest is defined.

From a United States perspective, there are two types of trade reform. The first involves northern countries; the second involves southern countries.

North-North reforms. This type concerns countries with broadly similar socio-economic characteristics (that is, employment conditions, social security laws, pollution rights, and so on). This similarity is important because it means that their impact on costs is broadly equal across countries so that free trade confers no competitive advantage or disadvantage on either party.

At the level of individual goods markets, the abolition of tariffs and quotas lowers the price of imports: this is a source of increased well-being for all consumers. The liberalization of domestic markets also serves to strengthen product market competition, which promotes lower prices and improved quality on domestically produced goods.[3] This is another source of benefit. Finally, by creating a larger unified market, this allows for economies of scale which can support lower prices and greater product variety.

From a macroeconomic standpoint, the removal of foreign tariffs and protections increases the demand for exports. Since export demand is part of total demand, this stimulates employment and output. However, balancing this is the fact that the elimination of tariffs and quotas increases imports. Since imports represent a diminuition of demand for domestically produced output, this reduces employment. The net effect on total demand, therefore, depends on the relative size of demand diversion into imports, compared to the creation of new export demand.

The extent of export demand creation depends importantly on the availability of international liquidity to finance expanded international trade. Without this liquidity, realizing the putative gains from free trade reform is problematic. However, northern countries have good access to international liquidity because of their high standing in international credit markets, so that this does not appear to be an obstacle impeding trade.

In sum, from a left Keynesian vantage, free trade liberalizations involving northern countries appear to carry significant benefits. Inevitably, there is some sectoral dislocation since enhanced product market competition leads to elimination of inefficient domestic producers. This dislocation adversely impacts specific groups of workers, but for workers as a whole the liberalization appears beneficial.[4] The net result is likely to be an expansion of demand, employment, and output in the participating countries. It is this reasoning that leads one to conclude that had the acronym NAFTA stood for North Atlantic Free Trade Agreement, its passage would have been largely unopposed. Far from being protectionist, the left Keynesian gaze strongly advocates free trade between northern economies.

North-South reforms. Whereas north north liberalizations are largely unproblematic, the left Keynesian perspective suggests the opposite for north-south liberalizations. Now the economies have radically different wage levels and socio-economic structures, which means that these factors no longer cancel out and instead have significant effects on absolute and comparative costs.

Once again, trade opens the possibility for both increased exports and imports, and the demand effects of this are potentially the same as in the north-north case. However, now access to international liquidity to finance trade is problematic. This is because southern economies have lower standing in international financial markets owing to their lower levels of wealth. Southern countries are bound, therefore, by a "finance" constraint that limits their ability to purchase northern exports, thereby reducing the putative benefits of free trade.

Differences in capital:labor ratios between northern and southern economies also set up incentives to re-allocate production. These effects are well recognized in orthodox theory, which predicts that production of labor intensive goods will be transferred to southern countries where wages are low, while production of capital intensive goods will be transferred to northern countries where costs of capital are low. Of course, orthodox theory also assumes full employment so that there can be no unemployment as a result of the trade liberalization. However, even orthodox analysis predicts that the share of output paid to labor will fall in the northern country, and the share of output paid to capital will rise. Consequently, from a distributional standpoint, labor suffers in the northern country while capital gains.

Within orthodox theory, wages are established by reference to the productivity of workers, and competition protects workers against exploitation. However, for left Keynesians, wage determination represents the complex outcome of bargaining between workers and firms. This bargain is framed by reference to firms' abilities to hire replacement workers at lower wages, balanced by the costs of firing existing workers, hiring and training new workers, and living with the consequences of a demoralized work force. It is in this dimension that the effects of north-south trade liberalizations may have their greatest impact, and it is this dimension that is completely absent in orthodox readings of trade reform.

These bargaining effects work by raising the threat of employment termination. Costs of production are lower in southern countries owing to lower wages and lower social overhead costs.[5] Though southern workers also tend to be less productive owing to differences in human capital and differences in the extent of public "infrastructure" capital, these productivity differences are often more than offset by the extent of the wage and social overhead cost advantages. The net result is that the replacement threat of firms in northern economies is credibly enhanced by north-south trade liberalizations. This worsening of labor's relative bargainning position then places downward pressure on wages. In a full employment world, this has distributional consequences but no employment consequences; in a left Keynesian world it has both, since worsened income distribution is bad for demand for output.

How real is this bargaining threat? There is certainly evidence that regional cost disparities have mattered within the United States. Thus, one of the principal consequences of the 1970's oil shocks was to set up labor competition within the United States between the "sun" belt and the "rust" belt. This competition weakened labor's position, and it is no accident that the lion's share of subsequent productivity growth has accrued to capital. Another recent example of such bargainning effects was in Connecticut in 1993, when United Technologies used the threat of moving production to Maine or Georgia as a means of getting both tax concessions from the state and wage concessions from the union. If such effects can operate within national economies, there is no reason to believe they will not operate across economies, since international trade is just trade with the added feature of goods being transported across national boundaries.

From a welfare standpoint, not only do north-south liberalizations potentially disadvantage labor, they may also have adverse consequences for the socio-economic structure. This may be termed the "lowest common denominator" effect of free trade. Thus, to the extent that high costs of environmental protection, worker safety standards, health care, or social security are seen as the cause of lost jobs or reduced wages, this will unleash political pressure to lower these politically determined costs. In this fashion, free trade can become a force for remodelling the socio-economic structure.

NAFTA.[6] NAFTA represents a special case of north-south liberalization, and the above analysis therefore applies to NAFTA.[7] Thus, the import-export effects, the issue of a finance constraint on Mexico, the threat of job replacement and a deterioration in labor's bargaining position, and the problem of differential social overhead costs are all present. However, there are some additional issues raised by Mexico's geographic contiguity to the United States. This is likely to strengthen the threat of job replacement since transportation costs from Mexican plants to the United States market will be smaller. Such costs represent an important source of protection to labor in northern countries, and the fact that these costs have been declining in recent years may partially help explain the deterioration in labor's position.

The contiguity of Mexico also raises issues related to the nature of Mexico's demand for United States exports. Since Mexican incomes are so low, it is unlikely that there will be significant export of consumption goods. Instead, exports are likely to be made up of capital goods and semi-finished goods shipped for finishing and re-export to the United States. Semi-finished goods first show up as a United States export, and then show up as a United States import, so that they increase the volume of both United States exports and imports.

However, to the extent that value is added in Mexico, they must ultimately give rise to a worsening of the trade balance since the value of the final import exceeds that of the initial export. More importantly, such semi-finished exports represent stripping out a stage of production (the finishing stage) from the United States economy and a transfer of that stage to Mexico.

The export of capital goods also raises a number of issues. First, there is the question of Mexico's finance constraint, and whether Mexico will be able to secure the liquidity needed to finance such purchases. Second, there is the issue of investment diversion.[8] Such diversion arises if exports of capital goods to Mexico are the result of substitution of investment in Mexico for investment in the United States. Thus, United States and foreign corporations may decide to build plants in Mexico to take advantage of the lower production costs and correspondingly reduce investment in the United States. To the extent that this occurs, the gain in United States exports is offset by a decline in investment in the United States. Moreover, the United States loses the lasting benefits of job creation and permanently enhanced production capabilities that would have occurred in the absence of such diversion.

Conclusion: A Left Keynesian Trade Policy for the United States

The above analysis indicates how the welfare effects of trade liberalizations depends on whether they are between northern countries, or whether they are between northern and southern countries. This contrasts with orthodox trade theory which makes makes no such distinctions and treats all liberalizations as unambiguously beneficial. Indeed, orthodox theory deems the greatest benefits come from liberalizations between northern and southern countries where the differences in capital:labor ratios are greatest.

Given this left Keynesian analytic framework, what policy conclusions can be drawn for United States trade policy? The analysis would suggest the following:

(1) Free trade between countries which have similar wage levels and socio-economic structures is desirable.

(2) Free trade between countries which have fundamentally different wage levels and socio-economic structures is problematic. Such trade requires case by case evaluation, according to the principles enumerated in (3)—(5) below.

(3) Where there are differences in technical ability to produce goods, trade should be free on the grounds of "technical efficiency." Thus, it makes no sense for the United States to produce coffee when climatic differences confer naturally a technical advantage in the production of coffee on Latin America. This is the traditional Ricardian theory of comparative advantage, which emphasizes differences in technology as the basis for trade.

(4) Where there are conditions of domestic monopoly, there should be free trade as a means of enforcing competitive behavior. In this case, free trade serves to prevent domestic monopolists from earning monopoly profits at the expense of domestic consumers. The application of this principle is readily understood in terms of the history of the "Big Three" United States auto producers. Here, the introduction of free trade in autos has conferred billions of dollars of benefits for consumers by producing lower prices and improved quality.

(5) Where the only reason for trade is the low wage structure and absence of social overhead costs, then trade should be managed through imposition of a "social tariff." The purpose of this tariff is to compensate for low wages and lack of committment to social goals regarding the environment and worker health and safety. Where countries meet these minimum standards, there should be no tariff; where they do not, the social tariff should be imposed.[9] The revenues from this social tariff could be paid to the United States treasury or paid into a fund to benefit the developing countries. There are many ways in which this fund could work: revenues could be paid to the World Bank or some like organization; alternatively, revenues could be used to provide free export credits, thereby actually stimulating United States exports while furthering southern development. Most importantly, the social tariff system provides a self-interest incentive for southern countries to improve wages and socio-economic structures by offering the prospect of

unrestricted market access if they do. Efficiently correcting the inequities of development has long been an intransigent policy problem; the social tariff offers a plausible and efficient means of doing so.

Underlying these principles of trade is the fundamental notion that it is unacceptable for trade to be based exclusively on wage competition and competition over social welfare standards. Thus, trade should not serve as a means of undermining the bargaining position of American labor in its wage bargain with capital, nor should trade serve as a force for rolling back laws and regulations regarding the environment, worker safety, and social security. The goal of international trade should be to export American prosperity, rather than import developing country poverty. This is the core moral principle guiding a left Keynesian gaze. It contrasts with the orthodox position, in which competition that sets foreign workers against domestic workers as a means of lowering domestic wages is deemed a good. This is because orthodox anlaysis assumes full employment and assumes that workers get paid back by sharing in the higher profits. When the economy is equally owned by all, it does not matter whether one is paid in wages or through profits; however, when ownership is as radically skewed as it is, shifting income from wages to profits has enormous implications. Likewise, when there is full employment, shifting jobs overseas does not matter since workers just find new and better jobs; however, when there is unemployment, this is not the case.

The deception in orthodox trade theory is that it begins with the persuasive Ricardian theory of trade based on differences in technical efficiency attributable to differences in climatic and natural resource endowments but then ends up justifying trade on the basis of relative wage costs. Free trade between the developed and under-developed worlds, therefore, implicitly becomes a means of indirectly pitting workers in developing countries, who have no protections or bargaining power, against workers in developed countries, who have had the historical good fortune to establish a relatively strong bargaining position.

Economics is a contested social science, and there are few areas of widespread agreement. However, one such area is "the law of one price," which states that where commodities and services are traded in an open market, there will be a tendency for similar commodities and sevices to trade at a single uniform price. Applied to free trade between the developed and under-developed world, it is labor that is implicitly being traded through its embodiment in imports, and the pressure for price equalization will be felt on wages, conditions of employment, and attitudes toward pollution in production.

Making the left Keynesian case for a sensible trade policy requires care. This is because left Keynesians recognize that not all free trade is the same, and there is a need to distinguish trade between developed economies and trade between developed and under-developed economies. This introduces an element of complexity which places left Keynesians at a rhetorical disadvantage vis-à-vis orthodox free trade theory, which just asserts that all trade is the same and trade benefits all. Moreover, implementing a left Keynesian trade regime calls for administrative interventions in the setting of standards. This opens the danger of rent-seeking, but it would be a tragedy if such arguments were used to prevent the development of intelligent economic policy; rather, they should serve to make policy analysts aware of the sources of policy failure so that they can be guarded against.

How important is trade policy? For European economies with their larger economic involvement in trade, it is likely to be extremely important. What about the United States? Here trade is a much smaller part of total economic activity, and trade with southern countries only a small part of that. Despite this, trade policy is still important. Though trade may be small compared to the economy, leverage exerted at the margin can have significant effects on distributional outcomes: it is the credible threat of movement rather than actual movement by companies that matters. The general worsening of income distribution in the United States is attributable to both domestic market forces and unbridled international wage competition; the former are difficult to counter, which makes it all the more important to embrace other opportunities.

Notes

[1] Gordon (1994) points out that there is often considerable slippage between economic theorizing and the formation of economic policy. Incorporating increasing returns to size within orthodox trade theory means that there is no longer a theoretical presumption in favor of free trade. A similar observation is made by Eatwell (1994). This objection to free trade is different from that associated with a left Keynesian gaze. However, what is interesting is that orthodox economists continue to unquestioningly promote free trade policy despite doubts about its benefits even within their own theoretical paradigm.

[2] If higher wages significantly reduce the profit rate, they can adversely affect investment spending which then reduces aggregate demand. This tension prevents increases in wages from always being a sure means of expanding economic activity.

[3] Workers in industries with domestic monopoly power may suffer from such liberalizations to the extent that they have been able to capture some of the monopoly rents earned by firms. However, since these high wages are derived from product market monopoly, they effectively come at the expense of all workers in the rest of the economy. This situation is illustrated by the United States auto and steel industries, where unions were able to extract high wages in the period to 1970 when international competition in these in industries was weak.

[4] The normative criterion used to assess the welfare effects of trade reforms has been that of the well-being of workers. In some countries, it is harder to talk about a representative worker. This is particularly true of countries with large agricultural sectors (such as France), in which case there may be a divide between the well-being of rural and urban workers. However, in the United States,

agricultural employment now represents a small fraction of total employment, so that this problem is not salient.

[5] Per orthodox trade theory, these differences can also matter. Thus, production of goods that are pollution or safety intensive will be shifted to southern countries where the cost of pollution or safety is lower. Since there is also full employment, northern countries benefit additionally to the extent that the "bads" associated with pollution and personal injury are shifted to the southern countries.

[6] The December 1993 issue of the *Review of Radical Political Economics* contains a symposium on the problems posed by NAFTA. Koechlin (1993a) also provides an overview of the left Keynesian position on NAFTA.

[7] The welfare effects of north-south liberalizations for southern countries are not the clear-cut symmetric opposite of those for northern countries. In the case of NAFTA and Mexico, there is a division between urban and rural workers, so that the device of a representative worker will not suffice for analyzing NAFTA's welfare effects on Mexico. Urban workers potentially gain from NAFTA, while rural workers lose owing to the liberalization of trade in agricultural products. Moreover, even if there is an increase in urban sector jobs, this does not mean that urban sector wages will increase. Mexico is a labor surplus country with a rapidly growing workforce, and the loss of jobs in the agricultural sector will compound the problem of urban unemployment. The one clear group that wins is the oligarchy which owns Mexican industry. This illustrates the need to analyze trade liberalizations on a country by country basis.

[8] This issue is emphasized by Koechlin (1993b).

[9] Obviously, this raises questions of what these minimum standards should be. A suggestion for the wage standard might be 40 percent of the United States minimum wage, but this is obviously open to negotiation.

Bibliography

Eatwell, J., "Institutions, Efficiency, and the Theory of Economic Policy," *Social Research* 61:1 (Spring 1994):35–53.

Gordon, D.M., " 'Twixt the Cup and the Lip: Mainstream Economics and the Formation of Economic Policy," *Social Research* 61: 1 (Spring 1994):1–33.

Koechlin, T., "A Critical Assessment of the Debate over NAFTA,"

Review of Radical Political Economics 25 (September 1993a): 113-21.

Koechlin, T., "NAFTA and the Location of North American Investment: A Critique of Mainstream Analysis," *Review of Radical Political Economics* 25 (December 1993b):59–71.

[13]

The economics of globalization: problems and policy responses[1]

I. Globalization and the relevance of Catholic social teaching on labor

Nations and communities around the world are today confronting the process of globalization. This process refers to the creation of a unified global economy through the breaking down of barriers between national economies. Globalization is creating both new opportunities and problems. The opportunities include the possibility of raising global economic productivity and advancing economic development in under-developed countries, thereby raising standards of living around the world. The dangers include the introduction of new sources of economic instability, and a shift in the relative bargaining power of labor and capital that risks lowering wage incomes for the benefit of profit. These dangers have been brutally illustrated by the suffering caused by East Asia's economic crisis, and by the subsequent spread of the crisis to Russia and Brazil.

The concerns raised by globalization resonate deeply with the long history of Catholic social teaching on labor.[2] This teaching emphasizes the concept of a "right to work" at a "just wage", with work being such that it is consistent with "human dignity" and contributes to "fulfillment as a human being." Globalization has unleashed forces that potentially impinge negatively on every dimension of this teaching. Thus, increased international integration has unleashed forces of wage competition which have contributed to lowering wages in industrialized countries, and this threatens the payment of just wages. It has also facilitated companies taking advantage of retrograde employment conditions in countries where workers are denied rights of free association and collective bargaining, thereby threatening the realization of human dignity through work. Finally, international financial integration has unleashed new forces of economic instability that have undermined the ability to achieve and sustain full employment, and this threatens the notion of a right to work.

How to make Catholic social teaching on labor an economic reality is a major task. To this end, the church has acknowledged a need for dialogue with the social sciences. In participating in this dialogue, economists are implicitly asked to adopt an instrumentalist approach whereby their understanding can be used to help make Catholic teaching a concrete reality. It is in this spirit that the current paper has been written. Thus, the paper analyzes the economic foundation of globalization, and proposes a series of policy responses designed to preserve the opportunities of globalization while curtailing the threats.

II. The origins of globalization

Globalization refers to the increased international integration of national goods, financial, and labor markets. This process of integration is being driven by firms' competitive search for new markets and by the law of market arbitrage which has profit-maximizing firms equalizing the price of similar goods and services across markets.

In many regards, globalization represents a logical extension of the processes that have driven domestic economic development. Thus, the formation of a unified national market in 19th century America was also driven by the search for new markets and the law of market arbitrage. Similarly, the emergence of wage competition between the U.S. economy's "sun" and "rust" belts in the 1970s, has parallels with wage competition between developing and industrialized countries today. However, globalization transcends national boundaries, whereas earlier periods of economic integration tended to take place within the context of the national unit.

The process of globalization is girded by technological and organizational innovations that enhance the mobility of capital, thereby allowing business to operate on a global scale. These innovations are the product of "Schumpeterian" market forces that reflect the workings of a dynamic capitalist economy. Business seeks to maximize and grow profits, and it does so through technological and organizational innovation. Firms can gain a competitive advantage over rival firms by capturing a greater share of the existing market, or they can create a new market that destroys the old. They can also innovate in ways that redistribute income from labor to capital. This latter form of innovation amounts to re-slicing the economic pie rather than growing it. Both forms of innovation are visible in the process of globalization. Thus, firms use the global economy both to lower their costs to gain competitive advantage over rivals, and they also use the threat of international job relocation to win wage concessions from domestic labor.

Globalization has also been fostered by economic policy which has removed barriers to international trade, investment, and financial flows. Though these policies appear to be exogenous changes, they can also be viewed as the endogenous outcome of corporate "political" innovation. Just as business has an incentive to innovate with regard to products, technique, and location of production, so too it has an incentive to capture government policy so as to change existing laws and regulations to its competitive advantage. Such political innovation is clearly evident in business's advocacy of the North American Free Trade Agreement, "fast track" trade negotiating authority, and the Multilateral Agreement on Investment (MAI).

Over the last decade, globalization has become an increasingly contested matter. The impulse behind this new found contested status is the spreading realization that globalization creates both winners and losers, that in many instances the losers are large in number, and that the winners seldom compensate the losers. On the positive side, globalization has increased international goods market competition, thereby lowering consumer prices, increasing consumer choice, and increasing productive efficiency. The integration of financial markets has also facilitated the provision of financing to developing countries, which has opened the potential for them to grow faster. On the negative side, it has contributed to the transfer of U.S. manufacturing jobs to developing countries, wage stagnation, and the worsening of income inequality. It has also promoted the emergence of extreme financial instability in the international economy.

The fact that globalization brings both benefits and costs has made it a contested issue. Almost all agree that the process of globalization cannot be stopped, and nor is it desirable to do so. The real debate is about the balance of benefits and costs under the existing process, and the policy adjustments needed to enhance the benefits and reduce the costs. One view – call it the optimists' view – maintains that the benefits clearly outweigh the costs under existing arrangements, and that these benefits would be even larger if national economies were more open and markets more flexible. A second view – call it the realists' view – sees the process of globalization as problematic, with the balance of benefits and costs more finely balanced. Moreover, the costs are large, and could get larger as globalization matures. What is needed is a change in the rules and institutions of the international economy that would alter existing patterns of incentives, thereby discouraging economic actions that generate costs and promoting actions that bring benefits.

III. A view from the optimists: globalization as perfection of the market process

The optimists' position on globalization is eloquently stated by Tietmeyer (1998). For Tietmeyer, the existing process of globalization represents a positive and largely unproblematic development. The opening of national capital markets and their integration into the international financial system ensures that scarce capital is allocated to its globally most productive use, and this improved allocation raises global welfare. The globalization of goods markets, brought about by increased international trade, is also unproblematic. Countries are induced to specialize in the production of those goods and services in which they have comparative advantage, so that resources are used more efficiently. At the same time, there is never a shortage of demand because the act of production always ensures that sufficient income is forthcoming to buy whatever is produced.

Though much less affected than goods and financial markets, globalization is also largely unproblematic for labor markets. This is because the forces of competition guard against exploitation and ensure that workers are paid their worth. If there is a problem with unemployment, then it is to be found in imperfections and rigidities within labor markets. These result from excessive minimum wages, laws granting workers excessive job protections, trade unions that price workers out of jobs, and from the immobility of workers who refuse to move where the jobs are. To the extent that globalization competes away these imperfections and rigidities, it is even more beneficial.

IV. A view from the realists: globalization and the problem of economic leakiness[3]

An alternative view of globalization casts the process in terms of the creation of a "leaky" economic environment in which national economies are no longer sealed off from one and other (Palley, 1998). This new environment is marked by a pattern of incentives that can give rise to bad economic outcomes, as well as making it difficult to implement effective policy responses. Three different types of leakiness can be identified:

(1) *Macroeconomic leakiness* refers to the tendency for aggregate demand to leak out of national economies owing to a larger propensity to import. It is the result of increased international trade which has changed patterns of spending. The increase in macroeconomic leakiness is captured in Table 13.1 which shows the degree of country "openness" as measured by the ratio of imports plus exports to total gross domestic product. A measure of 0 corresponds to a totally closed economy which has no imports or exports. Economic openness has increased almost everywhere, and in the U.S. it has increased 151% over the last 30 years.[4]

Table 13.1 Openness of OECD countries, 1966–1997

Country	1966 (%)	1997 (%)	Change 1996–1997 (%)
US	9.9	24.9	151.00
Canada	39.1	78.7	101.30
Japan	19.4	21.0	8.25
Germany	51.1	49.8	–2.54
UK	37.8	57.3	51.60
France	25.0	49.4	97.60
Italy	28.1	46.3	64.80
Austria	51.4	85.0	65.40
Belgium	73.5	139.3	89.50
Denmark	58.5	68.7	17.40
Finland	41.3	70.8	71.40
Netherlands	89.8	104.0	15.80
Norway	83.2	75.5	–9.30
Portugal*	54.1	63.6	17.60
Spain	20.2	54.8	171.00
Sweden	43.8	80.6	83.90
Switzerland	58.7	74.9	27.60
G-7	23.4	36.2	54.70
Europe	40.3	58.9	46.20

Note: Openness = [Exports + Imports]/GDP. G-7 and Europe computed using population weights. * = 1996 data.
Source: Author's calculations using IMF statistics.

(2) *Microeconomic leakiness* refers to the tendency for jobs to leak out of an economy if labor markets aren't sufficiently flexible, labor costs are too high relative to other countries, or profit taxes are relatively unfavorable. This form of leakiness has greatly increased owing to greater mobility of production, itself the product of reduced transportation costs and changed technologies that have facilitated new structures of production. Costs of transporting goods have fallen dramatically. In the 1960s, the cost of sea freight was 5–10% of the value of goods: today, it is around 1.5%. Costs of foreign production have fallen because tariff barriers have been reduced, thereby making it less costly to produce goods in one country and sell them in another. Costs of coordinating production in different locations have also fallen owing to improved communication and production technologies. Thus, whereas factories used to be marked by management's offices sitting directly above and looking out over the factory floor, today, management can be located in New York while production takes place in Guangdong, China.

(3) *Financial leakiness* refers to the increased international mobility of financial capital. Innovations in electronic communications and money transfer, combined with the abolition of capital controls, have made it easier to shift money between countries. As

a result, financial capital now moves in response to small differences in cross-country interest rates and perceived future rates of return, and to differences in national economic policies and inflation rates.

These three forms of leakiness have changed significantly the economic structure and the pattern of incentives facing business. They have also made the conduct of domestic economic stabilization policy more problematic, as well as creating perverse incentives for policymakers to follow contractionary policies. The new pattern of incentives has similarities with the prisoner's dilemma. The market sends signals encouraging a particular type of behavior, and when one market participant adopts such behavior they are made better off: however, when all adopt the behavior, all are made worse off.

IV.a Macroeconomic leakiness

Increased international trade means that exports and imports now constitute a larger share of GDP. This has numerous important implications. First, the increased reliance on exports as a source of aggregate demand (AD) means that countries are more exposed to economic shocks originating in other countries. This is visible in the manner in which East Asia's recession has impacted U.S. manufacturing employment.

Second, increased reliance on imported goods results in a greater leakage of demand out of national economies. Consequently, expansionary fiscal policy is less effective in stimulating domestic economic activity and has a larger negative effect on the trade balance. As is discussed below, this, in combination with increased financial leakiness, sets up an incentive for policymakers to shift toward less expansionary policies.

Third, with imports constituting a larger share of spending, imports also constitute a larger share of the consumer price index. Domestic inflation is therefore more subject to the vagaries of foreign inflation and movements in the exchange rate. In 1998, the U.S. inflation rate fell from 2.7% to 1.5% despite a 25-year low unemployment rate of 4.5%. This inflation performance significantly reflected the lower price of imports resulting from a strong dollar and severe recession in East Asia. However, just as inflation can now fall when unemployment is low, so too it may rise in future when unemployment is high, thereby presenting a significant policy dilemma.

Exposure to foreign inflation and exchange rates has been further exacerbated by the stance of anti-trust policy which has allowed greater concentration of industry on the grounds that markets are now global in scope. However, the price discipline of foreign competition depends on exchange rates, and a weakening of the dollar could result in increased monopoly pricing power for domestic producers.

IV.b Microeconomic leakiness

Increased mobility of production has increased the options available to business, and this has increased the bargaining power of firms vis-à-vis both labor and government. This increased bargaining power has in turn been used to win concessions from both labor and government. The result has been to shift the distribution of income in favor of profits over wages, and to shift the burden of taxes away from capital income on to wage income.

The impact of changed bargaining power on wages and the distribution of income is formally examined in the appendix using a Kaleckian mark-up pricing model. The effects of increased microeconomic leakiness operate through three different channels. The increased threat of job transfer lowers both the real wage and the wage share of income. The presence of such an effect has been documented by Bronfenbrenner (1996) who shows that after the enactment of NAFTA, American firms increased their use of the threat of relocation to Mexico to win wage and benefit concessions. The foreign price competition effect raises both the real wage and wage share. It does so by giving consumers additional choice options in goods markets, thereby reducing domestic producers' monopoly power and lowering prices. Finally, the foreign competition production efficiency effect also raises both the real wage and wage share, with enhanced foreign competition prompting domestic firms to seek out more efficient production techniques and eliminate Leibenstein (1978) X-inefficiencies.

Such an analysis shows how increased microeconomic leakiness brings both benefits and costs. The benefits are associated with the introduction of more competition in goods markets which lowers prices and stimulates productivity and quality improvements, while the costs are associated with the ability of firms to place domestic wages in competition with foreign wages. Globalization optimists tend to emphasize the former, whereas pessimists emphasize the latter.[5]

Increased mobility of production has also had negative effects on government's ability to tax capital. Increased mobility gives capital the option to exit, taking with it jobs. Capital can therefore use this threat to win tax concessions, and government is also given an incentive to pursue policies that lower taxes on capital with the hope of becoming relatively more attractive to business.

There is solid evidence that such a process is underway. Rodrik (1997) documents the decline since the early 1980s of tax rates on capital relative to labor in France, the U.S., the U.K., and Germany. Palley (1998a) details how European governments and state governments in the U.S. have engaged in tax auctions to attract new investment. These auctions involve giving tax relief to companies in return for new investment. The key feature is that business plays one government off against another, thereby engaging them in a tax relief bidding war. Such tax competition has significant macroeconomic and distributional effects. The government's budget constraint is given by

$$D = G - T_W - T_K \qquad (13.1)$$

where D = budget deficit/surplus, G = government spending, T_W = taxes on labor incomes, and T_K = taxes on capital incomes. Tax competition drives down T_K. If government is constrained in its ability to deficit finance, then spending (G) must decrease or taxes on wages (T_W) increase. If T_W increases, then capital's ability to move results in a shifting of tax burdens that lowers after tax wages and worsens the distribution of income. Alternatively, government can cut down on its provision of services. However, both reduced G and increased T_W have deflationary macroeconomic consequences. Reduced government spending reduces aggregate demand, while lower wages depress household consumption demand.[6]

Analytically, tax competition corresponds to a prisoner's dilemma. It is illustrated in Figure 13.1. Countries can choose either to hold capital taxes at existing levels or to lower them. If one country lowers and the other holds, then it gains investment from the other country and is made better off, while the country that holds loses investment and is made worse off. The optimal outcome is if both hold, as tax revenues are maintained and neither country loses investment. The sub-optimal outcome is when both lower, as both lose tax revenues and neither gains investment from the other. Unfortunately, the structure of incentives is such that each country has a private incentive to lower, thereby realizing the sub-optimal equilibrium.

		Country A	
		Hold the line on taxes	**Cut taxes**
Country B	**Hold the line on taxes**	A. Tax harmonization	B.
	Cut taxes	C.	D. Tax Competition

Figure 13.1 Tax competition as an example of the prisoner's dilemma

Microeconomic leakiness also promotes a tendency which can be termed "systems competition".[7] Economies are complex social systems that embody different forms of labor market governance and social protection. Examples of difference include the scope of employee rights and employment protections, work place safety regulation, environmental protection legislation, and requirements on firms to provide health and pension benefits. These system differences significantly impact costs of production, and they can confer a competitive disadvantage on firms in international markets. To stay competitive, firms in countries with higher systems costs will try to lower costs, and this can unleash pressures for the undoing of arrangements that provide social protections. Capital will either tend to exit so as to avoid meeting requirements, or it will blame such requirements for loss of jobs in the hope of generating political momentum for their repeal. This possibility is evidenced in Europe where there is much debate over the viability of the European model of social protection. Lastly, the proclivity toward systems competition rises as the degree of economic openness increases because gaining international cost advantage becomes ever more important. This indicates how different types of leakiness may interact synergistically.

As with tax competition, systems competition also partakes of the prisoner's dilemma. Each country has an incentive to try and attract capital and win a competitive advantage in international markets by lowering standards. This is the hallmark of the "race to the bottom".

IV.c Financial leakiness[8]

The third form of leakiness is financial leakiness. It too has been driven by technological innovations and policy changes. Improvements in electronic communications and money transfer technologies have greatly lowered the cost of transferring funds between countries, which has hugely increased the extent of such transfers. Elimination of official controls on capital flows between countries has also increased the extent of transfers. Thus, according to the Bank of International Settlements, the ratio of foreign exchange (FX) trading to world trade was 10:1 in 1980; by 1992 it was 50:1, and by 1995 it was 70:1.

This expansion of international financial flows has increased the risk of financial instability and reduced the scope for economic policy autonomy. The increased risk of instability arises because of greater speculation in capital markets. Sudden changes in portfolio preferences can cause abrupt changes in asset prices. A loss of investor confidence in one country can cause a capital outflow, and as investors sell off their holdings they drive up interest rates while their currency sales drive the exchange rate down. Such shifts are particularly problematic if a country is a net foreign debtor whose debts are denominated in foreign currency. In this case, the fall in the exchange rate increases the burden of foreign debt service.

Moreover, it is not just the country from which investors are exiting that suffers. The exchange rate rises in countries experiencing capital inflows, and this can profoundly affect their competitiveness in international goods markets. Consequently, employment in trade-related sectors may be severely impacted despite no change in factory floor productivity.

Keynes (1936) described speculation through a metaphor whereby financial investing was akin to the newspaper beauty contest in which contestants picked the person they thought other contestants thought the most beautiful, rather than the person they truly thought the most beautiful. The same may hold in stock markets where the trick is to buy stock that others are buying rather than the stock of the soundest company. The theory of rational asset price bubbles explains how asset price bubbles can be self-sustaining through expectations that become self-fulfilling. De Long et al. (1990) explain how "noise" traders, who trade randomly and disrupt market signals, can survive in the long run: all that is needed is that noise traders be less risk averse than "fundamentals" traders and therefore purchase assets with slightly higher expected returns. The problems of speculation are compounded by herd behavior that is rooted in rational maximizing behavior. Banerjee (1992) presents a model of herd behavior in which the actions of others are believed to convey information that is valuable in one's own private decision making, and this results in "follow the leader" behavior. Palley (1995) presents an alternative "safety in numbers" model of herd behavior whereby managers have an incentive to behave like other managers to avoid the risk of being singled out for bad performance. All that is needed is some degree of risk aversion and that pay be based on relative performance.

These microeconomic accounts of speculation and herd behavior provide the behavioral foundation that explains why international financial speculation can be a significant threat to economic stability. This claim is strongly supported by recent events in East Asia. In the early 1990s, financial investors acquired a taste for "emerging markets". They were initially rewarded with spectacular rewards, which attracted even larger flows of funds and produced a herd-like move into East Asia. These moves were facilitated by the elimination of controls on capital flows into and out of many countries in the region. In 1997, a combination of growing current account deficits and a realization that much of the capital inflow consisted of short-term lending that was up for repayment, prompted investors to begin to exit. This then triggered a rush for the exits, with investors seeking to protect the value of their holdings by reconverting them back into hard currencies. This selling drove asset prices down and depreciated East Asian exchange rates, thereby raising the burden of East Asia's foreign currency denominated debt. The increase in debt burdens caused widespread bankruptcy and pushed East Asia into deep recession.

Another problem resulting from increased financial leakiness is loss of national policy autonomy. The precise nature of the limitations on policy depend importantly on the exchange rate regime. In the Fleming (1962)–Mundell (1963) model, when exchange rates are fixed international financial capital mobility neutralizes monetary policy but leaves fiscal policy intact. Conversely, when exchange rates are flexible, fiscal policy is neutralized but monetary policy remains effective.

Fixed exchange rates mean that monetary policy is ineffective. The gain is supposed to be that they bring exchange rate stability. However, financial leakiness can undo this and render a system of fixed exchange rates highly unstable. One source of difficulty is that countries differ in their rates of inflation and productivity growth, and this necessitates periodic exchange rate adjustments to ensure that countries do not become internationally uncompetitive. These adjustments in turn open the door to speculation. In effect, speculators are offered a "one-way" option. The weak currencies are easily identifiable on the basis of economic fundamentals. Consequently, there is an incentive to sell these currencies and buy back-in after the devaluation. If a devaluation occurs, speculators win big: if not, all they lose are the transactions costs which are increasingly negligible. This one-way option is what Mr. Soros exploited in 1992 when he speculated against the pound sterling.

The above argument is that speculation can force premature abandonment of a fixed exchange rate, but fundamentals would have required this anyway at a later date. Morris and Shin (1998) show that speculation can force abandonment of a fixed exchange rate even where it would have been sustainable on a fundamentals basis. Given the finite holdings of reserves by central banks, speculators can simply out-sell the bank forcing a devaluation. Moreover, this has become easier to do given the decline in transactions costs and the growth in financial markets' capacity to leverage assets. Thus, under current procedures for defending currencies whereby each central bank defends its own currency, fixed exchange rates may no longer be a viable option.

Flexible exchange rates preserve the effectiveness of monetary policy, but here too financial leakiness is problematic. Increased economic openness means that countries are more prone to imported inflation caused by sudden exchange rate depreciation. To guard against depreciation, governments are prompted to follow policies that are viewed favorably by financial markets. Given financial markets dislike inflation, policymakers therefore incline toward policies that are more anti-inflationary and carry slightly higher unemployment. Moreover, to the extent that financial markets dislike budget deficits, policymakers also incline toward greater fiscal austerity. To the extent that financial markets dislike trade deficits, this provides an additional incentive toward austerity. Moreover, this incentive is strengthened by increased macroeconomic leakiness because now expansionary policy has a smaller impact on domestic employment, so that the benefits foregone are smaller. Finally, there may also be a prisoner's dilemma regarding interest rate policy. Each central bank has an incentive to raise interest rates marginally above the global average to guard against capital flight and support its exchange rate. However, when all pursue this policy, the result is higher interest rates everywhere. None gain a relative advantage, and all are pushed in a deflationary direction.

Finally, these arguments reveal how the three different types of leakiness interact in a negative fashion. Macroeconomic leakiness reduces the scale of the employment multiplier which reduces the benefit while raising the cost of expansionary macroeconomic policy. It also makes economies more subject to imported inflation. Financial leakiness, in combination with macroeconomic leakiness, then gives policymakers an incentive to tilt policy in a deflationary direction. This includes an incentive to reduce budget deficits in order to placate financial markets. Reduced budget deficits then amplify the problem of tax burden shifting posed by microeconomic leakiness, requiring either less government spending or higher taxes on labor.

V. Policy responses to increased leakiness

Increased economic leakiness poses serious challenges for policymakers. Each type of leakiness is a problem in its own right, but the problem is worsened by the fact that the different forms of leakiness interact synergistically. This means that a comprehensive policy response is required.

The benefits of globalization are real. They result from increased international trade, and from the channeling of funds to worthwhile investment projects in the developing world. Such investments are profitable for investors and contribute to economic development. However, absent a response to the problems of leakiness, these benefits of globalization may be overwhelmed by costs. Increased leakiness threatens to exert a deflationary influence on economic policy that raises unemployment through higher interest rates and lower government spending. It also threatens to shift the burden of taxes away from capital income on to labor income, and this may occur at a time when the wage share of income is already subject to downward pressure. Systems competition also threatens to gradually degrade national systems of social protection. Lastly, there is evidence that increased financial openness has created greater financial instability.

Increased macroeconomic leakiness means that economic activity is more inter-linked across countries, and this calls for improved macroeconomic policy coordination. This need is further increased owing to greater financial leakiness which makes financial capital more responsive to small interest rate differentials. In this new environment, coordinated interest rate adjustment becomes particularly important in order to avoid destabilizing capital inflows and outflows.

Increased macroeconomic leakiness has also made it more difficult to unilaterally pursue policies of domestic demand-led growth, and this has encouraged a switch to policies of export-led growth. However, though such policies can work for one country acting in isolation, they cannot work when all pursue them. One country's exports represent another's imports, so that not all can run trade surpluses. If all try to grow on the basis of demand in other countries, none expand demand and the result is a global shortage of demand and recession.[9] Furthermore, export-led growth also tilts firms' strategic focus toward wage cutting to gain a competitive cost advantage, and it exacerbates "race to the bottom" systems competition for similar reasons. Workplace standards, employee protections, and environmental standards can raise costs, giving firms an incentive to lobby for their elimination on the grounds that they result in reduced international competitiveness.

For these reasons, policymakers should abandon their focus on export-led growth and switch to policies encouraging domestic demand-led growth. This applies particularly forcefully to the IMF which has consistently recommended that developing countries pursue export-led growth strategies. This has contributed to job loss in developed countries, enhanced the extent of global wage and systems competition, and aggravated the long-standing trend deterioration in developing country terms of trade. A new policy mix that fosters economic development through domestic demand growth is needed.

One component of this new policy mix must include debt relief and the provision of credit on easier terms. This is necessary to finance the import of capital goods needed for development, and to provide relief from interest service payments which force countries to export to earn the necessary income. There are also benefits to developed economies in the form of increased demand for exports of capital goods.

Having developing countries move to a domestic demand-led growth path also requires rising wages to support domestic consumption, and this necessitates leveling the playing field between business and labor. Core labor standards that give workers rights of free association and allow them to form unions and bargain collectively are essential. Rather than being a market distortion, independent trade unions are the private sector solution to the current imbalance of power created by capital's new found mobility. Evidence that democracy and labor standards positively affect economic outcomes is provided by Rodrik (1998) and Palley (1998b). Rodrik reports clear evidence that democracies pay higher wages. Palley reports evidence showing that countries instituting changes giving workers the right of free association experience faster growth.

Core labor standards also benefit workers in developed countries by lessening the incentive for firms to engage in systems competition. This stands to subtly alter the dynamics of trade in a welfare-improving fashion since the focus of competition would be pushed away from wages and workplace standards toward labor productivity, product quality, and business mark-ups.

Finally, labor rights and the right to form strong independent trade unions are also vital for reasons of governance. The IMF has increasingly emphasized the problem of political corruption and economic cronyism, which has given rise to misallocation of borrowed resources. It has proposed solving this problem through greater market discipline imposed by increased financial transparency and further financial liberalization. The argument is that market competition will compete cronyism away. However, to the extent that cronysim is politically sponsored, eliminating it requires political reform that puts in place counter-veiling forces that can block it. Human and labor rights, that give workers the right to free association and confer the ability to organize independent trade unions, are the foundation of such reforms.

Microeconomic leakiness also pits business against government, and it endangers the public sector by undercutting governments ability to tax capital income. This also worsens the distribution of income, as well as giving a deflationary tilt to fiscal policy. Tax competition is the problem, and eliminating such competition requires greater harmonization of tax rates across countries.

Financial leakiness is the third area demanding a policy response, and East Asia's financial crisis has clearly shown the dangers of such leakiness. The conventional wisdom is that the crisis resulted from inadequate financial transparency, and the problem can be fixed by improved accounting standards, increased transparency, and further capital account liberalization. However, this diagnosis fails to recognize the problems of increased financial instability and loss of policy autonomy posed by increased financial leakiness.

Improved transparency and accounting standards are desirable, but they do not address the problem of financial leakiness. There is a need to reduce speculation and get investors to invest with an eye to the long term with proper regard to risk. Tobin taxes (Tobin 1978) that reduce currency market speculation are needed, as are Chilean style speed bumps that oblige investors to commit for a minimum time period. Not only do these measures reduce the incentive for destabilizing speculation, they can also help restore domestic policy autonomy. By adding a small friction, financial capital will be rendered less mobile and therefore less able to veto policies it dislikes. Asset-based reserve requirements (Palley, 1997b) can also help enhance domestic monetary control, as well as being useful for discouraging short-term international lending which has proved so destructive in East Asia.

Finally, new arrangements are needed for defending currencies against speculative attack. Under the existing system, each central bank is responsible for defending its own currency, and this places the onus of defense on weak currency central banks. Given their finite holdings of foreign reserves, and given the capacity of modern financial markets to leverage positions, central banks can now be bankrupted of foreign reserves by market speculators. A new system is needed. If the onus of defense were placed on central banks whose currency is appreciating, then central banks would be restored to a dominant position. In place of defending a currency with limited supplies of foreign reserves, central banks would have the unlimited supply of the printing press, thereby restoring dominance over foreign currency speculators.[10]

VI. Establishing the foundation for consensual response to globalization

In many regards, the process of globalization is a logical extension of the economic process that created unified national economic systems. In the U.S., the creation of a successful national economy that delivered widespread and stable prosperity required national economic institutions. Labor law was codified through the Wagner Act, the National Labor Relations Board was established to govern relations between business and labor, a national minimum wage was established to prevent worker exploitation, and national child labor laws were established to prevent exploitation of children. The Occupational Health and Safety Administration was established to ensure work place safety, while the Environmental Protection Agency works to secure a clean environment. In financial markets, the Securities Exchange Commission helps ensure probity in financial markets, while the Federal Reserve is responsible for the governance of the banking system. These institutions contributed to the making of an efficient unified national economy. In a sense, they addressed the problems of macroeconomic, microeconomic, and financial leakiness as they applied within the domestic economy. Just as the creation of a unified national economy required new institutions of economic governance, so too does the new global economy. Such institutions are needed to bar unacceptable dimensions of competition and behaviors which generate destructive instability.

Recognition of this need leads to recognition of a larger abstract point. Proponents of the existing model of globalization argue for more open trade, greater deregulation, reduced government involvement in the economy, and more liberalized financial markets. These calls are couched in terms of creation of a global free market, which carries great rhetorical appeal. However, the reality is that they too aim to establish new institutions and rules such as the World Trade Organization and the Multilateral Agreement on investment. All economies require rules, and this applies as much to a global economy fashioned under the Washington Consensus as it does to the economy fashioned under the New Deal. The implication is clear: globalization is not a natural process that has to be fatalistically accepted. In the words of John Sweeney, President of the AFL-CIO, "The global economy is not a natural outgrowth of the workings of an invisible hand. It is an act of man, not of god." The problem is that the new global economy has been made to benefit some at the expense of others. Hence, President

Sweeney notes that it has been "created by government muscle, wielded behind closed doors, largely on behalf of the most powerful corporate and financial interests."

This leads to a closing point. The new institutions required by the global economy depend critically on how we understand the economic world. Economists tend to assume that markets are perfectly competitive, and in such markets power is absent. It is not a matter of agents being equally powerful, but rather a matter of complete absence of power on the part of all. In such an environment, market competition serves to protect market participants from exploitation. Agents get paid their economic worth because perfect information ensures competitors will bid for their services, and because perfect mobility allows them to move and do business with others if they face exploitation. In this world, frictions are undesirable because they inhibit mutually beneficial exchange and because they inhibit mobility. It is this thinking that has prompted economists to push for elimination of tariff barriers, capital market openness, and deregulation of labor markets that includes lowering minimum wages and weakening unions.

However, if the real world is characterized by power and bargaining rather than perfect competition, frictions and transactions costs acquire a totally different economic significance. Simply eliminating frictions, as has been the policy recommendation of the Washington Consensus, does not create an efficient perfectly competitive market. Instead, it serves to redistribute bargaining power and alter patterns of incentives. In this environment, frictions can be a good thing that remedy market failure arising from grossly unequal distributions of market power. The forces of technological and organizational innovation have been tearing down barriers and frictions that previously restrained capital, and policymakers have indiscriminately abetted this process. However, in a world of bargaining power, the proper policy response is to discriminate between frictions, distinguishing between those that diminish public well-being and those that enhance it. In some areas policy should aim to reduce friction, in other areas it may need to augment them. This is an intellectually very different conception of the economy from that which guides policy today.

Appendix

The appendix presents a simple Kaleckian mark-up pricing model that illuminates how changes in bargaining power impact the distribution of income. The definition of variables is as follows:

P = price level, m = mark-up, W = nominal wage, w = real wage
a = average product of labor y = real output n = employment
t_1 = job relocation threat effect on labor
t_2 = effect of foreign competition on pricing in goods market
t_3 = effect of foreign competition on production efficiency

Signs above functional arguments represent signs of partial derivatives. Prices are a mark-up over average unit labor costs, and are given by

$$P = [1 + m(\overset{+}{t_1},\overset{-}{t_2})]W/a(\overset{+}{t_3}) \tag{13A.1}$$

Output is determined by a linear production process given by

$$y = an \qquad (13A.2)$$

Rearranging equation (13A.1) yields the real wage which is given by

$$w = a(t_3)/[1 + m(t_1, t_2)] \qquad (13A.3)$$

Combining (13A.2) and (13A.3) then yields the wage share which is given by

$$s_w = 1/[1 + m(t_1, t_2)] \qquad (13A.4)$$

The effects of increased microeconomic leakiness are captured by the variables t_1, t_2, and t_3. These effects operate through three different channels. The increased job threat effect resulting from increased mobility of production operates through t_1, and it serves to lower both the real wage and the wage share of income. The foreign price competition effect operates through t_2, and it raises both the real wage and wage share. It does so by giving consumers additional choice options in goods markets, thereby reducing domestic producers' monopoly power and lowering prices. Finally, the foreign competition production efficiency effect operates through t_3, and it also raises both the real wage and wage share.

Notes

1. This chapter was prepared for the plenary meeting of the Pontifical Academy of Social Sciences held at the Vatican, March 3–6, 1999. It was subsequently published in *Toward Reducing Unemployment*, 5th Plenary Session of the Pontifical Academy of Social Sciences, Vatican City, 1999, pp. 185–205.
2. The history of Catholic social teaching on labor is surveyed by Schasching (1998).
3. This section is based on the chapter titled "Structural Keynesianism and Globalization" in Palley (1998a).
4. For Europe as a whole, the degree of openness is similar to that of the U.S. Individual European countries engage in significant intra-European trade which raises European country levels of openness. Once these intra-European trade flows are netted out, European openness reduces to U.S. levels.
5. The above analysis is aggregate in nature. In practice, the extent of product versus wage competition likely differs according to the countries one trades with, as well as differing by sector. Trade between developed countries likely tends to generate greater price competition and efficiency gains, whereas trade between developed and developing countries likely has a stronger wage competition dimension.
6. The net effect of such tax shifting depends on the relative marginal propensities to consume out of wage and profit income. Palley (1997a) provides several theoretical arguments as to why the MPC out of wage income likely exceeds that out of profit income.
7. The notion of systems competition is introduced in Palley (1998a).
8. The problems of financial leakiness and possible solutions are examined in detail in Palley (1998c).
9. Once again, the incentives correspond to the prisoner's dilemma. Export-led growth is favorably received by financial markets, and it therefore has a private incentive to shift toward export-led growth, but when all do it becomes mutually destructive.
10. A comprehensive reform program for addressing the problem of international financial flows is detailed in Palley (1998c).

References

Banerjee, A.V. (1992), "A Simple Model of Herd Behavior," *Quarterly Journal of Economics*, 108, 797–817.

Bronfennbrenner, K. (1996), "Final Report. The Effects of Plant Closing or Threat of Plant Closing on the Right of Workers to Organize," New York State School of Industrial and Labor Relations, Cornell University, Ithaca, NY

De Long, J.B., Shleifer, A., Summers, L.H., and Waldman, R.J. (1990), "Noise Trader Risk in Financial Markets," *Journal of Political Economy*, 98, 703–38.

Fleming, J.M. (1962), "Domestic Financial Policies under Fixed and under Flexible Exchange Rates," *International*

Monetary Fund Staff Papers, 9 (Nov.), 369–79.
Keynes, J.M. (1936), *The General Theory of Employment, Interest, and Money*, London: Macmillan.
Leibenstein, H. (1978), *General X-Inefficiency Theory and Economic Development*, London: Oxford University Press.
Morris, S., and Shin, H.S. (1998), "Unique Equilibrium in a Model of Self-Fulfilling Currency Attacks," *American Economic Review*, 88 (June), 587–97.
Mundell, R. (1963), "Capital Mobility and Stabilization Policy Under Fixed and Flexible Exchange Rates," *Canadian Journal of Economics and Political Science*, 29 (Nov.), 475–85.
Palley, T.I. (1995), "Safety in Numbers: A Model of Managerial Herd Behavior," *Journal of Economic Behavior and Organization*, 28, 443–50.
Palley, T.I. (1997a), "Keynesian Theory and AS/AD Analysis," *Eastern Economic Journal*, 23 (Fall), 459–68.
Palley, T.I. (1997b), "Asset Based Reserve Requirements: An Unappreciated Instrument of Monetary Control," Technical Working Paper, T007, AFL-CIO Public Policy Department, Washington, D.C.
Palley, T.I. (1998a), *Plenty of Nothing: The Downsizing of the American Dream and the Case for Structural Keynesianism*, Princeton: Princeton University Press.
Palley, T.I. (1998b), "The Beneficial Effect of Core Labor Standards on Economic Growth," Technical Working Paper, T010, AFL-CIO Public Policy Department, Washington, D.C.
Palley, T.I. (1998c), "International Finance and the Problem of Capital Account Governance," Economic Policy Paper, E017, AFL-CIO Public Policy Department, Washington, D.C.
Rodrik, D. (1997), "Trade, Social Insurance, and the Limits to Globalization," NBER Working Paper Nos. 5905.
Rodrik, D. (1998), "Democracies Pay Higher Wages," NBER Working Paper Nos. 6364.
Schasching, J. (1998), "Catholic Social Teaching and Labor," in *The Future of Labor and Labor in the Future: Pontificiae Academiae Scientiarum Socialium Acta*, 2, 53–80.
Tietmeyer, H. (1998), "Financial Markets in Relation to Employment and Unemployment," in *The Future of Labor and Labor in the Future, Proceedings: Pontificiae Academiae Scientiarum Socialium Acta*, 2, 211–44.
Tobin, J. (1978), "A Proposal for International Monetary Reform," *Eastern Economic Journal*, 4, 153–59.

[14]

Great Controversies

Developing the Domestic Market

Thomas Palley

The model on which the world's most influential financial institutions base their development policies emphasizes export-led growth and supply-side development. It pays no attention to developing the domestic demand of economies, yet it is critical to growth. A fundamental political obstacle to incorporating demand-side development concerns into policy is that it would place the IMF and the World Bank at odds with their global political paymasters.

EVERY FALL AND SPRING, the International Monetary Fund (IMF) and the World Bank hold meetings in Washington, DC, which provide the occasion for policy critics to target the Fund and the Bank. However, all too often it seems a case of the critics and the Fund talking past one another as much as a case of disagreement. Behind this failure to communicate lies an unarticulated difference in perspective about development economics.

The current moment is an especially opportune time to engage

THOMAS PALLEY is an economist in Washington, DC. He is the author of Plenty of Nothing: The Downsizing of the American Dream and the Case for Structural Keynesianism *(Princeton University Press, 2000). His articles and papers are available at www.thomaspalley.com.*

Challenge, vol. 49, no. 6, November/December 2006, pp. 20–34.

ISSN 0577–5132 / 2006 $9.50 + 0.00.
DOI: 10.2753/0577–5132490602

with these big-picture issues. Both the Fund and the Bank (especially the Fund) are in periods of transition, and the Fund is grappling with implementing a medium-term strategy. However, the "Managing Director's Report on Implementing the Fund's Medium Term Strategy" (IMF 2006) makes no mention of these deeper issues, and instead takes the existing paradigm as sealed and delivered. That is a mistake.

There is much to be learned from the last two decades of development experience, but little of that experience has been factored in to the managing director's report. The Fund is more modest today than it was a decade ago (which is good), but it is little changed in terms of intellectual vision (which is bad). Put bluntly, governance reform is not enough. The Fund and the Bank also need to change their theoretical approach to the economics of development.

Both are currently guided by a combination of export-led growth theory and neoclassical economic growth theory. Export-led growth theory has been important in guiding their thinking about international trade and trade liberalization. Neoclassical growth theory has framed their construction of the underlying development problem, which is defined as one of capital accumulation—be it private business capital, public capital (such as infrastructure), or human capital.

The problem is that this export-led growth–capital accumulation frame is flawed and incomplete. Consequently the Fund and the Bank do some things right, some things wrong (sins of commission), and miss doing some things that they should (sins of omission). The missing conceptual element in their economic model concerns the demand side of economies. The underlying assumption in the Fund–Bank view is that the demand side takes care of itself. The reality is that it does not, and failure to attend to the demand side generates stillborn development.

Export-Led Growth and the IMF–Bank Approach to Development

The export-led growth approach to development triumphed in the late 1970s, when it replaced import-substitution–based development.[1] That earlier paradigm emerged after World War II and recommended that countries develop domestic manufacturing capacity to replace imports.

Import substitution relied heavily on state economic involvement, with the state providing financing and tariff and quota protection against international competition. Initially, the import substitution approach was hugely successful, and in the twenty-five years after 1945, growth and development accelerated dramatically in countries adopting it. However, by the mid-1970s there was evidence that it was growing tired and that excessive and permanent protection may have fostered inefficiency.

Rather than seeking to reform the paradigm by implementing enhanced domestic and regional competition measures, import substitution was abandoned in the late 1970s and early 1980s in favor of export-led growth. The IMF and the World Bank took a lead role in promoting the new paradigm, and three sets of arguments were put forward in its favor. First, classical trade theory suggested there were gains to be had from focusing on exports in which a country had comparative advantage, rather than on replacing imports in which it did not. Second, import substitution led to inefficiency because of protection and lack of competition, so that repealing it would generate immediate efficiency gains. Third, the economic success of Japan and the four East Asian tiger economies (Taiwan, Hong Kong, Singapore, and South Korea) supposedly provided empirical confirmation of the model. The tacit assumption was that exports were the cause of their success and that the model could be easily replicated elsewhere.

These economic rationalizations fitted neatly with the changed political climate, and export-led growth quickly became a central component of the new neoliberal approach to development that became known as the "Washington Consensus." At the heart of the neoliberal paradigm is an antipathy to state economic intervention and support for liberalized markets. Export-led growth fitted this political paradigm, whereas import-substitution did not. The new political climate therefore elevated arguments in favor of export-led growth and disregarded arguments in favor of import substitution.

The shift to export-led growth represented a dramatic turn in policy and can be viewed as inaugurating the contemporary stage of globalization. This shift was especially pronounced in Latin America, which had earlier adopted the import-substitution model most deeply. State economic intervention was reduced, and economic development was turned over to the market. Whereas import substitution made the domestic economy the engine of development for manufacturing, export-led growth made foreign markets the engine. This change quickly became visible in the behavior of multinational corporations that had previously set up shop to supply domestic markets in countries like Brazil and Mexico but now started using these countries as export production platforms.

Whereas the export-led growth model worked in East Asia, it has not worked when applied on a global scale. In East Asia there were national peculiarities regarding relatively egalitarian societies, and these countries were also the first to embark on this route. In addition, East Asia relied on heavy state investment to create comparative advantage in industries that subsequently became large exporters. None of these conditions has been present with the Latin American experiment, and the failure of the export-led growth experiment is evidenced by the decline in the rate of economic growth in Latin America since 1980.

Latin America's experiment has revealed a number of pathologies within the export-led growth model.[2] First, it tilts development away from the domestic market and instead creates shallow export enclaves that are the modern analogue of the plantation economy. These enclaves lack deep linkages with the domestic economy and often rely heavily on imported inputs. Moreover, enclaves are often given special legal standing as export processing zones in which national labor and tax laws are suspended and companies given special rights. An example of such development is Mexico. Under import substitution, manufacturing development was clustered around Mexico City in the center of the country. With the shift to export-led growth, manufacturing has moved to the maquilladora region on the U.S. border, and it relies heavily on imported U.S. inputs.

Second, the focus on exports makes the model bitterly competitive, creating a tendency toward race-to-the-bottom competition between developing countries. International competitive advantage is key to success, and countries therefore have an incentive to do whatever is necessary to secure that advantage. That may mean suppressing worker rights, holding wages down despite productivity growth, giving companies tax abatements and soft subsidies, disregarding environmental costs, and promoting undervalued exchange rates. All of these features have come to the fore over the last twenty years as countries have adopted the export-led growth paradigm.

Third, export-led growth tends to promote global excess capacity and deflation, because its focus is on increasing supply for sale on global markets, rather than promoting growth of demand in tandem with supply. In earlier eras, developing countries were afflicted by declining terms of trade resulting from their reliance on exports of primary products. Today, developing countries face a risk of declining terms of trade because of their collective reliance on manufacturing exports. In this new hyper-competitive environment, developing-country manufacturers and workers capture less and less value. Instead, economic value is captured increasingly by distributors and retailers at the end of the value chain in developed-country markets.

China is the one country that appears to have successfully used export-led growth. However, many of the problems identified above are clearly present in China—including wage suppression, disregard of worker rights, and environmental degradation. China has also resorted to undervalued exchange rates. Moreover, China's version of export-led growth involves heavy state involvement in terms of mercantilist policies that provide subsidies and limit imports. Finally, though China has been successful, it has crowded out development in other countries, as evidenced by the loss of Mexican manufacturing jobs. This result highlights the underlying conflictual tilt of the export-led growth model.

Capital Accumulation and the IMF–Bank Model

The second pillar of the Fund–Bank approach to development is the neoclassical growth model (Solow 1956), which has dominated modern development economics. This model represents the economy as a production process (aggregate production function) that uses capital and labor. The development problem is therefore one of accumulating more capital via investment, which adds to the capital stock.

Later versions of neoclassical growth theory have stuck with this core vision, though the model has been refined to include additional forms of capital. One such form is human capital, whereby labor is distinguished by level of skill. Development then involves raising the average skill level, since skill is associated with higher productivity owing to the ability to make better use of the capital stock. The notion of human capital then leads to a focus on health and education as part of the development process. A third form of capital is public capital, such as infrastructure. This, too, needs to be accumulated, and it opens the way for government-financed investment in public capital.

The latest generation of neoclassical growth models looks to place the physical and human capital-accumulation processes in the context of markets and then examines how decisions to accumulate capital may be adversely affected by market imperfections. With regard to physical capital accumulation, there is a focus on imperfect information in financial markets that limits lenders' willingness to lend. There is also a policy focus on the need to create a favorable investment climate. The good side of this focus on investment climate is the promotion of rule of law and the reduction of corruption. The bad side is the push for low wages, absence of business accountability, and general hostility toward the public sector. With regard to human capital, there is a similar focus on why financial markets may be unwilling to finance self-investment in education, and why firms may be unwilling to provide adequate training because they do not own the trained individual.

This neoclassical growth approach dominates economists' thinking, and it dominates thinking at the IMF and the World Bank. Its core analytic feature is an emphasis on supply constraints (availability of capital) that restrict the ability to produce. The same thinking lies behind supply-side economics, with its emphasis on cutting taxes on profits and incomes to increase the incentive for economic activity. Both emphasize supply constraints and disregard the demand side, simply assuming that demand will take care of itself. This assumption is known as Say's law. The claim is that supply creates its own demand. In effect, the act of production is assumed to create the income that ensures that production can be purchased.

However, Say's law does not hold in developed economies or in developing economies. That means policy must also focus on developing the demand side, which is something the Fund and the Bank have failed to do.

Developing the Demand Side: The Missing Element in Development Policy

In contrast to classical macroeconomics, Keynesian economics has long emphasized the importance of demand constraints.[3] Keynesian economic analysis rests on two core propositions. First, the level of demand matters for the determination of the level of economic activity. Second, market economies do not automatically generate a level of demand sufficient for full employment.

Keynesian economic theory was developed in the context of industrialized economies in which systems of income and demand generation are well established. Within the Keynesian model, this situation left a role for government to fill in temporary shortfalls of demand through expansionary fiscal and monetary policy. From a developing-country perspective, the problem is that Keynesianism may not work because the country's system of income and demand generation is undeveloped. Consequently, if developing countries try to secure full employment by standard monetary and fiscal policy measures, they risk ending up with government debt crises and the inflation that results from printing money to cover government deficits.

The Keynesian challenge in developing countries is to develop "structures" of income and demand generation. This is the challenge that the United States addressed in the first half of the last century during the Progressive and New Deal eras (1900–1940). It is this piece that is missing in the IMF and World Bank paradigm. More broadly speaking, it is missing from academic thinking about economic development, which also errs in the direction of assuming that the demand side of economies takes care of itself.

Developing the demand side of the economy should be viewed as a complement to developing the supply side. Productive capacity is needed to produce, but demand is needed to ensure that productive capacity is used. Strong demand is also an incentive to add to capacity. Moreover, additions to capacity in the form of investment spending are themselves part of demand.

Likewise, trade is a complement. Exports are a component of demand, and all countries need to exports to cover their imports, making international competitiveness a critical concern. Problems only arise when export competitiveness and incentives for capital accumulation are the exclusive focus of attention, and development of domestic demand structures is neglected.

The implications of a demand-development perspective can be traced out by considering five areas of policy and seeing how that perspective generates different policy recommendations from those of the IMF and the Bank. These areas are:

1. Income distribution
2. International financial liberalization
3. Trade policy
4. Privatization
5. Policy space and democracy

Income distribution is key to developing domestic markets, yet until recently it has figured little in Fund and Bank thinking. Today, to the extent that it does figure, it is in terms of the neoclassical growth model and how unequal income distribution can harm capital accumulation by limiting collateral to secure investment financing or limiting private investment in education (human capital). The core problem of wages and exploitation is sidestepped because of the belief that markets pay workers what they are worth. However, if this is not the case, and wages are determined by economic power, political power, and social perceptions, there is a case for institutions that remedy imbalances of power. These institutions include labor standards, trade unions, minimum wage laws, and systems of social protection. To Fund and Bank economists, these measures are labor market distortions that lower employment. From a Keynesian demand-development perspective, they are needed to establish a solid process of income and demand generation.

International financial liberalization was a key policy recommendation of the IMF in the 1990s. The fallout from the East Asian financial crisis of 1997 has somewhat tamed Fund enthusiasm for capital market opening, and it now talks of the need for careful sequencing of measures that open capital markets. However, the underlying view remains strongly favorable to capital market liberalization and hostile to measures that interfere with free international financial capital flows.[4] In stark contrast, a demand-development perspective is far more cautionary. Financial market openings can expose countries to speculative inflows of hot money that leave them financially exposed when speculators' ardor cools. In addition, financial openness poses problems for management of domestic interest rates and exchange rates, which are two of the most important prices in an economy. Keynes (1980) was aware of this, writing in 1942: "In my view the whole management of the domestic economy depends upon being free to have the appropriate rate of interest without reference to the rates prevailing elsewhere in the world. Capital control is the corollary of this."

Trade policy is another area that has undermined development of the demand side. The Fund and the Bank have strongly endorsed the current model of export-led growth, which most developing countries are now simultaneously pursuing. As noted earlier, this model suffers from critical pathologies when applied on a global scale, promoting global deflation by adding to global supply without tending to the growth of global demand. This pattern is evident in today's global financial imbalances, with the United States serving as global buyer-of-last-resort and running a huge trade deficit that makes up for the shortage of demand elsewhere. In addition, export-led growth promotes competitive undervaluation of exchange rates as countries try to secure a competitive advantage. Such competitive undervaluation is also deflationary, because it promotes exports and undermines purchasing power for imports.

From a Keynesian demand-development perspective, the export-led growth model is especially problematic because of the downward pressures it puts on wages. Holding down wages to gain a competitive advantage, despite gains in productivity, prevents the development of a local middle class. More generally, the export-led growth model promotes race-to-the-bottom tendencies that are antithetical to development of needed demand-side structures. In an export-led world, these structures are a cost, whereas in a domestic demand-centered model, they are a benefit.

The export-led growth model is intimately connected with the World Trade Organization (WTO), which has played a critical role in implementing the model on a global basis. Labor standards and trade unions are key to getting income distribution right and developing the demand side, yet the WTO is staunchly opposed to making such standards part of the rules of the game. Too often these standards are represented as undercutting the competitive advantage of low-wage developing countries, when in fact they may help developing countries to capture more of the value they produce. This is because the current system allows mobile international buyers to play countries off against each other and drive down wages and prices. Labor standards can provide a floor that prevents such competition, and thereby benefit all developing countries.

Another piece of the WTO trade agenda, also promoted by the IMF and the World Bank, concerns the promotion of multilateral trade agreements over regional trade agreements. However, regional trade agreements may be more suitable for developing countries moving up the industrialization ladder. Such agreements can expand the size of the market and increase competition. However, they do not create a mismatch of competition, because regional partners tend to be at similar levels of development, nor do they promote race-to-the-bottom competition for similar reasons. Finally, regional agreements tend to retain the benefits of commercial development within the region, unlike the export-led growth model with its reliance on imported inputs and export processing zones.

A third piece of the WTO agenda concerns intellectual property rights (IPR). The agenda imposes a universal set of IPR based largely on U.S. law. These IPR are hugely expensive for developing countries that must use scarce foreign exchange to pay for permission to use ideas. There is absolutely no economic justification for this system. Developing countries are sovereign states that are entitled to their own intellectual property (IP) laws. Moreover, there are strong grounds for believing that U.S. laws are suboptimal from a U.S. perspective, and they are even more suboptimal from a developing-country perspective. These countries are unlikely to be significant IP producers in the near- or medium-term future, and they would therefore benefit from having differently structured IP laws. In a world of economically diverse countries, economic theory says that optimal IP laws will differ across countries. The attempt by the WTO, aided and abetted by the World Bank, to impose a uniform global IPR legal regime is nothing short of economic imperialism theory. It also siphons income out of developing countries, thereby inhibiting domestic demand.

A final critique of the WTO agenda concerns tariff revenues and their implications for government funding. In many developing countries, tariff revenues are an important source of government revenue. That means their reduction or abolition poses grave problems and can undermine the provision of government services and needed public goods. These countries often lack the administrative capacity to raise tax revenues in other ways, so that tariffs are the economically efficient way to fund government. These concerns have been largely ignored in the past, and they undermine government spending that is needed on both the supply and demand sides of market economies.

Privatization represents another policy that has been pushed by the

IMF and the World Bank, though this push is drawing to an end as the cherries have largely been picked. In retrospect, the costs and benefits of privatization were poorly assessed. There were undoubtedly microeconomic efficiency gains to be had, but many of these gains might have been reaped by management reengineering rather than privatization.

Moreover, privatization has often ended up being associated with massive corruption, and it has not been easy to regulate the privatized entities that have often had significant monopoly power. In addition, privatizations have occasionally failed (e.g., the privatization of Mexico's banks) and then required hugely expensive bailouts. Most important, from a demand-development perspective, unions and pay structures were most advanced in state-owned industries. They therefore constituted the logical base from which to develop a modern industrial relations structure.

Policy space and democracy is the final area where the Fund–Bank development paradigm has caused problems. Policy space affects the ability of governments to undertake macroeconomic stabilization policies, and it is a vital element of Keynesian economics. Market economies are powerful producers of wealth and income, but they can also be highly unstable and subject to shocks. Government monetary and fiscal policies can help counter macroeconomic shocks, while regulatory policies can contribute to building fairer microeconomic outcomes. Unfortunately, not only have the policies of the Fund and the Bank opposed needed social and labor market regulation, they have also contributed to closing down policy space.

In particular, the combination of international capital mobility and free trade has given business the power to veto policies that it deems unpalatable. The result is that countries seeking to impose progressive systems of taxation are likely to be penalized by international investors. More than that, investors will game the system to drive down taxes on capital incomes and weaken business regulation by putting governments in competition with each other in their quest to secure investment and job creation. These effects have been empirically confirmed by Rodrik (1997), who reports that within the Organization for Economic Cooperation and Development, increases in international economic openness drive down both tax rates on capital incomes and government spending as a share of the gross domestic product.

Finally, the issue of policy space raises the issue of quality of governance. Policy space is vital for achieving good economic outcomes in both developed and developing economies. However, policy space can be used to good or bad effect, and corrupt government can do great economic harm. That means government transparency and accountability are critical. In addition, democracy is critical as a means of holding governments accountable and in check. In every organization there is always the problem of "who will guard the guardians," and democracy is central to controlling government. However, both the Fund and the Bank have been reluctant to promote democracy, arguing that they do not engage in political interventions. This defense is false. The reality is that they have sought to use markets to discipline governments, so that in effect they have been engaging in undemocratic political intervention.

Where Next for Development Policy at the Fund and the Bank?

The IMF and the World Bank are powerful institutional forces in the world of economic development. Their financial resources give them direct policy influence, and this power is leveraged by the fact that financial markets are influenced by the Fund and Bank's willingness to lend. The Fund and the Bank also play a critical role in forming and shaping elite policy opinions on trade, development, and globalization. The Fund and the Bank therefore act as powerful coordinating institutions that get countries on board for a particular version of globalization based on deregulation, shrinking government's economic presence, and the absence of social and labor standards. Moreover, their huge research and public relations resources are used to push this agenda among the broader public. This makes changing the Fund and Bank's economic view critical.

The IMF and the World Bank are currently politically weak. That has made them more modest and willing to consider change to their internal voting structures. However, governance reform alone is inadequate. It must be accompanied by engagement with intellectual restructuring that challenges their basic economic model. That model rests on a combination of export-led growth and supply-side development, and lacks attention to developing the demand side of economies. Consequently, it cannot produce equitable growth and prosperity. Unfortunately, a fundamental political obstacle to incorporating demand-side development concerns is that it will change the trajectory of globalization by making it more egalitarian and democratic. That would place the IMF and the World Bank at odds with global corporate interests that currently dominate the policy landscape.

Notes

1. This section draws heavily on Blecker (2000) and Palley (2003).
2. See Ocampo (2002) for a comprehensive review of the impact the economic reforms of the last two decades had on Latin America.
3. This section draws on Palley (2002), which also contains suggestions regarding what a demand-side development program would look like.
4. The IMF's view reflects a capital accumulation and allocation perspective, rather than concern with demand-side issues. The flavor of the IMF's thinking is captured in the following remarks of Stanley Fischer (1997), made when he was deputy managing director of the IMF: "Put abstractly, free capital movements facilitate a more efficient global allocation of saving and help channel resources into their most productive uses, thus increasing economic growth and welfare. From the individual country's perspective, the benefits take the form of increases in both the potential pool of investible funds and the access of domestic residents to foreign capital markets. From the viewpoint of the international economy, open capital accounts support the multilateral trading system by broadening the channels through which developed and developing countries alike can finance trade and investment and attain higher levels of income."

For Further Reading

Blecker, R.A. 2000. "The Diminishing Returns to Export-Led Growth." Paper prepared for the Council of Foreign Relations Working Group on Development, New York.

Fischer, S. 1997. "Capital Account Liberalization and the Role of the IMF." International Monetary Fund, Washington, DC, September.

International Monetary Fund (IMF). 2006. "Managing Director's Report on Implementing the Fund's Medium-Term Strategy." Washington, DC, April 5.

Keynes, J.M. 1980. "Letter to R.F.Harrod, 19 April 1942." In *The Collected Writings of J.M. Keynes,* ed. D. Moggridge, vol. 25, chap. 3. London: Macmillan.

Ocampo, J.A. 2002. "Lights and Shadows in Latin American Structural Reforms." Paper presented at a conference of the Center for International Studies Program on Latin America and the Caribbean, University of Toronto, Toronto, April 19–20.

Palley, T.I. 2002. *A New Development Paradigm: Domestic Demand-Led Growth.* Foreign Policy in Focus Web site, September (www.fpif.org).

———. 2003. "Export-Led Growth: Is There Any Evidence of Crowding-Out?" In *Globalization, Regionalism, and Economic Activity,* ed. P. Arestis et al. Cheltenham, UK: Edward Elgar.

Rodrik, D. 1997. *Has Globalization Gone Too Far?* Washington, DC: Institute for International Economics.

Solow, R.M. 1956. "A Contribution to the Theory of Economic Growth." *Quarterly Journal of Economics* 70, no. 1: 65–94.

[15]

investigación económica, vol. LXXI, 280, abril-junio de 2012, pp. 141-161

The Rise and Fall of Export-led Growth

Thomas I. Palley*

Introduction

For the past thirty years development policy has been dominated by the paradigm of export-led growth. That paradigm is part of a consensus among economists about the benefits of economic openness which has been used to promote and justify globalization.

The Great Recession has surfaced contradictions that were always inherent in export-led growth and globalization and the global economy now confronts a troubling outlook of significant demand shortage. In developed economies the shortage is explicit in high rates of unemployment and large output gaps. In emerging market (EM) economies it is implicit in their reliance on export markets.

Received November 2011; accepted March 2012.

* New America Foundation, <mail@thomaspalley.com>. This paper was presented at a conference on the Mexican Economy organized by the Economics Department of the University of Puebla, Puebla, Mexico, November 17-19, 2010 and at a conference on Brazil-China-United States. Relations held at the Federal University of Rio de Janeiro, Rio de Janeiro, Brazil on June 10, 2011. I thank participants and two anonymous referees of *Investigación Económica* for helpful comments. All errors and opinions are those of the author.

This paper argues the case for trade openness and export-led growth was always over-simplified and over-sold. As a result of the widespread turn to openness and export-led growth the global economy confronts an extended period of asymmetric stagnation marked by slower growth in EM economies, stagnation in developed economies, and increased economic tensions between EM and developed economies.

THE RISE OF EXPORT-LED GROWTH

The export-led growth paradigm rose to prominence in the late 1970s when it replaced the import-substitution paradigm that had dominated development policy thinking (especially in Latin America) in the thirty years after World War II. Export-led growth is a development strategy aimed at growing productive capacity by focusing on foreign markets. It is part of a new consensus among economists about the benefits of economic openness that took hold in the 1970s.

This new consensus rests on a fusion of three strains of argument that is illustrated in Figure 1. The first strain, based on Heckscher-Ohlin-Samuelson comparative advantage theory, is about the gains from trade between economies with different capital –labor ratios (Ohlin, 1933; Samuelson, 1948; Dornbusch, Fischer and Samuelson, 1980). The second strain concerns the benefits of openness for controlling rent seeking, a problem that import-substitution development was strongly criticized for (Krueger, 1974). The third strain, which developed later, is the benefits of openness for growth. The claim is trade encourages technology diffusion and knowledge spillovers that contribute to faster productivity growth (Grossman and Helpman, 1991).

Export-led growth represents a subsidiary branch within this new consensus that applies to developing countries. The argument is self-conscious policy focused on external markets helps capture the economic benefits of openness for developing countries by encouraging best practice adoption; promoting product development; and exposing firms to competition. The success of the four East Asian Tiger economies (South Korea, Hong Kong, Singapore, and Taiwan) appeared to provide empirical support for these claims.

Figure 1
Arguments supporting the new consensus on openness

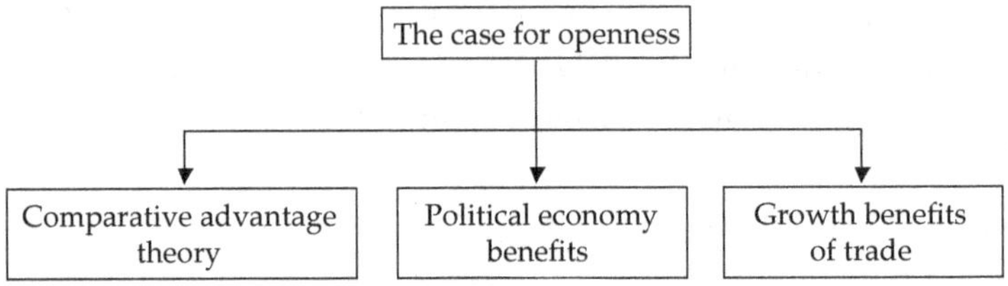

According to economists export-led growth generates a win –win outcome for developing and industrialized economies. All benefit from the global application of the principle of comparative advantage, while developing countries gain extra benefit from an external focus. Moreover, industrialized economies supposedly benefit even if developing countries subsidize their exports so as to win additional exports. That is because countries which subsidize their exports are giving a gift to countries receiving those exports. However, that latter claim rests on two highly questionable assumptions. First, there is no long-term dynamic cost to industries displaced by such subsidies. Second, there is scarcity of resources and full employment (*i.e.* no Keynesian unemployment) which makes the subsidies a gift.

These arguments about the benefits of trade and economic openness played an important role in propelling the new agenda of international economic integration. That is because they dovetailed with the economic interests of large corporations who were looking to establish a new global economic structure that has since become known as globalization. Corporations therefore embraced economists' ideas as they helped power their global economic agenda. That created a corporate –elite opinion alliance which bonded trade theory with corporate globalization, and that alliance drove expansion of the General Agreement on Tariffs and Trade (GATT) and the subsequent establishment of the World Trade Organization (WTO) in 1996.

With regard to developing countries, the International Monetary Fund (IMF) and World Bank played a special role spreading the new agenda. That is because developing countries needed financial assistance after the 1970s oil shocks and the IMF and World Bank made access to assistance conditional on governments embracing the openness agenda.

CRITIQUES OF THE NEW OPENNESS AGENDA

Though the new "openness" agenda swept academic economics, it was also always opposed and the insights and arguments of this opposition have become increasingly prescient. Figure 2 identifies four strains of critique of the openness paradigm. The first strain is the comparative advantage critique. There has always been a small internal neoclassical critique that focuses on potential pathologies of trade liberalization. These pathologies included Johnson's (1954, 1955) terms of trade deterioration critique; Bhagwati's (1958) immiserizing growth critique that extended Johnson's critique to a dynamic context; the Stolper and Samuelson (1941) critique about trade and income distribution; and Lipsey and Lancaster (1956-57) based critiques about unintended negative effects of trade liberalization in a world of market imperfections (see for example Brewer, 1985). However, this internal critique is a collection of rare pathologies and in many regards it is a confusing distraction to more systemic critiques. That is because it accepts the fundamental logic of neoclassical trade theory rather than challenging it.[1]

The second strain is labeled the Keynesian critique and it has its roots in macroeconomics and Keynes rejection of comparative advantage (Prasch, 1996; Milberg, 2002). In a Keynesian world of demand shortage trade can reduce domestic demand, leading to reduced output, employment, and national welfare. An implicit corollary proposition is that in a Keynesian world export subsidies are not a gift but may instead poach demand and employment.

[1] Progressive activists sometimes appeal to arguments such as the Stolper and Samuelson (1941) theorem to criticize free trade. This is a dangerous tactic as it implicitly accepts the logic of neoclassical trade theory with its claims about the benefits of trade arising from application of the principle of comparative advantage.

FIGURE **2**

Critiques of the new openness agenda

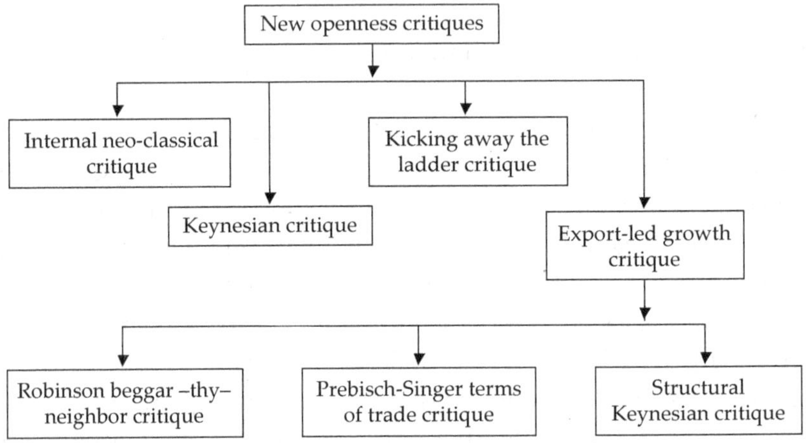

The Keynesian aggregate demand shortage critique also makes exchange rates a trade issue because undervalued exchange rates impact demand by altering the relative price of imports and exports. Classical open economy macroeconomics, which is the twin of neo-classical trade theory, asserts any employment effects of under-valued exchange rates are at worst temporary. That is because monetary factors are supposedly neutral. Either the real exchange rate adjusts to offset the effects of money, or the money supply adjusts via the specie-flow mechanism in response to trade deficits. However, this logic falls apart if there are hysteresis effects related to patterns of demand and the organization of production (Palley, 2003a). In that case exchange rates are non-neutral in both the short- and long-run, and these non-neutralities make the benefits of trade contingent on appropriate exchange rate arrangements. Absent such arrangements trade may reduce welfare.

The Keynesian demand shortage argument also carries over to situations with economies of scale. In the presence of economies of scale, measures that increase demand (including protection) can increase exports by lowering the average costs of producers. That can provide another reason to limit free trade (Krugman, 1984).

The third strain of critique is labeled "kicking away the ladder" after the book of that title by Chang (2002). This critique traces back directly to the post-World War II import-substitution school of thought and argues trade protection, industrial policy, and the ability to conduct macroeconomic policy are necessary for successful development. Chang (2002) argues no country has successfully industrialized without such policies. Whereas the Keynesian critique of openness is generic and holds for both developed and emerging market economies, the kicking away the ladder critique applies only to emerging market and developing economies.

The fourth strand of critique is specifically about export-led growth and it consists of three separate elements. The first element is labeled the Robinson beggar-thy-neighbor critique after Joan Robinson's (1947 [1937]) observations about macroeconomic mercantilism. This argument is Keynesian and stems from the competitive devaluation experience of the 1930s. The logic is countries that try to export their way out of demand shortage implicitly harm their neighbors by poaching demand and employment. Applied to export-led development, the Robinson critique suggests there may be a fallacy of composition and developing countries may crowd out each-others exports (Blecker, 2000; Palley, 2003b; Blecker and Razmi, 2010).

The second element is labeled the Prebisch (1950) and Singer (1950) critique. It focuses on supply and price effects of export-led growth in contrast to the Robinson critique which focuses on demand and quantity effects. Sixty years ago Raul Prebisch (1950) and Hans Singer (1950) identified a problem of declining terms of trade for commodity exporting countries. Today, the problem has shifted from commodities to manufactured goods and countries that engage in export-led growth may exacerbate the problem by increasing the global supply of such goods (Sarkar and Singer, 1991; Kaplinsky, 1993; Sapsford and Singer,1998).

The third element is labeled the structural Keynesian critique (Palley, 2002, 2004). The argument here is export led growth promotes economic structures that deliver low quality growth and prevent the development of deep prosperity. Within countries, development has shallow roots because it is externally focused –a phenomenon exemplified by export processing zones and Mexico's maquiladora zone–. Internationally, export-led growth promotes a race to the bottom as countries try to gain competitive advantage by any means. That results in wage suppression, disregard for labor and environmental standards, disregard of workplace conditions, and weak regulation aimed at pleasing capital.

The development of wages in Mexico (see Salas and Zepeda, 2003) exemplifies the wage suppression that comes with the adoption of an export-led growth strategy. Severe wage moderation aimed at increasing international competitiveness also afflicts Germany and has contributed to Germany's macroeconomic stagnation (see Hein and Truger, 2005, 2010). Moreover, because of Germany's economic standing and power it has also pressured wage developments throughout Europe, which illustrates the negative externalities that adoption of export-led growth can impose on global aggregate demand.

A BRIEF HISTORY OF EXPORT-LED GROWTH

The last thirty years have seen tremendous spread of the export-led growth paradigm. The strategy was pioneered by Germany and Japan in 1950s and 1960s. In the 1970s and 1980s it was adopted by the four East Asian Tigers –South Korea, Taiwan, Hong Kong, and Singapore–. In the 1980s and 1990s it spread further, being adopted in South East Asia by Thailand, Malaysia, and Indonesia. In Latin America it was adopted by Mexico. In the 2000s China has exemplified the paradigm.

The model has not been constant, but has instead evolved to fit changing global circumstances and to fit individual country conditions. This evolution can be thought of as involving four stages.

Stage I was kicked off by Germany and Japan and can be thought of as running from 1945-1970. Both countries had their own indigenous industrial base and export growth was driven by an under-valued exchange rate. Growth also benefitted from U.S. aid made available after World War II as part of reconstruction and the Cold War.

Stage II captures the experience of the four East Asian tigers - South Korea, Taiwan, Hong Kong and Singapore –and runs from 1970-1985–. Once again countries relied on an under-valued exchange rate but now there was need for more foreign technology acquisition. This was done via strategic planning and benefitted from the fact that technology was becoming more mobile.

Stage III is epitomized by Mexico's engagement with export-led growth. The major change from stage II is that countries now started turning themselves into export production platforms for foreign multi-nationals rather than developing their own indigenous industrial capacity. This changed strategy was feasible because of increased mobility of technology and capital. The key elements of the new strategy were *a*) integration into the global economy; *b*) an undervalued exchange rate; *c*) suppression of wages and social standards. The goal was to enhance international competitiveness so as to become attractive to multi-national corporations (MNCs) as a site for foreign direct investment (FDI) that was export-oriented. However, the benefits have also proved much more elusive.

The new strategy is exemplified by Mexico's experience which began with the trade liberalization of 1986. That set the path to North American Free Trade Agreement (NAFTA) and the creation of a North American free trade area in 1994. The inauguration of NAFTA in January 1994 was marked by a peso crisis that resulted in massive devaluation of the peso vis-à-vis the US dollar, providing Mexico with an under-valued currency.

This third stage of export-led growth represents the beginning of the modern era of corporate globalization, and a critical feature is that export-led growth is no longer a purely national strategy. Instead, it is a partnership between developing countries, multi-national corporations, and developed countries. Governments and multi-nationals promoted the new system using the traditional language of free trade and claimed the goal was creation of a global market place. However, the real goal was not to promote traditional trade, but rather to create a global production zone in which corporations could establish export production platforms that would export back to developed country markets.

NAFTA is the template for the new model and it is massively significant from a historical standpoint. By unifying the United States (U.S.), Canada, and Mexico into a single free trade zone NAFTA created for the first time a free trade production zone that unified developed and developing economies. This template was then extended globally via the establishment of the WTO in 1996 and the admission of China into the WTO in 2001.

There are three important features of the NAFTA –corporate globalization model–. First, it promotes trade but not the classical trade of balanced exports and imports. Second, it promotes a new type of export-led growth based on relocating existing production and diverting new investment. That benefits emerging market economies by creating jobs, transferring technology, and relieving balance of payments constraints on growth. However, these economies do not own the industrialization process as was the case in stages I and II. Third, it does considerable damage to developed economies via deindustrialization, creation of international financial imbalances, and undermining the wage –productivity growth link which in turn undermines the coherence of the domestic income and demand generation process.

Stage IV is an extension and augmentation of the stage III model and is exemplified by China. China's model makes three major adjustments to Mexico's NAFTA model. First, it is characterized by asymmetric global engagement with China maintaining greater tariffs on imports. Second, there is managed under-valuation of the exchange rate that is maintained with capital controls. Third, there is a strategy for building an indigenous national technological base via forced technology sharing, joint-ventures in which MNCs may be minority shareholders, and technology theft. China's policies toward banking and automobile production are prime examples of this.

MNCs have also changed their strategy. Thus, they are now willing to engage in joint-ventures and also license and source from foreign producers rather than own facilities. In the case of China that is the price of entry, with corporations hoping they will be paid back by future profits from China's large market. Licensing and joint-ventures also benefit corporations by reducing their capital investment.

However, the basic structure of dependence on multinationals for exports remains intact so that stage IV Chinese export-led growth remains distinct from the earlier stage I and II experiences of Germany, Japan, and the East Asian Tigers. This dependence is illustrated in Table 1 which provides a decomposition of Chinese exports and imports by ownership structure. Foreign-owned firms account for 50.4% of Chinese exports, and that rises to 76.7% if joint ventures are included.

TABLE 1
Decomposition by firm ownership structure of Chinese exports and imports in 2005

	All firms	*State-owned*	*Private domestic*	*Joint ventures*	*Foreign-owned*
Exports	100%	10.3	13.1	26.3	50.4
Imports	100%	21.7	7.1	24.1	47.2

Source: Manova and Zhang, 2008.

THE FALL OF EXPORT-LED GROWTH

So far the analysis has been backward looking. This section peers into the future. For past several decades export-led growth has been a relatively successful development strategy, but there have also been clear signs of fraying. Though China has done well, stage III participants (like Mexico) have been less successful. This is illustrated in Table 2 which shows China has had rapid Gross Domestic Product (GDP) growth, rapid labor productivity growth due to rapid capital accumulation, and rapid total factor productivity (TFP) growth reflecting a dynamic economy characterized by technical advance. In contrast, Mexico has not recovered its strong performance of 1960-1980. Since 1980 GDP growth has been sluggish, labor productivity has been unchanged, and TFP growth has been negative.

TABLE 2
Relative performance of Mexico (stage III) and China (stage IV)
(percentages)

	GDP growth		*Labor productivity growth*		*Total factor productivity growth*		
	1950-1980	*1980-2008*	*1950-1980*	*1980-2008*	*1960-1980*	*1980-1989*	*1990-2004*
Mexico	6.4	2.6	3.1	–0.1	1.6	–2.4	–0.6
China	4.9	8.5	2.0	6.7	0.6	4.2	4.7

Source: Palma (2010).

Looking into the future, there are reasons to believe the export-led growth strategy is exhausted for all. The reason is changed conditions in both the developing economies and the developed economies.

The financial crash of 2008 and the accompanying Great Recession represent a watershed moment and have created an over-arching structural condition of global demand shortage. The U.S. economy is debt saturated. Europe is constrained by fiscal austerity and is itself wedded to export-led growth via Germany. Japan continues to suffer from and weak internal demand, has an aging population, and it is also still hooked on export-oriented growth. This combination augurs for stagnation in the industrialized economies.

Emerging market economies have continued growing on the back of their export-led growth strategies but the positive factors are likely to prove temporary. EM economies benefitted significantly from recovery of trade after the trade collapse of 2009. They are also benefitting from high commodity prices that have bounced back with trade, and commodity prices have further strengthened because commodities are viewed as a speculative hedge against inflation. Lastly, EM countries are benefitting from interest rate compression produced by the crisis. This rate compression will likely be a permanent benefit, but the trade bounce is a one-off benefit and realization of the prospect of stagnation will likely take the inflation premium out of commodities. At that stage, EM economies as a group will face structural impediments that make export-led growth collectively impossible.

The export-led growth model is now afflicted with several structural problems. Problem number one is the debt saturation of U.S. consumers. The model relied on robust consumer markets in developed economies (particularly the U.S.) to buy the exports and justify FDI. For twenty-five years those markets were artificially strong, fuelled by rising debt and asset price inflation. That pattern was unsustainable and it is now over, leaving a hole in the logic of the export-led model.

Problem number two is the relative size of the EM economies. They have become such a large share of the global economy that their exports are now driving a hole in the industrialized economies and sabotaging the recovery of those economies. This is illustrated in Tables 3 and 4. Table 3 shows the evolution of developed economy and emerging market plus developing economy shares of global GDP. The latter's share has risen from 30.1 percent in 1980 to 50.8 percent in 2008. Their share of global economic activity therefore makes it difficult for the group to rely on export-led growth.

TABLE 3
The changing composition of global GDP based on purchasing power parity (PPP)
(billions of current dollars)

	1980	*1990*	*2000*	*2008*
World	12.961	26.988	45.205	77.109
Advanced economies	7.896 (60.9%)	16.242 (60.2%)	26.071 (57.7%)	37.900 (49.2%)
EM and developing countries	5.064 (39.1%)	10.746 (39.8%)	19.133 (42.3%)	

Source: IMF, *World Economic Outlook Database*, October 2007 and author's calculations.

Table 4 shows the changing composition of world trade. Non-Organization for Economic Co-operation and Development (OECD) country exports have risen from 25.1% of total in 1995 to 36.4 percent in 2008. Their share of world imports has risen more slowly from 26.2 to 33.2 percent. As a bloc these countries are running trade surpluses and they are still significantly dependent on exports for growth despite their larger size.[2]

TABLE **4**
The changing composition of world trade
(percentages)

		1995	*2000*	*2005*	*2008*
Exports	G-7	48.9	46.4	40.1	36.4
	OECD	74.9	72.2	66.9	63.6
	Non- OECD	25.1	27.8	33.1	36.4
Imports	G-7	48.7	50.0	45.0	40.1
	OECD	73.8	75.0	71.1	66.8
	Non- OECD	26.2	25.0	28.9	33.2

Source: OECD, *Economic Outlook 87 database,* June 2010.

In effect, the NAFTA globalization model has created a divided world where the consumers are in the North and producers are in the South. In the era of globalization expanding productive capacity is now relatively easy owing to technological innovations that have increased the mobility of capital and managerial expertise. The more difficult challenge is the structural Keynesian challenge of creating an income and demand generation process that supports productive capacity (Palley, 2006).

Nor is China likely to become the engine of growth because its growth model is still that of an assembler focused on supplying industrialized country consumers. This is illustrated in Figure 3 which provides a stylized representation of the new China-centric global supply chain. East Asian

---

2 In Table 4 non-OECD proxies for EM and developing economies. However, Mexico, South Korea and Turkey are members of the OECD. If their exports and imports were subtracted from the OECD and added to the non- OECD, the trade share of EM and developing economies would increase further.

country exports go to China and China's exports then go to the industrialized economies.

FIGURE 3
Stylized representation of the new China-centric global supply chain

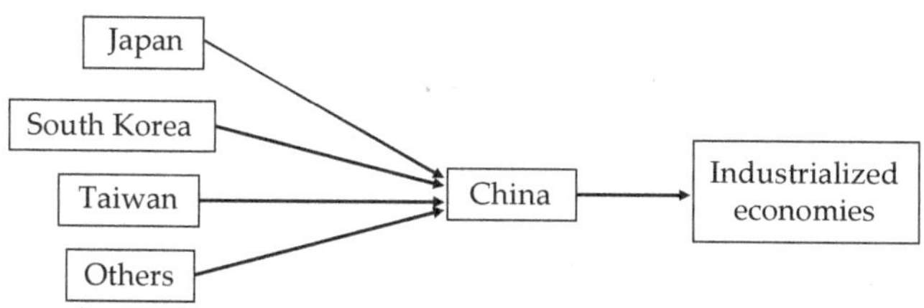

This pattern of trade is supported by evidence in Table 5 which analyzes the changing composition of East Asian exports. The share of East Asian exports going to China has been rising, reflecting China's assembly role. However, the share of Chinese exports going to East Asia has been falling, reflecting China's reliance on consumers in industrialized economies.

TABLE 5
The changing pattern of East Asian trade: percent of total exports going to East Asia and China
(percentages)

Exporter	*East Asia 1990-1994*	*East Asia 2000-2004*	*China 1990-1994*	*China 2000-2004*
East Asia	44.1	49.0	6.4	11.1
China	60.5	45.3	n.a.	n.a.

Source: Haddad, M., 2007. Trade integration in East Asia: the role of China and production networks. World Bank Policy Research Working Paper no. 4160.

Problem number three is the declining relative price of manufactured goods. With the export-led growth strategy being so widely adopted, this is contributing to a new Prebisch (1950) and Singer (1950) declining terms of trade problem similar to the one that afflicted commodity producing developing countries in the first half of the 20th century. During that period the relative price of primary commodities fell as supply increased. Now the problem is increased supply of low technology manufactured goods (Sarkar and Singer, 1991).

Problem number four is what globalization critics term the "global race to the bottom". Because it is so easy for MNCs to shift production between countries, that has created a "race to the bottom" dynamic in which developing countries undermine each other. Each country is trying to get competitive advantage through a combination of wage suppression; suppression of labor, environmental and social standards; suppression of business regulation; shifting of tax burdens onto labor income away from capital income; creation of extra-judicial export processing zones; and competitive devaluations that create financial instability. Since all do it, none gains significant competitive advantage. Instead, this destructive competitive dynamic undermines the development of standards, institutions, income equality and wage growth that are needed for deeply rooted development. The only beneficiaries are MNCs whose profit margins are increased.

Finally, problem number five is the adoption of export-led growth by China. Because China's labor force is so large and its wages so low, and because the prospect of producing for China's large domestic market is so commercially attractive, China is siphoning FDI and demand away from other emerging market economies. That is undermining their industrialization and development. China's emergence poses two problems for other developing and EM economies. First, its size blocks access to the traditional ladder of development for newcomers. Second, its entrance on the global stage has introduced South-South competition to go along with North- South competition. That explains why the benefits of export-led growth have been so limited for stage III countries like Mexico.

One benefit from China for developing economies is that China's relentless urbanization is likely to create persistent upward pressure on commodity prices. The urbanization process will require energy resources for power and transportation, and iron ore, copper, and lumber for construction.

However, even that is a mixed blessing. First, it will only benefit EM and developing economies with these resources. Second, it stands to create "Dutch disease" in these economies by appreciating their exchange rates, something that is already clearly visible in Brazil and Chile. That will actually undermine these countries' industrialization and development and recreate an international division of labor paralleling that created in the 19th century by British industrialization.

In sum, for a developing country beginning the process of industrialization thirty years ago, export-led growth offered a reasonable bet. Its endowment and resources would have been significantly different from developed economies, and the U.S. economy was about to embark on a thirty year consumption spree. Now, a newcomer must compete with many EM countries that are already on the ladder of industrialization and have similar resource endowments. Above all, it must compete with China. Moreover, that competition must take place in an environment where developed economies are debt-saturated in both the private and public sector.

THE CASE FOR DOMESTIC DEMAND-LED GROWTH

The implication of these arguments is the export-led growth paradigm is exhausted for developing countries. It also risks serious harm to the global economy. That means there is need to shift from export-led growth to a domestic demand-led growth model. This does not mean the abandonment of exporting. Countries will always need exports to pay for needed imported inputs and final goods they do not produce. However, it does mean building up the domestic demand side of the economy and reducing reliance on strategies aimed at attracting export-oriented FDI.

The outline elements of a domestic demand-led strategy are clear (Palley, 2002):

a) Build social safety nets that diminish need for precautionary saving.
b) Raise wages and link wages to productivity growth by implementing a minimum wage, improving labor protections, and increasing collective bargaining via unions.

c) Increase public infrastructure investment and fill the backlog of public investment opportunities resulting from twenty-five years of neglect imposed by the neoliberal Washington Consensus development model.
d) Increase the provision of public goods –like healthcare and education.
e) Rebalance tax structures by increasing taxes on higher income groups and lowering them on lower income groups.

In the international economy there is need to:

a) End under-valued exchange rates and adopt a system of managed exchange rates aimed at avoiding global imbalances in trade.
b) End policies of international labor competition via implementation of global labor standards.
c) Implement global environmental and social standards that block international competition on these margins.
d) Limit incentives to attract export-oriented FDI.

However, though it is clear what is needed, there are tremendous political obstacles preventing change. First, EM economies are unwilling to give up a strategy that has worked so well and has not yet been proven to fail. If a policy is successful, political calculus suggests it is unlikely to be abandoned until it fails. That is because abandonment means costs now for the sake of avoiding hypothetical future larger costs, which is not politically compelling.

Second, there is also resentment that EM economies are being asked to change when they still have far lower income per capita income. Third, no individual country has an incentive to abandon export-led growth and adopt these types of policy measures for fear of being the only country to do so. Indeed, each individual country has an incentive to cheat on such measures and pursue an export-led growth strategy by itself. In effect, there is a collective action problem. The only way to get a global shift to a new growth model is to establish and enforce multilateral rules on exchange rates, and standards on acceptable labor, tax and environmental competition. However, getting agreement on such rules and standards is unlikely.

In addition to these political obstacles to change, there are also structural obstacles. Once countries embark on the path of export-led growth it seems to be very difficult to change strategies. For example, Germany and Japan are still focused on exporting, continuously running large trade surpluses fifty years after having adopted the export-led model and long after they have become top tier high income countries. One possible explanation is that once export-oriented industries acquire dominance they gain political control, while the institutions and political interests that would promote domestic demand-led growth remain weak.

CONCLUSIONS AND PREDICTIONS

The above analysis suggests four conclusions and three predictions. Conclusion number one is the export-led growth paradigm is exhausted because of changed conditions in both EM and developed economies.

Conclusion number two is EM economies are mistaken in their belief that they can collectively continue to grow on the basis of export-led growth. It will not deliver success for them and it will further impede the task of economic recovery in the developed countries.

Conclusion number three is there is need for a major recalibration of the global economy that abandons export-led growth and replaces it with a new paradigm of domestic demand-led growth.

Conclusion number four is globalization has so diversified global economic activity that no country or region can act as the lone locomotive of global growth. A diversified global economy requires that all regions pull together.

These conclusions support the following three predictions. Prediction number one is for political reasons, it is highly unlikely that EM countries will shift away from export-led growth, and nor will the international community agree on the international arrangements needed to make a domestic demand-led growth paradigm work. The fact is once a country has adopted export-led growth it appears near impossible to abandon it.

Prediction number two is failure to recalibrate the global economy is likely to produce a political backlash in the industrialized countries, particularly in the U.S. where the public has lost political patience because adjustment by China has been delayed too long.

Prediction number three is the global economy is likely to experience asymmetric stagnation marked by slower growth in EM economies, stagnation in developed economies, and increased economic tensions between EM and industrialized economies.

REFERENCES

Bhagwati, J., 1958. Immizerizing growth: a geometrical note. *Review of Economic Studies*, 58, pp. 201-5.

Blecker, R.A., 2000. The diminishing returns to export-led growth. Paper prepared for the Project on Development, Trade, and International Finance the Council of Foreign Relations Working Group on Development. New York: Council on Foreign Relations.

Blecker, R.A. and Razmi, A., 2010. Export-led growth, real exchange rates and the fallacy of composition. In: Setterfield, M., ed. *Handbook of Alternative Theories of Economic Growth*, Cheltenham: Edward Elgar.

Brewer, A., 1985. Trade with fixed real wages and mobile capital. *Journal of International Economics*, 18, pp. 177-86.

Chang, H.-J., 2002. *Kicking Away the Ladder: Development Strategy in Historical Perspective.* London: Anthem Press.

Dornbusch, R., Fischer, S. and Samuelson, P.A., 1980. "Heckscher- Ohlin Trade Theory with a continuum of goods. *Quarterly Journal of Economics*, 95, pp. 203-24.

Grossman, G.M. and Helpman, E., 1991. Trade, knowledge spillovers and growth. *European Economic Review*, 35 (May), pp. 517-26.

Hein, E. and Truger, A., 2005. A different view of germany's stagnation. *Challenge*, 48, pp. 64-94.

Hein, E., and Truger, A., 2010. Finance-dominated capitalism in crisis: the case for a Keynesian New Deal at the European and the global level. Berlin School of Economics and Law Working Paper no. 6. Berlin: Berlin School of Economics and Law.

Johnson, H., 1954. Increasing productivity, income-price trends and trade balance. *Economic Journal*, 64, pp. 462-85.

Johnson, H., 1955. Economic expansion and international trade. *Manchester School of Economic and Social Studies*, 23, pp. 95-112.

Kaplinsky, R., 1993. Export processing zones in the dominican republic: transforming manufactures into commodities. *World Development*, 21, pp. 1851-65.

Krueger, A. O., 1974. "The political economy of rent-seeking society. *American Economic Review*, 64, pp. 291-303.

Krugman, P., 1984. "Import protection as export promotion: international competition in the presence of oligopoly and economies of scale. In Kierzkowski, H., ed. *Monopolistic Competition in International Trade.* Oxford: Oxford University Press, pp. 180-93.

Lipsey, R.G. and Lancaster, K., 1956-57. The General Theory of the Second Best. *Review of Economic Studies*, 24, pp. 11-32.

Manova, K., and Zhang, Z., 2008. "China's exporters and importers: firms, products, and trade partners. [unpublished manuscript]. June 2008. Stanford, CA: Department of Economics, Stanford University.

Milberg, W., 2002. Say's Law in the open economy: Keynes' rejection of the Theory of Comparative Advantage. In: Dow S. and Hillard, J. eds. *Beyond Keynes*, Aldershot: Edward Elgar.

Ohlin, B., 1933. *Interregional and International Trade.* Cambridge, Massachusetts: Harvard University Press.

Palley, T.I., 2002. Domestic demand-led growth: a new paradigm for development. In: Weaver J. and Baker, J. eds. New Rules for Global Finance. Washington, DC: New Rules for Global Finance. (Also published as: A new development paradigm: domestic demand-led growth [online]. September 2002. Foreign Policy in Focus (FPIF) Discussion Paper. Washington, DC: FPIF. Available in: <http://www.fpif.org/>).

Palley, T.I., 2003a. International trade, macroeconomics, and exchange rates: re-examining the foundations of trade policy. Paper presented at a Conference on Globalization and the Myths of Free Trade held at the New School for Social Research, April 18. New York: New School for Social Research.

Palley, T.I., 2003b. Export-led growth: evidence of developing country crowding-out? In: Arestis, P., Baddeley, M. y McCombie, J. eds. *Globalization, Regionalism, and Economic Activity.* Cheltenham: Edward Elgar.

Palley, T.I., 2004. The economic case for International Labor Standards. *Cambridge Journal of Economics*, 28 (January), pp. 21-36.

Palley, T.I., 2006. Capital accumulation is not enough: developing the domestic market. *Challenge*, November-December, pp. 20-34.

Palma, G., 2010. "Why has productivity growth stagnated in most Latin American countries since Neoliberal reforms? Cambridge Working Papers in Economics no. 1030. Cambridge: Department of Applied Economics, Cambridge University.

Prasch, R.E., 1996. Reassessing the Theory of Comparative Advantage. *Review of Political Economy*, 8(1), pp. 37-54.

Prebisch, R., 1950. *The Economic Development of Latin America and its Principle Problem*. Santiago: United Nations Economic Commission for Latin America (UNECLA).

Robinson, J., 1947 [1937]. *Essays in the Theory of Employment*, 2nd edition, Oxford: Basil Blackwell.

Salas, C. and Zepeda, E., 2003. Employment and wages in contemporary Mexico. In: Salas, C. and de la Garza, E. coords. *State of Working Mexico, 2003*. Washington, DC: Solidarity Center.

Samuelson, P.A., 1948. International trade and equalisation of factor prices. *Economic Journal*, 58, p. 163-84.

Sapsford, D. and Singer, H., 1998. The IMF, the World Bank, and commodity prices: a case of Shifting Sands?" *World Development*, 26, pp. 1653-60.

Sarkar, P. and Singer, H., 1991. Manufactured exports of developing countries and their terms of trade since 1965. *World Development*, 19, pp. 333-40.

Singer, H., 1950. The distribution of gains between investing and borrowing countries. *American Economic Review (Papers and Proceedings)*, 40, pp. 473-85.

Stolper, W.F., and P.A. Samuelson, 1941. Protection and real wages. *Review of Economic Studies*, 9, pp. 58-73.

[16]

A Labor Perspective on Globalization

THOMAS I. PALLEY

The Debate on Globalization

Globalization is an enormously controversial subject that is usually presented in terms of technical economic arguments. Aside from being difficult to grasp, conventional economic arguments tend to misrepresent the issue by painting it as a simple pro- versus anti-globalization debate, when the reality is more complex.

For these reasons, the debate on globalization is better viewed through a political lens, in terms of which different political camps emphasize different economic concerns. Considered in such a way there are three major perspectives, as illustrated in Figure 1. At the most fundamental level there is a divide between those who see the current structure of globalization as »sound« and those who see it as »problematic.«

Figure 1
The Debate on Globalization

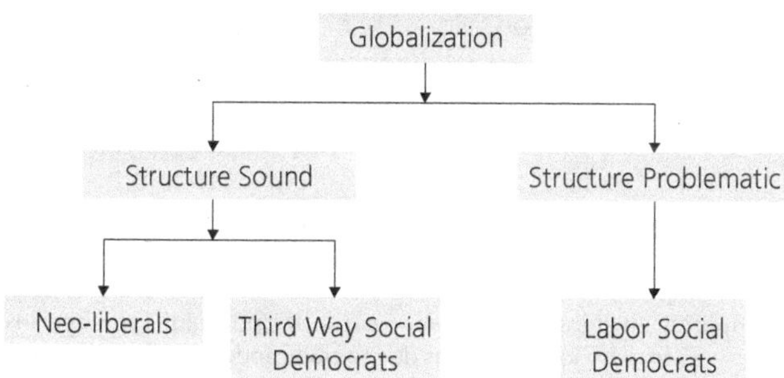

Those viewing globalization as sound can be subdivided into »neo-liberals« and »Third Way social democrats.« Neo-liberals believe that globalization is delivering its promised benefits, that in general all benefit, both within and between countries, and that globalization should continue full steam ahead in its current form.[1]

Third Way social democrats also believe that globalization is fundamentally sound and delivers positive net benefits to all countries.[2] However, within countries there are some losers, although total losses are less than total gains. For Third Way social democrats the policy implication is that globalization should continue as is, subject to making compassionate »helping-hand« policy adjustments that target help to those who lose out.[3]

Balanced against these two perspectives is a »labor social democrat« perspective that maintains that the current structure of globalization is fundamentally problematic and therefore needs deeper architectural change. The main features of a labor social democrat perspective are:

1. The current pattern of globalization is hurting many working families and widening social divisions by increasing income inequality.
2. The debate on the size of net gains or losses from globalization misses the point; nor is it an issue of stopping globalization. Instead, the issue is that globalization is being wrongly constructed, and the challenge is to construct a better globalization.
3. Globalization alone does not explain the adverse changes in growth and income distribution, and globalization should not be looked at in isolation. Instead, globalization should be seen as a core element in a new neo-liberal economic paradigm that has been implemented post-1980.

   That means that the debate on globalization is ultimately about replacing the larger economic paradigm, which includes the current approach to globalization.

The analytical split among social democrats regarding globalization creates major political difficulties for labor because it internally splits the parties that have traditionally represented labor's interests. This holds for

1. The neo-liberal perspective is exemplified by the US Chamber of Commerce.
2. The Third Way social democrat perspective is exemplified by the Brookings Institute in Washington, DC.
3. An example of »helping-hand« policy is the US proposal for wage insurance, whereby workers who lose their jobs due to trade and suffer wage losses would be compensated by government (Kletzer and Rosen 2005). The argument is that the costs of such programs can be paid for by taxes levied on those who have benefited from globalization. That way everyone can win since the overall gains exceed the losses.

the Social Democratic Party in Germany, the Labour Party in the United Kingdom, and the Democratic Party in the United States.[4]

As a result, social democrats have been put in a position of structural weakness as regards neo-liberal political parties, and this split confronts labor with a major political conundrum. For labor, the political choices are: (a) have social democrats stick together in fractious union and face the likelihood of steady erosion of historic social democratic aspirations; (b) split and risk full-blown neo-liberal political triumph; or (c) recapture social democratic parties by establishing a new economic consensus.

Economic Trends in the Era of Globalization

It is difficult to talk meaningfully about the global economy because of its diversity. One important fact (see Tables 1 and 2) is that average annual global economic growth has been slower post-1973 than in the period 1950–73 (Madison 2001). With regard to income distribution the consensus is that income inequality has been widening within countries (Anand and Segal 2008: 86) and across most countries (Milanovic 2005).[5]

Africa has experienced special political and governance difficulties related to corruption and civil strife, and it has suffered especially sharp deterioration in economic performance despite international economic

4. This split emerged with the political triumphs between 1979 and 1982 of Margaret Thatcher, Ronald Reagan, and Helmut Kohl. That triumph initiated the two-decade-long political dominance of conservative economic ideology, and some social democrats made the decision to embrace part of that ideology. Their argument was that it provided a needed modernization of social democratic thinking, as well as a tactical avenue for regaining political power. The Third Way conversation of Prime Minister Blair, President Clinton, and Chancellor Schröder can be viewed as an attempt to permanently seal this tactical decision by making it the official social democratic creed.
5. China and India have grown very rapidly since 1980. Their large size increases the overall weighted average global growth rate, and also reduces inequality between countries. However, both countries have experienced major increases in inequality within their borders. These two enormous countries complicate the discussion because they grew fast without adopting neo-liberal policies; they did adopt market reforms, however, and also joined the global economy. Their strong performance raises questions concerning whether their growth has been due to adopting market economy principles, their particular combination of state planning plus market forces, or globalization.

Table 1

Growth of GDP: World and Major Regions, 1950–98 (%)

	1950–73	*1973–98*
US	3.96	2.90
Western Europe	4.81	2.11
Japan	9.29	2.97
Asia ex-Japan	5.18	5.46
Latin America	5.33	3.02
Africa	4.45	2.74
World	4.91	3.01

Source: Madison (2001), 126 and 138.

Table 2

Growth of Per Capita GDP: World and Major Regions, 1950–98 (%)

	1950–73	*1973–98*
US	2.50	2.00
Western Europe	4.08	1.78
Japan	8.05	2.34
Asia ex-Japan	2.92	3.54
Latin America	2.52	0.99
Africa	2.07	0.01
World	2.93	1.33

Source: Madison (2001), 126 and 132.

opening. This shows that openness and global integration do not reduce corruption. Instead, opting for global integration may even worsen corruption by increasing the financial stakes and thereby aggravating the »natural resource curse« that afflicts so many developing countries.

Regional income inequality has increased almost everywhere. Table 3 shows how income shares for the fifth and tenth (top) deciles of the income distribution evolved between 1980 and 2000 in the OECD, Latin America and the Caribbean, East Asia and the Pacific, Africa, and Central and Eastern Europe. In all regions the income share of the fifth decile decreased between 1980 and 2000, while the income share of the tenth decile increased. This pattern resulted in further income inequality measured by the ratio of the incomes of the fifth to tenth deciles. Africa has the highest income inequality, followed by Latin America and the Caribbean. The OECD has the lowest income inequality, but inequality has been increasing.

Table 3

Evolution of Fifth and Tenth (Top) Decile Income Shares, 1980–2000

	OECD	*LAC*	*EAP*	*AFR*	*ECE*
Decile 5 – 1980	7.6 %	4.9 %	5.6 %	4.0 %	8.1 %
Decile 5 – 2000	7.2 %	4.7 %	5.4 %	3.1 %	6.5 %
Ratio 2000/1980	0.95	0.96	0.96	0.77	0.80
Decile 10 – 1980	25.7 %	41.6 %	41.2 %	51.6 %	22.7 %
Decile 10 – 2000	28.3 %	43.6 %	41.3 %	54.4 %	30.9 %
Ratio 2000/1980	1.10	1.05	1.00	1.05	1.36
5/10 Ratio 1980	0.30	0.12	0.14	0.08	0.36
5/10 Ratio – 2000	0.25	0.11	0.14	0.06	0.21

Note: LAC = Latin America & Caribbean, EAP = East Asia & Pacific, AFR = Africa, ECE = East & Central Europe.

Source: Dikhanov (2005) and author's calculations.

In many regards the US exemplifies the problematic trends of the last three decades. US median family income evolved relative to an index of productivity over the period 1947–2005. Until the late 1970s the two series moved together, but since then median family income has become detached from productivity (Figure 2).[6]

Figure 3 shows how average hourly compensation of production and non-supervisory workers evolved relative to productivity between 1959 and 2005. Such workers represent 80 percent of employment, and total compensation encompasses all benefits, including health insurance. Once again, compensation and productivity tracked closely until the late 1970s, but thereafter compensation stagnated while productivity continued to grow.

6. Figures 2, 3, and 4 are from the Economic Policy Institute, Washington, DC.

Figure 2

Median Family Income and Productivity, 1947–2005

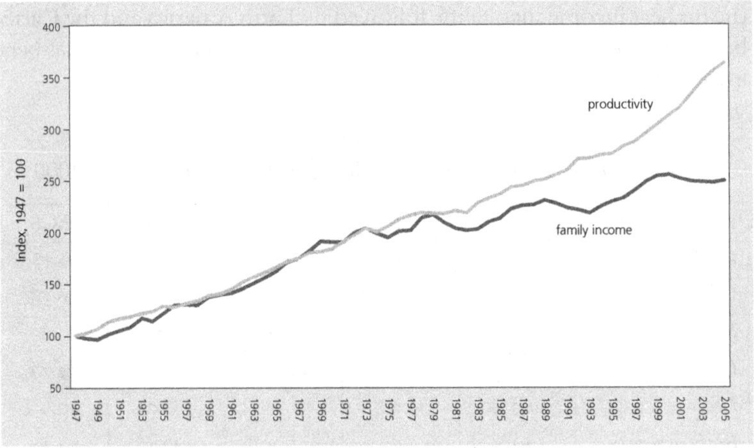

Figure 3

Index of Productivity and Hourly Compensation of Production and Non-supervisory Workers, 1959–2005

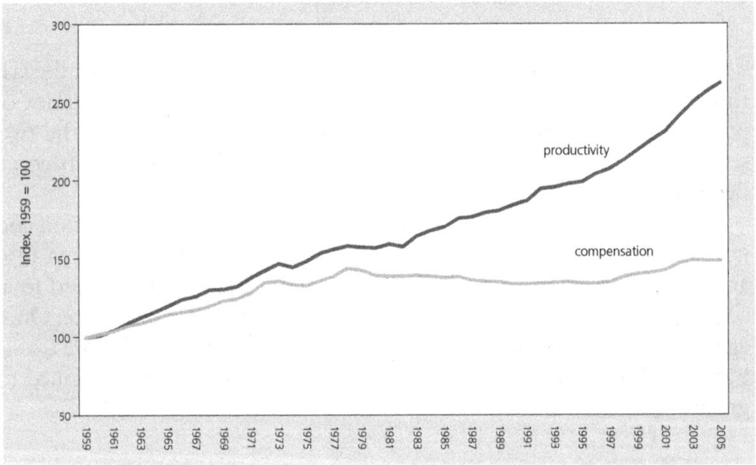

Figure 4

Index of Low Family Income & High Family Income, 1947–2005

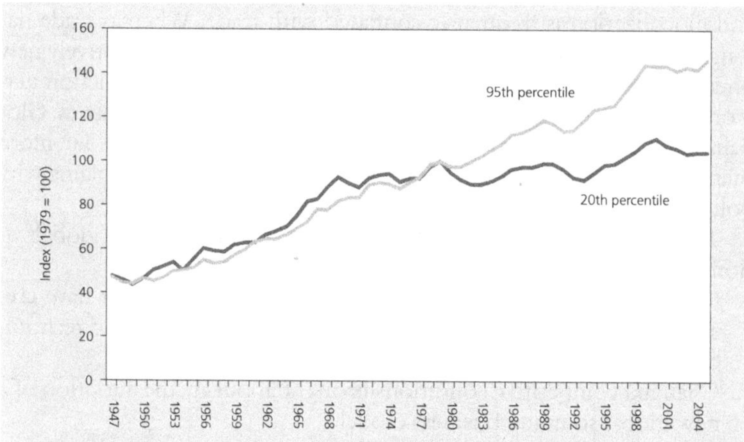

Source: Mishel et al. (2007): *The State of Working America 2006/2007*, an Economic Policy Institute book. Ithaca, NY: Cornell University Press.

Finally, Figure 4 illustrates the evolution of low family income (20th percentile) and high family income (95th percentile) for the period 1947–2005. Again, the two tracked together until the late 1970s, but since then low family income has stagnated while high family income has grown rapidly. The result of this divergence has been a widening of income inequality.

The core problem afflicting the US economy is the disconnection of worker wages from productivity post-1980. That disconnect explains wage stagnation and rising income inequality, and a similar disconnect probably affects many other industrialized countries. Restoring the link between wages and productivity growth represents labor's central challenge in the era of globalization.

The New Economics of Globalization

Globalization is widely believed to be a contributory factor in these adverse wage and income inequality developments, and the implementation of appropriate policy remedies therefore requires an understanding of the economics of globalization.

Unfortunately, the economics of globalization is not well understood and globalization is frequently conflated with trade. Whereas trade has long been part of the global economy, globalization is a qualitatively new phenomenon involving the creation of globally flexible production networks in which production can be readily shifted between countries. Globalization could not proceed without it, but globalization is far more than trade. Treating globalization as if it was simply trade explains why policy has come up short and failed to address the challenges.

The new global production networks that are the essence of globalization involve three main building blocks:

1. Changed technological and organizational conditions that have created a new world of »barge economics« in which capital and technology are globally mobile.
2. Changed competitive conditions brought about by the adoption of a new global sourcing business model.
3. Neo-liberal trade and financial policies that have removed barriers to international movements of goods and money.

The troubling effects of these systemic changes have been further amplified by the addition of two billion workers to the global labor supply owing to the end of economic isolationism in China, India, and the former Soviet bloc (see below).

Barge Economics: The New Model of Production[7]

According to classical theory the pattern of trade is explained by the principle of comparative advantage: all can benefit when countries specialize in producing those things in which they have a comparative advantage. A key assumption is that the means of production (capital and technology) are internationally immobile (that is, fixed in each country).

Globalization challenges this assumption, thereby deconstructing classical trade theory's foundation. Jack Welch, former CEO of General Electric, captured the new reality when he talked of ideally having »every plant you own on a barge.« Welch envisioned factories floating between countries to take advantage of the lowest costs, be they due to undervalued exchange rates, low taxes, subsidies, or low wages.

7. This section draws on Palley 2008a, 2008d.

Globalization has made Welch's barge a reality, creating a new world of »barge economics.« In this new world, capital mobility determines the pattern of trade rather than comparative advantage, with factories moving to wherever costs are lowest. As a result, so-called »free trade« increasingly trades jobs, which move with the barge.

Additionally, barge economics promotes downward equalization of wages and standards by fundamentally changing the balance of bargaining power between workers and corporations, and by changing the margins of competition between countries. Think of two swimming pools with different levels of water: barge economics joins the pools together, causing the water to equalize at the lower level.

Global Sourcing: The New Model for Buying[8]

Global sourcing is a second critical element of globalization. Barge economics represents a new model of global production (the supply side). Global sourcing represents a new model of buying (the demand side). Together they leverage each other and fundamentally change the nature of global competition.

Global sourcing has evolved gradually over the past sixty years, beginning with the growth of multinational corporations in the 1950s and 1960s. The role of multinationals has received much attention, but less noticed and equally important is the »retail revolution« based on so-called »big box« discount stores, exemplified by Wal-Mart. These stores have been a key driver of globalization.

Wal-Mart was established in 1962, and it immediately created a »national buying« model in terms of which it bought goods from manufacturers all around the US, thereby placing manufacturers in a nationally competitive market. In the 1980s big box discounters like Wal-Mart shifted to a global buying model, changing the scale of the phenomenon. This global buying model has big box discount retailers scour the world for the lowest price (the so-called »China Price«), which puts countries in competition. This creates North-North competition, North-South competition, and South-South competition, and puts each country's entire manufacturing sector in international competition. As a result, the global buying model erodes manufacturing jobs and wages, and its commercial success forces all retailers to adopt it or face elimination.

8. This section draws on Palley 2008c.

Offshore outsourcing represents an application of the retailers' global sourcing model to manufacturing. It is exemplified by recent developments in the US auto-parts industry that have affected companies such as Delphi and Visteon. These companies were originally subsidiaries of General Motors and Ford. In the 1990s they were spun off and placed in national competition with other US parts makers, but still retained some preferential supply-standing with their former corporate parents. That standing has now been abandoned and Delphi and Visteon have been placed in international competition, with General Motors and Ford asking their former in-house parts suppliers to meet the »China Price« or lose the business.

The same process is occurring in aerospace, with Boeing's new 787 Dreamliner being sourced on a global basis. Peering into the future, trade in services looks like being the next area of application of the global sourcing model, and the Internet means even retail can potentially be out-sourced.

The Role of International Economic Policy

The third critical element in the creation of the new global economic system is trade and international financial policy. Trade policy has worked to remove barriers to cross-country movement of goods, while financial policy has worked to remove barriers to cross-country movement of finance. Trade policy has also worked to secure property rights and investors' rights.

These policy developments have been essential for globalization, and they have leveraged and multiplied the effects of barge economics and global sourcing. Absent these policy changes, global production networks would be far less viable owing to the costs of moving goods, lack of investor confidence, and inability to finance these arrangements.

Two Billion Additional Workers

By itself the abovementioned economic cocktail would have produced downward pressure on wages and income distribution. However, these structural changes have been accompanied by the addition of two billion additional workers resulting from the end of economic isolationism in India, China, and the former Soviet bloc, which makes their effect even greater. Moreover, this labor supply impact can be expected to continue for years as the process of absorbing so many workers will take decades. China has played an especially significant role as it alone has approximately 750 million active workers and is a preferred location for MNC production. That has resulted in a flood of capital and technology into China, which has made it the global low price supplier for big box retailers and increasingly for manufacturing outsourcing. This impact is exacerbated by China's specific economic policies that encourage export-led growth and inflows of foreign investment through an undervalued exchange rate, wage suppression, and unfair trading practices such as subsidies, domestic content requirements, and production offsets.

Finally, China's impact afflicts both North and South. With regard to the North, China competes with large segments of Northern manufacturing, causing job losses and reduced investment. With regard to the South, China attracts foreign investment that might otherwise have gone to other developing countries, while its policies of export-led growth lower the price of low-end manufactured goods that are also produced by other developing countries. China's huge labor surplus pulls down wages in the North, while preventing them from rising in the South.

Globalization as Part of Neo-liberalism

Globalization is often talked of as if it were a natural phenomenon. Such talk distorts understanding and diminishes the political space for alternatives. Not only is globalization significantly a policy creation, but it should also be understood as an integral part of a larger neo-liberal policy agenda. Thus, globalization fits into a larger economic policy program developed by corporate elites and aimed at benefiting business. That makes globalization as much a product of corporate planning as of the invisible hand.

The neo-liberal policy program can be described as »boxing in« workers, as illustrated in Figure 5.[9] Workers are put inside the box and are then pressured on all four sides. The left side of the box has globalization pressuring workers through international competition. The right side has workers pressured by the push for small government, which aims to shrink the size of the public sector, lower public sector wages, and reduce

9. The notion of the neo-liberal box is attributable to Ron Blackwell of the AFL-CIO (American Federation of Labor and Congress of Industrial Organizations).

Figure 5

The »Neo-liberal« Policy Box

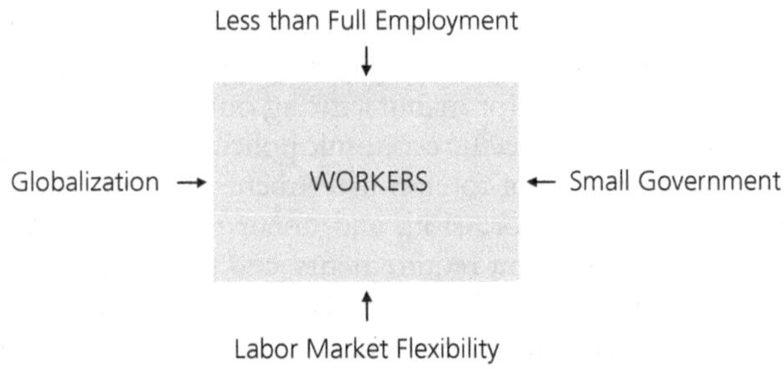

public sector provision of services. The upper edge has workers pressured by a retreat from the commitment to full employment, which is replaced by a focus on low inflation that is justified ideologically on the grounds of a »natural rate of unemployment.« Finally, the lower edge of the box pushes for labor market flexibility that principally aims to weaken unions and labor market protection, thereby increasing the threat effect of unemployment and weakening workers' bargaining power.

Workers cannot outrun the consequences of this box, and both private and public sector workers are boxed in. All workers feel the pressure of labor market flexibility and the retreat from full employment, while private sector workers are pressured in particular by globalization and public sector workers by the push for small government. Southern workers are also pressured because the neo-liberal agenda has been applied in developing countries, too, and globalization (that is, barge economics and global sourcing) also puts Southern workers in competition with each other, as described earlier.

Governments are also boxed in. Mobility of investment and production creates fears of employment losses, while mobility of finance creates vulnerability to financial disruption. These conditions deter progressive policies (such as fair taxation and unionization) by raising their »political cost.« Moreover, it also creates »lock-in« whereby the longer a policy is in place the harder it is to reverse.

Some Comments on Germany: The Problem of Export-led Growth

The neo-liberal box provides a generic description of the neo-liberal paradigm, but there are also country-specific differences. Among industrial countries Germany represents a special situation, though it may be shared to some degree by Japan. In particular, Germany has remained a manufacturing powerhouse and is also a heavily export-oriented economy, which might lead one to believe that it benefits from neo-liberal globalization. However, closer inspection shows that globalization is problematic for Germany, too.

First, like other countries, Germany has been subject to wage competition from less developed economies, especially those in Central Europe. Thus, even Germany's famed auto and engineering sectors have felt the threat effects of manufacturing relocation to Poland, Hungary, the Czech Republic, and Slovakia.

Second, Germany's export-led paradigm poses problems for the global economy that ricochet back to Germany. This is because one country's exports are another's imports, which means that not all countries can rely on export-led growth. If all try to run trade surpluses the result must be a global shortage of buyers that produces global unemployment and deflation. Moreover, even if a few try it, those few inflict a negative externality on other countries by poaching their demand.[10] Thus, Germany, which relies on the global economy to provide demand, may have weakened growth in other countries and contributed to the global financial imbalances that are behind the current financial crisis.

With global growth now weakening, Germany is feeling two significant negative effects. First, its reliance on exports and neglect of German domestic demand mean that it is vulnerable to the global economic slowdown. Second, Germany's trade surplus has made it vulnerable to financial contagion. This is because its trade surpluses were invested in US financial assets, thereby providing a corridor of contagion into the German financial system.

10. This fundamental problem was identified long ago by the economist Joan Robinson (1966) who characterized it as »beggar-thy-neighbor« economics, whereby countries rely on other countries for growth. Export-led growth also poses a problem for developing economies as they crowd each other out in trying to gain market share in industrialized economies (Palley 2003)

Ironically, Germany's trade surplus required giving up consumption, yet Germany now finds itself afflicted by financial instability and the financial assets it received for its exports are considerably reduced in value. That suggests a better outcome for Germany would have been to export less and consume more – but that requires dismantling the neo-liberal policy box so that German workers can bargain the higher wages needed to support higher consumption.

How Should Labor Respond?

The neo-liberal box is built upon economic policy, which means that changing economic policy is critical. Social policy, in the form of helping-hand policies for displaced workers, is always welcome but it cannot substitute for changing economic policy.

Repacking the Box

For labor the goal must be to replace the neo-liberal policy agenda with a social democratic agenda that repacks the box, taking workers out of the box and putting corporations and financial markets in. Such an alternative box is illustrated in Figure 6. It involves globalization with standards and restrictions on adverse forms of competition; full employment policy; restoring workers' bargaining power; and reviving a social democratic vision of government that provides generously for education, social and health insurance, public goods, and public infrastructure.

Figure 6
Repacking the Box

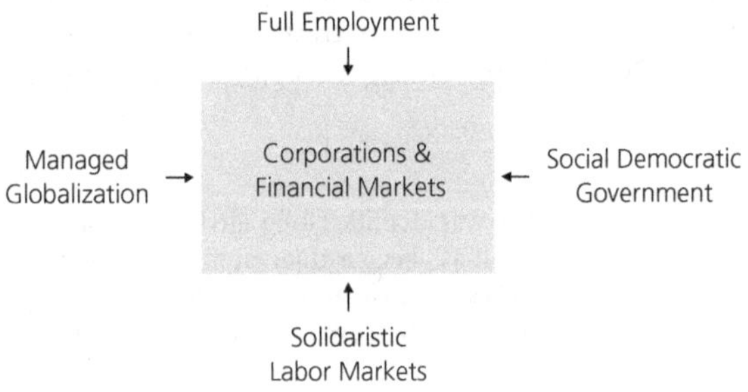

Financialization

The neo-liberal policy box represents the face of neo-liberalism, and it is tempting to immediately jump to standard policy recommendations. However, that would be a mistake. Instead, it is necessary to understand more deeply what holds the box together, and then to address those aspects.

Figure 7
Lifting the Lid and Unpacking the Box

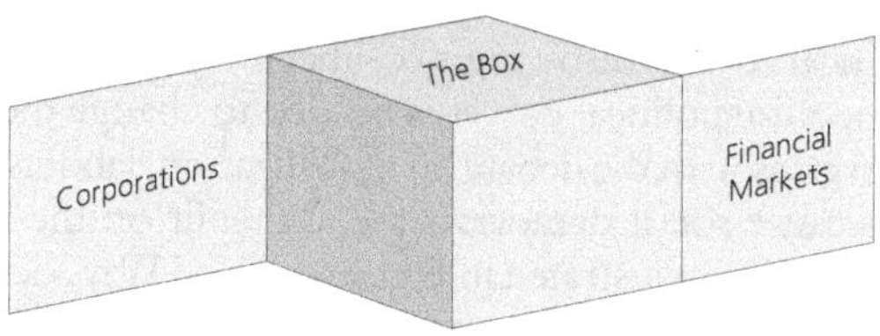

Figure 7 shows how the neo-liberal box rests on the power of corporations and financial markets, which combine in a new phenomenon that has been labeled »financialization« (Epstein 2001; Palley 2008b). Absent these side-supports the box would fold.

Figure 8
Dynamics of Financialization

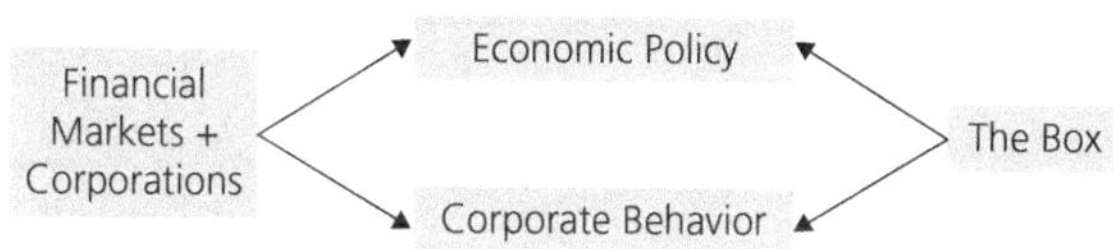

Figure 8 illustrates how financialization operates. Financial market interests have seized control of corporations, and the combination of the two drives neo-liberal policy in the political arena and short-term financially-oriented behavior in the corporate arena.

Such behaviors undermine long-run growth, put persistent downward pressure on wages, and worsen income distribution. The full nature of their deleterious effects was masked for many years by asset price inflation and rising debt that maintained demand, but they are being starkly revealed by the current financial crisis.

Analytically, the important implication is that it is not enough to re-pack the box by changing the »policy mix.« There is also need for a deeper policy agenda addressing financial markets and corporations. In a sense, financialization is the economic foundation of neo-liberalism, which means that reversing the neo-liberal paradigm requires a policy agenda addressing financial markets and corporations. That agenda must aim to re-align the behaviors of both financial markets and corporations so that they incorporate a greater public interest.

Changing the Climate of Economic Opinion

Politics is critical to overthrowing neo-liberal policy and repacking the box. This is because political power is needed to change the direction of policy. However, as with the debate on globalization, labor is again poorly positioned because social democrats are also split on the issue of neo-liberalism. This split is illustrated in Figure 9. Third Way social democrats think that the neo-liberal policy paradigm is basically sound, but is in need of some compassionate »helping-hand« policies to assist the »invisible hand.« Conversely, labor social democrats think that the neo-liberal paradigm is fundamentally misguided and the box needs repacking.

Figure 9
The Political Dilemma of Neo-liberalism

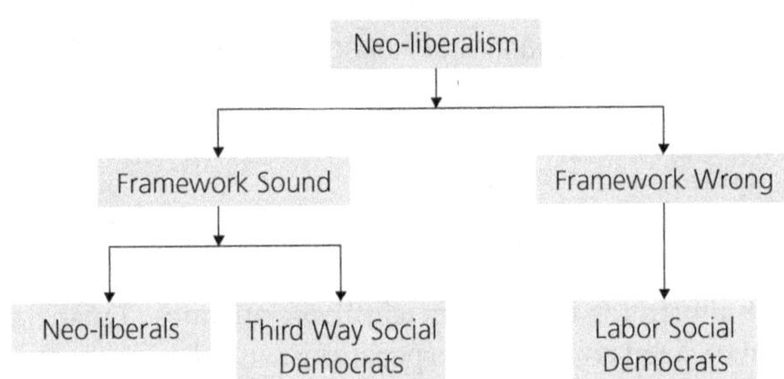

This split means that electing social democratic governments in the current environment is at best a holding strategy. More likely, neo-liberalism will continue to entrench itself inch by inch, even when social democrats are in government.

That points to the fact that standard electoral politics are insufficient. Rather, there is a need to fundamentally change the national economic policy debate. Such change requires transforming the ideas that frame economic thinking – what Friedman called the »climate of opinion.«

To use a sports metaphor, for the past thirty years neo-liberals and market fundamentalists have controlled the political playing field by conducting the national economic conversation. That control has given neo-liberals an enormous advantage, placing labor persistently on the policy defensive. It compares with the thirty years from 1945 to 1975 when the ideas of Keynes and Franklin Roosevelt's New Deal dominated thinking. During that earlier period social democrats defined the policy playing field and neo-liberals were on the defensive.

Labor's challenge is to reconfigure the political and policy playing field by recapturing the national economic conversation. That is a deeper and broader task than conventional economic policy analysis. It involves constructing a compelling economic vision supported by economic logic that justifies the policies labor advocates.

The political experience of the past two decades shows that technically good policy alone is unconvincing. Policy also needs to be connected to a logically compelling economic vision that has widespread public understanding and support. Labor has to promote and communicate that vision. History shows that if labor persuades people about how the economy works, political support will quickly be forthcoming for its policies.

The current moment of crisis and accumulated discontents opens a window for political change. However, change will be deep and long-lasting only if labor regains control of the climate of opinion. Absent change in deep economic understanding, political victory is likely to prove fragile and temporary, and easily swept away by everyday political misfortunes or sudden bad economic news. Bringing about such a change calls for a new intensive engagement with economics and economic policy by labor. That engagement has been missing for the past thirty years.

Conclusion

Labor is not opposed to globalization. It is opposed to the current pattern of globalization that too often harms working families and has contributed to the disconnection of wages from productivity growth.

This pattern of globalization is part of a larger neo-liberal economic policy paradigm that boxes workers in, undermining their bargaining power and putting persistent downward pressure on wages and working conditions. That means that the debate over globalization is ultimately part of a larger debate on neo-liberalism. The neo-liberal paradigm not only persistently pressures workers, but also tells a story that legitimizes this pressure by claiming that the economy can work only if wages are suppressed. From a neo-liberal perspective the price of employment is wage suppression. Moreover, managers are also pressured by the system so that even those firms that might want to choose a different path cannot do so because of global competitive threats. This illustrates the systemic nature of the problem. It is not a matter of fine-tuning existing policy, but rather of replacing neo-liberalism with a new economic paradigm.

References

Anand, S. and P. Segal (2008): »What Do We Know about Global Income Inequality?,« in: *Journal of Economic Literature,* 46:1: 57–94.

Dikhanov, Y. (2005): *Trends in Global Income Distribution 1970–2000, and Scenarios for 2015,* Occasional Paper, Human Development Report Office, UNDP.

Epstein, G. (2001): »Financialization, Rentier Interests, and Central Bank Policy,« manuscript, Dept. of Economics, University of Massachusetts, Amherst, MA.

Kletzer, L.G. and H. Rosen (2005): »Easing the Adjustment Burden on Workers,« in: C.F. Bergsten (ed.): *The United States and the World Economy: Foreign Economic Policy for the Next Decade.* Washington DC: Institute for International Economics.

Madison, A. (2001): *The World Economy: A Millennial Perspective,* Paris: OECD.

Milanovic, B. (2005): *Worlds Apart: Measuring International and Global Inequality.* Princeton and Oxford: Princeton University Press.

Palley, T. I. (2003): »Export-led Growth: Evidence of Developing Country Crowding-out,« in: Arestis, Badley, and McCombie (eds.): *Economic Integration, Regionalism, and Globalization.* Cheltenham: Edward Elgar.

—— (2008a): »Barge Economics: The New Economics of Globalization,« Testimony presented to the Subcommittee on Investigation and Oversight, House Committee on Science and Technology, U.S. Congress, Washington DC (June 24, 2008).

—— (2008b): »Financialization: What It Is and Why It Matters,« Working Paper 04/2008, IMK Macroeconomic Policy Institute; Düsseldorf, Germany.

—— (2008c): »The Economics of Outsourcing: How Should Policy Respond?,« in: *Review of Social Economics,* 66:3: 279–95.

—— (2008d): »Institutionalism and New Trade Theory: Rethinking Comparative Advantage and Trade Policy,« in: *Journal of Economic Issues,* XLII (March): 195–208.

Robinson, J. (1966): *The New Mercantilism. An Inaugural Lecture.* Cambridge: Cambridge University Press.

Chapter 7

LABOR IN THE GLOBAL ECONOMY

Article 7.1

THE GLOBALIZATION CLOCK

BY THOMAS PALLEY

May/June 2006; revised November 2018

Over the past forty years real wages have stagnated in developed economies, and there has also been a massive increase in income and wealth inequality. Those developments are substantially attributable to the neoliberal economic policy paradigm which has dominated policymaking. Globalization is a critical element of that paradigm, and it has been a major contributing factor to wage stagnation and increased inequality.

The neoliberal policy era did not happen in a vacuum. Instead, it needs to be explained by political economy, which shows how particular economic interests triumphed in capturing political power and the world of economic ideas (i.e. economic theory), and how those ideas and policies were accepted by society. The Globalization Clock provides a metaphor for understanding that political process as it relates to globalization. It helps explain why globalization has been so politically difficult to turn back despite its injurious effects. A key reason is globalization's adverse impact on political solidarity, with globalization aggravating the pre-existing decline in solidarity caused by the rise of the consumer society.

Political economy has historically been constructed around the divide between capital and labor, with firms and workers at odds over the division of the economic pie. Within this construct, labor is usually represented as a monolithic interest, yet the reality is that labor has always suffered from internal divisions—by race, by occupational status, and along many other fault lines. Neoliberal globalization has in many ways sharpened these divisions, which helps to explain why corporations have been winning and workers losing.

One of these fault lines divides workers from themselves: since workers are also consumers, they face a divide between the desire for higher wages and the desire for lower prices. Historically, this identity split has been exploited to divide union from nonunion workers, with anti-labor advocates accusing union workers of causing higher prices. Today, globalization is amplifying the divide between people's interests as workers and their interests as consumers through its promise of ever-lower prices.

Consider the debate over Walmart's low-road labor policies. While Walmart's low wages and skimpy benefits have recently faced scrutiny, even some liberal commentators argue that Walmart is actually good for low-wage workers because they gain more as consumers from its "low, low prices" than they lose as workers from its low wages. But this static, snapshot analysis fails to capture the full impact of globalization, past and future.

Globalization affects the economy unevenly, hitting some sectors first and others later. The process can be understood in terms of the hands of a clock. At one o'clock is the apparel sector; at two o'clock, the textile sector; at three, the steel sector; at six, the auto sector. Workers in the apparel sector are the first to have their jobs shifted to lower-wage venues; at the same time, though, all other workers get price reductions. Next, the process picks off textile sector workers at two o'clock. Meanwhile, workers from three o'clock onward get price cuts, as do the apparel workers at one o'clock. Each time the hands of the clock move, the workers taking the hit are isolated. In this fashion, globalization moves around the clock, with labor perennially divided.

Manufacturing was first to experience this process, but technological innovations associated with the Internet are putting service and knowledge workers in the firing line as well. Online business models are making even retail workers vulnerable—consider Amazon.com, for example, which has opened a customer support center and two technology development centers in India. Public-sector wages are also in play, at least indirectly, since falling wages mean falling tax revenues. The problem is that each time the hands on the globalization clock move forward, workers are divided: the majority is made slightly better off while the few are made much worse off.

Globalization also alters the historical divisions within capital, creating a new split between bigger internationalized firms and smaller firms that remain nationally centered. This division has been brought into sharp focus with the debate over the trade deficit and the overvalued dollar. In previous decades, manufacturing as a whole opposed running trade deficits and maintaining an overvalued dollar because of the adverse impact of increased imports. The one major business sector with a different view was retailing, which benefited from cheap imports.

However, the spread of multinational production and outsourcing has divided manufacturing in wealthy countries into two camps. In one camp are larger multinational corporations that have gone global and benefit from cheap imports; in the other are smaller businesses that remain nationally centered in terms of sales, production and input sourcing. Multinational corporations tend to support an overvalued dollar since this makes imports produced in their foreign factories cheaper. Conversely, domestic manufacturers are hurt by an overvalued dollar, which advantages import competition.

This division opens the possibility of a new alliance between labor and those manufacturers and businesses that remain nationally based—potentially a potent one, since there are approximately 7 million enterprises with sales of less than $10 million in the United States, versus only 200,000 with sales greater than $10 million. However, such an alliance will always be unstable as the inherent labor-capital conflict over income distribution can always reassert itself. Indeed, this pattern is already evident in the internal politics of the National Association of Manufacturers (NAM), whose members have been significantly divided regarding the overvalued dollar. As one way to address this division, the group is promoting a domestic "competitiveness" agenda aimed at weakening regulation, reducing corporate legal liability, and lowering employee benefit costs—an agenda designed to appeal to both camps, but at the expense of workers.

Solidarity has always been key to political and economic advance by working families, and it is key to mastering the politics of globalization. Developing a coherent story about the economics of neoliberal globalization around which working families can coalesce is a key ingredient for solidarity. So, too, is understanding how globalization divides labor. These narratives and analyses can help counter deep cultural proclivities to individualism, as well as other historic divides such as racism. However, as if this were not difficult enough, globalization creates additional challenges. National political solutions that worked in the past are not adequate to the task of controlling international competition. That means the solidarity bar is further raised, calling for international solidarity that supports new forms of international economic regulation. ❑

PART IV

THE WAR OF IDEAS

real-world economics review, issue no. 49

After the bust:

The outlook for macroeconomics and Macroeconomic policy*

Thomas I. Palley [Levy Economics Institute, USA]

Introduction: crisis, economists, and change

The current moment of financial crisis and the prospect of deep recession offer a historic window of opportunity for change in economics and in economic policy. The combination of crisis and accumulated popular resentments following two decades of wage restraint, widening income inequality, and increased economic insecurity makes for a political atmosphere conducive to change.

In the 1930s and '40s, the Great Depression and World War II provided the launch pad for the Keynesian revolution in economics. In the 1970s, monetarists and New Classical economists used the economic crisis created by the OPEC oil shocks to launch a counterrevolution (Johnson 1971).

Milton Friedman, the intellectual godfather of American neoliberal economics, understood the role of crisis in fostering change:

> There is enormous inertia—a tyranny of the status quo—in private and especially governmental arrangements. Only a crisis—actual or perceived—produces real change. When that crisis occurs, the actions that are taken depend on the ideas that are lying around. (Friedman 2002, pp. xiii–xiv)

He went on to describe the role of economists as follows:

> . . . to develop alternatives to existing policies, to keep them alive and available until the politically impossible becomes politically inevitable. (Friedman 2002, p. xiv)

The good news is, current conditions may have created a crisis moment in which policy and thinking can change. The bad news is, deep recession means there will likely be enormous economic suffering, and the economics profession will be profoundly resistant to change.

The post-bust policy challenge

European governments and the U.S. president face three challenges:

(1) *Stop the bleeding*—which means stopping the liquidation trap (Palley 2008a) that currently grips markets. This requires putting a floor under the financial crisis by stopping further wholesale asset price deflation and restoring credit flows.

(2) *Jump-start the economy*—which means getting the economy and employment growing again. This requires further monetary easing and massive fiscal expansion.

(3) *Ensure that future growth is characterized by full employment and shared prosperity*—which means having wages grow with productivity and reducing current high-income inequality to levels that prevailed 30 years ago, before the neoliberal economic policy experiment.

Among policymakers, there is significant agreement on challenges (1) and (2), but significant disagreement on challenge (3).

Regarding the first two challenges, any differences are largely a matter of degree—such as, What is the best way to thaw credit markets and stabilize asset prices? How far should interest rates be lowered and how fast? How much should taxes be cut, and whose taxes should be cut? How much should government spending be increased and what form should it take?[1] These are important differences, but as President Nixon famously observed in 1971, "We are all Keynesians now." The truth of that statement is being confirmed by current policy developments, though Nixon should more accurately have said, "In a recession, we are all Keynesians."

However, there is significant disagreement regarding the challenge of ensuring economic growth with shared prosperity. For most mainstream economists, the crisis is being represented as a perfect storm, the result of a rare probability event. From a post-Keynesian perspective (Godley 2000, 2001, 2005; Palley 1998, 2001, 2005, 2006a, 2006b), it is a predictable outcome of the economic paradigm that has driven growth since the neoliberal era was inaugurated, in the early 1980s, by Prime Minister Thatcher and President Reagan. That paradigm is now exhausted. It was never able to generate growth with shared prosperity; now it is unable even to generate growth with inequality.

Figure 1 Index of Productivity and Hourly Compensation of Production and Non-supervisory Workers, 1959–2005

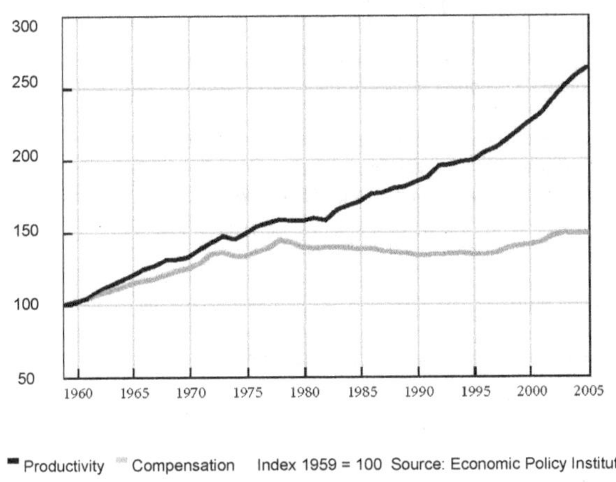

Index 1959 = 100 Source: Economic Policy Institute

The neoliberal paradigm and mainstream economics

The single most salient feature of the neoliberal economy is the disconnect between wages and productivity growth, as exemplified by the U.S. experience. Figure 1 shows an index of U.S. productivity and average compensation (which includes all benefits) of non-supervisory workers, who represent 80 percent of the workforce. Until the late 1970s, the two series grew together; since then, they have grown apart, with compensation stagnating even as productivity has continued to rise. Figure 2 tells the same story for the relation between U.S. median family income and productivity.

Figure 2 Median Family Income and Productivity, 1947–2005

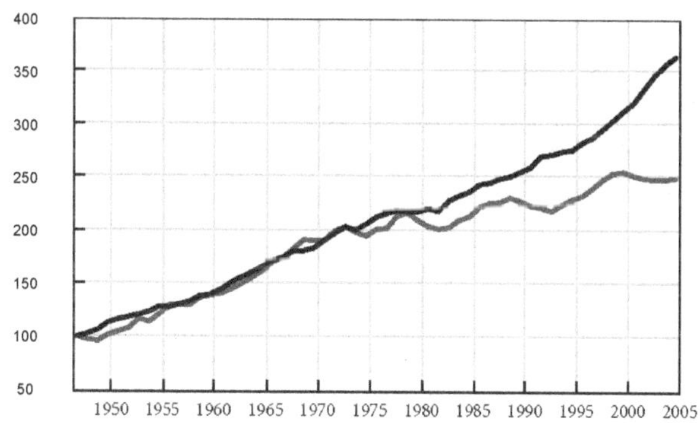

Productivity Compensation Index 1959 = 100 Source: Economic Policy Institute

This disconnect in turn explains widening income inequality. With wages stagnating at the bottom of the distribution but productivity still rising, income has been shifting to the top of the distribution. This pattern is captured in Figure 3, which shows income growth at the 20th and 95th percentiles of the U.S. income distribution. The two income series grew in tandem until the late 1970s but separated after 1980, when inequality also started rising.

The neoliberal economic policy paradigm can be described in terms of a box, as illustrated in Figure 4.2 Workers are "boxed in" on all sides by a policy matrix consisting of globalization, labor market flexibility, a focus on inflation rather than full employment, and the erosion of popular economic rights (as exemplified by the 1996 welfare reform act) in the name of "small government." Similarly, there has been an erosion of government's administrative capacity and its ability to provide services, with many government functions being outsourced to corporations. This has created a "predator state" (Galbraith 2008) in which corporations enrich themselves on the back of government contracts while the workers who provide these privately produced–publicly funded services are placed in a more hostile work environment. The result is the appearance of Big Government. The reality is a government whose capacity has been significantly cannibalized

Figure 3 Index of Low Family Income and High Family Income, 1947–2005

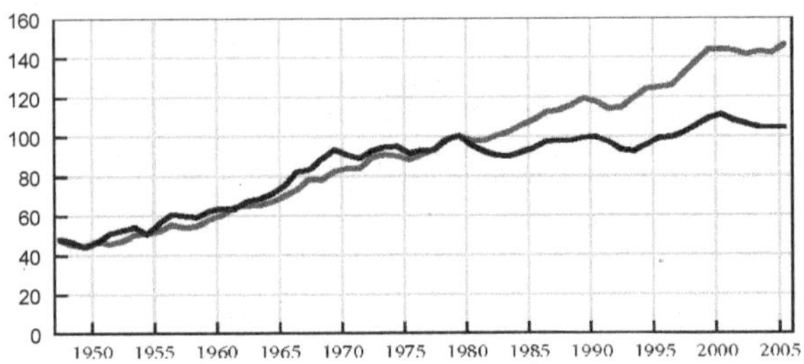

■ 20th Percentile ■ 95th Percentile Index 1959 = 100 Source: Economic Policy Institute

Figure 4 The "Neoliberal" Policy Box

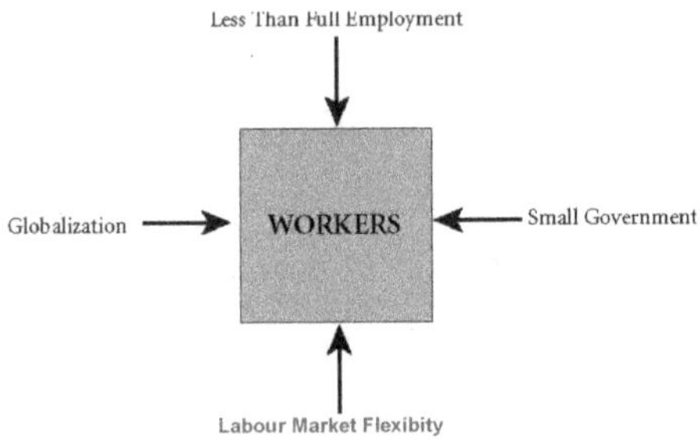

The strength of the neoliberal policy box derives from a new relationship between the "side supports" of corporations and financial markets, as illustrated in Figure 5. This new relationship has been termed "financialization" (Epstein 2001, Palley 2008b), and the box would collapse without it.

Figure 6 shows the economic workings of financialization. The basic logic is that financial markets have captured control of corporations, which now serve market interests along with the interests of top management. That combination drives corporate behavior and economic policy, creating an economic matrix that puts wages under continuous pressure and raises income inequality. Viewed from this perspective, financialization is the economic foundation of neoliberalism. Reversing the neoliberal paradigm therefore requires a policy agenda that addresses both financial markets and corporations, with the aim of bringing their behavior in line with the greater public interest.

The structure of the policy box has been supported by mainstream economic theory,which has provided justification for these outcomes. Neoliberal globalization has been justified by appeal to the theory of free trade based upon comparative advantage, and to neoclassical arguments for deregulating financial markets and allowing uncontrolled international capital flows.

Figure 5 Lifting the Lid and Unpacking the Box

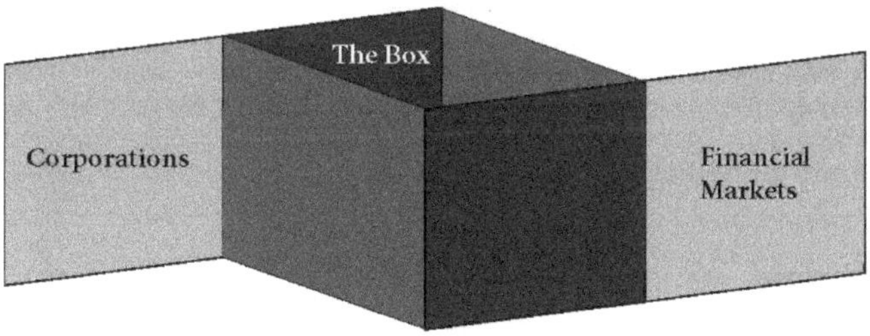

Figure 6 Dynamics of Financialization

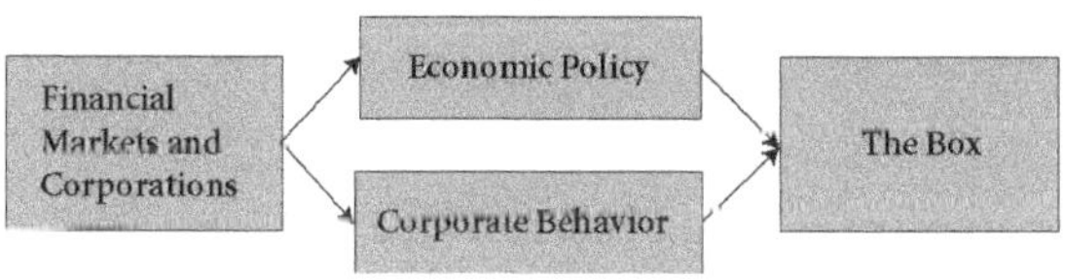

The case for small government is based on Friedman's (2002) arguments for a minimalist, or night watchman, state. Moreover, the Chicago School of Economics recommends that even market failures be ignored, since government intervention to fix them can give rise to even more costly failures.

The retreat from full employment has been driven by New Classical macroeconomics, which substituted the notion of a natural rate of unemployment and a vertical Phillips curve for the negatively sloped long-run Phillips curve (Friedman 1968). In the process, concern with inflation has replaced concern about employment. The theoretical justification is that policy can have no permanent impact on employment, and that the market by itself gravitates quickly to full employment.

The push for so-called "flexible" labor markets has been driven by the neoclassical construction of labor markets based on marginal productivity theory (e.g., that competitive markets ensure labor is paid fairly for its contribution to production). That theory has fueled an attack on unions, the minimum wage, and employment protections, all of which are characterized as labor market "distortions."

Increased corporate power has been justified by the shareholder-value model of corporations, which claims that wealth and income are maximized if firms maximize shareholder value without regard to other interests. To the extent that there is a principal-agent problem with managers not maximizing shareholder value, this is to be solved by aligning managers' interests with shareholder interests via bonus payments and stock options.

Lastly, expansion of financial markets has been promoted by appeal to the theory of efficient markets (Fama 1970), claims that speculation is stabilizing (Friedman 1953), and the notion of a market for corporate control that ensures firms are disciplined by shareholders (Jensen and Meckling 1976). Kenneth Arrow and Gerard Debreu's (1954) contingent-claims approach to financial markets has been used to justify exotic financial innovations in the name of risk spreading and portfolio diversification, while q theory (Tobin and Brainard 1968) has been used to support the claim that financial markets do a good job of directing investment and the accumulation of real capital.

Figure 7 Repacking the Box

An alternative, progressive box

The neoliberal policy box is suggestive of an alternative, "progressive Keynesian" box that would supplant workers with corporations and financial markets, as shown in Figure 7. This requires redesigning and repacking the box as follows:

(1) Globalization, with labor and environmental standards that promote upward harmonization instead of a race to the bottom. Additionally, international economic governance arrangements are to be strengthened, especially regarding exchange rates, so as to prevent a repeat of the recent huge global imbalances. Capital controls must also be a legitimate part of the policy tool kit.

(2) A balanced approach to government that ensures government efficiently provides public goods, health insurance, social insurance, education, and needed infrastructure.

(3) Restoration of full employment as a policy priority.

(4) The promotion of labor markets that encourage creation of high-quality jobs that pay fair wages, which grow with productivity.

(5) A corporate agenda that restricts managerial power by enhancing shareholder control, places limits on managerial pay, limits unproductive corporate financial engineering, and represents other stakeholders.

(6) Financial market reform that consolidates and strengthens regulation, limits speculation, increases transparency, and provides central banks with tools (such as asset-based reserve requirements) to address asset price bubbles.

An opportunity for Post Keynesian economics

Mainstream macroeconomics completely failed to understand the fragility and unsustainability of the current macroeconomic regime. The extent of this failure cannot be overstated and it provides an opportunity for Post Keynesian economics. That is because Post Keynesians (Godley 2000, 2001, 2005; Palley 1998, 2001, 2005, 2006a, 2006b) predicted the outcomes that have come to pass.

The economics profession has talked widely of "the Great Moderation." According to that hypothesis, the economy has become more stable and the business cycle tamed through a combination of improvements in monetary policy driven by improved economic theory, and innovations in financial markets and business management that have spread risk, stabilized credit flows, and reduced inventory fluctuations. Federal Reserve Chairman Ben Bernanke is himself a strong proponent of the Great Moderation thesis: "My view is that improvements in monetary policy, though certainly not the only factor, have probably been the most important source of the Great Moderation" (Bernanke 2004, p. 2).

Yet, the current financial crisis has shown the Great Moderation to have been a period of artificial calm. Moreover, the crisis also lends credence to an alternative Post Keynesian interpretation (Palley 2008c) that the Great Moderation was driven by a retreat from full employment that reduced the income distribution conflicts that surround full employment, and by reliance on the temporary but unsustainable stimulus of borrowing to fuel growth.

Nothing epitomizes the mainstream's failure more than former Fed Chairman Alan Greenspan's admission to Congress, on October 23, 2008, that his economic ideology was flawed and that the self-interest of lending institutions had failed to protect shareholders. Greenspan's approach to financial regulation and the conduct of monetary policy was widely endorsed by the economics profession. Thus, when he retired from the Federal Reserve, in 2006, he was feted by the profession, with the liberal New Keynesian economists Alan Blinder and Ricardo Reis declaring that Greenspan "has a legitimate claim to being the greatest central banker who ever lived" (Blinder and Reis 2005).

The Federal Reserve, the International Monetary Fund (IMF), and leading economists on both sides of the Atlantic all provide clear evidence of the lack of understanding. In March 2007, current Fed Chairman Bernanke testified before the Joint Economic Committee of Congress that "the impact on the broader economy and financial markets of the problems in the sub-prime market seems likely to be contained" (Bernanke 2007). And throughout 2007 and into 2008, district Federal Reserve Bank Presidents Jeffrey Lacker (Richmond), Charles Plosser (Philadelphia), and Thomas Hoenig (Kansas City) all consistently played up the danger of inflation rather than financial crisis and slump.

The IMF has laid claims to being the global economy's early warning system. Yet in July 2007, just as the crisis was about to erupt, the IMF (2007) revised its global growth forecast upward, emphasizing that inflation risks had edged up and central banks would likely need to further tighten monetary policy. Even more than the IMF, the European Central Bank seems to have misunderstood the financial crisis, which explains its resistance to lowering interest rates in 2007 and much of 2008. The same also holds for the Bank of England.

Harvard professor and former IMF Chief Economist Ken Rogoff (2008b) also focused on inflation, writing as late as July 2008 that the global economy was a "runaway train" requiring tighter monetary and fiscal policy. Moreover, Rogoff (2008c) misunderstood the significance of the collapse of Lehman Brothers, celebrating it with an article titled "No More Creampuffs" that argued Lehman's failure would put an end to moral hazard and restore healthy business incentives.

British economist Willem Buiter (2008) also failed to see the system's instability, virulently criticizing the Federal Reserve for its decision in January 2008 to cut the federal funds rate by 75 basis points, from 4.25 to 3.50 percent. Likewise, the politically liberal Paul Krugman (2008) failed to appreciate the extent of speculation in oil and commodity markets, rationalizing the surge in oil and commodity prices in 2008 as the result of market fundamentals rather than speculation.

With regard to the global economy, proponents of the so-called "Revised BrettonWoods" (RBW) hypothesis (Dooley, Folkerts-Landau, and Garber 2003) claimed the huge global financial imbalances associated with the U.S. trade deficit were stable and sustainable. Another argument for sustainability came from Harvard professor and former Inter-American Development Bank Chief Economist Ricardo Hausman (2005), who, with his colleague Federico Sturzenegger, claimed the U.S. trade deficit was a non-issue because of "dark matter" investments that yielded huge excess returns to U.S. overseas investments.

Where there was mainstream criticism regarding the U.S. trade deficit, it was strikingly wrong. Thus, some economists (Eichengreen 2004; Obstfeld and Rogoff 2007; Rogoff 2007, 2008a; Bergsten 2005) predicted a run on the dollar, while others (Goldstein and Lardy 2005) predicted China's inflation would force a rebalancing.

None of this has come to pass. Instead, the U.S. economy has imploded from within as predicted by Post Keynesians, sending shock waves around the world. Far from collapsing, the dollar has actually strengthened during the crisis, as the extent of global economic dependence on the U.S. consumer as buyer of last resort has become clear.

Mainstream economists have been intellectually honest and guided by their theoretical models. The problem is, events have conclusively shown their theoretical analysis to be fundamentally flawed. Both in its theory and empirical analysis, mainstream macroeconomics failed to connect the dots linking the weak U.S. expansion, the U.S. trade deficit, and the U.S. housing bubble. It also failed to connect long-term developments in the U.S. economy concerning expanding debt, wage stagnation, and worsening income distribution.

This contrasts with Post Keynesian economics, which got it right and provides clear justification for the type of fiscal and monetary policies being implemented. For Post Keynesians, the challenge is to win recognition for this record, as the mainstream profession will try to airbrush the past and rewrite history by burying its own failures and ignoring the success of its critics.

Figure 8 The Political Dilemma of Neoliberalism

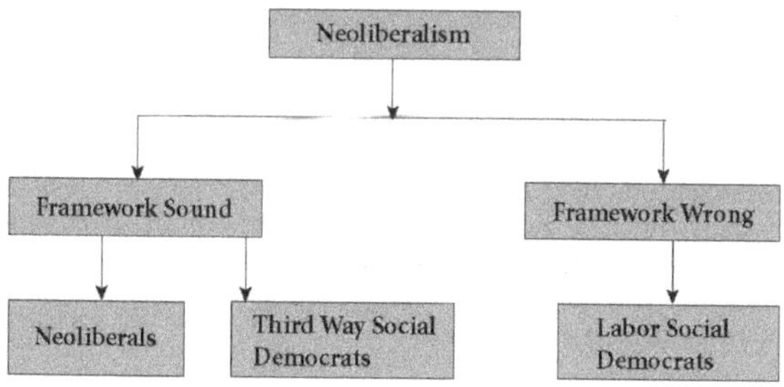

Obstacles to change

Though the current moment provides an opportunity for change in both economics and economic policy, there are a number of major obstacles to overcome.

A. Politics and the split among social democrats

A first obstacle concerns politics, and the fact that social democratic political parties—including the Democratic Party in the United States, the Labour Party in the United Kingdom, and the Social Democratic Party in Germany—are split regarding the neoliberal economic paradigm.

Figure 8 illustrates this split. At the most fundamental level there is a divide between those who see the neoliberal economic paradigm as sound (e.g., neoliberals and Third Way social democrats) and those who see it as intrinsically flawed (labor social democrats). The political problem is that these opposing views split social democrats, making it harder to dislodge the paradigm. Neoliberals continue to promote the paradigm, and their response to the crisis has been to try and shift blame onto government, arguing that the crisis is another example of government failure. For instance, U.S. conservatives (see, for example, Schiff 2008) are falsely blaming the government-sponsored mortgage giants Fannie Mae and Freddie Mac for causing the crisis. The Community Reinvestment Act (1977), which aims to promote homeownership among disadvantaged communities, has also been falsely blamed.[3]

Third Way social democrats also remain committed to the neoliberal model. The key difference separating them from neoliberals is that they support stronger financial regulatory reform as well as "helping hand" programs to assist those adversely affected by the market. In the United States, the Third Way "New Democrat" explanation of the Bush Administration's economic failure is that it abandoned budget discipline and pursued inegalitarian tax and social policies. That is a critique of policy rather than a critique of the paradigm.

This Third Way acceptance of the neoliberal economic paradigm creates a division with labor social democrats who support progressive Keynesianism. That division in turn creates a major political conundrum. On the one hand, if labor social democrats split from Third Way social democrats, they risk bringing about a full-blown neoliberal triumph. On the other hand, if they maintain their fractious union, the risk is a gradual entrenchment of neoliberalism. The only satisfactory solution is the creation of a new, progressive Keynesian consensus that places economics front and center on the political stage.

B. Intellectual opinion

The importance of economics points to a second obstacle to change: the intellectual dominance of neoliberal economics in academic and public policy discourse. Though the current crisis has created an opportunity to unseat neoliberalism and bring the "Age of Milton Friedman" to an end, events are running ahead of the climate of opinion, which remains dominated by neoliberalism. The political environment may have become more favorable, but a generation of miseducation impedes change. That miseducation affects policymakers, economic advisers, think tanks, and the media alike.

The dominant analytical framework among economists is the neoclassical, dynamic, general equilibrium, real-business-cycle model, which is adjusted to include price rigidities by so-called "New Keynesians." The assumptions of this model—competitive market clearing, the "loanable funds" theory of interest rates, and the neoclassical theory of labor markets—lace both professional and public discourse. These assumptions generate the conventional neoliberal prescriptions regarding labor market flexibility; balanced budgets; the desirability of unimpeded international financial flows and free trade; monetary policy guided by the natural rate of unemployment; and supply-side economics, which emphasizes tax cuts.

The implication is that, as long as economic thinking remains dominated by the neoclassical, dynamic, general equilibrium, real-business-cycle framework, mainstream economics will continue to be amajor obstacle to change.

C. The sociology of economics

The importance of intellectual understandings in turn spotlights a third obstruction to change: the sociology of the economics profession, which operates to exclude and ignore alternative points of view. This practice is justified by appealing to a myth that claims neoclassical economics is a scientifically proven truth, while opposing views are scientifically wrong.

The neoclassical "science" myth plays a critical function, which explains the repeated claim that neoclassical economics *is* science. This function supports the sociological practice that has mainstream economists labelling dissidents as wrong. That in turn justifies purging dissidents from orthodox economics departments and ignoring them in heterodox departments, thereby stripping dissidents of intellectual standing and diminishing their capacity to challenge the neoliberal paradigm.

The deeper sociological problem is that academic economics is a club in which new members are elected by existing members. Today, club members only elect those who subscribe to the current dominant paradigm, as this behavior is justified by the science myth. This poses an intractable sociological obstruction to alternative points of view and the possibility of fundamental change (Palley 1997).

D. Cuckoo economics

Lastly, there is the obstacle of "cuckoo" economics. The cuckoo bird surreptitiously places its eggs in the nests of other birds, which then raise its young. In many regards, neoliberal economics does the same to Keynesian economics. This serves to create confusion, blur distinctions, and promote the claim that Keynesian ideas are already fully incorporated in mainstream economic thought and have nothing further to contribute.

The practice of cuckoo economics is evident in the tendency of mainstream economists to recommend Keynesian policies in times of economic crisis. Thus, many economists support expansionary discretionary fiscal policy and robust interest rate reductions in such situations, even though their theoretical models are hard pressed to justify such actions.

New Keynesianism is the ultimate example of cuckoo economics. It is impossible to read John Maynard Keynes's *General Theory* (1936) and believe that his theory of unemployment rests on the combination of imperfect competition and price adjustment "menu" costs. However, that is the New Keynesians' claim, and their adoption of the "Keynesian" label serves to confuse debate and dismiss authentic Keynesian claims about the exclusion of Keynesianism (see, for instance, DeLong 2007). The reality is that New Keynesian economics is a form of real-business-cycle theory. It should really be called "New Pigovian economics," as it is firmly in the tradition of Arthur C. Pigou rather than Keynes.

The latest example of cuckoo economics is "hip" orthodoxy and behavioral economics (Hayes 2007). Thus, some mainstream economists are now embracing ideas from social psychology that critics of the mainstream have long talked about. These ideas include concerns with relative standing (Veblen 1899, Duesenberry 1949), fairness, and less-than-perfect rationality. The trick behind the new behavioral paradigm is that it draws on arguments made by critics of the mainstream but adopts only those ideas that leave unchanged the core analytical assumptions driving modern neoclassical macroeconomics (Palley 2007).

This capacity to selectively incorporate ideas reflects the amoeba-like character of neoliberal economics, which, though dented by recent events, has an astounding capacity to reinvent itself without real change. The implication is that neoliberal economics has not been staked through the heart, and it therefore promises to rise again, like a zombie, when times stabilize.

Conclusion: The outlook for macroeconomics and macroeconomic policy

The depth of the current economic crisis means there will almost certainly be a policy turn in a Keynesian, or even a Post Keynesian, direction. However, there are profound political, intellectual, and sociological obstacles blocking any fundamental change to macroeconomics. In particular, the economics profession and its ideology remain unreformed. There is little indication of shifts in core understandings concerning labor markets, globalization, and the theory of the natural rate of unemployment. The only place where there is evidence of substantive intellectual change is in attitudes toward financial regulation (though even here, "market transparency" recommendations dominate "quantitative requirements"). These obstacles will mute the policy response to the crisis, and, if a deep economic downturn is averted, will tend to encourage a return to the existing policy paradigm, which has failed disastrously.

Notes

* This paper was previously published by the Levy Economics Institute.

1. With regard to jump-starting the economy, one major disagreement concerns the treatment of debt. Progressive Keynesians prefer policies and legislation that facilitate cancelling household debts, whereas neoliberals strongly oppose this action and seek government bailouts of financial institutions without obligating those institutions to cancel outstanding debts.

2. The box analogy is attributable to Ron Blackwell, chief economist for the AFL-CIO.

3. See Ritholtz (2008a, 2008b) for a rejection of the claim that the housing crisis was caused by the Community Reinvestment Act and a failure to regulate the government-sponsored mortgage lenders Fannie Mae and Freddie Mac.

References

Arrow, K. J., and G. Debreu. 1954. "Existence of an Equilibrium for a Competitive Economy." *Econometrica* 22: 265–90.

Bergsten, C. F. 2005. "A New Foreign Economic Policy for the United States," in Bergsten, ed., *The United States and the World Economy: Foreign Economic Policy for the Next Decade*. Washington, D.C.: Institute for International Economics.

Bernanke, B. S. 2004. "The Great Moderation." Remarks presented at the meetings of the Eastern Economic Association, Washington, D.C., February 20.

———. 2007. "The Economic Outlook." Testimony before the Joint Economic Committee, U.S. Congress, Washington D.C., March 28.

Blinder, A. S., and R. Reis. 2005. "Understanding the Greenspan Standard" Working Paper No. 114. Brussels: Centre for European Policy Studies. September.

Buiter, W. 2008. "The Bernanke Put: Buttock-clenching Monetary Policymaking at the Fed. "Maverecon blog, comment posted January 22, http://blogs.ft.com/maverecon/2008/01/the-bernanke-puhtml/.

DeLong, B. 2007. "What Are We, Chopped Liver?" TPM Café blog, comment posted May 31, http://tpmcafe.talkingpointsmemo.com/007/05/31/what_are_we_chopped_liver/.

Dooley,M. P., D. Folkerts-Landau, and P. Garber. 2003. "An Essay on the Revised Bretton Woods System. "Working Paper No. 9971. Cambridge, Mass.: National Bureau of Economic Research. September.

Duesenberry, J. S. 1949. *Income, Saving, and the Theory of Consumption Behavior.* Cambridge, Mass.: Harvard University Press.

Eichengreen, B. 2004. "The Dollar and the New Bretton Woods System." Lecture presented at the Cass Business School, City University, London, December 15.Manuscript housed at the University of California, Berkeley.

Epstein, G. 2001. "Financialization, Rentier Interests, and Central Bank Policy. "Working paper. Department of Economics and Political Economy Research Institute, University of Massachusetts Amherst. December.

Fama, E. 1970. "Efficient Capital Markets: A Review of Theory and Empirical Work." *Journal of Finance* 25, no. 3 (May): 383–417.

Friedman, M. 1953. "The Case for Flexible Exchange Rates," in *Essays in Positive Economics*. Chicago: Chicago University Press.

———. 1968. "The Role of Monetary Policy." *American Economic Review* 58 (May): 1–17.

———. 2002. *Capitalism and Freedom*. 40th anniversary ed. Chicago: University of Chicago Press.

Galbraith, J. K. 2008. *The Predator State: How Conservatives Abandoned the Free Market and Why Liberals Should Too*. New York: Free Press.

Godley, W. 2000. "Drowning in Debt." Policy Note 2000/6. Annandale-on- Hudson, N.Y.: The Levy Economics Institute. June.

———. 2001. "As the Implosion Begins..." Strategic Analysis. Annandaleon- Hudson, N.Y.: The Levy Economics Institute. August.

———. 2005. "Some Unpleasant American Arithmetic." Policy Note 2005/5. Annandale-on-Hudson, N.Y.. The Levy Economics Institute. June.

Goldstein,M., and N. R. Lardy. 2005. "China's Role in the Revived Bretton Woods System: A Case of Mistaken Identity." Working Paper No. WP 05-02.Washington, D.C.: Institute for International Economics. March.

Hausman, R., and F. Sturzenegger 2005. "Dark Matter Makes the U.S. Trade Deficit Disappear." *Financial Times*, December 8.

Hayes, C. 2007. "Hip Heterodoxy." *The Nation*. June 11. International Monetary Fund. 2007. "The Global Economy Continues to Grow Strongly. "World Economic Outlook Update. Washington D.C. July.

Jensen,M. C., and W. H.Meckling. 1976. "Theory of the Firm: Managerial Behavior, Agency Costs, and Ownership Structure." *Journal of Financial Economics* 3, no. 4 (October): 305–60.

Johnson, H. 1971. "The Keynesian Revolution and the Monetarist Counter-Revolution." *American Economic Review* 61, no. 2 (May): 1–14.

Keynes, J.M. 1936. *The General Theory of Employment, Interest, and Money*. London: Macmillan.

Krugman, P. 2008. "The Oil Non-bubble." *The New York Times*, May 12.

Obstfeld,M., and K. Rogoff. 2007. "The Unsustainable U.S. Current Account Position Revisited," in R. H. Clarida, ed., *G7 Current Account Imbalances: Sustainability and Adjustment*. National Bureau of Economic Research Conference Report Series. Chicago: University of Chicago Press.

Palley, T. I. 1997. "The Academic Jungle: Social Practice and the Survival of Economic Ideas." *Review of Radical Political Economics* 29, no. 3 (September): 22–33.

———. 1998. *Plenty of Nothing: The Downsizing of the American Dream and the Case for Structural Keynesianism*. Princeton, N.J.: Princeton University Press.

———. 2001. "Contradictions Coming Home to Roost? Income Distribution and the Return of the Aggregate Demand Problem." Working Paper No. 332. Annandale-on-Hudson, N.Y.: The Levy Economics Institute. June.

———. 2005. "The Questionable Legacy of Alan Greenspan." *Challenge* 48, no. 6 (November–December): 17–31.

———. 2006a. "The Weak Recovery and the Coming Deep Recession." *Mother Jones*. March 17.

———. 2006b. "The Fallacy of the Revised Bretton Woods Hypothesis: Why Today's International Financial System is Unsustainable." Public Policy Brief No. 85. Annandale-on-Hudson, N.Y.: The Levy Economics Institute. June.

———. 2007. "Challenging Orthodox Economics—Part 1." TPM Café blog, comment posted May 29, http://tpmcafe.talkingpointsmemo.com/007/05/29/challenging_orthodox_economics/

———. 2008a. "The Liquidation Trap." *Asia Times Online*, September 18.

———. 2008b. "Financialization: What It Is and Why It Matters." Working Paper No. 04-2008. Dusseldorf, Germany: IMK Macroeconomic Policy Institute.

———. 2008c. "Demythologizing Central Bankers and the Myth of the Great Moderation." *Asia Times Online*. http://www.atimes.com/atimes/Global_Economy/JI19Dj03.html, April 8.

Ritholtz, B. 2008a. "Misunderstanding Credit and Housing Crises: Blaming the CRA, GSEs." The Big Picture blog, comment posted October 2, http://bigpicture.typepad.com/comments/2008/10/misunderstandin.html.

———. 2008b. "Fannie Mae and the Financial Crisis." The Big Picture blog, comment posted October 5, http://bigpicture.typepad.com/comments/2008/10/fannie-mae-and.html.

Rogoff, K. 2007. "Dog Days for the Super Dollar." Project Syndicate. December. www.project-syndicate.org/commentary/rogoff37

———. 2008a. "Goodbye to the Dollar." Project Syndicate. April. www.project-syndicate.org/commentary/rogoff41.

———. 2008b. "TheWorld's Runaway Train." Project Syndicate. July. www.project-syndicate.org/commentary/rogoff44

———. 2008c. "No More Creampuffs." *The Washington Post*, September 16.

Schiff, P. 2008. "Don't Blame Capitalism." *The Washington Post*. October 16.

Tobin, J., and W. Brainard. 1968. "Pitfalls in Financial Model Building." *American Economic Review* 58 (May): 99–122.

Veblen, T. 1899. *The Theory of the Leisure Class: An Economic Study in the Evolution of Institutions*. New York and London: Macmillan.

SUGGESTED CITATION:
Thomas I. Palley, "After the bust: The outlook for macroeconomics and Macroeconomic policy", *real-world economics review*, issue no. 49, 12 March 2009, pp. 22-35, http://www.paecon.net/PAEReview/issue49/Palley49.pdf

[19]

The war of ideas: a comparison of the U.S. and Europe[1]

1. Ideas matter

The financial crisis of 2008, the Great Recession it triggered, and the great stagnation that followed, have spawned a "war of ideas". On both sides of the Atlantic, progressives and trade unionists are engaged in a war of ideas, the outcome of which will greatly influence the future.

The war of ideas is present in the debate over whether fiscal and monetary stimulus is the right policy response to the crisis, or whether the right response is fiscal austerity and rejection of quantitative easing by central banks. The war of ideas is also reflected in the explanation we give for the crisis.

In the U.S. there are three competing explanations (Palley, 2012, chapter 3). The first is the hardcore neoliberal explanation that can be labeled the *government failure hypothesis*. According to it, the crisis is due to the implosion of a house price bubble caused by the Federal Reserve and government housing policy. The Federal Reserve supposedly pushed interest rates too low and held them there too long in the period 2001–2007, while politically motivated government intervention in the home mortgage market encouraged unwise and unsupportable levels of home ownership. The second explanation is the softcore neoliberal explanation which can be labeled the *market failure hypothesis*. According to it, the crisis is the result of a financial implosion caused by the combination of excessive financial deregulation, lax financial regulation that permitted dangerous speculation, and so-called "black swan" effects resulting from excessive financial complexity. The third explanation is the structural Keynesian "*destruction of shared prosperity hypothesis*" whereby the crisis is the logical outcome of thirty years of neoliberal policy. Those policies caused wage stagnation and widened income inequality, the adverse effects of which were covered over by a generation long credit bubble that eventually burst.

In Europe, there are also three explanations for the euro zone's crisis. The first is it is a public debt crisis caused by government fiscal profligacy (Lachman, 2010). The second is it is a balance of payments crisis caused by Germany's pursuit of export-led growth based on domestic wage suppression which has undermined both European aggregate demand and the competitiveness and sustainability of Southern Europe's economies (Bibow, 2012). The third is it is the result of Europe's adoption of a neoliberal policy regime that undermined aggregate demand by creating wage stagnation. Europe's policymakers also implemented a flawed design for the euro that created a form of analogue gold standard, thereby exposing countries to the types of financial fragility that afflicted the gold standard a century earlier (Palley, 2013).

The war of ideas is relevant to both Europe and the U.S. because how we explain the crisis will determine how we respond to it. It is already affecting the character of the monetary and fiscal policy response, and it will also affect the content and direction of future policy.

If you accept the hardcore neoliberal position, the recommended policy response is fiscal austerity now and "doubling-down" on the neoliberal policies of the past 30 years. Those policies include deregulation of financial and product markets; deepening the *laissez-faire* version of globalization; shrinking government and social welfare protections; flexibilizing labor markets by dismantling unions, worker protections, and the minimum wage; and strict inflation targeting. From a hardcore neoliberal standpoint, the crisis proves prior neoliberal reforms were not pure enough, which prevented the market from functioning properly.

If you accept the softcore neoliberal position the recommendation is to modernize financial regulation to avoid a repeat of the financial crisis of 2008. In addition, because the crisis caused a deep recession, strong monetary and fiscal stimulus is needed to jumpstart the economy again. However, once recovery is on track, fiscal austerity and downsizing of the welfare state will be needed to offset fiscal stimulus expended. Other than that, little else needs change as the basic neoliberal economic model is sound.

Lastly, if you accept the structural Keynesian destruction of shared prosperity hypothesis the policy recommendation is stimulus now plus structural reform that reverses the neoliberal attack on workers and social democratic government. That means establishing rules for globalization that prevent an international race to the bottom; restoring full employment as a key policy objective of macroeconomic policy; rebuilding labor market institutions like unions and the minimum wage that ensure wage are tied to productivity growth; and restoring social democratic government that provides public goods, education, health care, and a basic level of retirement income security.

These different recommended policy responses to the crisis show the importance of ideas. How the crisis is explained and interpreted will affect the choices society makes in response. That makes the war of ideas critical.

2. The war of ideas in the U.S. and Europe: a comparison

Because neoliberalism is a global ideology, the war of ideas is being fought on a global scale. However, the terrain and challenges differs across countries because history, politics, and culture differ across countries. It is therefore interesting to compare the challenge in Europe, exemplified by Germany, with that in the United States.

The state of the policy debate

In Germany, mainstream political opinion (Christian Democrats versus Social Democrats) appears less divided. That is reflected in the relatively small differences that characterized the recent (2013) election contest between the incumbent Christian Democrat Chancellor, Angela Merkel, and the Social Democratic challenger, former Finance Minister Peer Steinbrück. In Germany, the microeconomic social contract about the strong merits of the welfare state remains largely intact. However, the macroeconomic social contract about the role and significance of counter-cyclical Keynesian policy has been largely discarded by both sides of the political aisle.

In the U.S., political opinion is much more sharply divided, as reflected in the vitriolic challenge waged by Republicans against the Obama administration. The microeconomic social contract about the welfare state is under profound attack, with the Republicans seeking to annihilate it completely. A small but powerful group of Democrats is also willing to go along with shrinking its scope and depth. However, the macroeconomic social contract about Keynesian counter-cyclical policy remains intact. Democrats are strong supporters but, surprisingly, so too are Republicans. It is easy to be fooled by Republican rhetoric against counter-cyclical policy and their obstruction of the Obama administration's requests for fiscal stimulus. However, that reflects tactical politics aimed at sabotaging the Obama administration. If Republicans were in power they would use plutocratic counter-cyclical policy, as they did in the recession of 2001 under President George W. Bush. Their current opposition to fiscal stimulus derives from a combination of opposition to egalitarian counter-cyclical policy plus a desire for President Obama to fail.

In a sense, Europe and the U.S. are symmetric opposites. Debate is more contested in the U.S. and the microeconomic welfare state social contract is under attack. Debate is less contested in Germany and it is the macroeconomic counter-cyclical social contract that is under attack.

The state of understanding

In the U.S., neoliberal opposition is far stronger and success requires much deeper change regarding society's views about the economy. Neoliberal "free market" ideology has taken much deeper root in the public's political imagination, making it harder to reverse. Contrastingly, in Europe the dominant social and intellectual ethos remains social democratic. What is needed is that Social Democrats rediscover their social democratic heart and belief in the merits of both the microeconomic and macroeconomic social contract.

In many regards, the challenge posed by the war of ideas is greater in the U.S. than in Europe. That is because neoliberalism has deeper roots in American culture and the American public's imagination. But even though the overall challenge is greater, the direction of movement is also more favorable. In the U.S. political engagement has at least begun, as evidenced by the more vitriolic political discourse. In Germany and Europe it has not, as measured by the very modest differences of political style and program. Across the continent, Social Democrats have shied away from offering a substantively different explanation of the economic crisis with a correspondingly different policy program.

There is a lot of complaint about the contested and divided nature of U.S. political discourse. Those complaints are misplaced. At this historical moment, contest and division is a good thing, not a bad thing. It is the hallmark of the beginning of change. If anything, the problem is Democrats have not differentiated themselves enough from Republicans and have not yet offered policies that match the scale of the problem.

Current dangers

It is also the case that Europe is in a more dangerous position. In the U.S. economic growth is sub par but it is positive, employment has increased substantially since the end of the recession in 2009, and there is nothing equivalent to the euro zone crisis. In contrast, Europe is trapped in stagnation and has experienced double-dip recession. The periphery countries of Greece, Ireland, and Portugal are in depression. So too is Spain, which is Europe's fourth largest economy. Italy is teetering on renewed recession and financial markets have grave doubts about the state of Italy's public finances. Economic conditions and public finances are weakening in France, and the U.K. has also experienced a double-dip recession and appears stuck with near zero growth. Even Germany is in a dangerous situation as it is significantly oriented to export-led growth, which exposes it to European stagnation. It is also exposed to slowing growth in China.

These conditions are objectively bad enough. But things could get far worse if the euro disintegrates under country economic and political pressures. In that event, the economic and political fallout could be very ugly. That makes it urgent that European Social Democrats take up engagement with war of ideas.

Though the neoliberal impulse is weaker and the social democratic impulse stronger, Europe faces special political challenges because individual countries do not have the same level of control over their economic futures as the United States. That is because of the euro and monetary union. The euro needs reform but that is a European level task. In particular, the European Central Bank must take on the role of government banker for euro member countries so that it acts like the Federal Reserve already does on behalf of the U.S. government. The role of government banker is to help the government manage its debts and finance budget deficits at reasonable interest rates.[2]

Second, given the lack of a single national government for the continent, Europe needs to introduce shared rules to ensure fiscal and wage coordination across countries. In slumps, countries must engage in coordinated fiscal stimulus. And in normal times wages must grow at roughly the same pace to discourage countries from engaging in a deflationary race to the bottom aimed at gaining competitiveness.

Third, Germany must be weaned from its export-led growth model based on wage suppression. As Europe's largest economy, Germany must shift to a domestic demand-led growth model based on rising wages so that it can play its proper role of locomotive for larger European economy.

These are massive political challenges. They require agreement among countries. They also require Germany's agreement as only Germany can change its own policies. That means the future of shared prosperity in Europe depends significantly on Germany's willingness to change and adopt a new European economic model. Unfortunately, even though German voters have a strong social democratic inclination, German political elites may be the most neoliberal in Europe.

3. Europe's global significance in the war of ideas

Europe's political history and culture makes it intrinsically less neoliberal. At the same time, it faces far greater political and institutional obstacles because of its fragmented governance structure.

Unfortunately, Europe's economic under-performance has major global consequences in the war of ideas. That is because Europe is widely viewed as the standard bearer of social democracy and Keynesianism. Thus, in public debate the European economic model is often posited as the social democratic alternative to the neoliberal U.S. economic model. Consequently, when Europe fails, neoliberals use that failure to argue that social democratic Keynesianism does not work.

The great tragedy is that Europe's failure is self-inflicted. It is failing because Europe's policymakers have been even more captured by neoliberal macroeconomic policies than the United States. The European Central Bank (ECB) and European finance ministries are dominated by economic policymakers trained in Chicago school neoliberal economics. In contrast, the pragmatism of U.S. politicians has supported budget deficits and Keynesianism. In the past that has held for both Republican and Democratic administrations though, recently,

Republicans have become fiscal policy obstructionists as part of their strategy for wounding President Obama.

In economics, macroeconomic policy trumps microeconomic policy. Consequently, Europe's adoption of hardcore neoliberal macroeconomic policy has trumped its more social democratic microeconomic policy. As a result, the European economy has under-performed the U.S. economy, giving rise to perceived failure of the social democratic model when it has not been given a chance to succeed.

The true measure of the social democratic model is the period 1950–1980 when Europe pursued a combination of Keynesian macroeconomic policies and social democratic microeconomic policies. That era was a golden age for Europe and the European model was shown to deliver. The past 30 years saw European policymakers abandon Keynesian inclinations. That undercut Europe's economic performance and undermined the appeal of the European model, making it harder to challenge the neoliberal model.

4. Conclusion: a better future is possible

Neoliberalism is a global ideology that has infected the U.S., Europe, and Germany. From a structural Keynesian standpoint, neoliberal economic policy design is the ultimate cause of the global slump. The global challenge is to bend the arc of history away from neoliberalism and back toward social democratic Keynesianism that has proved capable of delivering shared prosperity and full employment. Meeting this challenge requires winning the war of ideas.
<np>Just over 30 years ago wages started to stagnate and income inequality started to explode in both the U.S. and Europe. A big reason was working families lost the war of ideas. The economic crisis provides an historic opportunity to reverse that defeat and thereby enable the restoration of shared prosperity and full employment. It can be done.

Notes

1. Originally published as Chapter 2, "The war of ideas: a comparison of the U.S. and Europe," in Thomas I. Palley and Gustav A. Horn (eds.), *Restoring Shared Prosperity: A Policy Agenda from Leading Keynesian Economists*, CreateSpace.com, 2013.
2. That will require introducing some form of euro bond, the revenues from which and the attached obligations are shared among all governments. Only such an arrangement can ensure that the European Central Bank treats countries equally and is not drawn into unfairly assisting individual countries at the expense of others.

References

Bibow, J. (2012), "The euro debt crisis and Germany's euro trilemma," Working paper No. 721, Levy Economics Institute of Bard College, Annandale-on-Hudson, New York.

Lachman, D. (2010), "Euro will unravel, and soon: collapse could imperil U.S. economy," American Enterprise Institute for Public Policy Research, Washington, D.C., No. 2, September.

Palley, T.I. (2012), *From Financial Crisis to Stagnation: The Destruction of Shared Prosperity and the Role of Economics*, Cambridge: Cambridge University Press.

Palley, T.I. (2013), "Europe's crisis without end: the consequences of neoliberalism," *Contributions to Political Economy*, 32, 29–50.

Challenge, 62(2):128–143, 2019

ISSN: 1558-1489 print/0577-5132 online
DOI: 10.1080/05775132.2019.1592843

Routledge
Taylor & Francis Group

Inequality and Stagnation by Policy Design: Mainstream Denialism and Its Dangerous Political Consequences

THOMAS PALLEY

This important paper argues that the mainstream economics profession has utterly failed to address the financial crisis and ensuing stagnation. The author makes a direct assault on the defensiveness of mainstream economics today. To the contrary, he argues, mainstream policies contributed significantly to the economic shocks. Constructive critiques of policy have been made in light of events, but there has been overwhelming mainstream resistance to such ideas. This critique of mainstream economists is not about "values" or lack of "change." It is about academic practice that suppresses ideas that are threatening to its survival.

IDEAS AND INTERESTS: THE DEBATE OVER INEQUALITY AND STAGNATION

The scientific method rests on the principle of falsification (Popper 1959), but science does not operate in a vacuum. Instead, it operates in a social context in which competing interests can interfere with the process, and the history of science is replete with examples of such. If a theory is sufficiently threatening to the status quo it may be denied a hearing, or even actively suppressed, and this may be done all the while invoking the name of science. Such behavior is a real possibility in economics, as the distribution of income and wealth rests, in part, on the explanations economists provide to rationalize and justify existing patterns.

This paper argues that the increase in inequality, the financial crisis of 2008, and the ensuing stagnation are substantially attributable to neoliberal policy design. Design must be distinguished from intention. The triumph of neoliberalism means that economic policy over the past forty years has been designed according to neoliberal ideas and that policy design

Thomas Palley is an independent economist living in Washington, DC, USA.

contributed significantly to the current situation. However, though aiming to increase the profit rate and the power of capital relative to labor, neoliberal policymakers did not intend to create financial crisis and stagnation. The latter were unintended consequences of neoliberal policy.

The fact that neoliberal economic policy has created those damaging outcomes now creates a scientific dilemma for mainstream economists. Those economists are existentially threatened by theories that explain the financial crisis and stagnation as resulting from policies they justified and recommended. Merely acknowledging the possible legitimacy of those theories would be analogous to signing one's own death warrant. Consequently, mainstream economists resist engaging them to avoid legitimizing them.

That resistance has contributed to blocking the politics and policies needed to address stagnation, thereby contributing to a political vacuum that is being filled by odious forces. Those ugly political consequences are also unintended, but they are still there. When wrong-headed ideas get to rule the roost, powerful sociological and economic interests may keep them in charge, and the unintended consequences can be ugly.

Pluralism is the great social defense against such outcomes. It works by promoting competition of ideas, thereby diminishing the likelihood that wrong-headed ideas will prevail. However, pluralism requires a level playing field, and that is no longer the case in economics, which is dominated by a neoclassical monopoly (Palley 2008). That monopoly makes the political challenge of reforming the current neoliberal order even more difficult, which in turn makes the current moment more dangerous and the threat to shared prosperity more enduring.

THE FAILURES OF MAINSTREAM ECONOMICS

A good starting point is recognition that the last decade has not been kind to mainstream economists. They have been repeatedly surprised by major economic developments that have forced economists to come up with "after the fact" explanations. First came the financial crisis of 2008. The failings of orthodox economists were symbolized by the inability of the faculty of the London School of Economics to answer the Queen of England's simple question (November 5, 2008) as to why no one foresaw the crisis. After that came the failure to recover from the Great Recession as predicted. Initially, the expectation among mainstream economists was for a quick V-shaped recovery. When that failed to materialize, expectations were downgraded to a slower U-shaped recovery. And when that also failed to materialize, talk turned to L-shaped recovery and then to chatter about stagnation.

The theoretical and analytical failures of mainstream economics are mirrored in economic forecasts. Figure 1 shows the Federal Reserve's

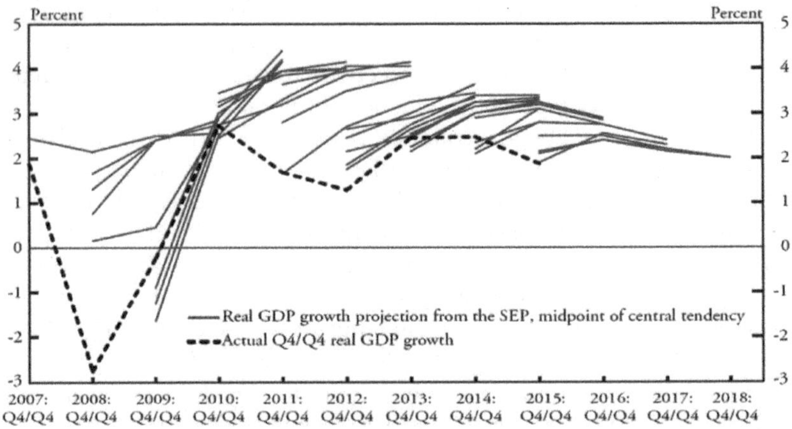

FIGURE 1 FOMC Projections of U.S. Real GDP Growth Versus Actual by Vintage. *Source*: Kahn and Palmer (2016).

Federal Open Market Committee (FOMC) projections of real GDP versus actual GDP by vintage, from 2008.Q4 through to 2015.Q4. Actual GDP is shown by the broken line. Predicted GDP is shown by the blue lines—with each blue line being a fresh updated prediction. The figure shows that the FOMC totally failed to anticipate the Great Recession (2007.Q4)—the starting blue line is far above the broken black V. During the recession (2008.Q1–2009.Q2), the FOMC systematically underestimated its severity—again the blue lines are above the broken black V. And once the recovery began (2009.Q3–2015.Q3), the FOMC systematically overestimated the strength of recovery—again the blue lines are all above the black line.

Figure 2 shows the FOMC's estimate of long-run growth of potential GDP. After being revised up fractionally in 2009, it has been persistently and significantly revised down, reflecting the slow embrace of the reality of stagnation.

Finally, Figure 3 shows that the International Monetary Fund (IMF) has also had to persistently revise down its forecast of global real GDP growth, and its forecasts have consistently been overly optimistic relative to actual growth. The solid line is actual global GDP growth. The broken lines are IMF forecasts of growth by vintage, and they consistently lie above the solid line.

In sum, these figures show that the forecasts of leading elite economic policymaking institutions have been systematically wrong. They all failed to anticipate the financial crisis, underestimated the severity of the Great Recession, and have all been persistently overly optimistic regarding recovery. The one-sided nature of the forecast errors suggests something is profoundly wrong with their models. The systematic forecast errors are the empirical twin of the analytical failure of mainstream economics to anticipate events.

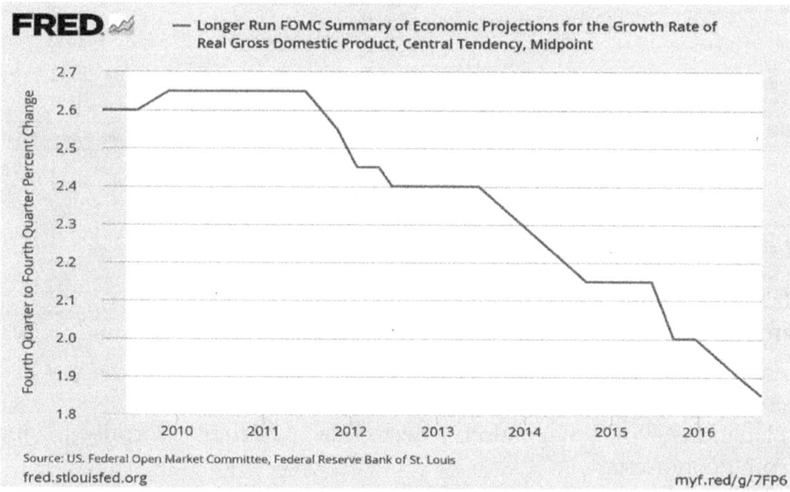

FIGURE 2 FOMC Projections of the U.S. Economy's Long-Run Growth Rate.

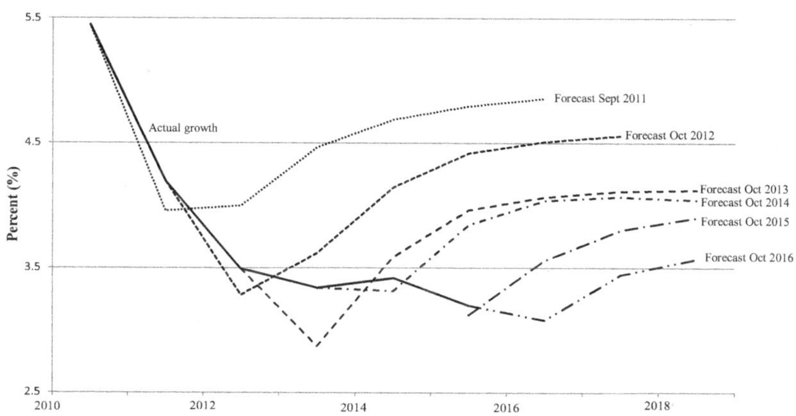

FIGURE 3 IMF's Forecast of Global Real GDP Growth by Vintage.

ECONOMISTS' RESPONSE TO THE CRISIS, INEQUALITY, AND STAGNATION

The failure of mainstream economics to anticipate developments has forced an ongoing process of catch-up. Stage 1 involved attempts to concoct ex-post explanations of the financial crisis and Great Recession. During this period, the issue of inequality began to seep into mainstream explanations of the crisis and recession. Stage 2 has involved developing

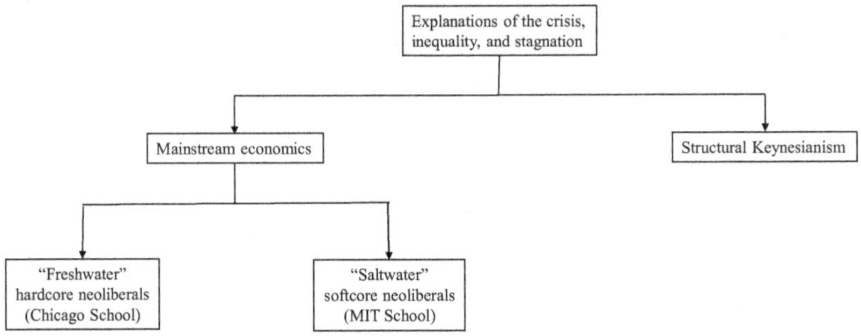

FIGURE 4 Understanding the Debate: Competing Explanations of the Crisis, Inequality, and Stagnation.

explanations of stagnation that has further surprised mainstream economists.

Figure 4 decomposes the different responses of the profession to the challenge of explaining the crisis, income inequality, and stagnation. The mainstream is divided between the "freshwater" hardcore neoliberal Chicago School response and the "saltwater" softcore neoliberal MIT school response. These twin mainstream responses are contrasted with the "structural Keynesian" account of events (Palley 2012).

Hardcore Neoliberalism

The hardcore neoliberal position can be labeled the "government failure hypothesis." This view is associated with the Republican Party and with the economics departments of Stanford, the University of Chicago, and the University of Minnesota.

Hardcore neoliberals argue that the crisis was rooted in the U.S. housing bubble. They claim the bubble was due to excessively prolonged loose monetary policy (Taylor 2007, 2009) plus politically motivated government intervention in the housing market aimed at increasing ownership (Rajan 2010).

With regard to monetary policy, the Federal Reserve pushed interest rates too low for too long following the recession of 2001. With regard to the housing market, government intervention via the Community Reinvestment Act and Fannie Mae and Freddie Mac supposedly drove up house prices and encouraged homeownership beyond people's means.

Hardcore neoliberals explain the rising inequality as the result of skill-biased technical progress, which means the labor market has been working as it should (Rajan 2010). The significance and importance of rising inequality is that it prompted politically motivated government intervention in the housing market, which supposedly caused the bubble.

Consequently, rising inequality is not an economic problem per se and does not reflect malfunctioning of the economy. Instead, it is an ethical concern and a political problem.

When it comes to explaining stagnation, hardcore neoliberals embrace a collection of arguments. First, there is an argument that the economy remains overregulated, and the situation has been worsened by post-crisis financial regulation such as the Dodd-Frank Act (2010). According to the hardcore view, the correct response to the financial crisis of 2008 should have been to double-down on neoliberal policies rather than to reform them.

Second, the recession and stagnation were deepened by mistaken expansionary fiscal policies that increased government debt, delayed needed economic adjustments, and worsened financial fragility. According to hardcore economists, expansionary fiscal policy is ineffective and stagnation is the result of failure to "bite the bullet."

Softcore Neoliberalism

The softcore neoliberal view can be labeled the "market failure hypothesis." It is identified with the Obama–Clinton wing of the Democratic Party and economics departments such as those at MIT, Yale, and Princeton.

The softcore neoliberal view is that the crisis was due to excessive financial deregulation and perverse incentive pay structures within banks. That permitted Wall Street to engage in "loan pushing" rather than "sound lending," which generated a housing bubble. When the bubble burst, it triggered a financial crisis that deepened an ordinary recession, transforming it into the Great Recession.

Softcore neoliberals initially ascribed no economic significance to rising inequality, which they also explained as due to skill-biased technological change. They also expected the economy to bounce back from recession, which did not happen. That has forced them to also develop a second-stage agenda that makes a collection of adjustments aimed at explaining the role of inequality and the failure to bounce back.

The main softcore argument for stagnation is the so-called zero lower bound (ZLB) to interest rates. The claim is that the ZLB has prevented monetary policy from lowering interest rates sufficiently to restore full employment (Eggertsson and Krugman 2012). Subsequently, softcore neoliberals have added an argument about hysteresis (Summers 2014). According to that argument, the financial crisis and Great Recession caused a "shock" that has permanently lowered the economy's growth rate and increased equilibrium unemployment. However, the details of the hysteresis mechanism are unclear, making the argument a black box.

What about income inequality? Initially, it was viewed as a nonfactor and just a political and social concern, but that has also changed under the pressure of facts. Krugman (2013a, 2013b) has made a political economy argument that worsened income inequality twisted politics against the use of fiscal policy. Consequently, the policy response to the Great Recession was inadequate, which contributed to failure to recover. Now, there are indications that softcore neoliberals may be turning to borrowing the long-standing Keynesian argument that increased inequality increases saving, which allows them to claim inequality has worsened the ZLB problem by pushing the full-employment interest rate even farther below zero (Palley 2016).

The bottom line is that both branches of mainstream economics have had to play catch-up and patch their theory. First, they had to come up with explanations of the crisis, which they had completely failed to anticipate. After that, they have had to come up with explanations of stagnation, which they also failed to anticipate.

Structural Keynesianism

The structural Keynesian hypothesis holds that the crisis was rooted in the neoliberal economic paradigm that was adopted in the late 1970s and early 1980s and has guided economic policy since (Palley 2009, 2012). The analytical implication is that the financial crisis, inequality, and stagnation are the result of policy design.

An important feature of the argument is that, though the United States is the epicenter of the crisis, all countries are implicated as they all participated in the adoption of a systemically flawed policy paradigm. That is why it was a global crisis.

For the period 1945–80 the U.S. economy was characterized by a "virtuous circle" Keynesian growth model built on full employment and wage growth tied to productivity growth. This model is illustrated in Figure 5 and its logic was as follows. Productivity growth drove wage growth, which fueled demand growth and created full employment. That provided an incentive for investment, which drove further productivity growth and supported higher wages. This model held in the United States, and it also held throughout the global economy—in Western Europe, Canada, Japan, Mexico, Brazil, and Argentina.

After 1980 the virtuous circle Keynesian growth model was replaced by a neoliberal growth model. There were two key changes. First, policymakers abandoned the commitment to full employment and shifted to targeting low inflation. Second, policy helped to sever the link between wages and productivity growth. Together, these two changes created a new economic dynamic. Before 1980, wages were the engine of U.S. demand growth. After 1980, debt and asset price inflation became the engine.

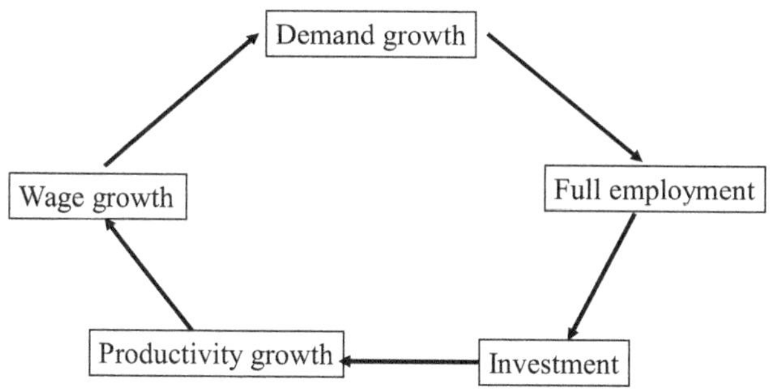

FIGURE 5 The 1945–80 Virtuous Circle Keynesian Growth Model.

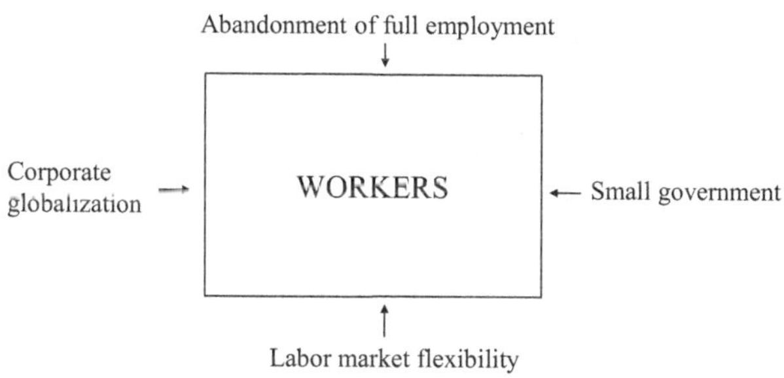

FIGURE 6 The Neoliberal Policy Box.

The new economic model was rooted in neoliberal economic thought. As shown in Figure 6, it can be described as a neoliberal policy box that pressures workers on all sides. On the left side, the corporate model of globalization put workers in international competition. On the right side, the "small" government agenda attacked the legitimacy of government and pushed persistently for deregulation regardless of dangers. From below, the labor market flexibility agenda attacked unions and labor market supports such as the minimum wage, unemployment benefits, employment protections, and employee rights. From above, policymakers abandoned the commitment to full employment. Like the postwar Keynesian growth model, the neoliberal policy box was also implemented on a global basis, in the North and the South. That global diffusion multiplied its impact and explains the importance of the "Washington Consensus" that was exported by the World Bank and International Monetary Fund.

The second critical component of the structural Keynesian story concerns financialization and the role of finance. As shown in Figure 7, finance had a dual role. First, it provided structural support to the neoliberal policy box. Second, it supported the AD generation process.

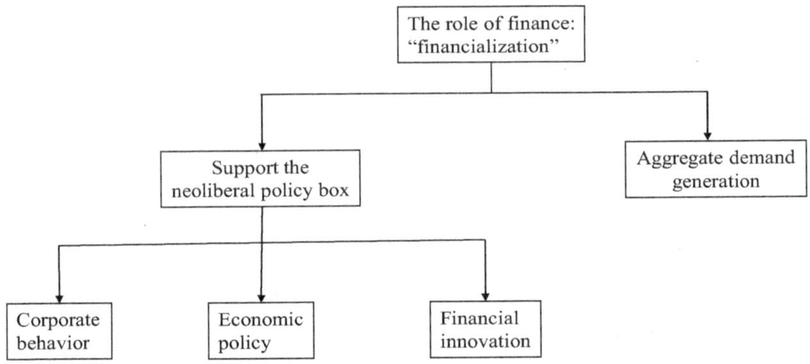

FIGURE 7 The Role of Finance in the Neoliberal Model.

With regard to structurally supporting the neoliberal policy box, finance did so in three ways. First, financial markets captured control of corporations via enforcement of the shareholder value-maximization paradigm of corporate governance. Consequently, corporations were reoriented to serve financial market interests along with the interests of top management. Second, financial markets and corporations lobbied politically for neoliberal policies, and they supported think tanks and economic research advocating those policies. Third, financial innovation facilitated and promoted financial market control of corporations via hostile takeovers, leveraged buyouts, and reverse capital distributions. By capturing and reengineering corporations, financial markets changed business behavior. Together with neoliberal economic policy, that produced an economic matrix that suppressed wages and raised inequality.

The second vital role of finance has been to support aggregate demand. The neoliberal model gradually undermined the income-and-demand generation process via wage stagnation and rising inequality, creating a growing structural demand gap. The role of finance was to fill that gap. Deregulation, financial innovation, speculation, and mortgage lending fraud enabled finance to fill the demand gap by lending to consumers and by spurring asset price inflation. Along the way, it also created a housing price bubble, the bursting of which became the trigger for the financial crisis and stagnation.

The Fallacy of the Great Moderation

Additionally, the structural Keynesian story provides an explanation of the so-called "Great Moderation" and why the crisis appeared out of nowhere. The Great Moderation refers to the period 1980–2007 when the U.S.

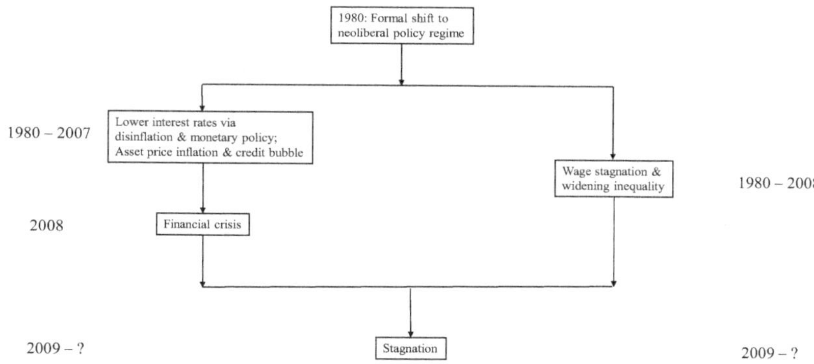

FIGURE 8 Deconstructing the Great Moderation: The U.S. Economy in the Neoliberal Era.

economy experienced disinflation, longer booms, and shorter, shallower recessions.

Mainstream economists believe the Great Moderation was because of improved monetary policy based on mainstream economists' improved theoretical understanding of the economy. That explains why they were so self-congratulatory before the crisis and why they were clueless regarding imminent major developments.

Structural Keynesianism always viewed the Great Moderation hypothesis as false, and this is explained in Figure 8. The shift to neoliberal policy in 1980 initiated a dual process. On one side there was wage stagnation and rising inequality that drove disinflation and slowly undermined the aggregate demand-generation process. On the other side, disinflation allowed lower interest rates, while financialization initiated an era of asset price inflation and a thirty-year-long credit bubble. That combination increased wealth and increased the quantity of easy credit, which covered over the emerging problem of demand shortage. Every time the economy got into trouble, the Federal Reserve lowered interest rates and restarted the credit bubble–asset price inflation mechanism, thereby generating the illusion of a Great Moderation.

Finally, the process in Figure 8 also explains why the saving rate fell despite rising income inequality. That is because the increased saving of the rich was offset as consumption and mortgage credit to lower-income households.

The Structural Keynesian Explanation of Stagnation: Exhausted Paradigm

The structural Keynesian hypothesis also provides a clear and simple explanation of stagnation. It has no need for invention of auxiliary theories like the zero lower bound (ZLB) or hysteresis.

The financial crisis of 2008 put a sudden stop to the credit bubble that had created the illusion of a Great Moderation. Policymakers then used bailouts to address the financial system's insolvency, and massive fiscal and monetary policy stimulus to prevent the Great Recession from becoming a second Great Depression. However, nothing was done to change the underlying neoliberal economic model described by the neoliberal policy box in Figure 6. Given that, stagnation was inevitable as the model inevitably produces structural demand shortage via wage suppression and increased income inequality.

When the neoliberal model was implemented in 1980, the income and AD-generation process were still robust and income inequality was much lower. Additionally, the economy had room for asset price inflation and extended credit growth as asset prices and indebtedness were both much lower. Those favorable initial conditions meant the economy could expand despite the stagnationist effects of neoliberal policy. However, now those conditions are exhausted so that debt and asset price inflation can no longer adequately fill the structural demand gap. Analytically, it was easy to predict stagnation. Here is the conclusion to a paper published in July 2009:

> (T)hough the economy may stabilize, it will likely be unable to escape the pull of economic stagnation. That is because stagnation is the logical next stage of the existing paradigm (Palley 2009, 33).

THE LINK BETWEEN MAINSTREAM ECONOMISTS AND THE CRISIS

The structural Keynesian hypothesis emphasizes the role of economic policy in causing the financial crisis, inequality, and stagnation. Scratch any side of the neoliberal policy box and you find a justification that comes straight from mainstream economics.

Corporate globalization has been justified by appeal to the theory of free trade based upon comparative advantage and by appeal to neoclassical arguments for deregulating financial markets and allowing uncontrolled international capital flows.

The small government agenda comes straight from Milton Friedman's (1962, 2002) arguments for a minimalist or "night watchman" state. The retreat from full employment policy is based on Friedman's (1968) theory of a "natural" rate of unemployment, which was adopted and endorsed by almost the entire economics profession. The theory says monetary policy cannot affect the long-run rate of unemployment and there is no tradeoff between inflation and unemployment. That provided policymakers with the justification for abandoning full employment and shifting to inflation targeting. Since monetary policy has no lasting impact on employment, policy should instead minimize inflation, which is undesirable and the only thing monetary policy can permanently affect. Employment should just be left to market forces.

The "flexible" labor markets agenda has also been driven by neoclassical economics. The argument is that competitive labor markets ensure that workers and CEOs are paid their contribution to value of production. That is the theory in all conventional textbooks, and it has fueled an attack on unions, minimum wages, and employment protections, all of which are characterized as labor market "distortions" that lower employment and increase unemployment.

Increased corporate power has been justified by the shareholder value model of corporations, which claims that wealth and income are maximized if corporations maximize shareholder value. Finally, expansion of financial markets has been promoted by appeal to the theory of efficient markets and claims that speculation is stabilizing. Portfolio theory was invoked to justify exotic financial innovation in the name of risk spreading. The claim was that such financial engineering effectively created additional wealth and provided a free lunch. Meanwhile, portfolio diversification would render a collapse near impossible.

Putting the pieces together, modern mainstream economics played a critical role in the making of the financial crisis and Great Recession. According to the structural Keynesian account, the fingerprints of mainstream economists and modern economic theory are all over the neoliberal policy box and financialization. Together, the neoliberal policy box and financialization caused the crisis and undermined the demand-generating process, which now causes stagnation.

THE HYPOTHESIS MAINSTREAM ECONOMISTS CANNOT CONSIDER: POLITICAL, PSYCHOLOGICAL, AND SOCIOLOGICAL BARRIERS TO OPENNESS IN ECONOMICS

The financial crisis and ensuing stagnation have compelled mainstream economics to come up with *ex-post* explanations of those events, which they failed to anticipate and initially lacked the capacity to explain. The need to play catch-up holds for both branches of the mainstream, the "freshwater" hardcore neoliberal branch and the "saltwater" softcore neoliberal branch.

In stark contrast, structural Keynesian economics provides a comprehensive account of events from the crisis to stagnation, anticipated the crisis, and predicted stagnation long before it was an issue. Yet despite this superior performance, the structural Keynesian account remains largely suppressed within the economics profession and economic policy circles. Why is that? The answer lies in powerful political, psychological, and sociological forces that support the status quo and block change.

Politics

With regard to politics, neoliberalism is a political project that has advanced the interests of business and wealthy elites. Those elites have an interest in maintaining the "Freshwater vs. Saltwater" construction of economics because it is supportive of neoliberal policy and justifies current economic arrangements. It also creates the politically useful impression that economics is open and intellectually contested by Freshwater and Saltwater economists, when in fact they both share the same core intellectual perspective. Like Coke and Pepsi, they are both colas.

Both freshwater and saltwater economics are rooted in Arrow and Debreu's (1954) competitive general equilibrium theory. Where there are differences, they are differences of degree regarding the extent and severity of market failures and the capacity of government to remedy those failures. That contrasts with the structural Keynesian view, which rejects competitive general equilibrium theory as the benchmark for theoretical economics, and it is politically threatening to dominant business interests. The support of elite interests for the intellectual status quo resonates with Karl Marx's abiding observation in *The German Ideology* (1845) on the social foundations of dominant ideas:

> The ideas of the ruling class are in every epoch the ruling ideas, i.e. the class which is the ruling material force of society, is at the same time its ruling intellectual force. The class which has the means of material production at its disposal has control at the same time over the mental means of production, so that thereby, generally speaking, those who lack the means of mental production are subject to it.

Psychology

With regard to psychology, the close connection between mainstream economics and the neoliberal policy box makes it near impossible for mainstream economics to even acknowledge the structural Keynesian story, which argues that increased income inequality and stagnation are the result of policy design. For mainstream economics to admit or even acknowledge the hypothesis as legitimate would be tantamount to admission of comprehensive intellectual failure. That is a very hard thing for any person to do.

Instead, the mainstream response has been consistent with social psychologist Leon Festinger's theory of cognitive dissonance, which he described as follows:[1]

> Suppose an individual believes something with all his heart . . . suppose that he is presented with evidence, unequivocal and undeniable evidence, that his belief is wrong; what will happen? The individual will frequently emerge, not only unshaken, but even more convinced of the truth of his beliefs than ever before. Indeed, he may even show a new fervor about convincing and converting people to his view.

Sociology

Finally, with regard to sociology, mainstream economists have an economic interest in preserving the intellectual status quo, and they have the power to do so. They are trained in neoclassical economics, have built their professional reputations on it, are well rewarded for their support by business and governing elites, and have nothing to gain from creating space for rival critical points of view.

Academic economics is also governed as a club in which existing members elect new members. Existing members control entry to the club via the tenure system. They also control elite journals that impact dissemination of ideas and professional visibility; they control the production of new Ph.D. economists that influence the intellectual allegiances and open-mindedness of next-generation economists; and they control the classroom, the curriculum, and the textbook that influences how society thinks about the economy and the knowledge claims of mainstream economics. Those tremendous powers are used to exclude and suppress the ideas of those who do not share the beliefs of existing club members (Palley 1997).

Instead, at best, the mainstream profession selectively borrows ideas from its critics and tries to capture and incorporate those ideas within its own discourse. However, that process of capture and incorporation takes the form of "Gattopardo" economics (Palley 2013)—change that leaves things the same as before. Thus, ideas like stagnation are incorporated and explained as the result of a technical glitch in the market mechanism, but the deep fundamentals of neoliberal theory remain unchanged. At the same time, no reference is made to existing prior work on stagnation by

[1]Cited by Mirowski (2010, 35).

critical economists as that would legitimize the critics. In this fashion, the idea is captured and defanged without giving legitimacy to other perspectives and outsider economists.

CONCLUSION: THE DANGEROUS UNINTENDED CONSEQUENCES OF THE DEATH OF PLURALISM IN ECONOMICS

Current political conditions echo the ugly conditions of the 1930s, with the economy being at the center of much political discontent and anger. Economic hardship and disappointment have been primary factors driving the success of Donald Trump in the United States, Marine Le Pen in France, and Brexit in the UK.

Those conditions speak to a need for a full and open discussion about the economy so as to identify what has gone wrong and what should change. However, that has not happened because forty years of neoliberal dominance have destroyed pluralism in economics, atrophied popular economic understandings, and curtailed society's economic conversation. Instead of opening discussion for an evidence-based assessment of the competing explanations, mainstream economics has come up with a series of patches that leave their theoretical model essentially unchanged. That has provided justification for establishment policymakers and politicians to stick with the policy status quo.

We should be crystal clear. The critique of most mainstream economists is not about "values" or lack of "change." Many mainstream economists share the same values as their structural Keynesian critics. Mainstream economics has also updated and changed its ideas in response to the challenges posed by the financial crisis and stagnation. Instead, the critique is of the intellectual practice of mainstream economics, which has replaced pluralism with a neoliberal-friendly neoclassical monopoly. That monopoly limits the economic policy conversation, thereby helping to block the politics and policies needed to address the perilous political moment.

REFERENCES

Arrow, K. J., and G. Debreu. 1954. "Existence of an Equilibrium for a Competitive Economy." *Econometrica* 22 (3):265–90. doi:10.2307/1907353

Eggertsson, G. B., and P. Krugman. 2012. "Debt, Deleveraging, and the Liquidity Trap: A Fisher-Minsky-Koo Approach. *Quarterly Journal of Economics* 127 (3):1469–513. doi:10.1093/qje/qjs023

Friedman, M. 1962, 2002. *Capitalism and Freedom*. Fortieth anniversary ed. Chicago: University of Chicago Press.

———. 1968. "The Role of Monetary Policy." *American Economic Review* 58 (May):1–17.

Kahn, G. A., and A. Palmer. 2016. "Monetary Policy at the Zero Lower Bound: Revelations from the FOMC's Summary of Economic Projections." *Economic Review, Federal Reserve Bank of Kansas City, First Quarter*: 5–37.

Krugman, P. 2013a. "Inequality and Recovery. The Conscience of a Liberal." New York Times, January 20.

———. 2013b. "Why Inequality Matters." New York Times, December 16, A25.

Mirowski, P. 2010. "The Great Mortification: Economists' Responses to the Crisis of 2007– (and Counting)." *Hedgehog Review, Summer* 12 :28–41.

Palley, T. I. 1997. "The Academic Jungle: Social Practice and the Survival of Economic Ideas." *Review of Radical Political Economics* 29 (3):22–33. doi: 10.1177/048661349702900303

———. 2008. "Breaking the Neoclassical Monopoly in Economics." Project Syndicate, January 31, and republished in T. I. Palley, "The Economic Crisis: Notes from the Underground," CreateSpace 2012, p. 145–47.

———. 2009. *America's Exhausted Paradigm: Macroeconomic Causes of the Financial Crisis and Great Recession*. Washington, DC: New America Foundation, July.

———. 2012. *From Financial Crisis to Stagnation: The Destruction of Shared Prosperity and the Role of Economics*. Cambridge: Cambridge University Press.

———. 2013. "Gattopardo Economics: The Crisis and the Mainstream Response of Change That Keeps Things the Same." *European Journal of Economics and Economic Policies* 10 (2):193–206. doi:10.4337/ejeep.2013.02.04

———. 2016. "Zero Lower Bound (ZLB) Economics: The Fallacy of New Keynesian Explanations of Stagnation." IMK Working Paper No. 164. Dusseldorf, Germany Institute for Macroeconomics, February.

Popper, K. R. 1959. *The Logic of Scientific Discovery*. New York: Basic Books.

Rajan, R. G. 2010. *Fault Lines: How Hidden Fractures Still Threaten the World Economy*. Princeton, NJ: Princeton University Press.

Summers, L. 2014. "US Economic Prospects: Secular Stagnation, Hysteresis, and the Zero Lower Bound." *Business Economics* 49 (2):65–73. doi:10.1057/be.2014.13

Taylor, J. B. 2007. "Housing and Monetary Policy." NBER Working Paper No. 13682, December.

———. 2009. "How Government Created the Financial Crisis." *Wall Street Journal*, February 3, A19.